The Emergence of the South African Metropolis

Focusing on South Africa's three main cities – Johannesburg, Cape Town and Durban – this book explores South African urban history from the late nineteenth century onwards. In particular, it examines the metropolitan perceptions and experiences of both Black and White South Africans, as well as those of visitors. Drawing on a rich array of city histories, travel writing, novels, films, newspapers, radio and television programmes and oral histories, Vivian Bickford-Smith focuses on the consequences of the depictions of the South African metropolis and the 'slums' they contained. The book also seeks to place South African cities comparatively alongside similar treatment of European and North American cities of the same period.

Vivian Bickford-Smith is Extraordinary Professor at Stellenbosch University, Emeritus Professor at the University of Cape Town and Visiting Fellow in the Institute of Historical Research at the University of London.

The Emergence of the South African Metropolis

Cities and Identities in the Twentieth Century

Vivian Bickford-Smith

Stellenbosch University and University of Cape Town

CAMBRIDGE
UNIVERSITY PRESS

CAMBRIDGE
UNIVERSITY PRESS

University Printing House, Cambridge CB2 8BS, United Kingdom

Cambridge University Press is part of the University of Cambridge.

It furthers the University's mission by disseminating knowledge in the pursuit of education, learning and research at the highest international levels of excellence.

www.cambridge.org
Information on this title: www.cambridge.org/9781107002937

© Vivian Bickford-Smith 2016

First published 2016

Printed in the United States of America by Sheridan Books, Inc.

A catalogue record for this publication is available from the British Library

Library of Congress Cataloguing in Publication data
Bickford-Smith, Vivian, author.
The emergence of the South African metropolis cities and identities in the twentieth century / Vivian Bickford-Smith, Stellenbosch University.
Cambridge ; New York : Cambridge University Press, 2016. | Includes bibliographical references and index.
LCCN 2015042448 | ISBN 9781107002937 (hbk)
LCSH: Urbanization – South Africa – History. | Cities and towns – South Africa – History. | City and town life – South Africa – History | Sociology, Urban – South Africa. | National characteristics – South Africa. | Group identity – South Africa | South Africa – Race relations – History.
LCC HT384.S6 B53 2016 | DDC 307.760968–dc23
LC record available at http://lccn.loc.gov/2015042448

ISBN 978-1-107-00293-7 Hardback

For Richard and James

Contents

Illustrations

Maps

Tables

Acknowledgements

The writing of this book was made possible through generous funding from the Leverhulme Trust (United Kingdom), National Research Foundation (South Africa) and University Research Committee of the University of Cape Town (UCT). I was fortunate indeed to be awarded a Visiting Leverhulme Professorship at the Centre for Metropolitan History (CMH), Institute of Historical Research (IHR), University of London, between 2008 and 2010. This gave me time to undertake a significant portion of the research and formulate ideas necessary for this book. Two further years of joint appointment with UCT was also enormously helpful in this respect. I would particularly like to thank Professor Matthew Davies and Olwen Myhill of the CMH, Derek Keene, who was my predecessor as Leverhulme Professor at the CMH and Miles Taylor, the then Director of the IHR, for their collegial and convivial support. Equally, thanks are also due to colleagues in the Department of Historical Studies and Faculty of Humanities at UCT, who not only tolerated my absence but also allowed me six months away for two further years during the IHR joint appointment. The same faculty kindly granted me sabbatical leave in 2014 that allowed eventual completion of the project. While on leave in the United Kingdom between 2008 and 2014, both St John's and Gonville and Caius colleges at Cambridge University offered me at various times generous hospitality and intellectual stimulation through membership of their Senior Common Rooms, while Birkbeck College, University of London, conferred an honorary Visiting Professorship.

A very large number of librarians and archivists were liberal and helpful with their time and knowledge, and I hope they will forgive me for not mentioning each of them by name while recording the institutions they belong to: African Studies Library and Special Collections, UCT; BBC Written Archives Centre, Reading; British Film Institute (BFI) National Archives, London; British Library, London; Cambridge University Library; Centre for Popular Memory Archives, University of Cape Town; Don Africana Central Reference Library, Durban; Gonville and Caius College Library, Cambridge; Killie Campbell Library, University of KwaZulu-Natal, Durban; Modern Records Collection, Warwick University; National Archives Repository, Cape Town; National Archives Repository, Pretoria; Senate House Library, University of London; South African National Film Video and Sound Archive, Pretoria; South African Public Library, Cape Town. Special thanks to Freddy Ogterop and Sue Ogterop, who drew on their extensive knowledge in the field to point me to many of the often little-known South African films referred to in the book as well as to Elizabeth Van Heyningen for finding Durban Publicity Association material and the comments she made on it. Neil Parsons also offered considerable help in sharing findings from his ongoing work on early South African cinema. Sandy Shell, head of the African Studies Library, UCT, supplied original maps on which some of the newly designed versions in this book were based and that of Cape Town in 1918 included as an illustration. Alli Appelbaum was similarly helpful in terms of several select committee reports while Eustacia Riley helped identify numerous city histories for subsequent exploration. Additional thanks for supplying photocopies of extensive magazine and newspaper material goes to Leah Nasson and Mischa Minne.

Paul Sloman and Guy Powell, the team at Subtract Design Limited (Brighton), were responsible for compiling the seven maps that appear at the front of the book. Paul Sloman together with Emily Angus also helped create an initial version of the bibliography from footnotes. My gratitude to all at Cambridge University Press responsible for publishing the book. Kate Gavino (New York), Maria Marsh and Sarah Green (Cambridge) guided the manuscript into the production stage where Ian McIver, Ramya Ranganathan and their team ensured its completion. Particular thanks to Diana Witt for her work on the bibliography and Lakshmi Krupa for the copy-editing.

Final and inadequate thanks is offered to colleagues, friends and members of my nuclear and extended family in South Africa, Britain and beyond who have offered the essential moral and material support needed by any author during the sometimes seemingly interminable time necessary to complete a book. Encouragement, hospitality and ideas were offered on numerous occasions when papers were delivered that became elements of this one. These occasions included seminar series at the universities of Cape Town, Stellenbosch, Cambridge, Leicester, Oxford and component parts of the University of London such as the Centre for Metropolitan History, Birkbeck and the School of Oriental and African Studies as well as conferences organised by the IHR, Lincoln University, the Indian Institute of Advanced Studies (Shimla), the Swiss South African Joint Research Project at Basel, the American Historical

Association, the European Association of Urban Historians and the Urban History Group (United Kingdom). Members of the latter who have offered particular support and friendship over many years include Roey Sweet, Richard Dennis, Richard Rodger, David Green, Simon Gunn, Helen Meller and Bob Morris. Wayne Dooling and Ruth Watson made particular efforts to make me feel welcome in London and Cambridge while Hilary Sapire generously offered insights into her innovative work on Royal Tours and British loyalism. Sage advice and sustenance has continued to be offered as ever by John Iliffe, Colin Bundy, Bill Freund and Richard Mendelsohn. My debt during the writing process itself became great indeed to two friends and colleagues in particular, Bill Nasson and Vic Gatrell, in terms of red wine and many other forms of succour, intellectual and beyond, which they have constantly proffered. Informative and sustaining too were the semi-regular London meals in the company of Vic Gatrell, Jerry White, Jennifer Davis, Jeremy Krikler and David Feldman. Also deserving of special mention has been the constantly splendid hospitality and collegial encouragement of Miri Rubin and Gareth Stedman Jones. Gareth read and commented on an early version of my writing about 'local colour' in South African cities. Miri Rubin together with Paul la Hausse demonstrated enormous kindness and fortitude by reading and making innumerable useful comments on the entire manuscript. The anonymous reviewers at CUP also made helpful suggestions, not least on the initial book prospectus, and my thanks for those. The blame for remaining shortcomings in the paragraphs that follow should clearly be attached to me alone.

Abbreviations

ABM	American Board Missions
ACVV	Afrikaanse Christelyk Vrouwe Vereneeging
AFP	African Film Productions
ANC	African National Congress
APO	African Political Organization
BMSC	Bantu Mens' Social Centre
CAFDA	Cape Flats Distress Association
CPPA	Cape Peninsula Publicity Association
CPSA	Communist Party of South Africa
DEIC	Dutch East India Company
DPA	Durban Publicity Association
DRC	Dutch Reformed Church
ESCOM	Electricity Supply Commission
GNP	Gesuiwerde Nasionale Party
HNP	Herenigde Nasionale Party
ICU	Industrial and Commercial Union
ILN	*Illustrated London News*
ISCOR	Iron and Steel Industrial Corporation
JPA	Johannesburg Publicity Association
NAD	Native Affairs Department
NCAW	National Council for African Women
NIC	Natal Indian Congress
NP	National Party
NPA	National Publicity Association
OB	Ossewabrandwag
PAC	Pan African Congress
SANNC	South African Native National Congress
SAP	South African Police
SAR&H	South African Railways and Harbours
SATOUR	South African Tourist Corporation
SDF	Social Democratic Federation
TBIC	Transvaal British Indian Congress
UP	United Party

Maps

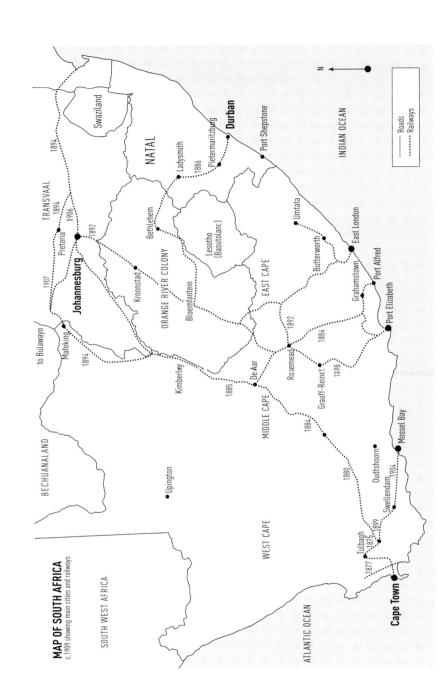

1 South Africa c.1910 showing main cities and railways

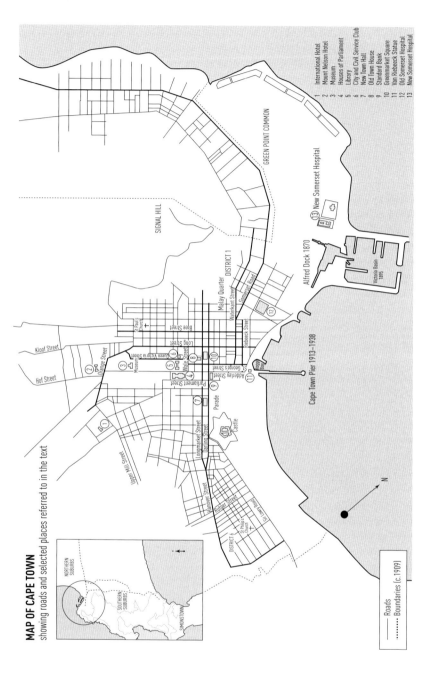

MAP OF CAPE TOWN
showing roads and selected places referred to in the text

1 International Hotel
2 Mount Nelson Hotel
3 Museum
4 Houses of Parliament
5 Library
6 City and Civil Service Club
7 New Town Hall
8 Old Town House
9 Standard Bank
10 Greenmarket Square
11 Van Riebeeck Statue
12 Old Somerset Hospital
13 New Somerset Hospital

Roads
Boundaries (c. 1909)

SIGNAL HILL

GREEN POINT COMMON

Alfred Dock 1870

Victoria Basin 1895

New Somerset Hospital

Malay Quarter

DISTRICT 1

Cape Town Pier 1913–1938

Somerset Road

Waterkant Street

Bree Street

Riebeeck Street

St Paul's Church

Kloof Street

Hof Street

Orange Street

Museum

Long Street

Queen Victoria Street

Wale Street

St George's Street

Adderley Street

Parliament Street

Castle

Parade

Buitengracht Street

Longmarket Street

Dalton Street

Upper Mill Street

Hanover Street

Tennant Street

Buitenkant Street

St Philip's Church

DISTRICT 6

NORTHERN SUBURBS

SOUTHERN SUBURBS

SIMONSTOWN

N

2 Inner Cape Town with places referred to in the text

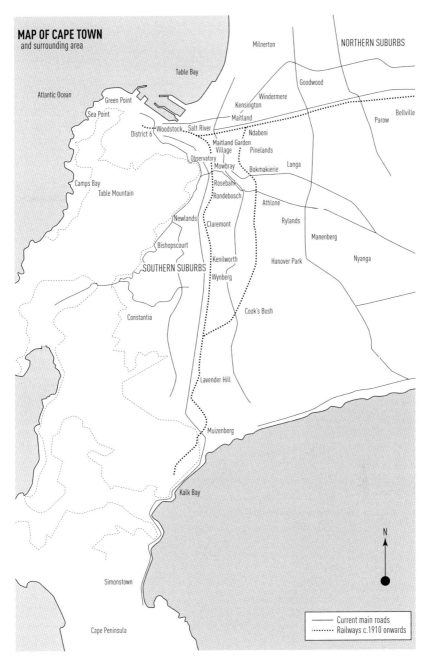

MAP OF CAPE TOWN
and surrounding area

Table Bay

NORTHERN SUBURBS

Milnerton

Goodwood

Atlantic Ocean

Green Point

Windermere

Sea Point

Kensington

Bellville

Maitland

Parow

Woodstock

Salt River

District 6

Ndabeni

Maitland Garden
Village

Pinelands

Observatory

Mowbray

Langa

Bokmakierie

Camps Bay

Rosebank

Table Mountain

Rondebosch

Athlone

Newlands

Claremont

Rylands

Bishopscourt

Manenberg

SOUTHERN SUBURBS

Kenilworth

Hanover Park

Nyanga

Wynberg

Constantia

Cook's Bush

Lavender Hill

Muizenberg

N

Kalk Bay

Simonstown

Current main roads
Railways c.1910 onwards

Cape Peninsula

3 Cape Town and surrounds with places referred to in the text

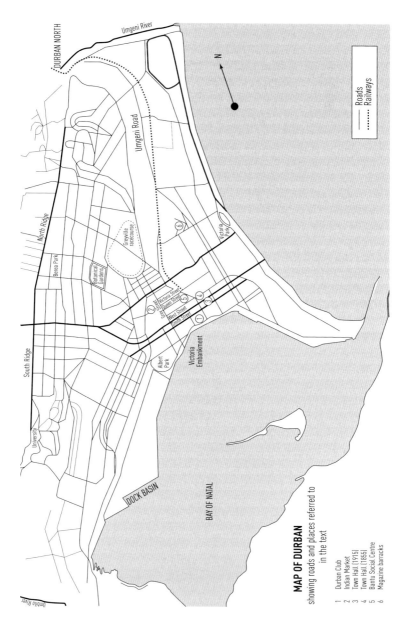

MAP OF DURBAN

showing roads and places referred to
in the text

1 Durban Club
2 Indian Market
3 Town Hall (1915)
4 Town Hall (1885)
5 Bantu Social Centre
6 Magazine barracks

4 Inner Durban with places referred to in the text

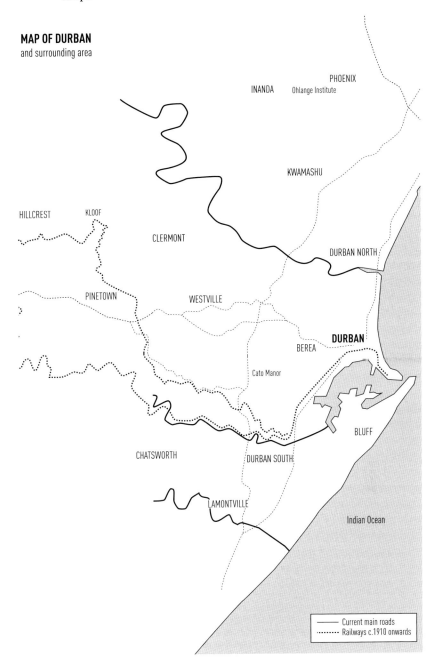

MAP OF DURBAN
and surrounding area

PHOENIX
INANDA   Ohlange Institute

KWAMASHU

HILLCREST   KLOOF

CLERMONT

DURBAN NORTH

PINETOWN   WESTVILLE

DURBAN

BEREA

Cato Manor

BLUFF

CHATSWORTH

DURBAN SOUTH

LAMONTVILLE

Indian Ocean

——— Current main roads
········· Railways c.1910 onwards

5 Durban and surrounds with places referred to in the text

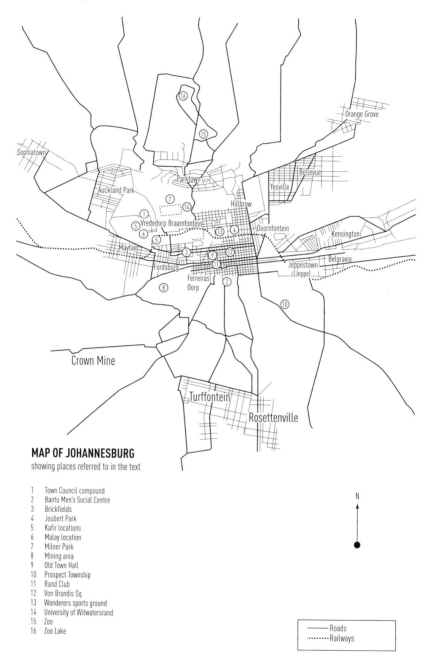

MAP OF JOHANNESBURG
showing places referred to in the text

1   Town Council compound
2   Bantu Men's Social Centre
3   Brickfields
4   Joubert Park
5   Kafir locations
6   Malay location
7   Milner Park
8   Mining area
9   Old Town Hall
10   Prospect Township
11   Rand Club
12   Von Brandis Sq
13   Wanderers sports ground
14   University of Witwatersrand
15   Zoo
16   Zoo Lake

N

——— Roads
········· Railways

6 Inner Johannesburg with places referred to in the text

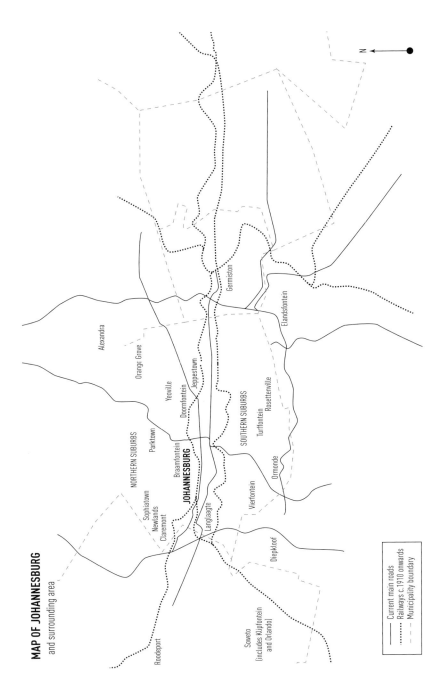

MAP OF JOHANNESBURG
and surrounding area

Roodeport

Sophiatown
Newlands
Claremont

NORTHERN SUBURBS

Parktown

Braamfontein

JOHANNESBURG

Langlaagte

Soweto
(includes Klipfontein
and Orlando)

Diepkloof

Vierfontein

Alexandra

Orange Grove

Yeoville

Doornfontein

Jeppestown

Jeppestown

SOUTHERN SUBURBS

Turffontein

Rosettenville

Ormonde

Germiston

Elandsfontein

N

— Current main roads
····· Railways c.1910 onwards
--- Municipality boundary

7 Johannesburg and surrounds with places referred to in the text

1   Introduction

In 1910 Maurice Evans sat thoughtfully on the veranda of his suburban home in Durban. Evans was a businessman, plant collector and erstwhile member of the Natal Legislative Assembly and Native Affairs Commission. His house, on the verdant Berea Ridge, commanded a magnificent view of the town centre and harbour below.

In Evans' opinion, the buildings he saw might have been anywhere in the British Empire. They expressed the 'taste and aspiration' of Western Europe. The large town hall, completed in 1885, was 'no whit different to what the final flowering of municipal life would be in Europe or America'. There were also broad streets, electric trams, huge department stores full of 'the products of European skill' and a harbour 'equipped with all the recent inventions of European science'. Durban's built environment was 'overwhelmingly European'.

As if to reinforce this perception, Evans could hear a youthful voice nearby singing from *Hymns Ancient and Modern*. But there were two other sounds that suggested Durban was not quite so European after all: 'the monotone of Abantu singing ... accompanied by the rhythmic beat of heavy feet stamping in unison' and, further away, 'the lighter reiteration of the Indian tom-tom'.[1] These three snatches of music brought to Evans' mind the existence of different 'races' in Durban: 'Whites' (or 'Europeans'); 'Abantu' ('Natives' or 'Africans'); and 'Indians' ('Asians').[2]

For Evans, thinking about a city in South Africa was synonymous with thinking about race. The origins, functions or symbolic significance of

---

[1] Maurice Smethurst Evans, *Black and White in South East Africa: A Study in Sociology* (London: Longmans and Co., 1911), 1–2.

[2] In using these terms, I do not wish to suggest that they are anything other than historically constructed ethnic labels or racialised categories. Capitalisation of initial letters when using such terms in the course of the book is intended to suggest as much. This will cut down on the need to use inverted commas. When not citing contemporary sources, I will use the term 'African' as a synonym for Native as the former is of course more acceptably used today. I use Black as a collective noun for people described by Whites or themselves, for instance and at times, as African, Coloured, Malay or Indian or as a synonym for 'Non-White', though Black was seldom a self-description in South Africa until the late 1960s.

1

town halls, broad streets, trams, harbours and department stores were soon forgotten as he devoted the more than three hundred pages of *Black and White in South East Africa* to pondering South Africa's race 'problem'. By 1910, most White opinion makers called this the 'Native Question', whose conundrum has been neatly summarised as follows:

how to organize society to provide for the mutual access of black labourers and white employers in the coming industrial age without having to pay the heavy social costs of urbanization or losing the dominance of white over black.[3]

Matters of race have dominated writing about South African cities ever since, not least within the historical academy. The resulting literature has numerous strengths, especially the thorough way in which it has explored and explained the history of urban racial segregation, 'Native' administration, popular culture, consciousness and resistance. Such work has greatly aided the task of writing this book.[4] A lacuna, though, is that there is seldom any direct discussion of what people thought about urbanisation, cities or urban life beyond the racial matter of how mine owners and municipalities of White municipal ratepayers saw segregation as solving urban 'problems' or serving their material self-interests, or both.[5] Much of this historiography is also confined to a focus on only one racial or ethnic group within a single city.

Consequently two historical geographers have said that writing about South African cities has displayed 'racial fetishism'; studying 'urban society does not begin with race – rather it reflects the creation of race as part of the intricate development of modern society'.[6] Their argument

---

[3] Maynard W. Swanson, 'The Sanitation Syndrome: Bubonic Plague and Urban Native Policy in the Cape Colony, 1900–1909', *Journal of African History* 18, 3 (1977), 394. See also Saul Dubow, 'South Africa and South Africans: Nationality, Belonging, Citizenship', in Robert Ross, Anne Mager and Bill Nasson (eds), *The Cambridge History of South Africa*, vol. 2 (Cambridge: Cambridge University Press), 17–65.

[4] Review articles on South African urban historiography reveal a great deal about its strengths and weaknesses, provide useful bibliographical surveys and contain some valuable comparative insights themselves. They include Gordon Pirie, 'South African Urban History', *Urban History Yearbook* (1985), 18–29; Chris Saunders, *Writing Urban History: South Africa's Urban Past and Other Essays* (Pretoria: Human Sciences Research Council, 1992), 3–68; *Journal of Southern African Studies: Special Issue on Urban Studies and Urban Change in Southern Africa* 21, 1 (March 1995); Bill Freund, 'Urban History in South Africa', *South African Historical Journal* 52 (2005), 19–31; and V. Bickford-Smith, 'Urban History in the New South Africa: Continuity and Innovation since the End of Apartheid', *Urban History* 35, 2 (2008), 287–315.

[5] For an excellent summary of this work that contains fine insights of its own, including the comment on the predominance of 'history-in-the-city', see Paul Maylam, 'Explaining the Apartheid City: 20 Years of Urban Historiography', *Journal of Southern African Studies* 21, 1 (March 1995), 19–38.

[6] Susan Parnell and Alan Mabin, 'Rethinking Urban South Africa', *Journal of Southern African Studies* 21, 1 (March 1995), 39–62.

was that focusing on racial matters led to an over-emphasis on South African urban exceptionalism that made enlightening comparative studies less likely. Academic particularism of this kind concealed international influence and global commonalities in the evolution of South African cities as well as in the experience, culture and consciousness of their inhabitants. The same observation holds true for contemporary perceptions of urban achievements, problems and solutions, of how the desire of elites for 'improvement' as well as power helped shape South African cities. Even when the intention has been to explain segregation, a focus on race alone can obscure parallels with other forms of exclusion based on class or gender, and their influence on devices like separate entrances or seating or complete exclusion in public and private facilities.[7]

The premise behind the writing of this book is that a study of perceptions and experiences of South African cities not focused solely on race, or on a single racial group or city, is overdue, even though race remains central to the story. There are numerous scholarly explorations of what Europeans and Americans have thought about the rise of big cities and the nature of city life in the past and the consequences of their judgements.[8] Yet, although there are now more people living in African cities than in those of North America, no equivalent study exists for any part of Africa.[9] For South Africa, with a few notable exceptions, most writing can still be described as 'history-in-the-city', the history of events or processes that have happened in cities.[10] 'History-of-the-city', in which the distinct

[7] The class dimension in particular informed V. Bickford-Smith, *Ethnic Pride and Racial Prejudice in Victorian Cape Town* (Cambridge: Cambridge University Press, 1995).

[8] See for instance R. Williams, *The Country and the City* (Oxford: Oxford University Press, 1975); Burton Pike, *The Image of the City in Modern Literature* (Princeton: Princeton University Press, 1981); Andrew Lees, *Cities Perceived: Urban Society in European and American Thought, 1820–1940* (Manchester: Manchester University Press, 1985); Emrys Jones, *Metropolis* (Oxford: Oxford University Press, 1990); Alan Mayne, *The Imagined Slum* (Leicester: Leicester University Press, 1993); Philip Kasinitz, *Metropolis: Centre and Symbol of Our Times* (London: Palgrave Macmillan, 1995); Caroline Arscott, 'Representations of the Victorian City', in Martin Daunton (ed.), *Cambridge Urban History of Britain: Volume Three (1840–1950)* (Cambridge: Cambridge University Press, 2000), 811–32.

[9] Bill Freund, *The African City* (New York: Cambridge University Press, 2007), provides a very useful overview and synthesis of the origins, functions, spatial orderings and economic underpinnings of his subject as well as suggested further reading. The latter includes two other broad takes on urbanisation and African urban experience: David Anderson and Richard Rathbone (eds), *Africa's Urban Past* (Oxford and Portsmouth, NH: James Currey and Heinemann, 2000) and Catherine Coquery-Vidrovitch, *Histoires des villes d'Afrique noire dès origins à la colonisation* (Paris: Albin Michel, 1993). But none of these books focuses on the perception, and consequences of perceptions, of African urbanity in the past, though Freund, both in his monograph and in the chapter he contributed to the Anderson and Rathbone collection, provides useful insights on pessimist and optimist views about the post-colonial city of recent decades.

[10] Maylam, 'Explaining the Apartheid City', 20.

urbanism or 'whole' history of individual cities takes centre stage, remains rare; work of this kind that has substantial comparative dimensions is rarer still.[11]

The intention is to begin to fill this gap by exploring what both insiders and outsiders thought about three of Africa's largest cities, Johannesburg, Durban and Cape Town. Wherever it has occurred, urbanisation has had enormous social, political, cultural and intellectual impact. Equally, perceptions of problems and possibilities of particular cities have had historical significance. They have influenced urban policies, planning, popular culture and the experience of urban belonging or alienation. Indeed, as suggested by Raymond Williams, debates about cities have generally been debates about the future because in most industrial societies a common image of the future is an image of cities.[12] Debates about South African cities frequently focused on the extent and nature of urban 'progress', sometimes thereby on the future of 'civilisation' itself.

My aim is to offer some answers to several overlapping and pre-eminently 'history-of-the-city' questions. How and according to what criteria were our three South African cities fashioned, perceived, experienced, promoted and judged? How and why did residents develop attachments to particular cities, or parts of cities, and what did this mean in terms of their self-identities? And why were cities or parts of cities perceived as having particular characteristics, and how were such senses of place created? The objective is also of course to demonstrate how such opinions and attachments may have mattered over time.

The Union of South Africa was a country created in 1910, the year of Evans' contemplation, out of two British colonies, the Cape of Good Hope and Natal, and two Boer republics, the South African Republic or Transvaal and the Orange Free State. Big cities arose early in this region because South Africa was the first part of sub-Saharan Africa to experience substantial industrialisation. The sizeable cities that emerged with this development were already attracting considerable comment, judgement and speculation in a wide variety of literary and visual forms by the time of Union.

The very number and nature of these sources bear witness to the early extent of economic and technological growth below the Limpopo, as well

---

[11] Attempts at whole city histories that have much to say about the urbanity of an individual city but not a great deal in terms of comparative observations are: Nigel Worden, Elizabeth Van Heyningen and Vivian Bickford-Smith, *Cape Town: The Making of a City* (Cape Town: David Philip, 1998); Vivian Bickford-Smith, Elizabeth Van Heyningen and Nigel Worden, *Cape Town in the Twentieth Century* (Cape Town: David Philip, 1999); Keith Beavon, *Johannesburg: The Making and Shaping of a City* (Pretoria and Leiden: University of South Africa Press, 2004).

[12] Williams, *The Country and the City*, 297.

as to the novelty of African and European urban encounter on such a significant scale. There are travellers' accounts, newspapers, government commissions, oral histories, popular 'city' songs and autobiographies as there would be for many other large African towns. But there are also, and in prolific numbers, local city histories, guides, novels, poetry and books about the 'state of the nation'. Additionally, there are numerous local as well as foreign newsreels, documentaries and feature films, because a domestic film industry was already established in South Africa before the First World War. Many of these sources have hitherto been little used by historians. Hence a further purpose of this book is to demonstrate that they provide rich evidence about South Africa's urban past.

In combination, and understood as providing mutually informing ideological debate, these sources facilitate an understanding of what residents and visitors alike thought about urbanisation and city life. This is the first of three main themes of this book. These thoughts, whether positive or negative or somewhere in between, were the product both of actual experience and the local, national and transnational circulation of ideas. Debate about the nature of acceptable or unacceptable urban life was not confined by national boundaries. One significant and enduring question for visitors as well as those in political and economic control of South Africa's cities – a question inevitably informed by international comparisons – was whether these places were truly metropolitan. In other words, were South African cities great not only in size but in cultural and social achievement; if not, what changes were needed to achieve such status; or if less impressive in some respects than their European or North American counterparts, were South African metropolises nonetheless more impressive in others?

Answers to such questions affected the ways in which South African cities were built and rebuilt and the nature of their architecture, amenities and spatial arrangement. Thus an early middle-class defence of South African cities against their British counterparts was that residents enjoyed more space and a decidedly *rus-in-urbe* existence, and that this was desirable. One example of such opinion was a poem first published in 1873 and republished in a *Readers' Digest*-style South African publication three-quarters of a century later. It argued that even relatively privileged inhabitants of London endured cramped living conditions compared to those experienced by middle-class South African city dwellers. The poem went in part:

> *Your* people are cribb'd and cabin'd,
> Like sprats in a sardine-tin –
> Each head on the tail of a neighbour,
> No room to wag a fin;

. . .
We live in cities of gardens,
Where the air is still serene,
And lines of oaks and acacias
Fringe open streets with green.[13] [Emphasis added]

The perceived desirability of 'our' urban existence was enduringly reflected in the way in which White middle-class South African urban life developed from the late nineteenth century onwards, as with the relatively large size of suburban plots. Lewis Mumford wrote that 'the cities and mansions that people dream of are those in which they finally live'.[14] In reality, material factors such as land values, levels of wealth and technology have been crucial not only in determining how or whether aspirations are realised but also what they may consist of in the first place. Yet aspirations, ideas or perceptions are not readily reducible to material factors. Ideological and material factors frequently interact, and ideas also have had a degree of autonomous agency in affecting the precise ways in which cities have been built, ordered and experienced.

A second major theme of this book is how perceptions of cities or discrete areas within cities contributed to creating or reinforcing social identities like nationality, ethnicity, race and class. Senses of urban territoriality and belonging have powerfully reinforced such identities, even if the circulation of ideas and different cultural traditions, as well as human mobility across cities for work or social purposes, was also a key part of South African urban existence, one usually ignored both in apartheid propaganda and much academic urban history. Senses of living in what was identifiably one's 'own' urban district while 'others' lived in theirs, whether this was through compulsion or volition, powerfully underpinned social identity.[15] Urban boundaries had to be imagined, and they could be frequently crossed, but there was constant interaction between imagined and experienced kinship networks, occupations, institutions and built or topographical features that could be associated with particular areas.[16] In the persuasive language of urban geographers, this interaction transformed spaces into places; and senses of belonging to particular places informed social identities.[17]

---

[13] H.M. Foot, 'Cape Sauce', *Cape Monthly Magazine* (February 1873) cited in Eric Rosenthal and Richard Robinow, *The South African Saturday Book: A Treasury of Writing and Pictures of South Africa, Old and New, Homey and Extraordinary* (London: Hutchinson, 1948), 130–1.

[14] Lewis Mumford, *The Story of Utopias* (New York: Boni and Liveright, 1922), 19.

[15] D. Delaney, *Territory: A Short Introduction* (Oxford: John Wiley & Sons, 2008).

[16] G. Bruno, *Atlas of Emotion: Journeys in Art, Architecture, and Film* (New York: Verso, 2002), 27–8.

[17] T. Cresswell, *Place: A Short Introduction* (Oxford: Wiley-Blackwell, 2004). Dolores Hayden, *The Power of Place* (Boston: MIT Press, 1995).

The argument then is that South African national, ethnic and racial identities were less imagined, more material, than Benedict Anderson's work on national identity might have us believe.[18] Such identities, whether advocated in print by ethnic mobilisers or nationalists, or informed by divisions of labour, were maintained and bolstered by parochial patriotism, or attachment to lived-in places with both real and imagined communal and territorial components. In the twentieth century, national and municipal governments both destroyed as well as created places in South Africa, and both processes affected people's self-identities. As Bloke Modisane, author and ex-resident of Sophiatown – a Johannesburg suburb destroyed by the Afrikaner Nationalist government in the 1950s – put it: 'Something in me died, a piece of me died, with the dying of Sophiatown.'[19]

If particular attention is given to anglophile South African identity in the chapters that follow, this is because, compared to Afrikaner or African identity, British South African identity and twentieth-century social experience have been relatively neglected in existing historiography; completely so in terms of their relationship to urban place.[20] This is surprising, given

---

[18] B. Anderson, *Imagined Communities: Reflections on the Origin and Spread of Nationalism* (London: Verso, 1983).

[19] Bloke Modisane, *Blame Me on History* (London: Thames & Hudson, 1963), 5.

[20] The emphasis of this recent attention, in which the work of John Lambert is particularly notable, has been on the political and institutional process of inculcating Britishness, 'Anglicisation' or British 'loyalism' for the nineteenth and early twentieth century, and for the South African War and First World War, rather than on its social dimensions or the later twentieth century. There is still no monograph on the topic, but see, for instance, James Sturgis, 'Anglicization at the Cape of Good Hope in the Early Nineteenth Century', *Journal of Imperial and Commonwealth History* 11, 1 (1982), 5–32; Vivian Bickford-Smith, 'Revisiting Anglicisation in the Nineteenth Century Cape Colony', *Journal of Imperial and Commonwealth History* 31, 2 (2003), 82–95; Vivian Bickford-Smith, 'The Betrayal of Creole Elites 1880–1920', in Philip D. Morgan and Sean Hawkins (eds), *Black Experience and the Empire* (Oxford and New York: Oxford University Press, 2004), 194–227; Bill Nasson, *Abraham Esau's War: A Black South African War in the Cape, 1899–1902* (Cambridge: Cambridge University Press, 1991); John Lambert, 'South African British? Or Dominion South Africans? The Evolution of an Identity in the 1910s and 1920s', *South African Historical Journal* 43, 1 (November 2000), 197–222; John Lambert, '"Loyalty Its Own Reward": The South African War Experiences of Natal's "Loyal" Africans', in G. Cuthbertson, A. Grundlingh and M.-L. Suttie (eds), *Writing a Wider War: Rethinking Gender and Identity in the South African War, 1899–1902* (Cape Town and Athens, OH: David Philip and Ohio University Press, 2002), 119–31; John Lambert, 'Britishness, South Africanness, and the First World War', in P.A. Buckner and R.D. Francis (eds), *Rediscovering the British World* (Calgary: Calgary University Press, 2005); John Lambert, 'An Identity Threatened: White South Africans, Britishness and Dominion South Africanism, 1934–1939', *Kleio* 37 (2005), 50–70; John Lambert, '"An Unknown People": Reconstructing British South African Identity', *Journal of Imperial and Commonwealth History* 37, 4 (December 2009), 599–617; Andrew Thompson, 'The Languages of Loyalism in Southern Africa, c.1870–1939', *The English Historical Review* CXVIII (2003), 617–50.

that Britishness was the 'prime nationalism of South Africa, against which all subsequent ones ... reacted'; and unlike Afrikaner or African identity, this nationalism could and did embrace both Black and White South Africans.[21] A focus on British South African identity that had both a civic and ethnic dimension also stems from the fact that all three cities by 1910 were places whose municipal governments, businesses and institutions were largely controlled by immigrants from Britain, or their progeny.[22] With the assistance of colonial and Imperial governments, and all the multimedia possibilities available to them in an urban environment, these immigrant elites set about fashioning Cape Town, Durban – and in time Johannesburg – as British cities, through the use of appropriate urban territorial naming, architecture, institutions, associations, recreation and traditions. Consequently it was in the major cities that British national identity and related values, and on occasion overt nationalism, was most successfully maintained across racial and ethnic divides. It was in these cities that Britishness had the majority of its adherents, even if their numbers and proportion of the urban population declined in the course of the twentieth century.

This process was aided by the history of individual cities, their suburbs and institutions provided in a variety of publications, radio programmes, documentaries and newsreels that emphasised their British South African elements. For White English-speaking South Africans in particular, this helped inculcate a sense of urban contribution and belonging, even as Britishness was giving way to a more purely ethnic anglophone South African identity. History could teach such South Africans, irrespective of class divides, that cities were 'our' places, explaining the local architecture, monuments, civic ceremonies and naming of streets and particular suburbs. Once understood in this way, they reinforced a sense of belonging. To explain how this happened, some historical explanation of such suburbs, explanation hitherto confined in most academic urban history to Black residential areas more commonly termed 'locations' or 'townships', is required.[23]

---

[21] Robert Ross, *Status and Respectability in the Cape Colony 1750–1870: A Tragedy of Manners* (Cambridge: Cambridge University Press, 1999), 43.

[22] My understanding of these terms is that whereas members of an ethnic group *will* assume that they have common ancestry or descent, those of a national group *may* do so but in some circumstances they might also believe that nationality is defined by citizenship that can be acquired, perhaps through naturalisation, birth or residence in the territory of the nation state. For similar understandings, see for instance Liah Greenfeld, *Nationalism: Five Roads to Modernity* (Cambridge, MA: Harvard University Press, 1992), 11–13; Steven Grosby, *Nationalism: A Very Short Introduction* (Oxford: Oxford University Press, 2005), 14, 33–5.

[23] One path-breaking paper that makes the academically neglected history of South African suburbs its subject is Alan Mabin, 'Suburbs on the Veld: Modern and Postmodern' (Unpublished paper, University of Witwatersrand, 2005).

Local history was also a significant conveyor of ideas about the identities of particular cities or parts of cities, so this identity *of* cities and their component parts, closely related to how inhabitants identify *with* them, is the third major theme of this book. Explaining the identity of individual cities has exercised the minds of many leading practitioners of urban history from its emergence as a subdiscipline in the 1960s. Yet what Jim Dyos, one of the founders of British urban history, called the 'individual characteristics' of cities remain little explored in South African historiography. This may be a matter of complexity. City identities have objective and subjective components. Both components, as well as the relationship between them, need to be understood.[24]

Objective components may include a city's or space within a city's geographical position, topographical features, economic, military, sacred or administrative functions, architecture, monuments, institutions, spatial arrangement, wealth, amenities, physical and demographic size. Yet subjectivity clearly also comes into play in how all of these factors are imagined, promoted or rejected. Major cities were places where opinions about urban life were on offer in greatest profusion and in the widest variety of aural, visual and literary forms. This was not simply because city life was the focus of discussion, but because cities also played host to the greatest array of opportunities and formats for the expression of opinions. By the early twentieth century, these included newspaper articles, novels, short stories, songs, travellers' accounts, photography, city histories, newsreels and stage and cinematic dramas. Equally, the intention of many of those who produced them was to explore urban spaces, conditions and lifestyles in 'experiential realist' fashion, by providing 'moment-by-moment experience – sensory, visceral, and mental'.[25]

A further intention of some was to attempt an overall 'sense-of-place'. In 1957 the British writer James (later Jan) Morris described Johannesburg as 'Steely hardness ... gaunt power'; Durban as 'A conjunction of the tomtom and the *Tatler*'; and Cape Town as 'A little of San Francisco ... and a whisper of France'.[26] Likewise Peter Abrahams, a 'Coloured' writer who grew up in and around several working-class areas of Johannesburg, described one of them in 1946: 'The pulsating motion of Malay Camp at night was everywhere. Warm and intense and throbbing.'[27] Studying the construction and transmission of such senses of particular urban places, and the sensory and emotional experiences

---

[24] H.J. Dyos (ed.), *The Study of Urban History* (London: Edward Arnold, 1968), 15.

[25] Robert Alter, *Imagined Cities: Urban Experience and the Language of the Novel* (New Haven and London: Yale University Press, 2005), x.

[26] James Morris, *South African Winter* (London: Faber & Faber, 1958), 20–1, 92, 186.

[27] Peter Abrahams, *Mine Boy* (London: Faber & Faber, 1946), 49.

involved, is now a burgeoning field of scholarship, even if much of the existing work has concentrated on the very recent past or on representations in one medium only, most often either novels or cinema.[28]

Giuliana Bruno's work has been more ambitious than most in this respect. She has demonstrated that both travelogues and fiction films draw on a long European tradition of representing cities in which literary depictions were giving way to visual forms such as photography or magic lantern shows by the end of the nineteenth century. Bruno argues that cinema, whose development coincided with rapid advances in travel technology, provided a virtual form of tourism with a mixture of spectacle, exotic 'otherness' and education.[29] Cinema's depiction of particular places has been 'both an extension and an effect of the tourist's gaze'.[30]

Individual cities and city spaces have been represented in fictional formats like novels, feature films and poetry as well as ostensibly non-fiction social surveys, guidebooks, travel writing, city histories, select committee reports and documentaries. The divide between these fictional and non-fictional forms in terms of accuracy of information provided has not always been readily discernible. Equally, representations of any kind generally reflect contemporary social attitudes to a particular urban place or to the urban in general.[31] They might in turn help shape or maintain those attitudes, and thereby contribute to conveying the place's identity to both visitors and residents. Creating and conveying the identity of a city

---

[28] Path-breaking general accounts of how novels have represented the city included Williams, *The Country and the City* and Pike, *The Image of the City*. Since then there have been numerous accounts of how particular individual cities have been imagined in literature, albeit many have focused on the near present. For a recent work that has looked at how a number of significant novelists like Flaubert, Joyce and Dickens have portrayed different cities see Alter, *Imagined Cities*. On sensory history and the history of emotions, see Joyce Davidson and Christine Milligan, 'Embodying Emotion Sensing Space: Introducing Emotional Geographies', *Social and Cultural Geography* 5, 4 (December 2004), 523–32 and Mark M. Smith, 'Consuming Sense, Making Sense: Perils and Prospects for Sensory History', *Journal of Social History* 40, 4 (Summer 2007), 841–58. Some key works that each examines how a range of cities have been represented in film are D.B. Clarke (ed.), *The Cinematic City* (London and New York: Routledge, 1997); M. Shiel and T. Fitzmaurice (eds), *Cinema and the City: Film and Urban Societies in a Global Context* (Oxford: Blackwell, 2001); Bruno, *Atlas of Emotion*. Krause and P. Petro (eds), *Global Cities: Cinema, Architecture and Urbanism in a Digital Age* (New Brunswick and London: Rutgers University Press, 2003).

[29] Bruno, *Atlas of Emotion*, 77–9, 191.

[30] Giuliana Bruno, 'City Views: The Voyage of Film Images', in Clarke (ed.), *The Cinematic City*, 47.

[31] Lees, *Cities Perceived* was a pioneering and monumental demonstration of how this happened in Britain, Germany and the United States in the late nineteenth and early twentieth centuries.

or part of a city, an imaginative process that usually draws on material realities, has in turn affected those realities. An area might be perceived to be a 'slum' and demolished, and, as a consequence, its inhabitants get forcibly relocated.[32] In response, some residents or ex-residents might denounce such judgements and actions and portray the place in more positive fashion, as has happened in South Africa.

How a particular city is perceived can influence – and has influenced – some who might want to live there, the extent of tourism or fixed investment and its material fortunes. This realisation made those who governed cities promote their attributes and achievements. It also made municipalities and local businessmen seek to 'improve' those attributes in material and cultural terms. As transport and communication systems generally grew in pace and sophistication with industrialisation, those in charge of city governance competed on a global scale to attract immigrants, tourism and investment.[33] 'Place-sellers', officials in charge of publicising a city's attractions, or amateur city boosters attempted to encapsulate a place's supposedly unique and attractive characteristics through a variety of literary and visual media such as guide books, city histories, brochures or advertisements. Importantly, in the process they built on, challenged or strove to change pre-existing judgements and popular perceptions.[34]

In their efforts to promote a city, 'place-sellers' and amateur boosters usually employed slogans or epithets. These epithets were intended to create some unifying and positive idea about each place. A city might of course be given more than one epithet, or different ones over time. This sometimes happened as place-sellers deliberately attempted to alter what they considered to have been previously damaging stereotypes. For instance, the 'Glasgow's Miles Better' advertising campaign was a conscious attempt to alter that Scottish city's image as 'The Red Clyde' or 'The Sparta of the North'. The idea was to transform a place previously associated in popular imagination with revolutionary socialism or harsh lifestyles of the working class into 'Glasgow City of Culture': a more refined and middle-class and safer place to live and invest in or visit.[35]

---

[32] The argument of Mayne, *Imagined Slum*.

[33] C.M. Law, *Urban Tourism: Attracting Visitors to Large Cities* (London and New York: Mansell, 1993); P. Kotler, D.H. Haider and I. Rain, *Marketing Places: Attracting Investment, Industry, and Tourism to Cities, States and Nations* (New York: The Free Press, 1993); B.M. Kolb, *Tourism Marketing for Cities and Towns: Using Branding and Events to Attract Tourists* (Burlington and Oxford: Butterworth-Heinemann, 2006).

[34] Stephen V. Ward, *Selling Places: The Marketing and Promotion of Towns and Cities 1850–2000* (London and New York: Spon Press, 1998); John Urry, *The Tourist Gaze* (London, Thousand Oaks and New Delhi: Sage Publications, 2002).

[35] Colin McArthur, 'Chinese Boxes and Russian Dolls: Tracking the Elusive Cinematic City', in Clarke (ed.), *The Cinematic City*, 19–21.

Attempting to provide cities with positive identities has commonly involved rather more than mere propaganda. From the second half of the nineteenth century, many cities in the industrial world were being physically rebuilt and 'improved' by municipal authorities in reaction to criticisms from doctors, novelists, clergymen, journalists and intellectuals. According to such criticisms, industrialisation had produced what Dickens dubbed a 'Coketown': a city that was unhealthy, ugly, dehumanising, immoral, over-crowded, dangerous and lacking in anything morally or physically uplifting in the way of recreation or entertainment.[36] Much thinking about cities subsequently involved suggesting remedies, not least in terms of how industry might be harnessed for the benefit of citizens, rather than citizens merely harnessed to industry. Efforts were made through the extended provision of drains and sewers, paved streets and pavements, electric light or trams and trains that allowed many more to escape crowded inner city areas.[37]

By the early twentieth century, it had become the objective – in some cases fulfilled – of civic authorities and local businessmen in much of the anglophone world and beyond to build aesthetically more pleasing cities, prompted by combined desire for commercial profit, private glory and communal benefit.[38] The writing of theorists, who were often also pioneering practitioners of town planning on both sides of the Atlantic, provided detailed guidelines on how they thought this might be best achieved.[39] Their ideas subsequently influenced urban development in the southern hemisphere.[40] So cities of the south, including Evans' Durban, were at least partially designed or redesigned in accordance with British and American perceptions of what would remedy urban defects and provide a supposedly desirable and attractive urbanity.

---

[36] Charles Dickens, *Hard Times* (London: Penguin, [1854] 2003).

[37] Lees, *Cities Perceived*; Peter Hall, *Cities of Tomorrow: An Intellectual History of Urban Planning and Design in the Twentieth Century* (Oxford: Blackwell, 1998).

[38] Asa Briggs, *Victorian Cities* (London: Odhams Press, 1963); Tristram Hunt, *Building Jerusalem: The Rise and Fall of the Victorian City* (London: Weidenfeld & Nicolson, 2004); Simon Gunn, *The Public Culture of the Victorian Middle Class: Ritual and Authority and the English Industrial City, 1840–1914* (Manchester: Manchester University Press, 2008).

[39] Well-known examples include Ebenezer Howard, *Garden Cities of Tomorrow: Being the Second Edition of 'Tomorrow: A Peaceful Path to Reform'* (London: Swan Sonnenschein & Co., 1902); Charles Mulford Robinson, *The Improvement of Towns and Cities; Or the Practical Basis of Civic Aesthetics* (New York and London: Putnam's Sons, 1901) and *Modern Civic Art* (New York: Putnam, 1918 [1903]); Patrick Geddes, *Cities in Evolution* (London: Williams & Norgate, 1915).

[40] Alan Mabin and Dan Smit, 'Reconstructing South Africa's Cities? The Making of Urban Planning 1900–2000', *Planning Perspectives* 12 (1997), 193–223. For Two works that explore how northern ideas spread to other parts of the southern hemisphere such as India and Australia are: Helen Meller, *Patrick Geddes: Social Evolutionist and City Planner* (London and New York: Routledge, 1990); Robert Freestone, *Designing Australia: Cities, Culture, Commerce and the City Beautiful, 1900–1930* (London: Routledge, 2007).

The three main themes of the book are explored within a thematic-chronological framework that deserves its own brief introduction. Its outer parameters stretch from the emergence of substantial cities in the late nineteenth century through to the beginning of the 1960s. The reason for ending at this point is not just the prosaic matter of length. The end of the 1950s, described by one Black writer who lived through it as 'the fabulous decade', a time of 'infinite hope and possibilities', marked a political sea change in the debate about the future of the country and its cities.[41] In 1960, the shooting of sixty-nine protestors by police at Sharpeville was followed by a national State of Emergency and the banning of the African National Congress (ANC) and Pan African Congress (PAC). The prospect of a peaceful end to White supremacy now seemed remote. The Afrikaner-dominated National Party entrenched its power by extending the state security apparatus. Also in 1960, White voters came down narrowly in favour of a republic and therefore the removal of the British monarch as head of state. The following year South Africa left the Commonwealth. Both developments were significant blows to the continued viability of Britishness as a possible South African identity, one given considerable attention in this book.

The next chapter, 'Inventing British cities in Africa', describes the growth and anglicisation of Cape Town, Durban and Johannesburg in the nineteenth and early twentieth century that ensured they became pre-eminently places that helped convey and maintain British identity and values. By the beginning of the twentieth century, enduring and important elements of each city's form of governance, economy, demographic composition and social geography were established. Describing this formative period also allows us to introduce a past, in the form of place-names, events and individuals, subsequently much drawn upon in the likes of twentieth-century city histories, travelogues and tourism material. These helped confer each city's uniqueness, as well as a sense of British belonging for at least some of their inhabitants.

Yet there were limits to this invention of British cities. British identity and traditions were not the only ones available and visible in South African cities. Traditions and behaviour that appeared to be different, and perhaps inimical to Britishness, caused anxiety among the more anglicised White and Black inhabitants. Urban ills such as crime, disease, 'immorality', economic depression, industrial unrest and other threats to desirable social order produced a similar effect. All raised intermittent doubts about South African urban 'progress' between the 1870s and early 1920s, with Johannesburg in particular frequently depicted as a 'New

---

[41] Lewis Nkosi, *Home and Exile* (London: Longman, 1965), 25.

Babylon'. These anxieties and how they were expressed in a wide variety of media, including literature, film and song, is the topic of Chapter 3, 'More Babylon than Birmingham?' Its chronological focus considerably overlaps with that of Chapter 2.

Although, in any period, South African cities were portrayed in both optimistic and pessimistic fashion, as was the case in most individual accounts, more positive depictions predominated from the mid-1920s to the mid-1940s. These grew in number and gained considerable international acceptance as greater urban 'order' was achieved, and as publicity associations were formed that actively promoted positive and 'unique' city identities within a still British South Africa. Publicity material was 'Selling sunlit Utopias', the title of Chapter 4. Members of the urban Black working class, to the extent that they featured at all, were portrayed as 'local colour': be it as Cape Town flower-sellers and New Year Carnival participants, Durban Rickshaw Pullers and Indian fire-walkers or Johannesburg Mine Dancers. A 'New African' identity that embraced modernity including elements of American culture was ignored.

Such publicity efforts continued as rural–urban migration accelerated rapidly during the Second World War and prompted renewed post-war anxieties in anglophone circles about the urban future in the late 1940s and 1950s. Government commissions, academic research and documentaries worried once more about the problem of slums, immorality and crime. Large conurbations of self-built shacks were now highly visible in or around the three main cities. Closer international scrutiny of South African urban life accompanied the advent of Afrikaner nationalist rule and the coming of apartheid in 1948. Many now in power and promoting such policies were republicans who supported Germany during the Second World War, particularly shocking to those with British identity within or outside the country. Such scrutiny helps explain the enormous global success enjoyed by Alan Paton's novel *Cry, the Beloved Country*, published the same year. *Cry, the Beloved Country* focused on the plight of the African urban poor in Johannesburg, and drew national and international attention to South African 'slums'. It did so in a fashion similar to middle-class concerns about the urban poor in Victorian Britain contained in Mearns' *Bitter Cry of Outcast London*.[42] Most 'state of the (South African) nation' literary and visual foreign assessments of South African cities in the 1950s referred overtly or implicitly to Paton and *Cry, the Beloved Country*. The three 'metropolises' – Durban, Cape Town and Johannesburg – were predictably central to this debate. They featured in

[42] Gareth Stedman Jones, *Outcast London* (Harmondsworth: Penguin, 1976).

negative verdicts proffered in books commissioned by the British publisher Victor Gollancz, as well as in films and television documentaries. Notable among these were Anglican priest Michael Scott's *Civilisation on Trial*, a film shown in Britain and informally at the United Nations; and *African Conflict*, a two-part production for Ed Murrow's CBS *See It Now* television series, in the United States.

By drawing attention to the existence of slums and condemning that existence in prose or celluloid, popular disseminators of South African 'Bitter Cries' helped politicians in central and local governments justify policies that led to actual slum condemnation and destruction, as seen in Sydney, Birmingham and San Francisco.[43] Many Black South African inhabitants of places described in this way felt that slum clearance involved the destruction of community. The first major wave of Black writing about South African cities in the late 1940s and 1950s may have contained far harsher denunciations of urban conditions than White 'Bitter Cry' portrayals. Yet authors like Can Themba, Bloke Modisane, Alex La Guma and Richard Rive challenged existing dominant White representations and described much creativity amid urban hardship. Those from Johannesburg in particular depicted their lives and times in almost Baudelairian fashion while evoking a strong sense of place and belonging. Their urban writing and friendships across the race divide affected the way that a minority of influential White writers and film makers such as Anthony Sampson, Nadine Gordimer and Lionel Rogosin experienced and portrayed South African cities. The title of Chapter 5 is 'Bitter cries and Black Baudelaires'.

Chapter 6, as its title states, provides an epilogue to the book by exploring urban 'Remembrance of things past' against the backdrop of a swift overview of change and continuity in depictions of South African cities since 1960. As 'slum' eradication intensified, and as a result of apartheid-era implementation of urban forced removals, Black reminiscences were evocations of communal urban life, frequently described in Utopian terms. In the fashion of Jane Jacobs bemoaning the results of modern planning in American cities in 1961, the likes of oral testimonies, novels and autobiographies lauded a finer urbanism of vibrant, albeit poor, culturally creolised and cosmopolitan communities now threatened or already dismantled.[44] The fact that they did so, and in the process evoked a nostalgic collective memory of lost place and times, had much to do with the political and social uncertainties of the urban present that produced them.

---

[43] Mayne, *The Imagined Slum* explores what happened in these non-South African cities.
[44] Jane Jacobs, *The Death and Life of American Cities* (New York: Random House, 1961).

2   Inventing British cities in Africa

Sixty years before Evans contemplated Durban from the Berea, the region that became the Union of South Africa was overwhelmingly rural. Cape Town had acquired city status through the appointment of an Anglican bishop in 1847, but only had around 20,000 inhabitants.[1] Durban was still a village called Port Natal, with little more than a hundred residents. Johannesburg did not exist.

The history of urban settlement in southern Africa stretched back well before colonial times, but such places were small and impermanent. One of the earliest was Mapungubwe, situated on the top of a hill in what is now South Africa's Limpopo province and first settled around 1000 AD. As with the better-known Great Zimbabwe to its north, Mapungubwe was probably linked to the Indian Ocean trade networks, a product of more intensive local cultivation and technological specialisation. Yet neither of these settlements survived beyond the middle of the fifteenth century. Much the same is true of the 'agro-towns' of modern-day eastern Botswana, some of which were encountered by Europeans in the late nineteenth century. As these towns grew beyond the capacity of their inhabitants to farm surrounding areas with sufficient success, they disappeared as their populations (up to 20,000) moved on to new locations.[2]

Far larger and more enduring cities of more than 100,000 inhabitants only appeared in southern Africa around 1900. The three largest by that date were Johannesburg, Cape Town and Durban (the demographic breakdown of their populations in 1911 is given in Table 2.1). Substantial urbanisation was a result of the Mineral Revolution, the discovery of diamonds at Kimberley in 1870 and gold on the Witwatersrand in 1886. The broader political and economic processes caused by the Mineral Revolution included accelerated conquest and annexation of independent African societies by the

[1] David Bloomberg, *The Chain Gang: Mayors Who Served in Cape Town's City Hall* (Cape Town: Ampersand Press, 2011).
[2] Freund, *African City*, 3–7.

Table 2.1: *Population of Johannesburg, Cape Town and Durban according to Census categories of 1911*

	'European or White'	'Bantu'	'Mixed and Other Coloured'	Total
Johannesburg	119,953	101,971	15,180	237,104
Cape Town	85,442	1,388	74,749	161,579
Durban	34,880	18,947	36,171	89,998

Union Government (UG) of South Africa, *UG 32: Census for 1911* (Pretoria: Government Printer, 1912), 86–7, 90–1. The figures include suburban populations but, like most census figures, should be treated as approximations.

British, and their subsequent use of taxation to extract African labour.[3] The Mineral Revolution was also central to changed social relations and values in African societies within the context of colonial expansion and ecological crisis: drought, cattle disease, diminishing land and animals. Travelling and working as migrant labourers in the mines or in other urban occupations became a desire or necessity for many young African men in southern Africa. Such work could pay for guns, clothes, blankets, ploughs and wagons, or mean money to pay bride wealth (*lobola*) or colonial taxes. Migrant work in the emerging cities became a new rite of passage, one initially aimed at maintaining viable rural households and traditions.[4]

By Union in 1910, significant components of the 'urbanism' of Cape Town, Durban and Johannesburg were in place. These components included long-enduring features of each city's built environment, spatial layout, demographic composition and social geography, as well as their 'social, economic, and cultural systems'.[5] All of these factors played a part in how each city was subsequently experienced, perceived and promoted, so they need to be delineated. Doing so requires discussing broader political, social and economic developments that preceded Union, and that also help to explain the nature of the three cities.

Knowledge of this pre-Union history is important for another reason. It was much described in travel literature, tourism material, travelogues and

---

[3] See for instance, Charles H. Feinstein, *An Economic History of South Africa: Conquest, Discrimination and Development* (Cambridge: Cambridge University Press, 2005), 22–73.

[4] William H. Worger, *South Africa's City of Diamonds: Mine Workers and Monopoly Capitalism in Kimberley, 1867–1895* (Johannesburg: AD. Donker, 1987), 64–109; Patrick Harries, *Work, Culture and Identity: Migrant Labourers in Mozambique and South Africa, c.1880–1910* (Portsmouth, NH, London and Johannesburg: Heinemann, James Currey and Witwatersrand University Press, 1994).

[5] Anthony D. King, *Urbanism, Colonialism, and the World-Economy: Cultural and Spatial Foundations of the World Urban System* (London and New York: Routledge, 1990), 1.

histories of the cities subsequently produced in abundant numbers in the twentieth century. These accounts cumulatively conferred a distinctive identity on each city. The authors of city histories in particular used the nineteenth-century past to provide a sense of place and belonging for urban residents who saw themselves as British.

The fact that many, Black as well as White, adopted a British identity stemmed from anglicisation, policies and processes aimed at inculcating Britishness, which commenced in the nineteenth century.[6] The complex relationship between South African cities and the anglicisation that ensued has hardly been explored.[7] This is surprising given that Afrikaner and African national identities were responses to Britishness.[8]

Unlike African or Afrikaner identity, the acquisition of Britishness was open to those within the Empire across possible racial or ethnic divides. This was because from its eighteenth-century inception Britishness had been established as a civic rather than an ethnic national identity to forge Britons out of the likes of the Scots, Welsh, English and Irish. Hence it was designed to serve as an umbrella nationalism over other actual or potential sub-nationalisms. Britishness could be an acquired identity, whether through naturalisation, birth or residence in the territory of Britain, its colonies or dominions.[9]

Even after Union, Britishness remained an available and sometimes attractive identity, even though at other times, or simultaneously, some who adopted it might see themselves as, for instance, South African,

[6] 'Anglicisation' has become the accepted term even if it obscures non-English (e.g. Scottish) contributions to the process of inculcating Britishness; there appears to be no short but more embracing equivalent. The same comment applies to terms like 'anglophone' or 'anglophile'. James Sturgis, 'Anglicisation at the Cape of Good Hope in the Early Nineteenth Century', *Journal of Imperial and Commonwealth History* 11 (1982), 5–32; Bickford-Smith, 'Revisiting Anglicisation in the Nineteenth-Century Cape Colony', 82–95.

[7] Though there has been work within the areas of architecture and design in capital cities and, for more recent times, the causes and nature of 'Divided Cities' such as Berlin, Jerusalem or Beirut. One notable exception, at least in terms of cities and nationalisms, is F. Driver and D. Gilbert (eds), *Imperial Cities* (Manchester: Manchester University Press, 1999). For others and further bibliographical information, see V. Bickford-Smith (ed.), 'Cities and Nationalisms', Special Issue, *Journal of Urban History* 38, 5 (2012). Usefully suggestive for South Africa, if not directly investigating the theme, is relatively recent works on Royal Tours such as Phillip Buckner, 'The Royal Tour of 1901 and the Construction of an Imperial Identity in South Africa', *South African Historical Journal* 41, 1 (1999), 324–48; Hilary Sapire, 'Ambiguities of Loyalism: The Prince of Wales in India and Africa, 1921 and 25', *History Workshop Journal* 73 (2011), 37–65; H. Sapire, 'African Loyalism and Its Discontents: The Royal Tour of South Africa, 1947', *The Historical Journal* 54, 1 (2011), 215–40.

[8] Robert Ross, *Status and Respectability*, used the synonym 'English' for 'British', like many in the nineteenth-century Cape Colony.

[9] See for instance Greenfield, *Nationalism: Five Roads to Modernity*, 11–13; Grosby, *Nationalisms: A Very Short Introduction*, 14, 33–5.

Coloured, Zulu, Dutch or Indian. Values associated with Britishness could also change over time, while 'Americanisation' became an increasingly important component of South African cultural creolisation in the twentieth century.[10] Nonetheless civic Britishness attracted Black adherents even as the majority of settlers from Britain itself espoused an ethnic variation. The assumption here was that being British required shared ancestry, history and culture, in other words pale skins and origins traceable to the British Isles. For a combination of material and ideological reasons, anyone without 'kith-and-kin' British characteristics was seen as inferior. This included creolised elites who had acquired the English language, British education and dress and who saw themselves as British. Distinction was made easier when such 'others' were perceptibly different in terms of skin colour.

Yet many 'others' who were dismissed or denounced in this way overtly retained a civic British identity. This was because of associations they continued to make between Britishness, modernity, occupational opportunity and their own career choices. The Cape offered ostensible equality before the law and the possibility of acquiring political rights. The hope for those that saw themselves as Black British was that such rights would be extended to all other parts of South Africa. There appeared to be few viable alternatives to British identity given British military might, the perception that Boer rule would be worse and the impracticality of returning to pre-colonial existence. Black British expectation, however foolish this may seem with hindsight, was that British Imperial governments, personified by the monarch, might offer some protection against settler racism and discrimination, whether Boer or British or a combination of the two.[11]

The process of anglicisation accompanied the emergence of cities in southern Africa in the nineteenth century. By the time of Union, most of those who saw themselves as British or British South Africans were clustered in these cities. As Imperial ties weakened in the course of the

[10] J.T. Campbell, 'The Americanization of South Africa', in E.T. May and R. Wagnleitner (eds), *Here, There, and Everywhere: The Foreign Politics of American Popular Culture* (Hanover, NH: University Press of New England, 2000), 34–63.

[11] The works that have most directly informed my understanding of (sub-, supra-) nationalism in general and Britishness in particular beyond Greenfield and Grosby are: Anderson, *Imagined Communities*; R. Colls and P. Dodd (eds), *Englishness: Politics and Culture 1880–1920* (Beckenham: Croom Helm, 1986); Eric Hobsbawm, *Nations and Nationalism since 1780: Program, Myth, Reality*, (Cambridge: Cambridge University Press, 1990); Linda Colley, *Britons: Forging the Nation, 1707–1832* (New Haven: Yale University Press, 1992); Partha Chatterjee, *Nationalist Thought and the Colonial World* (Minneapolis: University of Minneapolis Press, 1993); Nicole Piper, *Racism, Nationalism and Citizenship: Ethnic Minorities in Britain and Germany* (Aldershot: Ashgate Publishers, 1998).

twentieth century, the majority of those who retained at least a distinctly anglophile South African identity, irrespective of race, still lived in cities.

Anglicisation began after the British seized the Cape Colony from the Dutch during the Napoleonic Wars. The Dutch East India Company (DEIC) had initiated European settlement at the Cape by establishing a refreshment station there in 1652, for its fleets travelling between Amsterdam and its spice trade possessions in the East.[12] The Table Bay area had already been a place of barter between local 'Hottentot' (Khoisan) inhabitants and the crews of passing European ships for more than a century.[13]

Formative years for Cape Town, Durban and Johannesburg

The Cape station that evolved into Cape Town served as a trading centre between land and sea, hinterland and port. The extent of such trade, together with its functions as DEIC administrative capital and military headquarters, determined subsequent economic and demographic growth. For many decades both were very slow, and the small settlement became known as *Kaapstad* or Cape Town only in the eighteenth century. In not dissimilar fashion to Jamestown, Virginia, settlers faced desperate struggles with food shortages and indigenous inhabitants who tried to retain their land and independence. In the Cape, as in the early years of Durban, there were also encounters with wild animals.

Cape Town's location was in keeping with other colonial trade settlements that needed access to the sea and had to be defensible, considerations that led to topographical patterns conditioning axes of future growth.[14] The first streets of what would in time become the central business district were laid out in grid plan fashion close to the sea in an amphitheatre formed by Table Mountain (easily identifiable to passing ships) and Signal Hill. The putative town was placed next to a Vauban-style castle and on the seaward side of a vegetable garden established to help provision DEIC fleets. The main paths out of the mountainous amphitheatre formed arterial routes of future development: whether

---

[12] The most detailed modern account of Cape Town's growth and development before the twentieth century is provided by Worden et al., *Cape Town: The Making of a City*, and the summary here draws mainly from this source.

[13] Khoisan is the combined term used by scholars to describe Khoi herders and San hunter-gatherers.

[14] Gillian Tindall, 'Existential Cities', in R. Fermour-Hesketh (ed.), *Architecture of the British Empire* (New York: The Vendrom Press, 1986), 82. See also Robert Home, *Of Planting and Planning: The Making of British Colonial Cities* (London and New York: Routledge, 1997).

around the back of Table Mountain in a south-eastwards direction towards the DEIC's winter anchorage at Simon's Town, much further down the Cape Peninsula, or northwards and north-eastwards, across the sand-strewn and not easily passable Cape Flats, into the interior.

It was along the south-eastwards route behind Table Mountain that land was first granted to 'free burghers' for farming purposes in the first decade of settlement, presaging territorial expansion at the expense of the Khoisan. Such 'Dutch' free burghers came to include significant numbers of assimilated French and Germans of Protestant persuasion alongside those from the Netherlands. Slaves were almost immediately imported by the DEIC for both domestic and general labouring purposes, an early indication of enduring broad status divisions along racial lines. Initially slaves came mainly from the Dutch East Indies, and included Muslims from Malaysia and Indonesia; towards the end of the eighteenth century many were also imported from Madagascar and Mozambique.

The DEIC decision in the early 1670s that the Cape would be a permanent settlement led to the gradual but inexorable expansion of colonial borders over the next 150 years. As a consequence of military defeat, territorial dispossession and the ravages of smallpox, the Khoi herders were eventually reduced to servile status. The San (hunter-gatherer 'Bushmen') encountered by the Dutch were all but exterminated, often in deliberate genocidal raids by burgher commandoes. By the end of Dutch rule, the colony stretched hundreds of kilometres, from close to the mouth of the Orange River in the north-west to the Great Fish River in the east. The eastern frontier saw conflict between White settlers and Xhosa-speaking Africans over land and livestock for a further century.[15]

At the time of the second British conquest of the Cape in 1806, Cape Town was still the only sizeable urban centre in an overwhelmingly rural colony. The town's population was a mere 16,000 out of the colony's total of 75,000. Mirroring the major social division in the colony as a whole, there were equal numbers of lighter-skinned free burghers and the darker-skinned bonded, with only a small number of 'Free Blacks'. The built-up area of the town was clustered around the DEIC's vegetable garden and consisted of canteens and boarding houses, as well as white-washed, green-shuttered, thatched-roof homes, some of which contained shops or artisan workshops as homes did in Europe. The rest of the amphitheatre beneath Table Mountain and Signal Hill was occupied by sizeable estates with gabled 'Cape Dutch' style farmhouses.

---

[15] Still the best overall account of the Dutch period and the colonial social structure it produced is R. Elphick and H. Giliomee (eds), *The Shaping of South African Society* (Cape Town and London: Longman, 1989).

Elsewhere on the Peninsula there were farms and a few hamlets, mostly behind Table Mountain along the old wagon road route that ran for 40 kilometres to Simon's Town. The farms included Groot Constantia, established by Governor Simon Van der Stel in the 1680s. Its sweet Constantia wine gained some fame in Europe. Partly as a consequence, Groot Constantia farm was frequently visited by travellers to Cape Town from the late eighteenth century onwards.[16]

British control of the Cape from 1806 increased the pace of urban growth, in time turning the southern hamlets into more substantial and desirable suburbs. Their location behind Table Mountain offered protection from the wind-driven dust storms, greater heat and unpleasant smells of the town itself. It also offered verdant and spectacular scenery.

Economic activity was quickened by the removal of DEIC monopolies and by the fact that the town was brought within the networks and commercial orbit of the world's first industrial empire. The growth of agricultural exports, notably wool but also ostrich feathers and wine, resulted in harbour and railway construction in the 1860s. Government-funded railway lines linked Cape Town to the farmlands and, after the discovery of diamonds, to Kimberley by the 1880s. A privately financed line and horse-drawn omnibus service also connected the town to the southern suburbs by 1864.[17]

A steady immigration of merchants, tradesmen and artisans from Britain accompanied colonial control of the Cape. Their numbers, as well as those of rural–urban migrants to Cape Town from the interior, were significantly increased from the 1870s by the Mineral Revolution. Meanwhile, Cape Town's continued role as administrative capital and military headquarters meant the presence of considerable numbers of British colonial officials and military personnel into the early twentieth century. In addition, the city's important location on the sea route between India and Britain ensured not only that it was visited by many travelling that route on behalf of the British East India Company but that some of these 'Indians' (as they were dubbed) chose to retire to Cape Town.[18]

Influenced by a combination of the ideas of Adam Smith and William Wilberforce, the British gave greater freedom of movement to the Khoi in 1828 and conferred slave emancipation in 1834. This introduced official legal equality for all in the Cape Colony. Nonetheless, mid-

---

[16] Robert Ross, 'Cape Town (1750–1850): Synthesis in the Dialectic of Continents', in R. Ross and G.J. Telkamp (eds), *Colonial Cities: Essays on Urbanism in a Colonial Context* (Leiden: Martinus Nijhoff, 1985).

[17] Bickford-Smith, *Ethnic Pride and Racial Prejudice*, 11–14.

[18] Worden et al., *Cape Town: The Making of a City*, 96–7, 117, 131, 140–1, 163, 185, 252.

nineteenth-century census enumerators distinguished between 'Whites' (or 'Europeans') and 'Coloureds' (slave descendants, Khoi, Africans or darker-skinned people of 'mixed-race' descent). Later in the century 'Coloured' came to be used as a term that excluded Africans, who were by then more usually referred to as 'Natives' by Whites. All these terms were also commonly used as self-descriptions.[19]

Yet when the colonial government created a Cape Town municipality (1840), there were no racial restrictions on local officials or voters. Similarly, both Representative and Responsible Government in the Cape, bestowed by the British in 1853 and 1872 respectively, were based on non-racial franchises, albeit for men alone. This political and legal system came to be known as the 'Cape system' or the 'Cape liberal tradition' by the twentieth century. Property and wage qualifications for the vote were low, albeit high enough to ensure that Whites would be in a majority for the immediate future. To this end, financial qualifications were raised and a simple education test added in 1892.[20]

Because of slave emancipation, as well as other social and economic changes brought about by British colonial rule, about 15,000 pastoral 'Boers', White farmers who spoke Dutch or its creolised variation, Afrikaans, left the Colony in the 1830s. The Great Trek, as this exodus was called, led to Boer '*voortrekkers*' clashing violently with independent African chieftaincies like Shaka's Zulus in the interior. Nonetheless, the *voortrekkers* established the republics of Natalia (1838), the South African Republic or Transvaal (1852) and the Orange Free State (1854).[21] In each case, their constitutions clearly rejected the Cape system. Thus the Transvaal constitution of 1858 overtly stated that 'the people desire to permit no equality between coloured people and the white inhabitants of the country, either in church or state'.[22] Consequently, citizenship was limited to those categorised as Whites, even if some of those so described were in reality of mixed-race descent.

Greater freedom of movement for the Khoi and slave emancipation boosted the building of low-cost housing in Cape Town for them as for more recent rural migrants, in areas within easy walking distance of employment opportunities. These were small white-washed dwellings in Cape style, with flat roofs, after the danger of fire had sharply reduced the use of thatch in the town centre. They crept westward up the slopes of

---

[19] Ibid., 31, 186–209.
[20] Stanley Trapido, 'White Conflict and Non-White Participation in the Politics of the Cape of Good Hope, 1853–1910' (PhD thesis, London, 1970); Phylllis Lewsen, 'The Cape Liberal Tradition – Myth or Reality?', *Race and Class* 13 (July 1971), 65–80.
[21] Nigel Worden, *The Making of Modern South Africa* (Oxford: Blackwell, 1994), 11–17.
[22] Cited in Worden, *The Making of Modern South Africa*, 70.

Signal Hill creating the distinctive building stock of what became known as the 'Malay Quarter'. The term 'Malay' was not simply a reference to the geographical origins of slave descendants. From the mid-nineteenth century it was used as a synonym for 'Coloured' Muslims of whatever geographical origin. Despite its name, the Malay Quarter was multi-racial into the twentieth century even if a critical mass of Muslims resided there, reflected by the location of a Muslim cemetery, mosques and madrasas.

New and humbler house-building also took place eastward of the DEIC gardens and Castle, into the town's sixth district as delineated by municipal legislation in 1867, hence its enduring colloquial name of District Six.[23] Small workshops and factories gradually spread from the city centre, following flatter ground through District Six along or near the main road, and (from the 1860s) the railway lines out of town towards the north as well as to the southern suburbs. The migration of Africans from the Eastern Cape, and the arrival of East European Jewish artisans and labourers and Indian small-scale traders, furthered the development of a substantial and cosmopolitan, multi-racial working-class 'inner city' population. The desire for cheaper and more easily controllable labour caused many African stevedores to be accommodated by their employers in barracks at the docks in the late 1870s and again in the 1890s. Cape government legislation restricted immigration to those who spoke a 'European' language in 1902; and it was only largely through the efforts of a Jewish lawyer, Morris Alexander, that Yiddish was accepted as such and Jewish immigration continued. A high proportion of Cape Town's cosmopolitan working-class population lived in densely packed accommodation often with minimal water, light and sanitation in an area that eventually stretched from District Six through Woodstock to Salt River and Observatory. As transport facilities improved, the better-off, largely people of metropolitan British descent, increasingly opted for suburban life away from the dusty and noisy town centre. They moved to substantial villas in the southern suburbs or in Green Point and Sea Point municipality, just west of the town on the Atlantic Ocean. Yet in between or within these middle-class suburbs, pockets of largely working-class Coloured areas emerged like The Valley (Mowbray/Rosebank), Black River (Rondebosch), Harfield Village (Claremont), Lower Wynberg and Tramway Road (Sea Point).[24]

---

[23] Vivian Bickford-Smith, 'The Origins and Early History of District Six to 1910', in Shamil Jeppie and Crain Soudien (eds), *The Struggle for District Six Past and Present* (Cape Town: Buchu Books, 1990), 35–43.

[24] M. Marshall, 'The Growth and Development of Cape Town' (MA thesis, University of Cape Town, 1840); John Whittingdale, 'The Development and Location of Industries in Greater Cape Town' (MA thesis, University of Cape Town, 1973). For the development

Durban came into existence as an offshoot of British settlement at the Cape. It was initially called Port Natal and situated on the northern shore of the Bay of Natal. British traders and adventurers were allowed by the Zulu king Shaka to settle in a few 'kafir huts' made of wattle and daub to the south of his powerful kingdom in 1824. As in the case of Cape Town, the early years of Durban's existence were precarious and saw conflict between British settlers and both Zulus and Boers. Port Natal's inhabitants unilaterally renamed their settlement Durban in 1835, after the Cape's British governor Sir Benjamin D'Urban, largely in the hope that annexation by Britain and consequent greater security would ensue.

Instead in 1838, with Shaka's successor Dingane's initial approval, Boer *voortrekkers* established their own small settlement at Congella on the Bay of Natal's western shore, and it was the Boer *volksraad* of Natalia that commissioned a grid-iron plan for Durban's putative town centre in 1840. The British Imperial government, concerned with wider strategic issues, sent a force to reoccupy Durban, but this soon faced capitulation to the Boers. Only after a local British hunter called Dick King had made a subsequently famous 600-mile ride in 1842 to summon reinforcements were the Boers vanquished.

The British annexed what they called the 'District of Natal of the Colony of the Cape of Good Hope' the following year. Most of the *voortrekkers* consequently migrated to the two remaining Boer republics. When a British governor arrived in 1845, Port Natal's settler population was only fifty-six. The number steadily increased over subsequent decades through immigration. In 1854, Port Natal, now officially named Durban and with a settler population of 1,200, was granted municipal government. However Pietermaritzburg, rather than Durban, became the capital when Natal was granted Representative government in its own right in 1856.[25] Initially Natal had a non-racial franchise similar to the Cape's. Yet Natal's White settlers felt, indeed were, more vulnerable to electoral racial arithmetic than their counterparts in the Cape, and swiftly passed laws that severely restricted the possibility of African qualification.[26]

of Coloured pockets in White suburban areas, and the racial–spatial development of Cape Town more generally, see John Western, *Outcast Cape Town* (Cape Town: Human and Rousseau, 1981).

[25] Felix Stark, *Durban* (Johannesburg: Felstar Publishing Ltd, 1960), 14–27.

[26] T.R.H. Davenport, *South Africa: A Modern History*, 4th edition (London: Macmillan, 1991), 103. The restriction of the vote to very few Africans was accomplished by 1865 through a combination of an Exemption Law and a Native Franchise Act of Byzantine complexity. The former required any African wishing to be exempted from 'Native Law' and thereby eligible to vote to produce proof of literacy and take an oath of allegiance; the

In similar fashion to Cape Town, early tracks out of Durban to the north, south and west, as well as a fourth track that linked the first huts to a landing stage at Durban Point, near the entrance to the Bay of Natal, evolved into arterial routes in Durban's development. Omnibus, railway and tram routes subsequently reinforced these vectors of suburban growth. Predictably, this process (as with Cape Town) was influenced by topographical features that initially included swamplands and the 400-foot Berea Ridge that ran roughly parallel to the Indian Ocean. Westward and thus inland of the Berea, the ground sloped intermittently upwards to what in the twentieth century was called the Kloof-Hillcrest plateau of around 2,000 feet.[27] The road to Pietermaritzburg that ran up the Berea and across the Kloof-Hillcrest plateau became a nexus for later suburban development. So did the Berea itself, as higher ground offering sea breezes, views and distance from the town centre became much valued by British inhabitants like Maurice Evans. Grants of farms as well as the declaration of African reserves to the north and south of the city helped in time to confirm this British settlement pattern.

The rate of Durban's economic and demographic growth before the mineral revolution was associated with sugar milling and export, with the building of sugar mills as well as small factories for other food and clothing production. The first Natal railway lines were built with private capital, but the council made land available for the routes and terminus. Railway lines linked the harbour with the town, and the town with sugar plantations to the north and south by the 1870s.[28] These sugar planta-tions were worked by indentured Indian immigrants brought to Natal by the colonial government in large numbers from 1860. After five years these immigrants, mostly men, gained the right to stay in Natal as free people. Many sought economic opportunities either as independent sugar-cane producers or in Durban. Besides the ex-indentured, free or 'passenger' Indians, often experienced small traders, also came to Natal's main port after 1869.

---

latter stated that to be considered for the vote Africans had to have been residents of Natal for twelve years, have had proof of exemption from Native Law for seven years and have the approval of three Whites whose support was endorsed by a magistrate. Even after all of this, their admission to the electoral roll was still at the discretion of the lieutenant-governor.

[27] R.J. Davies, 'The Growth and Development of the Durban Metropolitan Area', *South African Geographical Journal* 45 (December 1963), 17–22.

[28] Jospeh Forsyth Ingram and Frank A. Sams, *The Story of an African Seaport: Being the History of the Port and Borough of Durban, The Seaport of Natal* (Durban: G. Coester, 1899); Stark, *Durban*, 28–34; Bill Freund, 'The City of Durban: Towards a Structural Analysis of the Economic Growth & Character of a South African City', in David M. Anderson and Richard Rathbone (eds), *Africa's Urban Past* (Oxford and Portsmouth NH: James Currey and Heinemann, 2000), 149.

Many Indian immigrants, especially passenger Indians, gravitated to an area near the swampy, less desirable 'Western Vlei'. By the early 1870s, this place of Indian residence, trade and small-scale manufacture was centred on Grey Street. The Grey Street area, just to the north-west of the town's main developing business district and close to Durban cemetery, was soon dubbed the Coolie Location by White Durbanites. Durban's first mosque was established there on the initiative of Abubaker Jabavi in the 1880s, and an Indian market was erected for fruit and vegetable sellers in 1900.[29] Yet the area was also inhabited by Africans and Whites. So Durban's Coolie Location, like Cape Town's Malay Quarter, may have had a critical mass of Indians but was still multi-racial. Indian migrants also lived slightly further north in a large 'Coolie Barracks' between the Umgeni Railway line and the Eastern Vlei, as well as in private accommodation elsewhere in the town.

Other Indians, including many post-indenture sugar plantation workers, often chose to live some distance from the city centre, beyond the municipal boundaries, even if this usually meant paying rent to White landowners and living in shanties of wood and iron or wattle and daub. This choice offered the possibility of supplementing family income derived from wages in town with additional revenue from small-scale market-gardening. Growing fruit and vegetables and owning small livestock benefited family diets. One early twentieth-century resident recalled walking into town over the Berea, and other relatives that worked in town, while the family also grew pineapples and bananas.[30]

Before the mid-twentieth century, there was no legislation that forced Indians to live in prescribed areas. The Town Council had wanted an Indian location as early as the 1870s, and was supported in this desire by the majority of White businessmen and shopkeepers whose racism was fuelled as it was among their Cape Town counterparts by commercial competition with Indians. However, official residential segregation was prevented before the granting of Responsible Government in 1893 as the British colonial government had opposed legislation that overtly discriminated against Indians as fellow British citizens. For the same reason, though racial restrictions could be and often were placed in the title deeds of White-owned private property as they were by Cape Town's Milnerton

[29] Fatima Meer, *Portrait of Indian South Africans* (Durban: Avon House, 1969), 188. They had been moved there from their previous more central site in Gardener Street.
[30] Maynard W. Swanson, '"The Asiatic Menace": Creating Segregation in Durban, 1870–1900', *International Journal of African Historical Studies* 16, 3 (1983), 403–5; Bill Freund, *Insiders and Outsiders: The Indian Working Class of Durban 1910–1990* (Pietermaritzburg, Portsmouth, NH, London: University of Natal Press, Heinemann and James Currey, 1995), 29–49.

and Camp's Bay development companies, the government also forbade legislation preventing municipal property being sold to Indians, or Indians from obtaining trading licences. So instead, municipal building regulation and sanitary by-laws were employed against Indian traders operating in the city's main streets, and they were forced to relocate to the Grey Street area.

But after Natal was granted Responsible Government, Britain paid far less attention to Indian rights. The Natal government was able to pass legislation in 1896 disenfranchising Indian and African voters. The following year further legislation allowed both the arbitrary refusal of trade licences to Indians and restriction on Indian immigration, the first of several laws with this intent. For instance, in 1906, the Natal government introduced a poll tax on every Indian resident over eighteen.[31]

The third key component of Durban's population was African and largely Zulu-speaking. Despite the fact that the Zulu Kingdom retained its independence until the Anglo-Zulu War of 1879 and was only fully incorporated into Natal in 1897, Africans were in a large majority in the colony from its inception. This fact led the British administration to assert political and social control over Africans in Natal through indirect rule and spatial separation, ostensibly to protect African society from exposure to European influences and land-grabbing. African rural reserves were established under chiefs and headmen who were answerable to the lieutenant-governor as 'Supreme Chief' and with inhabitants subject to 'Native Law'. Night curfews were imposed on Africans who came to towns, including Durban. Spearheaded by Natal's Secretary for Native Affairs, Theophilus Shepstone, these policies became known as the 'Shepstone system', and proved to be a highly influential ingredient in future urban segregationist ideas.[32]

Two African reserves were within walking distance of Durban, to the north-west and south-west of its centre. This meant that Africans, initially mostly young males, could and did oscillate between rural homesteads and temporary accommodation close to employment possibilities in the city centre.[33] They often sought short-term casual work stevedoring at the docks, as day labourers in the building industry, in laundry work or domestic service or, from the 1890s and in substantial numbers, as rickshaw pullers.[34] Further alternatives were either somewhat longer

[31] Swanson, '"Asiatic Menace"'.

[32] Worden, *The Making of Modern South Africa*, 71–2. Davenport, *South Africa*, 101.

[33] Freund, 'City of Durban', 150.

[34] Ros Posel, 'Amahashi: Durban's Ricksha Pullers', in Paul Maylam and Iain Edwards (eds), *The People's City: African Life in Twentieth Century Durban* (Pietermaritzburg and Portsmouth, NH: University of Natal Press and Heinemann, 1996), 202–21. Rickshaws

term (at least in theory) contract employment as domestic workers or self-employment in the informal sector, as small-scale traders or beer-brewers.[35]

In an attempt to control the rate of African migration to Durban, Shepstone introduced a day labourer or *togt* system in 1874 that required payment of fees, registration and the wearing of badges by African employees. The municipality, equally concerned about social control within its boundaries, yet as a body of employers keen to ensure a cheap labour supply, eventually made the registration of domestic servants compulsory as well by the 1890s. The municipality also established single-men's barracks to house day labourers.[36]

Yet the registration of African day labourers and domestic servants was disappointing and barrack accommodation unpopular. Most Africans preferred the comparative freedom that went with lodging in 'slums' and 'rookeries' in or near central Durban, or beyond the borough boundaries, like many Indians. From the Town Council's perspective, a way of financing more complete African residential segregation had still to be discovered.

Compared to other British colonial ports including Cape Town, Durban was best placed to benefit from the discovery of gold, particularly after a railway line from the city reached Johannesburg in 1895. Gold underpinned the growth of both Durban and Cape Town by the end of the nineteenth century. It was discovered in President Paul Kruger's South African Republic, also known as the Transvaal, in 1886. Within twenty-five years, the tented mining camp had become South Africa's largest city, and its main financial and industrial centre, though not without both military and financial alarms. After the future of gold-mining seemed assured with the development of more efficient extraction methods and deep-level supplies in the early 1890s, Johannesburg became the subject of violent contention between Britain and the Transvaal government that temporarily interrupted the city's growth.

The Jameson Raid in 1895–6 was the first skirmish. The Raid was an abortive coup planned by leading British magnates in Johannesburg and Cecil Rhodes, the then prime minister of the Cape, with the knowledge of the British government. Far more serious in both its immediate effects

were first introduced by sugar magnate Marshall Campbell. W.P.M. Henderson, *Fifty Years' Municipal History* (Durban: Robinson and Co., 1904), 341.

[35] Paul Maylam, 'Introduction', in Maylam and Edwards (eds), *The People's City*, 3–6; Paul La Hausse, 'The Struggle for the City: Alcohol, the Ematsheni and Popular Culture in Durban, 1902–1936', in Maylam and Edwards (eds), *The People's City*, 33–66.

[36] Maynard W. Swanson, '"The Durban System": Roots of Urban Apartheid in Colonial Natal', *African Studies*, 35, 3–5 (1976); La Hausse, 'The Struggle for the City', 39–47; Davenport, *South Africa*, 102.

and enduring legacy of bitterness on the Afrikaner side was the Boer War of 1899–1902. The war infamously led to the deaths of thousands of Boer women and children in British concentration camps. It destroyed the independence of both Boer republics, brought them under British rule and paved the way for the creation of the Union of South Africa by an act of the British Parliament in 1910. The two Boer republics together with the Cape and Natal became South Africa's four provinces.

By the eve of the Boer War, the Rand was producing around 27 per cent of the world's gold and had attracted capital investment of some £75 million. These figures had risen to 40 per cent and £125 million respectively at the advent of the First World War. By then Johannesburg's population was already about 250,000 within boundaries that covered 82 square miles.[37] By the early 1950s, Johannesburg was producing around 45 per cent of the country's net economic output and providing 45 per cent of its employment; in other words it swiftly became and remained South Africa's pre-eminent metropolis.[38]

The dominance of gold mining in Johannesburg's economy determined both its spatial development and social geography from the outset. On the instructions of the Transvaal government, leasehold stands that made up the future town centre were laid out on a rough grid pattern on a triangle of land belonging to the Randjeslaagte Syndicate. Believing that gold mining might be of short-term duration, the Kruger government ensured that as many stands as possible, eventually almost a thousand in all, were squeezed into the available area and that blocks of stands were small, intersected by numerous relatively narrow roads. This created a large number of more lucrative corner stands that the government could lease out. When the prediction of Johannesburg's early demise turned out to be wrong, the combination of asymmetrical layout, small blocks and narrow streets all contributed to future congestion problems.[39]

South of the original city centre were eight farms where the earliest noisy and dust-producing gold mining activity took place. This established an early association between southern Johannesburg, industrial production and labour, which lowered residential land values in the area. Large numbers of African migrant mineworkers were housed in compounds on land belonging to mining companies. Some White miners also lived on company land, albeit in better accommodation, while others

---

[37] Charles Van Onselen, *Studies in the Social and Economic History of the Witwatersrand, 1886–1914, Vol. 1 New Babylon* (Harlow: Longman, 1982), 2. Van Onselen's two-volume social history remains the most impressive account of early Johannesburg.

[38] Beavon, *Johannesburg*, 147–50.

[39] Beavon, *Johannesburg*, 23–4, 43–50. Beavon provides a uniquely detailed account of the spatial development of the city. The account that follows draws gratefully on this work.

moved into cheap boarding houses and hotels in the area between mine land and the town centre.

This territory was gradually subdivided into working-class 'townships'. Those in the south-east, such as Jeppestown and Belgravia, residential only and slightly more expensive, housed predominantly English-speaking miners and artisans. Afrikaans-speaking miners lived mostly in the emerging suburbs to the south-west, like Fordsburg and Ferreirasdorp, where housing was cheaper and small businesses were allowed alongside homes. In the 1890s, substantial numbers of Jewish artisans and traders from Eastern Europe also came to the suburbs of southern Johannesburg.[40] Although most subsequently moved eastwards and northwards, some still remained in the 1920s and 1930s, like the Hirsons, who lived in a ramshackle house on the corner of Fox and End streets in an area unimaginatively named City and Suburban, by then 'occupied by white workers, coloureds and Indians'.[41]

Land values to the west of the town soon pursued a similar downward trajectory through association with both poverty and racial difference. Kruger allowed impoverished Afrikaans-speaking Whites who were victims of drought, or who had been pushed off the land by commercial farmers, to gain employment by establishing brickfields on the nascent city's western edge. Developing into the insanitary residential area of Brickfields, it was also referred to as *Veldschoendorp* (Veld-shoes Village) because of its inhabitants.[42]

Johannesburg's Sanitary Board contributed to the slum-land reputation of the city's west end by demarcating areas to the west of Brickfields as 'locations' for 'Coolies', 'Malays' and 'Natives': in other words for Indians (largely from Natal), Coloured Muslims (largely from the Cape) and Africans (from many parts of southern Africa). In reality, the boundaries between all these intended spatial–racial divisions were far from rigid, the racial ownership and occupation of areas still fluid.[43]

Further urban migration of poor Afrikaans-speaking Whites followed to a new development, Vrededorp, to the north-west of these locations. Many of these Afrikaners had worked in animal-powered transport, now made redundant by the completion of railway lines from both Cape Town

---

[40] Beavon, *Johannesburg*, 53. Margot Rubin, 'The Jewish Community of Johannesburg, 1886–1939: Landscapes of Reality and Imagination' (MA thesis, University of Pretoria, 2004), 52–4, 80–2; Richard Mendelsohn and Milton Shain, *The Jews in South Africa: An Illustrated History* (Johannesburg and Cape Town: Jonathan Ball, 2008), 29–104.
[41] Baruch Hirson, *Revolutions in My Life* (Johannesburg: Witwatersrand University Press, 1995), 35.
[42] Van Onselen, *New Babylon*, 8.   [43] Beavon, *Johannesburg*, 49.

and Durban to Johannesburg by 1895, and turned their skills to cab driving in the increasingly sprawling town.[44]

As the comment that Vrededorp was intended as a White residential area might indicate, the term 'township' in the late nineteenth century was race neutral and referred to any area developed for residential or mixed purposes by private developers, including the most elite. Only gradually did 'township' become almost a synonym for a 'location' or Black residential area, while 'suburb' replaced 'township' if referring to a place of White residence. In turn, and as the case of the 'Coolie Location' in Durban's Grey Street area suggests, 'location' at this stage could refer to both de jure and de facto Black residential districts, especially, in de facto cases, places whose boundaries were unfenced and imprecise.[45] In the south-west area of Johannesburg, Black 'locations' and White would-be suburbs consisting mainly of Afrikaans speakers intermeshed.[46]

If the south-west corner of Johannesburg became home in anglophone middle-class minds to the equivalent of London's East End's 'dangerous' classes, it is understandable that Johannesburg's more prosperous suburban development was initially towards the north-east, away from industrial noise and grime. The first of the prestigious suburbs was Doornfontein, known as the 'snob suburb' or 'swagger suburb'.[47] Magnates initially chose to live there because it contained land climbing up a ridge above the town, offering distance from mining activity as well as views over the city. It had the added advantage of a reliable supply of spring water, and proximity to the town's two main parks. Some barren land nearby became the site of Johannesburg's first Wanderers' Athletic and Sporting Club in 1889.

Yet almost as soon as Doornfontein achieved pre-eminence in social prestige, it was displaced. In 1892 a large tract of land lying on the north side of a slightly more distant ridge than Doornfontein was officially proclaimed as the new township of Parktown. The north rather than north-east gradually became the preferred residential area for the professional and business elite, who were mainly of British origin, including soon-anglicised Jews from continental Western Europe. Doornfontein and nearby suburbs like Hillbrow, Yeoville and Bellevue were favoured by a cosmopolitan group of middle-class Whites. These included Eastern European Jews, many of whom moved to these suburbs after initially living in poorer areas to the south.[48]

---

[44] Van Onselen, *New Babylon*, 9.   [45] Beavon, *Johannesburg*, 75.
[46] Van Onselen, *New Babylon*, 27.
[47] L.E. Neame, *City Built on Gold* (Johannesburg: Central News Agency, 1960), 127.
[48] Margot Rubin, 'The Jewish Community of Johannesburg', 49–54, 80–2, 97, 142, 154.

So Johannesburg's northern suburbs became the equivalent in prestige to the southern and Atlantic suburbs of Cape Town, or some of the north-west suburbs of Durban. It was in such places that space, race and class most closely correlated and reinforced one another in terms of White identity. Yet in areas close to the emerging central business districts of all three cities, the correlation was far from absolute.[49] There remained a distinct cross-racial cosmopolitanism of the poor.[50]

This was particularly noticeable to Evans when he visited Cape Town around the time of Union. There was still far less social segregation even in its city centre than was the case for Durban or Johannesburg. Evans' detailed description conveys the extent and nature of the contrast.

To a Natal resident visiting Cape Town the mixed coloured population of that city and neighbourhood is a feature that deeply impresses him. He sees a mixture of races to which he is quite unaccustomed . . . fused, in varying proportions, to make the coloured people of today. At one end of the scale he sees men and women almost white, well educated, well spoken, well dressed, courteous and restrained in manner and at the other end of this colour scale some whom he considers inferior to the ordinary native or Indian coolie of his home. He hears that it is quite a common thing for the European immigrant introduced for railway and mechanical work to marry, even prefer to marry, women of colour . . . He sees a toleration of colour and a social admixture to which he is quite unaccustomed; it is evident on the streets, on the tramcars, in the railway stations, public offices, and in places of entertainment. Should he take a walk in Plein Street on a fine Saturday evening he will witness a sight impossible in an Eastern town such as Durban or Pietermaritzburg. The street is crowded, footway and roadway alike full of strollers, all shades and all colours . . . As a rule whites and coloured people keep apart and do not mix, but there are very many exceptions; . . . Young white men will be seen walking with well-dressed coloured girls, and an older European may often be seen with coloured wife and children of varying shades . . . The doors of a Bioscope [cinema] entertainment are open, and the crowd awaiting admission and jostling each other as they get tickets, includes representatives of every colour from the light-haired fair-complexioned Scandinavian sailor or English workman to the sooty-black of the Shangaan, and . . . [inside the Bioscope] he will find no distinction made, all and every colour occupy the same seats, cheek by jowl, and sometimes on each other's knees.[51]

Before the twentieth century, social geography in all three cities was still determined more by the natural environment and market forces than by planning. Albeit there were Whites-only clauses in some middle-class property deeds, racial residential separation largely consisted of White

---

[49] For a detailed analysis of the relationship between class and race in Cape Town in the late nineteenth century, see Bickford-Smith, *Ethnic Pride and Racial Prejudice*.

[50] James Moore, 'Between Cosmopolitanism and Nationalism: The Strange Death of Liberal Alexandria', *Journal of Urban History* 38, 5 (2012), 879–900.

[51] Evans, *Black and White in South East Africa*, 296–7.

employers housing Black employees in special quarters on their property, most notably in the mine compounds of Johannesburg. Durban's *togt* barracks housed only a tiny percentage of the city's African population. Despite the racial delineation found on contemporary maps, the intended segregation from the city's foundation of Black South Africans living outside mine compounds in Johannesburg was ineffectively enforced. Even when more thorough segregation of urban Africans was first attempted by municipal and central governments for all three cities in the early 1900s, it still met (as we shall see) with very limited success.

Anglicisation through immigration

By this time urban anglicisation was extensive. Jan Morris remarked that together with British sports and the English language 'urbanism was the most lasting of the British imperial legacies'.[52] Morris was referring specifically to the built environment, the 'stones' of Empire. Yet, if urbanism is understood to encompass a city's entire 'social, economic, and cultural systems', the built environment, English language and British sports were all part of that legacy.[53] All were products of anglicisation.

Anglicisation was initiated in earnest in the Cape Colony in the 1820s through a combination of 'direct' and 'indirect' means.[54] The former consisted of state policies such as making English the official language of government, education and the courts, and modelling central and local state institutions and traditions on their British counterparts. This meant that the Cape parliament in Cape Town, for example, featured a bewigged speaker, sergeant-at-arms, division by sides rather than ballot, clerk of the house, and standing rules and orders.[55] It also meant the introduction of British Imperial 'ornamentalism' like red post boxes, or coins and stamps displaying the monarch's head.[56] In addition, both the Cape and Natal governments pursued 'indirect' anglicisation by

[52] Jan Morris, *Stones of Empire: The Buildings of British India* (London: Penguin, 1983), 196.
[53] King, *Urbanism, Colonialism, and the World-Economy*, 1.
[54] Sturgis, 'Anglicisation', 25.
[55] J.L. McCracken, *The Cape Parliament 1854–1910* (Oxford: Clarendon Press, 1967), 138.
[56] Keith Jeffrey, 'Crown, Communication and the Colonial Post: Stamps, the Monarchy and the British Empire', *The Journal of Imperial and Commonwealth History* 34, 1 (2006), 45–70. The pre-Union Cape Colony was perhaps a surprising exception to the general rule of British territories issuing stamps from the Penny Black onwards with the monarch's profile, issuing instead the Cape Triangular with the coming of Representative Government in the 1850s, which featured the reclining female figure, Hope. Other British territories issued stamps with the Queen's or King's head, as did the Union of South Africa until 1924, after which a range of stamps with other depictions were also issued. Profiles of members of the Royal family disappeared when South Africa left the

encouraging British church and missionary activity as well as supporting immigration from Britain.

British emigration to southern Africa, tiny in scale compared to Australia or Canada, was nonetheless highly important in the process of anglicising its cities. It consisted of a mixture of independent migration and government and private immigration schemes. Initially, the latter were mainly intended to provide agricultural settlers. Both the 4,500 settlers brought to the Eastern Cape by the British government in 1820 and the privately financed Byrne settlement of 2,500 migrants in Natal between 1849 and 1851 fell into this category. In a similar vein the 850 London street children sent to the Cape between 1832 and 1841 were apprenticed to farmers. But many of these supposed agricultural settlers soon opted for the relative comfort and opportunities of town life.[57]

Later schemes were aimed as much, if not more, at supplying urban workers. Thus the Cape government-assisted immigration schemes from 1857 to 1862 and from 1873 to 1883 brought more than 32,000 artisans and domestic workers to the Cape, of whom a sizeable proportion settled in Cape Town.[58] There were also initiatives that focused on the emigration of single women to South Africa, whether 'gentlewomen' or servants. Organised by British-based Empire enthusiasts, these were aimed in large part at providing wives for the predominantly male British immigrant population and thereby 'out breeding' the Dutch or Boers. The most important of these was the British Women's Emigration Association, established in 1884. Its post-Boer War offshoot, the South African Colonisation Society, was responsible for introducing 5,176 single women immigrants between 1902 and 1912.[59]

Independent immigration, harder though it is to quantify, was probably far more significant in numerical terms than its private or publically funded counterparts, especially with the coming of the Mineral Revolution. A number of British soldiers also chose to seek employment in southern Africa after fighting against either Africans or Afrikaners in the many wars of the late nineteenth century, which also propelled some of the latter into the cities. By 1911, a sizeable minority of the White populations of all three of our cities had been born in Europe, probably most of them in Britain (as

Commonwealth in 1960. The first red fluted post boxes were imported to the Cape in 1860 from Smith and Hawkes, Birmingham.

[57] Marjory Harper and Stephen Constantine, *Migration and Empire* (Oxford and New York: Oxford University Press, 2010), 124–8.

[58] John Stone, *Colonist or Uitlander? A Study of the British Immigrant in South Africa* (Oxford: Clarendon Press, 1973), 111–12, 114.

[59] Cecille Swaisland, *Servants and Gentlewomen to the Golden Land: The Emigration of Single Women from Britain to Southern Africa, 1820–1939* (Oxford and Providence, RI: Berg Publishers, 1993), 23–5, 31–41.

Table 2.2: *Proportion of population of Cape Town, Durban and Johannesburg in 1911 born in Europe*

	Cape Town	Durban	Johannesburg
Born in Africa	53,955	17,662	61,285
Born in Europe	29,696	15,652	53,432
Elsewhere	795	426	1,768
Total	84,446	33,740	116,485
Born in Europe	35%	46%	46%

UG 32–1912 Census 1911 (Pretoria: Government Printer, 1912).

Table 2.2 indicates).[60] A considerable percentage of those inhabitants described as 'Born in Africa' would themselves have had parents or grandparents of British origins, given the earlier immigration already described. So it seems safe to infer that a sizeable majority of Whites in all three cities at this stage had British origins, with Durban having the largest such majority given its smaller number of Dutch/Afrikaner inhabitants.

Among these British immigrants were individuals and families involved in commerce, mining and industry who, thanks to wealth, skills and experience gained in Britain, came to dominate the political economy of South Africa's leading cities.[61] By 1914 almost half of the £3,800 million Britain invested overseas was placed within the Empire, and by 1931 two-thirds of Britain's exports by value went to the same destination.[62] Economic and social networks consequently linked businessmen of British origin not only within and across South African cities, but with their counterparts elsewhere in the Empire. In major cities, they were closely connected not only by joint business enterprises but also by kinship networks, same or similar school attendance, and shared membership of religious and secular institutions, associations and recreational pursuits. A strong sense of British community was given its territorial component in the form of shared residence in prestigious suburban areas.[63] 'Our' territory could most dramatically be distinguished from other parts of the city when most residents of the latter spoke different

---

[60] Harper and Constantine, *Migration and Empire*, 130, estimates that about 70 per cent of those born 'outside Africa' were born in Britain; allowing for the fact that some of these immigrants were born outside Europe (in North America, India or Australia for instance), perhaps around 75 per cent of those from Europe were British born.

[61] Details of how this happened are given in the many city histories cited in this book.

[62] King, *Urbanism, Colonialism, and the World-Economy*, 5–6.

[63] For academic historical studies that focus on early elites in Durban and Cape Town see: A.C. Bjorvig, 'Durban 1824–1910: The Formation of a Settler Elite and Its Role in the Development of a Colonial City' (PhD thesis, University of Natal, 1994); Digby Warren,

languages, had darker skins or possessed perceptibly different cultures and traditions.

Creating British suburbs

Residence in suburbs that were predominantly British in terms of their naming as well as in much of their broader cultural character conferred an everyday sense of territorial community for their inhabitants. This process occurred in each city for similar reasons. Hence many of the British immigrants to Cape Town chose to live in what became the southern suburbs because these were close to nature yet conveniently near to the elite social scene surrounding the British military camp at Wynberg. These suburbs were also attractively distant from the still predominantly un-British city centre.

The scenery was sublimely picturesque to British taste. As early as the first British occupation (1795–1802) of the Cape, Lady Anne Barnard, socialite and official hostess for the British governor, helped establish the desirable reputation of the area by choosing to live there and naming her house Paradise. Already by 1821 one observer noted that the road between Cape Town and Rondebosch 'was lined on either side with the villas of the merchants and more opulent tradesmen of the town, who drive their buggies to and fro like our London citizens and repose from the fatigues of the day in these rural retirements'.[64] This increasing possibility was chiefly the result of the purchase of former farmland by British immigrant businessmen like James Maynard in Wynberg or Thomas Matthews in Claremont.[65]

'Merchants, Commissioners and Ward Masters: Politics in Cape Town, 1840–1854' (MA thesis, University of Cape Town, 1986); Kirsten McKenzie, 'Gender and Honour in Middle-Class Cape Town: The Making of Colonial Identities: 1828–1850' (PhD thesis, University of Oxford, 1997); Ross, *Status and Respectability*. For a somewhat less analytical study, as its title suggests, but nonetheless useful, see also R.F.M. Immelman, *Men of Good Hope: The Romantic Story of the Cape Town Chamber of Commerce: 1804–1954* (Cape Town: Chamber of Commerce, 1955). Johannesburg is seemingly less well served in terms of academic analyses, but there are a host of antiquarian accounts of the early history of the city and its institutions which are indicative and will be discussed together with their Cape Town and Durban counterparts in more detail in the course of this book. But see A.P. Cartwright, *The Corner House* (Johannesburg and Cape Town: Purnell and Sons, 1965); Clive M. Chipkin and Shirley Zar, *Park Town: A Social and Pictorial History: 1892–1972* (Johannesburg: Studio Thirty-Five, 1972). Although focused on Pietermaritzburg and the Natal midlands rather than any of our three cities, a lucid examination of the establishment of a British South African colonial elite that focuses on male networks and ritual is provided by Robert Morrell, *From Boys to Gentlemen: Settler Masculinity in Colonial Natal, 1880–1920* (Pretoria: Unisa Press, 2001).

[64] Edward Blount, *Notes on the Cape of Good Hope* (London: John Murray, 1821), 9–10.

[65] H. Robinson, 'Beyond the City Limits: People and Property at Wynberg 1895–1927' (PhD thesis, University of Cape Town, 1995); H. Robinson, *Wynberg: A Special Place* (Cape Town: Formsxpress, 2001); Worden et al., *Cape Town: The Making of a City*, 201.

Early aristocratic acknowledgement of the merits of the southern suburbs was reinforced by the establishment of the British Governor's summer residence at Newlands and that of the Anglican Archbishop at nearby Bishopscourt.[66] What also enhanced the southern suburbs' reputation was endorsement by distinguished visitors like the British novelist Anthony Trollope and American writer Mark Twain in the late nineteenth century. Trollope commented that 'the district at the back of Table Mountain where are Mowbray, Rondebosch, Wynberg and Constantia' had almost unsurpassable scenery 'so grand are the outlines of the mountain, and so rich and bountiful the verdure of the shrubs and timbers'.[67] Twain referred simply to 'the paradise where the villas are'.[68] All of this underpinned the enduring social cache and consequent relatively high land values of the area.[69]

As access by carriage to these suburbs gave way to new forms of transport including the railway to Wynberg from 1864, British immigrants of lesser means also moved there, albeit to humbler abodes. Churches of various British denominations together with private or well-funded government schools reminiscent of their British counterparts, such as Wynberg Boys High (1841), Diocesan College or 'Bishops' (1847), Rustenberg Girls High (1894) and Rondebosch Boys High (1897), helped to ensure that the southern suburbs retained their attraction for British immigrants who could afford to live there.[70]

The anglicised naming of urban neighbourhoods, streets, facilities and institutions, and the way that such naming was explained to residents in subsequent city histories, was also important, as it was to be in Durban and Johannesburg. With the sole exception of Rondebosch, the names of

---

[66] Worden et al., *Cape Town: The Making of a City*, 117–18.

[67] Anthony Trollope, *South Africa* (Gloucester: Alan Sutton Publishing, [1877] 1987), 62.

[68] Mark Twain, *Following the Equator: A Journey around the World* (Hartford, CT: American Publishing Company, 1897), 710–11.

[69] Dorothea Fairbridge, *Lady Anne Barnard at the Cape of Good Hope 1797–1802* (Oxford: Clarendon Press, 1924). See also A.M. Lewin Robinson (ed.), *The Cape Journals of Lady Anne Barnard 1797–8* (Cape Town: Van Riebeeck Society, 1993); Margaret Lenta and Basil le Cordeur (eds), *The Cape Diaries of Lady Anne Barnard 1797–98*, vol. 1 (Cape Town: Van Riebeeck Society, 1998); Margaret Lenta and Basil le Cordeur (eds), *The Cape Diaries of Lady Anne Barnard 1799–1800*, vol. 2 (Cape Town: Van Riebeeck Society, 1999).

[70] Worden et al., *Cape Town: The Making of a City*, 152–207; Haymen W.J. Picard, *Grand Parade: The Birth of Greater Cape Town: 1850–1913* (Cape Town: Struik, 1969), 140–4; John Gardener, *Bishops 150: A History of the Diocesan College, Rondebsoch* (Cape Town: Juta, 1997); Doug Howard Thomson, *The Story of a School: A Short History of Wynberg Boys' High* (Cape Town: Wynberg Old Boys' Union, 1961); Reginald R. Langham-Carter, *Under the Mountain: The Story of St Saviour's Claremont* (Cape Town: Southern Press, 1973); K. Vos, *The Church on the Hill: St John's Parish Wynberg* (Cape Town: Struik, 1971).

suburbs were either British in origin (Woodstock, Observatory, Mowbray, Rosebank, Claremont, Bishopscourt and Kenilworth) or anglicised in either written version or pronunciation from the Dutch (Nieuw Land to Newlands, or Wynberg pronounced 'Wineberg' rather than 'Vainberg').[71] Naming and pronunciation in this fashion served to identify the territory the names encompassed as British, as did the giving of discernibly British names to institutions such as St Paul's Church, Rondebosch or St John's Church, Wynberg.[72]

There were additional ways in which these areas were overtly marked as British or British South African. While Cape Town's centre still remained perceptibly foreign territory, British residents successfully established separate suburban municipalities, each with its own modest town hall, for Claremont, Wynberg and Rondebosch.[73] This ensured a degree of British-controlled local government in Cape Town, in similar fashion to late nineteenth-century Dublin, where a Catholic Irish town centre was ringed by Protestant Anglo-Irish municipalities.[74]

Cecil Rhodes bought huge tracts of land in the Rondebosch area in the late nineteenth century. At Groote Schuur, his house designed by British architect of Empire Herbert Baker, Rhodes held court as Premier of the Cape and southern Africa's leading British Imperialist. In the 1890s, he was surrounded by fellow men of the Empire like Baker and Rudyard Kipling. After Rhodes' death, and on land that he had bequeathed to the Cape government, a memorial was erected in his honour. Financed in part by a local government grant, this was on the spot where Rhodes had supposedly gazed northwards dreaming of British territory from the Cape to Cairo.[75]

The Rhodes Memorial further marked its surroundings as British territory. Completed in 1912, it was positioned high above the southern suburbs, visible from afar not only to many of their residents but to anyone travelling between them and the city centre. Its design by Baker, in the style of a Greek Temple, included an equestrian statue by G.F. Watts titled Physical Energy. There was also a bust of Rhodes by John Swan that incorporated lines from Kipling's poem 'Burial', written for his departed friend:

[71] Worden et al., *Cape Town: The Making of a City*, 252–6; Ed Coombe, *Beard-Shavers' Bush: Place Names in the Cape* (Cape Town: Baardskeerder and Peter Slingsby, 2000).
[72] F.J. Wagener, *Rondebosch Down the Years, 1657–1957* (Parow: Cape Times, 1957); Vos, *The Church on the Hill*.
[73] Picard, *Grand Parade*, 52; Wagener, *Rondebosch*.
[74] Ciaran Wallace, 'Fighting for Unionist Home Rule: Competing Identities in Dublin 1880–1929', *Journal of Urban History* 38, 5 (2012), 932–49.
[75] Picard, *Grand Parade*, 122.

The immense and brooding Spirit still
Shall quicken and control.
Living he was the Land, and dead,
His Soul shall be her Soul.

In his speech at the opening ceremony, Earl Grey, director of Rhodes' British South Africa Company and former administrator of Rhodesia, drew a comparison with New York's Statue of Liberty. Grey declared that the memorial could plant desirable values in the mind of a British immigrant arriving in Cape Town. Such a person would 'find waiting for him at the gate of South Africa a message from Rhodes calling upon him for wholehearted and ungrudging service to South Africa, the Empire and humanity'.[76] Boy Scouts, suitably enough, laid wreaths at the memorial on the anniversary of Rhodes' death. A bequest by Rhodes also made possible the construction of the main campus of the English-language medium University of Cape Town beneath the Rhodes memorial after the First World War.[77] A statue of Rhodes adorned the campus itself by the 1930s.[78]

The Mineral Revolution gave rise to property development companies in the 1890s that operated beyond the southern suburbs, like the Milnerton Estates Company, developing an area to the north-east of the city centre. It was named after Sir Alfred Milner, the appointed British High Commissioner for South Africa in 1897, a further example of anglophile naming that consciously contributed to Imperial ornamentalism. Among the company's inaugural shareholders were Sir James Sivewright, John Hays Hammond and Major Frank Johnson, all close associates of Cecil Rhodes.[79]

Many elements of the way in which middle-class anglophone areas were created within Cape Town were echoed in the suburban development of Durban and Johannesburg. But in Durban's case, middle-class suburban development on the Berea overlooked, and was closer to, an already substantially anglicised city centre, with British municipal governance, street names and building styles. This, together with topographical considerations, helps explain why Durban's British residents felt able to locate their Greyville race course and main cricket and rugby

---

[76] Paul Maylam, *The Cult of Rhodes: Remembering an Imperialist in Africa* (Cape Town: New Africa Books, 2005), 48–54.

[77] Howard Phillips, *The University of Cape Town 1918–1948: The Formative Years* (Cape Town: University of Cape Town Press, 1993).

[78] Only to be removed in 2015 after protests (which included the flinging of faeces at the statue) by a small number of University of Cape Town students belonging to a RhodesMustFall movement. The movement's stated aim was to remove the statue as part of 'decolonising' the university.

[79] Eric Rosenthal, *Milnerton* (Milnerton, Cape Town: Milnerton Municipality, 1980).

grounds beneath the Berea and close to town. In Cape Town, these amenities were located in the southern suburbs at Newlands.

As with Cape Town, geography determined desirable elite residential location on Durban's Berea, with its breezes and views of city and sea. The Berea also provided elevation above the town's burgeoning cosmopolitan mixture of Whites, Indians and Africans. Again like Cape Town, the judgements of visitors confirmed British immigrant opinion in this respect. Trollope also visited Durban and commented,

> Immediately west of the town as you make the first ascent up from the sea . . . there is the hill called the Berea on and about which the more wealthy inhabitants of Durban have built their villas. Some few of them are certainly among the best houses in South Africa, and command views down upon the town and sea which would be very precious to many an opulent suburb in England. Durban is proud of its Berea and the visitor is taken to see it as the first among the sights of the place.[80]

Anglophone educational and religious institutions were established, in some cases relocated from the town centre, in and about the Berea from the late nineteenth century onwards. Early examples were Durban High School and Durban Young Ladies' Collegiate Evangelical Institution, which became Durban Girls' College, as well as St Thomas' and St Augustine's Anglican churches. Similar institutions were also built in other well-sited suburbs like Westville, Pinetown and Durban North.[81] A donor's bequest for a son killed fighting for king and country in the First World War paid for the first main structure of the Durban campus of Natal University College in 1922. Called the Howard College building, it was situated in an elevated position on the Berea Ridge, a more utilitarian and modest commemoration of Imperial Britishness than Cape Town's Rhodes Memorial.[82]

For the elite of Johannesburg, the attraction of Parktown was its distance from the noise, smells and dangers of the city itself. Residents were protected from having even to see Johannesburg by the barrier of Parktown Ridge, while the prevailing northerly winds ensured protection from urban odours. Instead, residents who bought elevated plots on the northern slopes of the Ridge could enjoy views over a valley newly planted with trees, towards the Magaliesberg range and beyond. Facing northwards also meant gaining winter sunshine. Position, reliance on private

---

[80] Trollope, *South Africa*, 201.
[81] Allister Macmillan, *Durban Past and Present* (Durban: William Brown and Davis Ltd, 1936); Hubert Jennings, *The D.H.S. Story 1866–1966* (Durban: Durban High School and Old Boys' Memorial Trust, 1966).
[82] Davies, 'Durban Metropolitan Area', 17–22; Freund, 'The City of Durban', 148–9; Janie Malherbe, *Port Natal* (Cape Town: Howard Timmins, 1965), 195–200.

carriage transport and minimum plot sizes of an acre meant that Parktown was expensive and soon highly desirable to the wealthy 'tiptops' of Johannesburg society.[83]

The Corner House group of mining houses, through a property development subsidiary, the Braamfontein Estate Company, began selling acre-sized plots in Parktown from 1892. The first of Johannesburg's wealthy to build there, on the north-facing slope of the ridge, was Lionel Phillips, Chairman of the Chamber of Mines.[84] His sprawling mansion Hohenheim had forty rooms and stood on twenty acres. In the aftermath of the Boer War, Parktown was soon dotted with the mansions of the English-speaking business and administrative elite.

The inauguration of an elite Country Club in Auckland Park, a township development near Parktown, confirmed the northern suburbs as socially desirable territory. As with the southern suburbs in Cape Town and the Berea in Durban, this association was reinforced by the establishment of churches, prestigious English-language schools like Roedean (1903, an offshoot of the eponymous school near Brighton) and St John's (1898), and, in 1922, the location of the University of the Witwatersrand.[85] Throughout the twentieth century, Johannesburg's expansive 'northern suburbs' remained the preferred residential choice of better-off anglophile Whites.

Parktown provides a variation on the theme of Imperial inscription. The style of its Herbert Baker houses included examples of mock Tudor, Georgian, Gothic and Scottish baronial.[86] These mansions were of monumental scale 'to be in harmony with the work of Nature', and contained elements such as arcaded cloisters, pergolas and walled terraces thought by Baker to be in keeping with the South African climate. They were built in part from local stone, in keeping with Baker's intention, as he put it, to provide 'architecture which establishes a nation'. Baker meant, of course, a nation within the British Empire, a British South African nation.[87]

Parktown street names like Empire Road, Victoria Avenue, Princess Place and Park Lane removed any possible misunderstanding in this

[83] Beavon, *Johannesburg*, 60–1.   [84] Beavon, *Johannesburg*, 61.
[85] Chipkin and Zar, *Parktown*, 21–2. Joan Raikes, *Honneur Aulx Dignes: Roedean School (S.A.) 1903–1978* (Johannesburg: Lorton Publications, 1978); John Brunette Wentzel, *A View from the Ridge: Johannesburg Retrospect* (Cape Town: David Philip, 1975).
[86] J. Foster, *Washed with Sun: Landscape and the Making of White South Africa* (Pittsburgh, PA: University of Pittsburgh Press, 2008), 144–77.
[87] Thomas Metcalf, 'Herbert Baker and New Delhi', in R. Frykenberg (ed.), *New Delhi through the Ages: Essays in Urban History, Culture and Society* (New Delhi: Oxford University Press, 1986), 392, 398.

respect.[88] Such gestures were enhanced by the presence of members of Sir Alfred Milner's 'kindergarten', the predominantly Oxford-educated protégés and aides of the British High Commissioner who administered the conquered Transvaal from 1901, following the Boer War. If Cape Town hosted that poet of Empire, Kipling, Johannesburg's kindergarten included one of its leading novelists, John Buchan. Another, Edgar Wallace, whose writings were greatly inspired by Kipling, also lived briefly in Parktown and became the first editor of Johannesburg's *Rand Daily Mail* in 1902.[89]

As with other predominantly British South African suburbs, the interiors and gardens of houses in Parktown were themselves often crowded with things from Britain, including cherished family heirlooms, which could provide imaginative connection to the Mother Country. Flora and even fauna were imported from Britain. Cecil Rhodes, for instance, introduced the common starling to Cape Town as he missed the sound of British songbirds.[90] The writer William Plomer grew up in a variety of houses in Johannesburg's northern suburbs, one of them in Parktown. Moving with the family were cutlery 'with deer-horn handles' and 'three silver owls with red eyes containing three different kinds of pepper, and sundry family plate, including a big-bellied soup tureen', once the possession of a Plomer who had been Lord Mayor of London.[91] Every day when they were in season, William's father picked roses from his garden to present to his wife.

The first house of Robert Atkinson, an immigrant British engineer, was a small cottage located on Crown Mine property in unfashionable southern Johannesburg. Photographs reveal a dining table covered with 'a heavy, brocaded cloth and … dining chairs … of solid construction, upholstered in leather attached with brass studs', a piano 'bedecked with ornaments, clock and candlesticks', and 'heavy side-board, ornately carved, covered by the family silver'.[92] When the Atkinsons moved to Parktown they built a far more substantial double-storied house they called 'Cragside', with an art nouveau stained glass window and dining room walls covered with expensively imported patterned wallpaper.[93]

---

[88] Beavon, *Johannesburg*, 62.
[89] Benjamin Pogrund, *War of Words: Memoir of a South African Journalist* (New York: Seven Stories Press, 2000).
[90] The attempted introduction of blackbirds, nightingales and thrushes was unsuccessful. For an evocative fictionalised account of Rhodes' efforts, see Anne Harries, *Manly Pursuits* (London: Bloomsbury, 2000).
[91] William Plomer, *The South African Autobiography* (Cape Town: David Philip, 1984), 103.
[92] William Gaul, 'The Atkinsons at Home', *Johannesburg Heritage Journal* 1 (June 2014), 4–5.
[93] Ibid., 20.

Anglicisation was enhanced within and beyond the prestigious suburbs by joint experience and membership of recognisably British institutions and societies with their accompanying imported or newly invented traditions. Together with other shared elements of Mother Country culture, these conveyed conceptions of gender, class and racial identity that were the essence of contemporary Britishness. John Noble, the clerk to the Cape's House of Assembly, provided insightful comment on how this happened and with what results in his observations on Cape Town in 1875:

Constant intercourse with, and continual accession of books, periodicals, and serials, from the mother country have naturally infused and extended English habits and ideas, which now generally prevail here. The home markets regulate the springs of trade and commerce; home fashions rule supreme in every circle; and almost all the popular institutions, and pleasures, sports and pastimes, are reproductions of home customs and home life … There are hospitals, orphanages, sailors' homes, savings banks, young men's institutes, and Christian associations. There are volunteer corps, and cricket, foot-ball and boating clubs. There are musical societies and theatrical entertainments; and lectures, concerts, and oratorios are frequently given in the assembly-rooms of the Mutual, or St. Aloysius Hall's. There are Masonic, Odd-Fellows', Foresters', and Good Templar lodges. There are comfortable and commodious hotels, a club, public dining-rooms, billiard-rooms, and reading rooms … There are cabs, traction engines, tram-cars, railways, and telegraphs.[94]

In other words, British traditions travelled to South African cities by means of migration, print and electronic media, and the transnational circulation of British 'things', people and ideas in mutually informing fashion.[95]

The invention of British South African traditions

Many of such traditions connected to civic associations and recreational activities, themselves the result of such travels, were in Eric Hobsbawm's categorisation 'social inventions' (unofficial or informal, created by citizens or subjects) rather than 'political inventions' (official or formal, established by the state).[96] The process of anglicisation can usefully be understood as

[94] John Noble, *Descriptive Handbook of the Cape Colony: Its Condition and Resources* (Cape Town and London: J.C. Juta and E. Stanford, 1875), 45.

[95] For both practical and theoretical elaborations of how this happened see, for instance, Alan Lester, *Imperial Networks: Creating Identities in Nineteenth Century South Africa and Britain* (London and New York: Routledge, 2001) and Astrid Erll, 'Travelling Memory', *Parallex* 17, 4 (2011), 4–18.

[96] Eric Hobsbawm, 'Mass-Producing Traditions: Europe, 1870–1914', in Eric Hobsbawm and Terence Ranger (eds), *The Invention of Tradition* (Cambridge: Cambridge University Press, [1983] 1996), 264.

including both political and social varieties *working in tandem*. Hobsbawm defined what he dubbed the 'invention of tradition' as:

A set of practises, normally governed by overtly or tacitly accepted rules and of a ritual or symbolic nature, which seek to inculcate certain values and norms of behaviour by repetition, which automatically implies continuity with the past ... The historic past into which the new tradition is asserted need not be lengthy...[97]

Yet this definition could surely apply to most traditions. Invented traditions, like elements of British monarchical ritual in the late nineteenth century, usually took their place alongside or incorporated or adapted older traditions. Scholars of rural Africa interested in 'tribal' traditions supposedly invented by colonial officials or missionaries have demonstrated that 'far from being created by alien rulers ... tradition was reinterpreted, reformed and reconstructed by subjects and rulers alike'.[98] Whenever rural or 'foreign' traditions were brought to the city, adaptation or reinterpretation frequently took place that included invention. Yet even for the modern metropolis, invented traditions had to be 'manufactured, or assembled, from an existing body of knowledge that, consciously or unconsciously, includes myth and symbol'.[99]

The adoption or invention of social traditions by members of the 'new' industrial classes in South African cities was often intended to boost their social status or promote their sectional interests, as Hobsbawm demonstrated for their contemporary counterparts in Europe. What many of these social traditions frequently also did in South Africa was to incorporate and support political traditions aimed at inculcating British national identity and values. There are many examples that can illustrate this point. For instance British social traditions, albeit often with local adaptations and additional inventions, travelled to South African schools because many such institutions were founded and initially staffed by teachers from Britain. This process is only most evident in elite schools.

---

[97] Eric Hobsbawm, 'Introduction: Inventing Traditions', in E.J. Hobsbawm and T.O. Ranger (eds), *The Invention of Tradition* (Cambridge: Cambridge University Press, [1983] 1996), 1–3. Hobsbawm associated 'customs' with 'traditional' societies and with the possibility of variation not present in invented traditions; and 'convention or routine' with the absence of 'significant ritual or symbolic function'. Yet he also allowed that conventions could acquire such significance, albeit 'incidentally' (in other words not obviously planned), and work on invented traditions associated with the British monarchy, for example, demonstrates that they could vary, or be reinvented, over time. See David Cannadine, 'The Context, Performance and Meaning of Ritual: The British Monarchy and the "Invention of Tradition", c. 1820–1977', in Hobsbawm and Ranger (eds), *Invention of Tradition*, 101–64.
[98] Thomas Spear, 'Neo-Traditionalism and the Limits of Invention in British Colonial Africa', *The Journal of African History* 44, 1 (2003), 4.
[99] Patrick Harries, 'Imagery, Symbolism and Tradition in a South African Bantustan: Mangosuthu Buthelezi, Inkatha and Zulu History', *History and Theory* 32 (1993), 106–7.

St John's, Johannesburg, almost inevitably featured magnificent Herbert Baker architecture aimed at promoting British South African identity. Its founder was the Rev. John Darragh, Rector of St Mary's Anglican Church, who installed his curate as the first headmaster. The writer William Plomer attended the school before the First World War and recalled some of its very British staff and traditions:

> The fathers were mostly excellent creatures, late-Victorian Englishmen from Oxford and Cambridge, dedicated to a somewhat austere Anglo-Catholicism … as soon as we were dressed of a morning we assembled in the chapel … After the brief early service we ran like stags, headed by an athletic, long-legged Resurrection father in a flapping cassock, across the main playing-field and back to our breakfast.

Whether founded by the State, British churches or private individuals, many anglophone schools, elite or not, had evocatively British, occasionally even Empire ornamentalist, names: King Edward VII and Roedean (Johannesburg), Diocesan College, Trafalgar and Livingstone High Schools (Cape Town) and Clifton (Durban).

Individual teachers like George Ogilvie, old boy of Winchester College in Britain and headmaster of Diocesan College in Cape Town between 1861 and 1885, brought to South Africa all the rituals, symbols (mottos, distinguishing uniform, coats of arms and so on) and recreations of their own educational establishments in the Mother Country. In Ogilvie's case, the latter included a Winchester version of football claimed as rugby's antecedent in the Cape, and famously severe physical punishments all aimed at instilling appropriate manliness. This intention may explain why Diocesan College headmasters turned a blind eye to initiation rites employed by pupils on new boys, ceremonies which involved beatings while the latter crawled under netting during obstacle races and heavy blows delivered to chamber pots placed on their heads in dormitories.[100] There were local variations in tradition, but Diocesan College proved to be typical of subsequent elite White boys' schools founded elsewhere in the country. All were designed to forge, through discipline, sport and often their own cadet corps, suitably muscular and patriotic human 'munition' for Britain's wars.[101]

---

[100] Gardener, *Bishops 150*, 11–12, 26, 33.

[101] John Lambert, '"Munition Factories … Turning Out a Constant Supply of Living Material": White South African Elite Boys' Schools and the First World War', *South African Historical Journal* 51 (2004), 66–86, the term 'Munition Factories' being coined by the headmaster of St Andrew's, Grahamstown, in the Eastern Cape. For a detailed account of similar intentions in schools and adult institutions in Natal see Robert Morrell, *From Boys to Gentlemen*.

It is not surprising therefore that the entire Durban High School first rugby fifteen enlisted for the Great War. The school's games board, placed alongside its memorial board, bore 'the names of those who are learning the game now, in order that they may be able someday, if called upon, to follow the example of those others who went before, and played a greater game'.[102] Enrolments from such schools ensured that mortality rates among their pupils were among the highest of all educational institutions in the Empire. Losses were commemorated as in Britain by chapel windows, clock towers, war memorials and Remembrance Day observation. There was also local innovation like the Comrades Marathon run between Durban and Pietermaritzburg.

Some of the traditions of White boys' schools were echoed in institutions across race, class and gender divides. This was true of elite Black schools like Zonnebloem College, Cape Town (1858), whose boys played cricket against both the Diocesan College and British army regiments in the 1860s; or of St Peter's Rosettenville, Johannesburg (1911), dubbed the Black Eton. Some, like Inanda Seminary School (1869) near Durban, (for African girls), only became elite institutions over time.[103]

Girls' schools had their own invented traditions, including those that taught appropriate female roles, including domestic skills. Others added the me-too feminist element of competitive sport. White girls at Roedean, founded by one of the sisters responsible for establishing its namesake in England, and again with buildings by Herbert Baker, even had a song that praised their cricket team: 'Oh, the cricket first eleven, we admire on every hand'. The school's 'A song of the Founders' honoured those who had

> Built up our walls at the birth of a city.
> Gathered us in and our banners bestowed
>   . . .
> Girls of Roedean, independent and thorough,
> Hold high the torch as we held it of old.[104]

---

[102] Lambert, '"Munition Factories"', 72.
[103] Janet Hodgson, 'Zonnebloem College and Cape Town: 1858–187', *Studies in the History of Cape Town* 1 (1879), 125–52; Heather Hughes, '"A Lighthouse for African Womanhood": Inanda Seminary, 1869–1945', in Cherryl Walker (ed.), *Women and Gender in South Africa to 1945* (Cape Town and London: David Philip and James Currey, 1990), 197–220. Zonnebloem was the product of the combined initiative of Cape Town's first Anglican Bishop, Robert Gray, and Governor, Sir George Grey, and aimed at educating the children of Xhosa chiefs. St Peter's was another Anglican establishment, a boarding school offshoot of the earlier St Martin's school. Inanda Seminary was an American Board Mission School, founded to complement Adam's College, which eventually, like St Peter's, attracted students from all over South Africa.
[104] Raikes, *Roedean*, 7.

Roedean's coat of arms was an adaptation of that of its sister school in Brighton, as some changes in its component parts reveal: a hinde became a springbok. A grid-iron in the words of the blazon became 'On a wreath Azure and vert, a Secretary Bird destroying a snake all proper'.[105] School plays were drawn from the British dramatic canon up to the late 1970s. A revealing partial exception was *Berkely Square* (1933), performed during the Second World War. This was a British adaptation of Henry James' *The Sense of the Past* (1926), about an American transported back to eighteenth century London to meet his ancestors.[106]

The transplanted traditions of St Cyprian's (1871), a girls' school in Cape Town, included the public celebration of St Cyprian's Day from 1889, with a procession down Government Avenue to Cape Town's St George's Anglican cathedral. Further ritual was described by an ex-pupil:

After Evensong we returned home and had a merry tea, at which the St Cyprian's Day cake occupied a central position. We all walked around it three times to ensure prosperity and happiness to S Cyprian's in the future [*sic*].[107]

In 1936, St Cyprian's inaugurated the Matric Dance, which spread and extended South African school tradition. In the early years at St Cyprian's at least, this ended with 'Auld Lang Syne' followed by 'God Save the King'.[108] Girls from both St Cyprian's and Roedean raised money to support prisoners of war in the First World War, and knitted clothes for soldiers in the Second World War. In addition, during the Second World War, Roedean girls sent not only clothing but sweets, cigarettes, books, records and musical instruments to HMS *Sondra*, a British whaling vessel converted to a minesweeper.[109]

Beyond the elite schools, there were already wide varieties of non-denominational government schools as well as mission schools for the 'poorer classes', almost all Black save those in Cape Town, that received government funding in the Cape and Natal by the 1890s. Whether institutions were elite or not, or for boys or girls, traditions invented by their predominantly White staffs mingled with sermons and school history lessons to inculcate British identity and behaviour. Only British history from 1066 to Waterloo, taught as part of the English syllabus, was on offer until the 1870s in the Cape. Subsequently, there were separate compulsory high-school courses in both 'colonial' and English

[105] Raikes, *Roedean*, 27.   [106] Ibid., 149, provides a list of the school plays.
[107] Elizabeth Broekmann and Gail Weldon, *There are Stories to be Told: St Cyprian's School 1871–1996* (Cape Town: Gavin and Sales, 1996), 25.
[108] Ibid., 78.
[109] Raikes, *Roedean*, 122–6; Broekmann and Weldon, *St Cyprian's*, 139–45.

history for the Cape Elementary, while history of any kind was only optional for the Higher.[110]

One of the earliest colonial history textbooks was Alexander Wilmot's *History of the Cape Colony for use in Schools*, published in 1871, in time for curriculum changes that followed Cape self-government in 1872.[111] Wilmot's history predictably provided a Whiggish account of European colonialism, but with significant progress presented as the result of British rather than Dutch governance. What was being conveyed was a British Cape Colonial identity. Individual Dutch contributions to Cape history could be judged positive, but DEIC rule was denounced as despotic. It was shown to be responsible for the likes of regressive Sumptuary Laws that dictated appropriate dress or carriage adornment according to social status, limited economic development and no real effort to 'civilize the heathen'. Indigenous societies were savagely disparaged. Though some positive qualities like 'fidelity in service' (by 'Hottentots') were acknowledged, traditions and actions were generally described in derogatory and racist fashion: 'Hottentots' were 'intensely fond of spirituous liquors', Bushmen possessed 'troublesome character' and displayed 'universally outrageous conduct', Xhosas had 'lawless and predatory habits'. It was only British rule that brought progress for all races, in terms of Christian evangelism, equality of status before the law, Western education, finance, infrastructure, agricultural methods and the non-racial franchise.[112]

The Rev. Joseph Whiteside's *A New School History*, first published in the mid-1890s, but which was much reprinted and extensively revised, provided a more diplomatic approach to the history of non-British societies (whether Black or White). The twelfth edition, published six years after South African Union, treated Dutch colonialism, as well as Dutch and Boer history in the nineteenth century, far more generously than Wilmot. Even the Sumptuary Laws were given a positive gloss, and detailed attention was given to the establishment and naming of 'Dutch' towns. Accounts of indigenous societies, though still pockmarked by comments about 'barbaric' people prone to idleness, ignorance, cruelty or superstition, now also made mention of courageous leaders and behaviour, on occasion even displaying some empathy for the conquered. Yet 'progress' still required the adoption by all of 'civilized' behaviour and beliefs, facilitated by British rule and adoption of British values. Marks of

---

[110] Anon, *Cape of Good Hope Teachers' Annual 1900* (Cape Town: J.C. Juta & Co., 1900).

[111] Alexander Wilmot, *History of the Cape Colony for Use in Schools* (Cape Town: J.C. Juta, 1871). Wilmot also wrote a history of the Cape Colony for adults, and further history and geography books that dealt with South Africa as a whole.

[112] Wilmot, *History of the Cape Colony*, 11, 32, 60 for quotations.

Progress sections, using the same kind of criteria as Wilmot, featured in the representation of Cape history under British rule.[113]

Such views mirrored those of most other contemporary histories influential within and beyond the classroom, like the works of George McCall Theal or the version of South Africa's past presented in a Cape Town pageant held on Green Point Common over two days to celebrate Union in 1910.[114] In combination they taught South African identity, but did so by also simultaneously transmitting the idea of its distinctive Dutch and British components. The pageant told the story of European engagement with Africa, beginning with Portuguese exploration and with the civilising mission and colonial enterprise as the binding ties between Dutch and British settlement. Conflict between the two was absent, as it was between French and British in a similar Canadian pageant, with the final tableau depicting the years 1854 to 1910 representing the defeat of Savagery by Civilisation and the development of South Africa's economy and society. Those of British descent or with acquired British identity might interpret the history on show as the creation of a new South African identity. But living as they did in a country under the British flag, the majority would believe, as did contemporaries in other British Dominions, that their new national identity was entirely compatible with the retention of a British one. This was certainly the intention of the pageant's largely English-speaking and pro-Imperial organising committee. The pageant had King Edward VII's brother, the Duke of Connaught, as its patron, who was present as part of his visit to open the first Union Parliament (see Illustration 2.1). The pageant suggested that if both the Dutch and the British contributed to civilisation in South Africa, the British were at its apogee, in keeping with the message of contemporary English-language history books.[115]

The history actually taught in schools to children across South Africa could vary, as might what they made of it, while very many (especially

---

[113] Rev. J. Whiteside, *A New School History of South Africa: With Brief Biographies and Examination Questions*, 12th edition, revised (Johannesburg and Cape Town: J.C. Juta & Co., 1916).

[114] Theal taught at the elite Lovedale Mission School in the Eastern Cape in the 1870s. On Theal and 'settler' history more generally, see Christopher Saunders, *The Making of the South African Past: Major Historians on Race and Class* (Cape Town: David Philip, 1988) and Ken Smith, *The Changing Past: Trends in South African History* (Johannesburg: Southern Books, 1988).

[115] Lesley Witz, *Apartheid's Festival: Contesting South Africa's National Pasts* (Bloomington, IN: Indiana University Press, 2003), 44–5; Peter Merrington, 'Pageantry and Primitivism: Dorothea Fairbridge and the "Aesthetics of Union"', *Journal of Southern African Studies* 21, 4 (1995), 643–56; Peter Merrington, 'Maps, Monuments and Masons: The 1910 Pageant of the Union of South Africa', *Theatre Journal* 49, 1 (1997), 1–14.

Illustration 2.1: Another royal occasion: Prince Arthur, Duke of
Connaught, on his way to opening the first Union Parliament in Cape
Town in 1910 (Mary Evans Picture Gallery)

African) children still received little or no Western education at all. On
occasion one can glimpse something of this variation. History as a 'compendium of names and dates' was still being taught in the 1930s at the
Jewish Government School, Johannesburg. Its pupils, including the
future Trotskeyite Baruch Hirson, 'did not question the text books or
our teachers'.[116] African girls at Inanda Seminary on the eve of the First
World War were taught about 'Dinizulu, Cecil Rhodes, President
Kruger, Lord Milner ... Victoria, Edward VII and George V', and the
Chief Inspector of Native Education in Natal took a personal interest in
the curriculum.[117] At much the same time, boys in Miss Joubert's Dutch
classes at Jeppe Preparatory School (Johannesburg) learnt 'a good deal of
the history of the Boers, their struggles, their aspirations and their

[116] Baruch Hirson, *Revolutions in My Life* (Johannesburg: Witwatersrand University Press,
1995), 39–40.
[117] Hughes, 'Inanda Seminary', 216.

sufferings', though most graduates of the High School were happy enough to join the cadets and sing 'God Save the King'.[118]

It is generally difficult to discern pupils' thoughts. Accounts of school days in biographies and autobiographies, as with all recollections, were subject to influence by post-school experiences and considerations. Opinions ranged from enthusiasm, through indifference to hostility, yet large numbers of Black South Africans adopted British values associated with respectability. For some at least, a sense of British civic national identity lingered on after South African Union. This was despite the fact that the non-racial Cape franchise had not been extended northwards, and that therefore British promises of 'equal rights for all civilised men south of the Limpopo', made before and during the Boer War, had been reneged on.[119]

One famous autobiographical account offers insight into how some Black schoolchildren could still be attracted by Britishness as late as the 1930s. It is by a pupil at Healdtown College, a Methodist school in the Eastern Cape, who lived in Johannesburg:

The principal of Healdtown was Dr Arthur Wellington, a stout and stuffy Englishman who boasted of his connection to the Duke of Wellington. At the outset of the assemblies, Dr Wellington would walk on stage and say, in his deep bass voice, 'I am the descendant of the great Duke of Wellington, aristocrat, statesman, and general, who crushed the Frenchman Napoleon at Waterloo and thereby saved civilization for Europe – and for you, the natives'. At this, we would all enthusiastically applaud, each of us profoundly grateful that a descendant of the great Duke of Wellington would take the trouble to educate natives such as ourselves. The educated Englishman was our model; what we aspired to be were 'black Englishmen', as we were sometimes derisively called. We were taught – and believed – that the best ideas were English ideas, the best government was English government and the best men were Englishmen.[120]

The pupil, who became a long-distance runner, boxer and prefect at the school, was Nelson Mandela. Even before he left Healdtown, Mandela recalled questioning Dr Wellington's philosophy. Mandela describes how he came to see himself as a Xhosa and, to an avowedly lesser extent, an African, but does not say whether he retained a British identity as well. In later life, Mandela remembered being uncomfortable about the African National Congress (ANC) Youth League's call for a boycott of the Royal Tour in 1947, a call ignored by older ANC leaders, and admitted

---

[118] Eddie and Win Roux, *Rebel Pity: The Life of Eddie Roux* (London: Rex Collings, 1970), 6–18.
[119] Bickford-Smith, 'The Betrayal of Creole Elites'.
[120] Nelson Mandela, *A Long Walk to Freedom* (Johanneburg: Macdonald Purnell, 1995), 35–6.

favouring the idea of monarchy. He apparently also prostrated himself at Clarence House in front of the somewhat startled Queen Mother in 1996.[121]

In contrast, fellow ANC Youth League member and Robben Island prisoner, Walter Sisulu, never saw himself as British and particularly enjoyed history that celebrated African warrior leaders, according to his daughter-in-law and biographer Elinor.[122] Another leader of the ANC, Chief Albert Luthuli, attended a Methodist institution at Edenvale, Natal, during the First World War. As with newcomers in many White boys' schools, he had to run the gauntlet of violent initiation as a form of invented tradition. Writing in the 1960s, he was angered by the

[African] Nationalist gibe nowadays that such schools as this one [Edenvale], or Adams College (near Durban), or St Peter's, Rosettenville, turned out "Black Englishmen" . . . Two cultures met and both were affected by the meeting . . . I am aware of a profound gratitude for what I have learned. I remain an African.[123]

Sixty years earlier, many among educated Black elites in southern Africa, as in anglophone West Africa, unashamedly projected themselves as Black British. They professed loyalty to the British monarch, someone who might be appealed to in time of need. They held ideas about self-improvement that included the benefits of acquiring the English language and adherence to the dichotomy between 'barbarism' and civilisation much used in contemporary school textbooks.[124]

This could still be true if the school they had attended was not British, though American Board Missions (ABM) schools like Adams College provided more exposure to alluring transatlantic possibilities. One who thought of himself as Black British, at least in the early part of his life, was Sol Plaatje, a founder member of the South African Native National Congress (or SANNC, which later became the ANC), who attended Pniel, a Berlin Mission school. There he was introduced to Shakespeare, the violin and *Nelson's Royal Reader*, an English primer used across the British Empire and replete with homilies against idleness like 'The Boy who was Always Late'.[125] On arriving in the mining town of Kimberley, and gaining employment with the post office, Plaatje became

---

[121] Sapire, 'African Loyalism', 237.
[122] Elinor Sisulu, *Walter and Albertina Sisulu: In Our Lifetime* (Cape Town: David Philip, 2003), 40–2.
[123] Albert Luthuli, *Let My People Go: An Autobiography* (London and Glasgow: Fontana, 1965), 27–9.
[124] Bickford-Smith, 'The Betrayal of Creole Elites' and Vivian Bickford-Smith, 'African Nationalist or British Loyalist? The Complicated Case of Tiyo Soga', *History Workshop Journal* 71 (Spring 2011), 74–97.
[125] Brian Willan, *Sol Plaatje: A Biography* (Johannesburg: Ravan, 2001), 21–4.

involved in numerous African societies and clubs that radiated British values and identity: the South Africans Improvement Society, the Eccentrics and Duke of Wellington cricket clubs, Rovers rugby club, and the Come Again Lawn Tennis club. The South Africans Improvement Society avowedly aimed 'to cultivate the use of the English language ... and to help each other by fair and reasonable criticisms in readings, recitations, English compositions etc'. At its second meeting, Plaatje read from *John Bull and Co.*, 'a humorous celebration of the glories of the British Empire' and became a central figure on social occasions involving Kimberley's Black elite. These usually incorporated British traditions, such as a loyal toast to the monarch and singing of the national anthem, as well as local innovations that might reveal other simultaneously held identities. In Plaatje's meeting, there were toasts to 'Africa' and 'Local Black Folk'.[126]

As Plaatje's Kimberley activities suggest, schools were not the only institutions that inculcated British identity in southern African cities. Among others were gentlemen's clubs modelled on those in London.[127] Women were only allowed in time to attend occasional social functions, and then sometimes only through separate entrances, a device similarly and simultaneously used for segregation based on class or race, which these clubs also incorporated.[128]

An attempt was made by British immigrants in Durban to form such a club as early as 1854, the inaugural year of the municipality. In the event, through lack of members and funds, the Durban Club had to be re-founded six years later with a membership that included mayors past and present, businessmen and Richard 'Dick' King of 'ride-to-relieve-Durban-from-the-Boers fame'. Three club houses built in increasingly extravagant fashion followed. The third, completed in 1904 at the cost of £63,000 (roughly £5 million today) and overlooking the Bay of Natal, was again in part a Herbert Baker design, baroque in style with Victorian ironwork additions. Treasured possessions included a snuffbox made from the hoof of a horse ridden by Trooper Able, who died in the Zulu War of 1879, and a painting by Thomas Baines of the *Sarah Bell*, the first ship that sailed directly from England to Durban. Menus were designed for special occasions during the Boer War; those for returning officers of

[126] Ibid., 37–41; see also Brian Willan, 'An African in Kimberley: Sol T. Plaatje, 1894–8', in Shula Marks and Richard Rathbone (eds), *Industrialisation and Social Change: African Class Formation, Culture, and Consciousness, 1870–1930* (Harlow and New York: Longman, 1982), 238–58.
[127] See Morrell, *From Boys to Gentlemen*, for this argument in respect of colonial Natal.
[128] See club histories cited later in the chapter: the Durban Club did not allow women to use its main entrance, and the City Club in Cape Town only refrained from building a separate entrance through considerations of cost.

the Natal Volunteers featured figures of Natalia and Britannia flanked by Union Jacks.[129]

Cape Town's City Club (1878), in Queen Victoria Street, was yet another Herbert Baker building, and formed twenty years after the Civil Service Club (1858), with which it eventually amalgamated. From 1888, City Club presidency was conferred on Cape Governor-Generals, and after 1910 on Governor-Generals of the South African Union. The membership list was predictably exclusive. Its interior evoked South African Britishness, as with its Johannesburg and Durban counterparts. In the City Club, depictions of Rhodes were everywhere; a bust over-looked the entrance hall and a portrait hung above the stairs leading to the first floor gallery, where there were two more. The library featured works by Scott, Dickens, Thackeray, Shakespeare and Churchill as well as prints of 'The Kaffir Wars'. In the lounge there were engravings of Lord Nelson, Trafalgar and Rorke's Drift, portraits of Prince Alfred and King Edward VII, and a large map of London displaying streets, squares, buildings and famous individuals associated with them and Churchill's words 'London, The Bastion of Liberty'.[130]

For Johannesburg, the Rand Club, established in the city centre in 1887 with Cecil Rhodes as one of its founder members, supplied a notable social and political centre for wealthy male Britons. Although other nationalities could and did join, the vast majority of the Rand Club's members in the early decades were British. The club duly became a centre for 'Reform Committee' political mobilisation against the Kruger govern-ment. Reform Committee members were arrested on club premises after the failure of the Jameson Raid and forced to hand over contraband firearms. Unremorseful, club members hosted a dinner in honour of Rudyard Kipling in 1898 that commenced with a patriotic song of the eighteenth century, 'The Roast Beef of Old England', which began:

> When mighty Roast Beef was the Englishman's food,
> It ennobled our brains and enriched our blood.
> Our soldiers were brave and our courtiers were good.

The meal ended with the national anthem.[131]

Singing the British national anthem or swearing an oath of loyalty to the monarch became a social tradition associated with many occasions in

---

[129] D.H. Strutt, *The Story of the Durban Club: From Bafta to Baroque* (Cape Town: Howard Timmins, 1963); Desiree Picton-Seymour, *Victorian Buildings in South Africa* (Cape Town and Rotterdam: A.A. Balkema, 1977), 236, 241, 244–5.

[130] W.E. Ranby, *The City Club, Cape Town: A Supplementary History to 1955* (Cape Town: Galvin & Sales, 1955).

[131] R. de Villiers and S. Brooke-Norris, *The Story of the Rand Club* (Johannesburg: The Rand Club, 1976), 64.

South African cities by the early twentieth century. Most theatre and cinema performances ended with the national anthem. Some institutional traditions with patriotic elements, like those of various Freemason branches connected to parent lodges in Britain, made their appearance before the Mineral Revolution, in similar fashion to gentlemen's clubs. Swearing allegiance to the monarch, rather less exotic than their other rituals invented in the early eighteenth century, became a condition of British lodge membership. Lodges also represented class status. British Masons, who grew to be far more numerous than their Dutch counterparts made frequent public appearances of Imperial, national and local import. In Cape Town, these included laying the foundation stones of the Sailors' Home, attended by Prince Alfred, and the Cape Parliament. On the former occasion at least, the Masonic anthem, 'When Earth's Foundations first were Laid', was sung to the tune of 'Rule Britannia'. Like gentlemen's clubs, lodges entertained officers of visiting British military units; like anglophone schools, they contributed to British war efforts. Perhaps unsurprisingly, Masons were suspected by Dutch Reformed Church ministers, closely associated with Afrikaner nationalism, of un-Christian and subversive practices between the 1940s and the 1960s, accusations vigorously denied.[132]

Other invented traditions that promoted Britishness, like those accompanying the Boy Scouts, Girl Guides or Vigilance Societies, emerged during or after the South African War, indeed were often products of that conflict. The Boy Scout movement, for instance, which demanded an oath of loyalty to the monarch, was inaugurated by Robert Baden-Powell, of Siege of Mafeking fame. His aim was to address the supposed physical and moral decay of young British men noticed during recruitment for the war, an aim shared by Anglican Boys' Brigades throughout the Empire.[133] Baden-Powell's *Scouting for Boys* was the manual of the movement's invented traditions. One section was on 'Scoutcraft and Scoutlaw, giving the Duties of Boy Scouts, their Secret Signs, Laws, Badges, War Dance, etc.' and contained Baden-Powell's design for uniforms: 'Shorts ... A kilt if you are a Scotsman'; 'Coloured handkerchief tied loosely round the neck'; 'Stockings, with garters made of green braid, with one end hanging down one inch'.[134]

In South Africa, there was considerable resistance both by White civilians, if especially in the ex-Boer republics, and by the Union government,

[132] A.A. Cooper, *The Freemasons of South Africa* (Cape Town: Human & Rousseau, 1986); Jessica L. Harland-Jacobs, *Builders of Empire: Freemasonry and British Imperialism, 1717–1927* (Chapel Hill: The University of North Carolina Press, 2007).
[133] Timothy H. Parsons, *Race, Resistance, and the Boy Scout Movement in British Colonial Africa* (Athens, OH: Ohio University Press, 2004).
[134] Lieut.-General R.S.S. Baden Powell, *Scouting for Boys: A Handbook for Instruction in Good Discipline* (London: Horace Cox, 1907).

to Black participation in the scouting movement. Black groups did not receive official recognition, despite the considerable enthusiasm of many mission teachers and their students. Only missionaries and liberals, often one and the same, were warmly in favour. Their collective efforts only led to the unofficial formation of parallel Scout and Girl Guide-style groups for Africans, Indians and Coloureds after the First World War.[135]

Scouting for Boys was subtitled *A Handbook for Instruction in Good Citizenship*, and contained a section on 'Patriotism and Loyalty'. This provided information on the growth of the Empire ('a large Map ... is useful for illustrating this'), the monarchy and the flag. It provided instructions on the right way to fly the flag, the words of the British, Canadian and Australian national anthems, and how the Empire should be defended. Scouts were instructed to 'be prepared' in this respect, by learning paramilitary skills and holding the right values: self-discipline, sobriety, thrift, honour, courage, chivalry (particularly towards women) and Christianity. Morally and physically healthy recreation and reading were suggested: woodcraft, flag raiding, and throwing an assegai. Re-enacting historical scenes was also recommended, like the Wreck of the Birkenhead (troops singing the national anthem on deck as the ship went down) or Wilson's Last Stand against Ndebele warriors in Rhodesia. The telling of instructional tales was advocated, like the tracking and summary execution of the Diamond Thief in South Africa; so was reading Walter Scott, Conan Doyle, Rudyard Kipling and Percy Fitzpatrick.[136] Sport was important too. Baden-Powell approved of football and cricket. He also supplied detailed instructions on how to play basketball, and what constituted fouls: 'holding, dashing, charging, shouldering, tripping'.

Although passages in *Scouting for Boys* now read like extracts from a Monty Python sketch, the book has been appreciated for the multimedia ways in which it demonstrates how British loyalty and values could be conveyed. The appearance and advocacy of regulated sports like basketball were shaped by the accelerated global pace of industrialisation and urbanisation. They were expected to help inculcate desirable national values, such as discipline, fitness and fair play, suitable for ordered city life. Enduringly, sport also transmitted appropriate gender behaviour and identity, even if feminist assertions gradually forced open a path for women's participation.[137]

---

[135] Parsons, *Boy Scout Movement*, 72–112. The Girl Guide movement faced similar segregation, though White and Coloured Guides and African 'Wayfarers' were nominally in one united movement rather than the parallel arrangement for scouts.

[136] Baden-Powell, *Scouting for Boys*.

[137] R. Holt, *Sport and the British* (Oxford and New York: Oxford Studies in Social History, 1990); V. Bickford-Smith, 'Leisure and Social Identity in Cape Town, British Cape Colony, 1838–1910', *Kronos: Journal of Cape History* 25 (1998/1999), 103–28.

Organised sports helped confirm and express numerous local, national and transnational identities. An annual cricket match between 'Mother Country and Colonial Born' inaugurated at Newlands as early as 1862, enhanced British or British South African identity. Many such occasions were attended by the colonial leadership, including the Governor. Sport was often incorporated into Imperial occasions: jubilee celebrations, regattas on the Queen's birthday or athletics during festivities to mark the marriage of Prince Alfred.[138]

Sporting activity in Boer-controlled Johannesburg helped promote British identity, with activity centred on the land on its northern edge used by the Wanderers' cricket and rugby clubs. In the late 1880s, the Wanderers' ground hosted a visit by Major Wharton's England cricket team, and in 1891 a gymkhana in which Sir Abe Bailey won the 'cigar and umbrella' race. The city's first cycling club met there in 1895, with its track laid around the cricket pitch. The Wanderers fittingly relocated to the northern suburbs after the Second World War, to make way for railway development and in keeping with changing social geography.[139]

Black elites established their own sports teams, whether Plaatje's Duke of Wellington cricket club or the Western Province Coloured Rugby Union in 1886, which like other civic associations promoted respectability. While transmitting British identity, they could at the same time reinforce African, Indian or Coloured identities, themselves products of British colonial categorisation.[140] Establishing and running sporting and other associations along these lines provided leadership and organisational experience, which was subsequently utilised in ethno-national political endeavours. Among these were the (Mohandas Gandhi-founded) Natal Indian Congress (NIC, 1894), the African Political Organisation (APO, 1902, which despite its name represented Coloured South Africans), the Transvaal British Indian Congress (TBIC, 1903) and the South African Native National Congress (SANNC, 1912), forerunner of the ANC. For decades, all were motivated by the desire to promote or protect members' and supporters' ethno-national interests and civil rights as British subjects; indeed throughout the Empire members of such organisations 'argued for equality and integration within a colour-blind empire, not for separation'. Most Western-educated Black elites whether in Africa, Asia or the Caribbean made this case 'with greater energy . . . as the tide of pseudo-scientific

[138] Bickford-Smith, 'Leisure and Social Identity', 103–28.
[139] Neame, *City Built on Gold*, 80–4.
[140] John Nauright, *Sport, Cultures and Identities in South Africa* (Cape Town and Johannesburg: David Philip, 1997).

racism gained ground', and as White racial discrimination hardened, well into the twentieth century.[141]

Beyond sport, teachers and clergymen taught British values and gender roles through song, prayer, sermons, lessons, textbooks, magic lantern shows, stained glass windows and informal conversations. In rural areas of southern Africa, conversion and absorption of Western culture more generally was an uneven process; but Black converts played an important role in the evangelical project as they did in the cities.[142] Recipients of rural missionary education who moved to the cities joined the Westernised and Christianised Black elites already there.

In Cape Town, for instance, an ecumenical mission under the auspices of the Presbyterian Church had been established in 1838 to minister to ex-slaves. From 1859, an Anglican clergyman, Canon Lightfoot, played a central role in instituting day-and-night schools for the poor in the western part of town connected to St Paul's Mission. When Lightfoot was asked what 'coloured' children gained by schooling, he replied, 'manners ... habits of diligence ... and order, and also respect and reverence'.[143] A church was eventually built there in the 1870s, and a Cape Town English Church Friendly Society and St Paul's Benefit Society established.[144] A further mission, St Philip's, was set up in District Six in 1884 to serve the rapidly developing eastern part of the city. For two decades before a Herbert Baker-designed church was built, services were held in private houses like those of a Mrs Holmes or of an ex-slave, Lydia. In 1893, Lydia was reported as 'keeping with festival the anniversary of the proclamation that abolished slavery [on 1 December 1834], and bears still on her back the marks of the slave whippings she got in her youth under Dutch regime'.[145] During an anniversary commemoration in 1901, a Cowley evangelist found Lydia in her 'one-roomed church and cottage... with a court of ladies all with white handkerchiefs on their heads, seated around'.[146]

So whether from rural areas or already in the city, Black Christian converts joined or founded secular and clerical associations and traditions, most connected to established churches but some as their own

[141] David Killingray, '"A Good West Indian, a Good African, and, in Short, a Good Britisher": Black and British in a Colour-Conscious Empire, 1760–1950', *The Journal of Imperial and Commonwealth History* 36, 3 (2008), 370.

[142] Two major contributions in this respect are Jean and John Comaroff, *Of Revelation and Revolution*, 2 vols (Chicago: Chicago University Press, 1991 and 1997); and Elizabeth Elbourne, *Colonialism, Missions, and the Contest for Christianity in the Cape Colony and Britain, 1799–1853* (Montreal: McGill-Queen's University Press, 2002).

[143] *South African Native Affairs Commission*, 1903–5, vol. 2, 191.

[144] H.P. Barnett-Clarke, *The Life and Times of Thomas Fothergill Lightfoot, BD, Archdeacon of Cape Town* (Cape Town: Darter, 1908), 110–85.

[145] *Cowley Evangelist*, September 1893.   [146] *Cowley Evangelist*, 1902, 36–7.

independent creations. One of the first was Ohlange Native Industrial Institute, near Durban. This was founded in 1900 by ABM-educated John Dube, first President of the SANNC. Ohlange was inspired by Booker T. Washington's Tuskegee Normal and Industrial Institute, which Dube had visited when studying in the United States. Washington stressed the need for Black self-reliance, as well as economic and educational advancement.[147]

Black teachers and clerics, and Black elite societies and sporting clubs became crucial conveyors of British values, and Black elites emulated or invented traditions in keeping with them.[148] The growth of Christianity played a key role in this process, accelerating among Africans after colonial conquest and the Mineral Revolution. Census returns show that around 25 per cent of Africans saw themselves as Christian in 1911, a figure that rose to over 50 per cent by 1946. The Methodist, Anglican and ABM churches all had African women's *manyano* Prayer Unions by 1910, which normally met on Thursday afternoons. Uniforms were created by members. For Methodists, these were modelled on British military redcoats; for Anglicans, dress included black headscarves and skirts, and white jackets. Uniforms that signified membership of Prayer Unions subtly indicated hierarchy and signified respectability. The meetings were occasions to share anxieties about the morality of children and express solidarity through sighing or weeping. Members organised savings schemes and gained self-confidence through a social support network.[149]

Black conversion to Christianity also fuelled the adoption, adaption or invention of suitably respectable music, dance and song. In and around Durban, *kholwa* (educated African Christians) formed the Motor Car Choir, Steam Roller Choir and Electric Light Choir, whose names expressed members' adherence to modernity and progress. Dube's Ohlange Institute, also known as the Zulu Christian Institute, played a central role in such developments, along with the ABM's Adams College and Catholic Mariannhill. ABM missionaries had facilitated Dube's studying at Oberlin College (United States). This American educational influence combined with that of African American musicians who visited South Africa in the late nineteenth century, like Orpheus McAdoo and his Virginia Jubilee Singers, to ensure that American as well as British and

---

[147] Heather Hughes, *First President: A Life of John L. Dube, Founding President of the ANC* (Cape Town: Jacana, 2012).
[148] Bickford-Smith, *Ethnic Pride and Racial Prejudice*.
[149] Debbie Gaitskell, 'Devout Domesticity? A Century of African Women's Christianity in South Africa', in Cherryl Walker (ed.), *Women and Gender in Southern Africa to 1945* (Cape Town and London: David Philip, 1990), 251–72.

African musical traditions featured in the repertoire for Black elites in Durban, Cape Town and Johannesburg.

The music included not only Christian hymns with an African musical inflection, but also American spirituals, sanitised forms of minstrelsy and British Music Hall-influenced ragtime, all performed at concerts or to accompany ballroom dancing. One popular song in the cities by 1900 was 'Oh Susanna', borrowed from American minstrelsy. Its lyrics mocked naive rural Blacks and allowed the concomitant praise of urban sophistication on both continents. This repertoire became part of the search by Black elites for status and identity in new and often challenging urban circumstances.[150]

Social inventions of tradition that conveyed British values were not the monopoly of White and Black elites. Members of the working class once imbued with such values through the likes of schools or church organisations could pass them on to their children by teaching respectability within the home. British working-class traditions included craft trade unionism, established by artisan immigrants around the 1870s. Carpenters, stonemasons, engineers, plumbers, bricklayers and plasterers – who often arrived in large groups through assisted-passage legislation 'ordered' by the same employer – brought traditions of work and association with them. These traditions included apprenticeship, the payment of membership fees, benefit payments during times of sickness or unemployment, and strike activities that involved street parading, songs and banners. Group outings or evening entertainment in Trades Halls were also based on British precedent, as was consciousness of craft pride and the desire to protect group privilege. The consequence of the latter, though, was that the vast majority of craft unionists, and almost all those outside the Cape, associated protection of their craft identity and privilege with race, with being White, and for many with being British. Thus the South African Labour Party, another imported Mother Country tradition, with the exception of some Coloured members in the Cape, was a predominantly White organisation from its establishment at the time of Union in 1910.[151] Nonetheless elements of craft union protest could be emulated by workers excluded from craft union membership.

---

[150] Veit Erlmann, *African Stars: Studies in Black South African Performance* (Chicago: Chicago University Press, 1991); Veit Erlmann, 'But Hope Does Not Kill: Black Popular Music in Durban, 1913–1939', in Paul Maylam and Iain Edwards (eds), *The People's City: African Life in Twentieth Century Durban* (Pietermaritzburg and Portsmouth, OH: Heinemann, 1996), 67–101.

[151] Bickford-Smith, *Ethnic Pride and Racial Prejudice*, 164–78.

Anglicisation by municipal governments

But it was the British elites, with their regional or transcontinental connections to commercial networks within a wider British world, who first gained local political power. Their control of municipal governments and their own private wealth were deployed in the creation or redesign of suburbs and city centres in recognisably British style. They also introduced British civic culture that included anglophone place-naming, monuments and ceremonies, a process one historian has dubbed 'imperial ornamentalism', aimed at inculcating and maintaining British national identity.[152]

Until the late nineteenth century, and unlike its southern suburbs, Cape Town's centre was perceived by many British residents and visitors to be distinctly un-British in its human mix and built environment. This was despite the existence of some familiarly British institutions such as the gentlemen's clubs and Masonic lodges mentioned above, as well as a commercial exchange and library fronted by the statue of former governor Sir George Grey. A number of street names had also been subject to anglicisation: notably the main thoroughfare's name was changed from the Hereengracht to Adderley Street. Yet many street names remained Dutch, and the architecture predominantly so. Consequently, in English-language depictions of Cape Town for much of the nineteenth century, the material conditions, architecture and inhabitants were portrayed as foreign and unworthy of a British colony. One such commentator was Anthony Trollope, who visited Cape Town in 1877. He blamed municipal officials for the inadequate state of the city and commented on its population:

It is as I have said ragged, the roadways are uneven and the pavements are so little continuous that the walker by night had better even keep the road. I did not make special enquiry as to the municipality, but it appeared to me that the officers of that body were not alert. A walk through the streets of Capetown [sic] is sufficient to show the stranger that he has reached a place not inhabited by white men, – and a very little conversation will show him further that he is not speaking with an English-speaking population.[153]

As Trollope's comments suggest, Imperial networks of individuals and ideas together with rapidly improving transport and communication systems disseminated metropolitan knowledge of urban life, its problems and its solutions with increasing rapidity.[154] Trollope was but one of

---

[152] David Cannadine, *Ornamentalism: How the British Saw Their Empire* (London: Penguin, 2001).

[153] Trollope, *South Africa*, 54–5.

[154] Lester, *Imperial Networks*; Alan Lester and David Lambert (eds), *Colonial Lives across the British Empire: Imperial Careering in the Long Nineteenth Century* (Cambridge: Cambridge University Press, 2006).

many British visitors and immigrants to decry Cape Town's dirty and insanitary condition, and the need for the local implementation of measures used in British cities: increased water supply, extended provision of drains and sewers, paved streets and pavements, and adequate street lighting. The transmission of these ideas was facilitated by the growth in number and circulation of English-language city newspapers, like the *Cape Argus* (1857) and *Cape Times* (1876) in Cape Town, Durban's *Natal Mercury* (1852), and the *Star* (1889), *Standard and Diggers' News* (1890) and *Rand Daily Mail* (1902) in Johannesburg.

These English-language newspapers continually asserted an association between Britishness, 'progress' and 'reform', whether the need for urban sanitation in Cape Town or for greater democracy in the Johannesburg of Kruger's Transvaal. In doing so, and by promoting the sense of shared local and transnational British community through a myriad of references to metropolitan British life, city newspapers fostered both British national identity and British nationalism in South Africa. They could even convey British identity when not overtly mentioning Britain, through the premise that anyone who read them and understood their anglophone allusions was 'one of us'.

Hence the first issue of the *Star* had a leading article titled 'Ourselves', an attack on Kruger's government for denying British immigrants the Transvaal franchise and preventing Johannesburg from acquiring proper municipal government. It concluded, 'to bring about reforms in these respects will be one of the aims of the *Star*'.[155] The *Lantern*, a weekly magazine robustly criticised Cape Town's insufficiently British municipality. A poem in an issue of 1881 opened with the lines, 'Waterless, rainless, sewerless and drainless, Surely our Bumbles are senseless and brainless'.[156] The first editorial of Durban's *Natal Mercury* stated that its opinions would be based on the fact that 'Natal is a British Colony and therefore her laws and institutions and the spirit of the Government should be gradually and carefully conformed to the characteristic of her position'. This meant that the majority population of 'barbarians congregated in dangerous masses' would need a 'wise and cautious system of government, administered with even-handed justice' to 'develop' their 'dormant labour' and 'elevate' their 'moral character'. Confident that this was desirable and achievable, the *Mercury* would 'exhibit to the world the singularly varied capabilities of the district of Natal as an eligible field for British colonisation'.[157]

---

[155] *The Star*, 17 October 1887.   [156] Cited in Picard, *Grand Parade*, 77–8.
[157] *The Natal Mercury*, 25 November 1852.

The *Lantern* poem's reference to Bumbles assumed that its readers had read Dickens. The poem was part of a vigorous local English-language press campaign waged from the 1870s to the 1890s aimed at wresting control of the Town Council from predominantly Dutch or Afrikaans-speaking property owners. Several of these property owners were associated with the Afrikaner Bond, an ethno-national movement initiated to protect Dutch/Afrikaner interests within a British-controlled Cape after the granting of Representative Government in 1872.[158] British South African nationalism that opposed it was given added bite by the rise of Imperial jingoism fuelled by British wars.[159]

Afrikaans or Dutch-speaking property owners serving on the Town Council were dubbed 'The Dirty Party' in the English-language press, and lampooned in column inches and cartoons as landlords who wished rates on property to remain low. Dirty Party candidates generally did resist substantial increases to municipal expenditure on sewage and water supply and manipulated elections, not least by putting pressure on their own tenants to vote for them. The *Lantern* and *Cape Times* threw their support behind a Clean Party of merchants and businessmen, predominantly of British background, bent on 'improving' the city along the lines of Joseph Chamberlain's approach to urban reform in Birmingham. Most Cleans lived in the southern suburbs, and helped establish the British-controlled municipalities there. As owners of businesses in the city, they believed that spending money on improving its centre would enhance commercial prospects.

The editors of English-language journals supported this aim and contrasted contemporary urban living conditions in the Cape unfavourably with those in Britain.[160] In the 1870s, the decade that saw the launch of the *Cape Times* and the *Lantern*, the prospect of wresting control from the Dirty Party had improved because of the growing British immigrant population within the municipality. By the end of the decade this element of Cape Town's population probably first crept ahead of its Dutch counterpart. But it was not until further immigration prompted by the gold-induced boom of the 1890s that Clean dominance of Cape Town municipal elections was secured, and with it control of local government throughout the greater Cape Town area.[161] For almost the whole of the next century, the Council

---

[158] T.R.H. Davenport, *The Afrikaner Bond 1880–1911* (Cape Town: Oxford University Press, 1966).

[159] Bickford-Smith, *Ethnic Pride and Racial Prejudice*.

[160] Vivian Bickford-Smith, '"Keeping Your Own Council": The Struggle between Houseowners and Merchants for Control of the Cape Town Municipal Council in the Last Two Decades of the Nineteenth Century', *Studies in the History of Cape Town* 5 (1984), 189–208.

[161] Bickford-Smith, *Ethnic Pride and Racial Prejudice*, 34, 38–9, 57–8, 60, 132–4.

remained under the control of representatives of White anglophone Cape Town, with mayors drawn overwhelmingly from this group.[162]

Clean rule with its transnational Imperial networks acted as a catalyst to the fashioning of central Cape Town along metropolitan British lines. Loans were raised on the London market, and money spent on parks, reservoirs, street surfacing and electricity supply. Advice was sought from a leading sanitary expert from Britain. Refashioning along British lines now encompassed street design, including the removal of most Dutch-style *stoeps*, and Victorian civic architecture, neoclassical business premises, neo-Gothic churches, and the ubiquitous use of wrought-iron adornment and signage imported from Britain. In 1905 the Council moved from the Old Town House, a small classically proportioned Dutch building of 1761, to an imposing Renaissance-style edifice on the Grand Parade.[163]

By the beginning of the twentieth century, the Cape Town Council had acquired the full range of British municipal regalia: mayoral robes, mace, chain and a coat of arms granted by the College of Arms with the Latin motto, *Spes Bono* (Good Hope). The mace was a combination of Cape and British civic splendour, the work of a Birmingham firm, and modelled on a mace presented to the corporation of Northampton by Charles II. It included the coats of arms of both Cape Town and the United Kingdom, its wood staff made of oak from Nelson's flagship *Victory*.[164]

Statues and monuments added to the growth of British civic material culture. A statue of Queen Victoria was placed in front of the Cape Parliament in 1890, and one of Edward VII on the Grand Parade in front of the town hall in 1902. One First World War memorial was placed in Adderley Street (1919), with another in the Gardens (1928) for the many who had fallen at the battle of Delville Wood.[165] Even before the opening of the Rhodes Memorial, a statue of this local hero of Empire was unveiled in the Gardens in 1910, facing northward; his left arm was raised and the inscription read, 'Your Hinterland is There'. This came eight years after elaborate rituals surrounding his death that included, for Cape Town alone, two ceremonies of lying-in-state, at Groote Schuur then Parliament; two funerals, at Groote Schuur and St George's Cathedral; and then the carrying of Rhodes' coffin in procession along Adderley Street to the railway station and eventual burial in Rhodesia. At the first

---

[162] For a somewhat rose-tinted account of these mayors and what they accomplished written by someone who was a Cape Town mayor himself in the twentieth century, see Bloomberg, *The Chain Gang*.

[163] Picton-Seymour, *Victorian Buildings*.

[164] John Shorten, *Cape Town* (Cape Town: John R. Shorten Limited, 1963), 145–6.

[165] Ibid., and Picard, *Grand Parade*, 164.

lying-in-state alone, over the Easter weekend of 1902, around 45,000 people filed by Rhodes' body. On view at the St George's service were wreaths from Queen Alexandra, Milner and Kitchener.[166]

Built environment and civic culture that promoted British identity drew comments from locals and visitors alike by the late 1890s.[167] An editorial in the *Cape Argus* thought that the 'new metropolis' was much better than the 'dirty white half-bred orientalism' of old Cape Town.[168] In the words of a British visitor, there was now 'something indescribably English in the atmosphere of Cape Town'.[169]

Cape Town was emulating Durban in this respect. From its inception in 1854, the Durban Town Council was controlled by British business-men. This reflected the fact that English-speaking Whites of British extraction far outnumbered their Dutch or Afrikaans-speaking counter-parts while only a small number of Indians qualified for the municipal voters' roll. Apart from building their own homes in colonial British style, and creating British institutions such as the Durban Club, businessmen as town councillors ensured that almost all main streets and suburbs were given British names, often those of prominent early residents.[170]

Visiting Durban after Cape Town, Trollope's comments were less critical. He attributed untidiness to lack of municipal funds rather than to foreignness. He said Durban's Town Gardens, located between the main business thoroughfares of Smith and West Street, was

not very well kept. I may suggest that it was not improved in general appearance when I saw it by having a couple of old horses tethered on its bare grass ... The combination when I was there suggested poverty on the part of the munici-pality ... There is also a botanical garden a little way up the hill very rich in plants but not altogether well kept.[171]

Influenced by such views, Durban's Council improved appearances as municipal revenues increased with growing trade and property values. This supported impressive commercial architecture similar to Cape Town's and, in time, Johannesburg's. As in Clean Cape Town, the council raised large loans on the London market and gave generous support to the provision or extension of water, drains, gas and electricity in the city centre and wealthier suburbs. It built a borough market and developed beach and swimming pool facilities. Money was also spent on road surfaces and extension, and on tramway systems and railway lines,

---

[166] There was another at Oriel College, Oxford, of which Rhodes was an alumnus. Maylam, *Cult of Rhodes*.

[167] Briggs, *Victorian Cities*; Gunn, *The Public Culture of the Victorian Middle Class*.

[168] *Cape Argus*, 25 January 1895.

[169] E.E.K. Lowndes, *Every-Day Life in South Africa* (London: S.W. Partridge, 1900), 29.

[170] Ibid., 28.   [171] Trollope, *South Africa*, 202.

often in co-operation with private companies. The drainage of local swamps increased the amount of usable ground within the borough and reduced the threat of malaria. When requisite skills were not locally available, suitably qualified 'experts' were recruited from Britain, like the Medical Officer of Health Dr Murison in 1903.[172]

Durban's first substantial town hall was built in 1885 on West Street opposite the Town Gardens, with an art gallery that housed paintings purchased from Britain. As with Cape Town, such ornamentalism could promote both British identity and local municipal prestige. The council acquired its own municipal regalia, including a coat of arms with the motto, *Debile Principium Melior Fortuna Sequeter* (Better Fortune will Follow a Difficult Beginning). In 1873, Victoria Park was laid out east of the town centre near the sea front, and Albert Park to its south-west on the shores of the Bay. In 1887, to commemorate Queen Victoria's Golden Jubilee, a fountain was placed in the Town Gardens. A statue of the Queen marking her silver jubilee followed just over a decade later, as well as a conservatory in the Botanical gardens, and a Victoria Embankment near Albert Park fronting the Bay. A statue of Durban's own hero of Empire, Dick King, adorned the Embankment from 1915. When Queen Victoria died, subscriptions were collected for a memorial portrait of her to be hung in the municipal gallery 'where every facility is afforded the students for studying and copying the pictures'.[173]

The Town Gardens gradually became the city's commemorative centre. By 1910, statues of the two first premiers, Sir John Robinson and Sir Harry Escombe, flanked a Durban Volunteers' Memorial in the form of Winged Victory set on a marble pedestal. In this year, an even grander town hall (see Illustration 2.2), the largest in South Africa, was built on Town Gardens' land to the east of these monuments, to whose number a First World War cenotaph was added in 1926. The old town hall was sold to the Natal government and became the main post office. The Natal government aided the creation of a perceivably British colonial town by constructing a substantial Victorian-style railway station to replace the previous rather ramshackle building in 1897, and by providing the Governor with a seaside alternative to his Pietermaritzburg residence in the form of the 'King's House' in 1904.[174]

Under Boer republican governance, British ornamentalism in the distinctly Boer-named Johannesburg was minimal compared to the coastal cities.[175] Many streets in the city centre had Boer names, as did Von

---

[172] Henderson, *Fifty Years' Municipal History*.
[173] Stark, *Durban*, 28–34; Henderson, *Fifty Years' Municipal History*, 325–7; Malherbe, *Port Natal*, 230.
[174] Stark, *Durban*, 28–34. Henderson, *Fifty Years' Municipal History*, 181.
[175] City histories have speculated on which of three Johannes it may have been named for.

Illustration 2.2: The second Durban Town Hall proudly advertised in a postcard of c.1920 (Mary Evans Picture Gallery)

Brandis Square and Kruger and Joubert Parks.[176] Before 1901, anglicisation was confined to private initiatives, as in the Rand Club, with its Rhodes Room and portrait of the Queen. As with Cape Town, improving Johannesburg was perceived by many English-speaking White residents to require British municipal government.

Although Kruger had belatedly conferred municipal governance on Johannesburg in 1897, a stipulation was that at least 50 per cent of the councillors would be Transvaal Burghers.[177] This changed under Milner's administration from 1901. He appointed Lionel Curtis, another

[176] Beavon, *Johannesburg*, 24–5 suggests that there are three main theories about the name Johannesburg. The first was that the city was named after two official surveyor-generals who selected the site, Christian Johannes Joubert and Johann Rissik; the second that it was named after the administrative officer of the district, Johannes Meyer; the third that it was named after King Joao of Portugal, because Kruger had just been honoured himself by that country. Many pages in histories of Johannesburg over the years were devoted to this question.
[177] Van Onselen, *New Babylon*, 14.

Oxford-educated member of his kindergarten, to draw up a British-style municipal constitution. The new Johannesburg municipality was given extensive powers to control urban development within much enlarged boundaries. Curtis became town clerk of a council that up until 1903 was appointed by Milner's administration. One of its first acts was to draw up a property assessment roll, and rates provided an annual income of more than £600,000 by 1904. So again it was a matter of loans floated on the London market, British experts consulted, and similar improvements embarked on, focused largely on the city centre and the more prosperous suburbs. Apart from an art gallery and the development of the public library, this delivered storm-water drainage and water-borne sewerage schemes with an outfall to the south-west of the city at Klipspruit, further confirming the south-west of the city as less desirable than the north.[178]

At the end of 1903 an elected Town Council took over, but with a municipal franchise confined to 'Whites'. The Labour Party enjoyed short periods of power, with a change to proportional representation briefly aiding its cause between 1909 and 1911.[179] But, as with Cape Town and Durban, and with ward boundary delineation that favoured middle-class residential areas, Johannesburg municipal government was controlled by the English-speaking middle class for almost the entire twentieth century.[180] In their efforts to improve Johannesburg, they were continually supported and cajoled by English language newspapers. An Afrikaans daily newspaper, *Die Transvaler*, was only established in 1937.[181]

The Council also embraced the possibility of enhancing British ornamentalism and its own prestige, especially in the northern suburbs. Before the First World War, newly acquired land was laid out as Milner Park in honour of the High Commissioner, one of ten new parks, and a Zoo and Zoo Lake were also constructed. A substantial Rand Regiment Memorial, designed by Sir Edwin Lutyens, was unveiled in 1910 in Saxonwold to commemorate soldiers killed fighting the Boers.[182] By then, Johannesburg Town Council had also acquired British ritual and regalia, with coat of arms incorporating three golden battery stamps and the motto *Fortiter et Recte* (Boldly and Well). In 1915, the Council moved

---

[178] John R. Shorten, *The Johannesburg Saga* (Johannesburg: John R. Shorten, 1970), 229, 232–5, 243.
[179] Beavon, *Johannesburg*, 72–5. Shorten, *Johannesburg*, 266, 280–1.
[180] For a list of these mayors and town clerks see Hedley A. Chilvers, *Out of the Crucible* (Johannesburg and Cape Town: Juta & Co. Ltd, [1928] 1948), 271–2.
[181] Shorten, *Johannesburg*, 239–40; Chilvers, *Out of the Crucible*, 283–5.
[182] Lutyens was an even more famous architect of the Empire than Baker, probably best known for his work in creating New Delhi. In the centenary anniversary year of 1999, the Rand Regiment Memorial was rededicated to all who had died in the Boer War.

out of its temporary corrugated-iron buildings, dubbed the Tin Temple, into its own large Victorian-style town hall.[183]

Anglicised cities and rituals of British Imperialism

Cities anglicised in these ways provided stages and audiences for the performance of major rituals associated with Imperial inventions of tradition. Static or more mobile spectacles, like processions or military reviews, could be held in places where large numbers of people already lived in daily contact with monuments, institutions and agents of the state likely to induce British national identity.[184] Such spectacles were staged in profusion for a variety of occasions. Many were Royalist, marking birthdays, weddings, accessions, jubilees, funerals and tours, from Prince Alfred's in 1860 through to the Royal Family's in 1947. They were accompanied by the granting of public holidays. Some of these holidays were annual, like 24 May, Queen Victoria's birthday, in nineteenth-century Cape Colony and Natal. From 1902, it was retained as Victoria or Empire Day throughout what was now British South Africa, with a King's Birthday holiday added for the first Monday in August.[185]

Rituals of British Imperialism were financed and planned in South Africa by both central and municipal governments. Those accompanying Queen Victoria's Diamond Jubilee, celebrated in cities throughout the British Empire and a few beyond between 20 June and 22 June 1897, were particularly spectacular. Johannesburg still lay within Kruger's Transvaal republic. Nonetheless, jubilee celebrations were organised by W.Y. Campbell, a prominent British businessman, and his Record Reign committee. Its slogan, just two years after the duplicitous Jameson Raid, was 'Britons, hold up your heads'. British-owned buildings in central streets were provocatively bedecked with Union Jacks and bunting, while a procession of floats, circus elephants and cyclists in fancy dress paraded through the centre of the mining town to the Wanderers' sports grounds for a carnival that lasted three days.[186]

The highlight of festivities in Durban was provided when the Mayor's wife, a Mrs Payne, switched on the town's first extensive electric lighting system. There were also 'monster' street parades, sporting events and

[183] Shorten, *Johannesburg*, 237, 244.
[184] Eric Hobsbawn, *Nations and Nationalism since 1780: Programme, Myth, Reality* (Cambridge: Cambridge University Press, 1990), 80–1.
[185] Empire Day and the King's Birthday remained public holidays until 1951. The former was then done away with by the (predominantly Afrikaner) National Party in 1952, though the second of July was retained as the Queen's Birthday until 1960 when South Africa became a republic.
[186] Neame, *City Built on Gold*, 140.

military reviews, a Masonic service with 400 members in full regalia, and a limelight exhibition depicting milestones in the Queen's reign. Banquets included a sit-down dinner for the poor in Spengler's Hotel, and a Diamond Jubilee Ball for the rich in the town hall. For the occasion, it was decorated with flags, flowers and Durban's coat of arms. Mrs Payne had determined that early Victorian costume was fitting for the occasion, and arrived by coach wearing ' black satin crimpoline skirt . . . a low bodice of black velvet, transparent white bishops sleeves, and a white lace kerchief'.[187]

In Cape Town, celebrations included combined church services, fireworks, military reviews, the laying of the foundation stone for the Victoria wing of the New Somerset Hospital, the firing of guns by sixty warships in Table Bay, and patriotic illumination and decoration of streets and buildings. But arguably the most spectacular element was the Grand Pageant. Detailed evidence exists for both its route and composition and allows for the following detailed description.

Two miles long, it wound its way from Green Point Common through thirteen of the main streets of the city centre, several now replete with grand new buildings of Victorian neoclassical grandeur, bedecked with flags and loyal slogans, to the Grand Parade, the largest of Cape Town's squares. The Pageant passed in front of the Governor of the Cape Colony, Sir Alfred Milner, who could hardly have failed to be impressed, if on occasion a little surprised, by what he witnessed. Leading the procession were mounted policemen, followed by contingents of Imperial troops. Towards the end were local regiments, members of the Jubilee Committee and the Town Council, with the Mayor a few paces behind. Bringing up the rear were more horses and men, in the form of a detachment of the Duke of Edinburgh's Own Volunteer Rifles.

In the middle of the procession was a wide representation of civil society, interspersed with an occasional float, like that of HMS *Victory*. Among those present were temperance societies, cycling clubs, eight wagon-loads of railway workers, the Society for the Prevention of Cruelty to Animals, Fraternities (such as Freemasons, Odd Fellows and the Ancient Order of the Druids), a large variety of Friendly Societies and 'Malay Hadjes [*sic*] with camels'. At the centre of the parade, placed on either side of a float containing a statue of Queen Victoria, were two sets of 'Malay gim cracks', one representing the year 1837 'Slavery', the other the year 1897 'Freedom'.[188]

---

[187] Malherbe, *Port Natal*, 85, 162–9, 231.
[188] Cape Archives (CA), 3CT 1/7/1/2 Mayor's Minutes, 17.

The 1897 jubilee celebrations, like Royal celebrations before and after, were invented political traditions clearly aimed at inculcating British national identity and loyalty. The enthusiasm they generated, if especially in Durban and Cape Town, was a product of the already extensively anglicised urban environments forged by anglophile elites in ways we have described. All Imperial rituals of celebration or commemoration in South African cities relied upon their existence and support. Generating enthusiasm for grand patriotic occasions was made easier by the numerous interlocking social traditions in civic associations and institutions among the urban population as a whole that helped inculcate British identity. So did private initiatives aimed at impregnating built environments with national symbolism, not least anglicised architecture and naming. Ostensibly un-British ethnic identities and traditions, like Malay identity in Cape Town or Zulu identity in Durban, could still be incorporated on ceremonial occasions within Empire-wide ideas of civic Britishness.

Jubilee celebrations were particularly dramatic examples of urban spectacle. Yet as such they demonstrate the range of ways in which urban sights and sounds, whether unusual or quotidian, provided both entertainment and information for illiterate and literate alike, irrespective of language. This information was conveyed through aural and visual means, through bands and anthems, ritual, regalia, dress, positioning in the parade, the presence of men and absence of women. The Pageant, as with other Jubilee festivities, aimed at legitimisation and commemoration, both of British Imperial rule as well as of more complex hierarchical relationships of authority within the city. At the same time it was meant to symbolise social cohesion, whether of Cape Town society as a whole, or of particular participating groups.

Jubilee events represented and conveyed beliefs and behaviour that Imperial and local elites wished to be associated with Britishness. These included military power, adherence to monarchy, hierarchical social order, patriotism, freedom, material and moral progress, and that preeminently Victorian virtue, 'respectability'. Hence the choreographed pomp and circumstance of parades and reviews, accompanied by the national anthem or 'Rule Britannia'; or the Mayoress of Durban inaugurating electric lighting; or bicycles on parade; or the 'Malay gim cracks' tableau of Slavery and Freedom; or the participation of Friendly and Temperance societies: an essential component of respectability was thrift and sobriety, if especially for the working class.

The Pageant's symbolism represented continuity but also change compared to earlier occasions. For instance, the wedding of Prince Albert in 1863 witnessed a 'Grand Procession' in Cape Town very similar to the

1897 Pageant. Yet bringing up the rear was a Carnival Parade that spoke of a more aristocratic and pre-industrial tolerance of what later in the century was considered 'unrespectable' popular culture. It was patriotic, with a float of 'Britannia in Triumphal Car attended by Tritons'. Yet there were other floats of 'Lady Godiva', played by a man, and the giants 'Gog and Magog', while clowns, harlequins and varlets ran around making fun of the crowd. In addition the town's poor were treated to a Grand Parade feast of roast ox, whose first slice was tasted by the Governor, and plentiful free wine. One of the most successful participants in the day's sports, old and new, was Simeon, 'a Kafir'. His participation would have been impossible in the more racially segregated 1890s.[189]

Precisely what a participant or spectator drew from any Royal celebration's 'publicly proffered myths' varied,[190] according to the likes of regional locality, education, ethnicity, class, gender and individual experience.[191] But wars gave rise to intense and widespread expressions of British patriotism that cut across these potential divides. These occasions were many: the departure and return of troops, dramatic wartime events like the relief of Mafeking, Rhodes' death, or the sinking of the *Lusitania*, the two-minute Midday Pause (initiated in Cape Town and observed daily in many other Imperial cities from May through to December 1918, and re-introduced in Cape Town in 1940), announcements of eventual victory, and Remembrance Day commemorations.[192] Conflict or international tension also spawned overtly pro-British political organisations such as the South African League in 1896 and the (Cape Colony) Progressive Party in 1898, established in the wake of the Jameson Raid, or the Guild of Loyal Women of South Africa in 1900 and Vigilance Societies, during the Boer War.[193]

Wars provided the opportunity for women from elite backgrounds to form welfare organisations like the Guild or the Victoria League that

---

[189] Bickford-Smith, 'Leisure and Social Identity', 103–28.

[190] Raphael Samuel and Paul Thompson (eds), *The Myths We Live By* (London and New York: Routledge, 1990), 15.

[191] Thompson, 'Languages of Loyalism'; Vivian Bickford-Smith, 'Writing about Englishness: South Africa's Forgotten Nationalism', in Graham McPhee and Prem Poddar (eds), *Empire and After: Englishness in Postcolonial Perspective* (Oxford and New York: Berghahn, 2007), 57–72; Bickford-Smith, 'Tiyo Soga'.

[192] Vivian Bickford-Smith, Elizabeth Van Heyningen and Nigel Worden, *Cape Town in the Twentieth Century* (Cape Town: David Philip, 1999), 50–9, 92–9.

[193] L. Thompson, 'Great Britain and the Afrikaner Republics', in M. Wilson and L. Thompson (eds), *The Oxford History of South Africa: 1870–1966*, vol. 2 (Oxford: Oxford University Press, 1971), 289–324; E. Van Heyningen and Peter Merrett, '"The Healing Touch": The Guild of Loyal Women of South Africa, 1900–1912', *South African Historical Journal* 47 (2003), 24–50. Thompson, 'Languages of Loyalism', 617–50.

tended war graves and promoted the reading of pro-Imperial history in schools.[194] Ethel Campbell, from a wealthy Natal family, sent semaphore signals to welcome and bid farewell to troop ships visiting Durban harbour during the First World War, and proffer them free refreshment, becoming known as the 'Angel of Durban'. Perla Siedle Gibson, described as a 'fine operatic soprano', sang well-known songs from music hall, theatre and cinema, ending her serenade of ships departing from Durban in the Second World War with 'Auld Lang Syne'.[195]

British world networks

Both during and beyond wartime, residents of major South African cities could feel more closely connected to British world networks through late nineteenth-century improvements in transport and communication. A weekly steamer service from Britain started in 1875, and within South Africa railways linked major cities by the mid-1890s.[196] Arrivals and departures of mail ships, and long-distance inter-city trains were carnival-like occasions of greetings and farewells. Newspapers reported on the comings and goings of local and metropolitan notables. The approach, then arrival, of the telegraph generated equal attention and excitement.[197] A sense of being part of a larger British community was enhanced by visiting acquaintances, British or Dominion sports teams and celebrities, as well as Royal Tours; travelling to parts of the British world beyond South Africa could have the same effect.

English-language newspapers, which garnered much of their editorial and other content from Britain well into the twentieth century, together with imported journals like the *Illustrated London News* (*ILN*), facilitated further communal connections, within and between South African cities and the wider British world. Indeed, the full range of print and electronic media made South Africans constantly aware of being part of this British world. This was not just a matter of shared Royal moments and accompanying traditions. Mass media facilitated reading, viewing and hearing about life in Britain on many other levels, including daily life, often highly idealised.

---

[194] Van Heyningen and Merrett, 'Guild of Loyal Women'; Archie L. Dick, *The Hidden History of South Africa's Book and Reading Cultures* (Toronto: University of Toronto Press, 2012), 54–61.

[195] Malherbe, *Port Natal*, 213–23.

[196] Picard, *Grand Parade*, 52. In this year the time for each voyage to Cape Town was twenty-five days, already reduced by 1876 to twenty-three days.

[197] See for instance Terry Wilks, *For the Love of Natal* (Durban: Robinson, 1977), which relates the history of Durban's *Natal Mercury* newspaper and its reporting of these matters for that city. For the carnival nature of mail ship arrivals and departures in Cape Town see George Manuel, *I Remember Cape Town* (Cape Town: Don Nelson, 1977).

Through newsreels, in particular, many South Africans gained 'prosphetic memory' of events and people elsewhere in the British world of which they had no direct personal experience: be they Imperial wars or members of the Royal family.[198] Feature films offered patriotic tales of Imperial derring-do. One South African offering of this kind was *Symbol of Sacrifice*, made at considerable cost during the First World War. [199] It was first screened on 27 March 1918 in Johannesburg's Town Hall and Palladium Theatre, where it had a three-week record run. It was then shown to 'enormous audiences' throughout the Union.[200] The film did not depict grim realities faced by British forces in Flanders' trenches, but the heroism, sacrifice of life and eventual triumph of those fighting for the British in the Anglo-Zulu War of 1879. The opening shot consisted of the following words superimposed over the Union Jack:

> I am the flag that braves the shock of war
> From continent to continent and shore to shore
> . . .
> You who for duty live, and who for glory die,
> The symbol of your faith and sacrifice am I.

The film aimed to appeal beyond those in the audience who saw themselves as ethnically British. One character in the film was Gobo, a faithful Zulu servant, prepared not only to help the wounded but to lay down his life for a White person, a common trope in many South African films and novels of the period.[201] In *Symbol of Sacrifice* Gobo first saves Marie, the daughter of a Boer called Gert Moxter, from the unwanted advances of an unpleasant German suitor; the suitor then beats Gobo with a *sjambok*. Later Gobo is killed saving Marie again, this time from the Zulus, and buried beneath the Union Jack. The message conveyed was that Britishness was a civic rather than ethnic national identity, which may have reassured some Black South Africans who saw the film. Its plot also attempted to win over Afrikaners. When Gert Moxter is killed in the conflict, the caption over a shot of his grave reads, 'A brave and gallant Dutch farmer who fought *for us*' [my emphasis].[202]

---

[198] Alison Landsberg, *Prophetic Memory: The Transformation of American Remembrance in the Age of Mass Culture* (New York: Columbia University Press, 2004).

[199] Dick Cruickshanks (dir.), *The Symbol of Sacrifice* (South Africa: African Film Productions, 1918).

[200] T. Gutsche, *The History and Social Significance of Motion Pictures in South Africa, 1895–1940* (Cape Town: Howard Timmins, 1972), 316–18.

[201] Peter Davis, *In Darkest Hollywood: Exploring the Jungles of Cinema's South Africa* (Johannesburg and Athens, OH: Raven and Ohio University Press, 1996), 7–12; Jacqueline Maingard, *South African National Cinema* (Abingdon, London and New York: Routledge, 2007), 36–45.

[202] A point made in Maingard, *National Cinema*, 37.

Extent of British urban identity by the early twentieth century

It still remains difficult to gauge the extent and variety of adherence to British identity and values in the early twentieth century. What people drew from public rituals of royalty was influenced by differing personal experiences shared with family, friends and co-workers as 'the currency of such relationships'.[203] Yet the 'stories' of many city dwellers by the early 1900s, including numerous Western-educated Black South Africans, reflected profound anglicisation. Many civic institutions, each with its own traditions, had worked with central and local state officials to secure this cultural hegemony.[204]

British identity was encouraged by a multitude of mundane sights and sounds in South African cities by the early twentieth century. Johannesburg, Durban and Cape Town were suffused with complex material traces of British traditions: red post boxes, stamps, coins, architecture, portraits, monuments, signs, institutions, dress, flags, anthems, bugles, music hall, sports and parades. Names of streets, buildings, parks and people reflected anglicisation: Royal and Queen's hotels; children of different 'races' with names like Albert, Albertina, Alfred, Victoria, Edward, George and Nelson; or Cape Town cabs with names like Telegraph, Victory, Electric and Sir James.[205]

The extent to which people felt British, and their motives for adopting this identity in the first place, varied as they responded to social dislocation or fateful moments like wartime. Expressions of adherence to Britishness across class, race, ethnicity and gender are legion: 'even the poorest of the Malays in the back streets illuminated their tenements' in Cape Town during Victoria's Golden Jubilee of 1887.[206] Ex-slave Lydia, like many other poorer urban residents well into the twentieth century, had a portrait of the British monarch hanging in her house: Edward VII's replaced Victoria's soon after the Queen's death.[207] Black British auxiliaries willingly risked their lives during the Boer War.[208] Gandhi, who lived just outside Durban, encouraged Indians to serve in the British Army both in that struggle and the Bambatha (Zulu) rebellion of 1906, in which he led a British Indian ambulance brigade.[209] The 'emergent

---

[203] Samuel and Thompson (eds), *The Myths We Live By*, 15.
[204] Anderson, *Imagined Communities*.
[205] Poultney Bigelow, *White Man's Africa* (London: Harper, 1898), 183.
[206] *Excalibur*, 24 June 1887.   [207] *Cowley Evangelist*, 1901, 126.
[208] Nasson, *Abraham Esau's War*; Bill Nasson, *The War for South Africa: The Anglo-Boer War 1899–1902* (Cape Town: Tafelberg, 1910).
[209] Arafat Valiani, 'Recuperating Indian Masculinity: Mohandas Gandhi, War and the Indian Diaspora in South Africa (1899–1914)', *South Asian History and Culture* 5, 4 (2014), 1–16.

bourgeoisie' among Jewish immigrants who embraced city life, soon providing mayors for all three major cities, adopted 'the standards and values of colonial Edwardian society', including membership of the Rand Club.[210] Gardener and ANC member Littin Mthetwa, formed a Zulu Union Choir to stage a concert in aid of war funds in Durban Town Hall in 1917.[211] Philip Roux, resident of Kitchener Avenue, Bezuidenhout Valley, Johannesburg, and Afrikaans-speaking from Aliwal North, scandalised his family by becoming 'an ardent supporter of the British government', fighting on that side in the Boer War. In 1910, he announced to his son, 'Eddie, your King is dead'.[212]

As these examples are intended to demonstrate, British identity frequently coexisted with other collective identities including ethnicities, sub-nationalisms and accompanying cultural diversities: Zulu, Afrikaner, African, Indian, Malay, Coloured or Jewish. Over time, an individual's British identity might change or be discarded. It became less jingoistic in the case of Philip Roux, a pacifist by the beginning of the Great War, and was rejected in favour of Bolshevism by Roux's son Eddie, who abandoned the Jeppe High School cadets.[213] Some Black South Africans promised equal rights for all 'civilised' men south of the Limpopo by Rhodes and Milner on the eve of the Boer War were disillusioned when victory brought British betrayal of the promise. Plaatje condemned post Union racial discrimination, not least the Land Act of 1913 that restricted Black ownership or leasing of agricultural land to the small portion of South Africa that comprised the reserves.[214] Elements of cultural anglicisation were appropriated within a 'New' and more assertive 'African' identity, eventually understood in nationalist and radically anti-Imperialist fashion. The British element of a British South African identity would in time disappear. These were lengthy and ambivalent processes, as detailed studies of Black responses to Royal Tours in 1925 and 1947 have revealed. Retaining British identity for Black South Africans must often have stemmed from contemplating a more fearful alternative in Afrikaner republicanism.[215]

In all three cities, Indian elites mobilised under the banner of British identity, but most Indian residents may have seen themselves far more insistently in ethnic terms, with caste, linguistic, religious and kinship ties that bound them not only to each other, but to their kith and kin in

---

[210] Mendelsohn and Shain, *The Jews of South Africa*, 65–8.
[211] Erlmann, *African Stars*, 126.   [212] Roux, *Rebel Pity*, 5.   [213] Ibid., 6–30.
[214] Sol T. Plaatje, *Native Life in South Africa* (Johannesburg: Ravan Press, [1916], 1982) was his lengthy denunciation.
[215] Sapire, 'Ambiguities of Loyalism', 37–58; Sapire, 'African Loyalism'.

India.[216] Living within the Cape Colony, more of Cape Town's Black inhabitants were likely to have been enthusiastic about British identity than their counterparts in Durban or Johannesburg, thanks to emancipation, the non-racial franchise and the comparatively less intense social segregation as witnessed by Evans. All of these made the idea of political as well as social 'progress' under British rule more tangible, even if it did not exclude White racism. Ex-slaves and their progeny had few attractive alternatives in 'national identity' terms, and African migrancy, with its attendant ties to non-British rural traditions, was less extensive than in Durban or Johannesburg.

The sympathies of many Whites who were not of British extraction, and who still spoke Dutch or Afrikaans, came to lie with the Boer republics rather than Britain, especially when conflict between the two increased after the Jameson Raid.[217] Numerous impoverished Afrikaners forced to seek work in Johannesburg after the Boer War, many with bitter experiences of the conflict, preferred the *Volkslied van Transvaal* to 'God Save the King'.[218] Equally, many migrant labourers in Durban and Johannesburg still closely connected to African rural traditions in Durban and Johannesburg might have felt little connection to Britishness.

So the following chapters examine a number of identities less concerned with British values or actively opposed to them. Doing so requires us to examine not just associated invented traditions that generated their own urban sights, sounds and symbols, but also how these affected the fashion in which South African cities came to be portrayed in different media in the early twentieth century. Fearful or hopeful, these visions established influential ways in which each city was perceived and understood.

---

[216] Freund, *Insiders and Outsiders*, 8–10.

[217] After many such Cape Colonists had been successfully wooed by Rhodes for the cause of British expansion northwards up to 1895: Mordechai Tamarkin, *Cecil Rhodes and the Cape Afrikaners: The Imperial Colossus and the Colonial Parish Pump* (London: Frank Cass, 1996).

[218] Jeremy Krickler, *White Rising: The 1922 Insurrection and Racial Killing in South Africa* (Manchester: Manchester University Press, 2005), 103–7.

3   More Babylon than Birmingham?

The creation of technologically advanced and ostensibly British cities in South Africa attracted opinions ranging from the highly favourable to the downright derogatory. Offered both by residents and visitors, these appeared in a wide range of literary, aural and visual forms that in combination became part of an enduring battle of ideas about the problems and possibilities of South African urbanisation.

This debate, whether explicitly or not, was about the nature and direction of South African society as a whole. To paraphrase Raymond Williams once more, in most industrial societies a frequent image of the future is an image of cities; images of the past are more commonly associated with the countryside.[1] Views on the nature of South African urbanisation mattered because of their potential to affect prejudices, policies and practices.

Though often very similar to debates in other industrial and, indeed, post-industrial cities, there was a local racial and ethnic emphasis to South African views. These resulted from colonial conquest and settlement, and accompanying ideologies of race and nation. In the early twentieth century, this included the idea in anglophone circles that South African cities were monuments to progress and modernity associated specifically with British rule and 'white civilisation'; cities were seen as places where those who could trace their origins to Britain rightly belonged, and were the equal of any modern counterpart in Europe and North America. Problems of urbanisation, be they poverty, disease or disorder in general, were commonly explained by Whites in racial terms. Consequently, so were possible solutions.

By the early twentieth century, opinions about city life were conveyed in both old and new ways in newspaper articles, novels, short stories, songs, travellers' accounts, city histories, actuality film, stage and cinematic dramas. In South Africa, as elsewhere, both fiction and non-fiction literature and films continually explored and reflected 'the distinctive

---

[1] Williams, *The Country and the City*, 297.

spaces, lifestyles and human conditions of the city'.[2] The intention of many who produced them was to do so in 'experiential realist' fashion, by providing 'moment-by-moment experience – sensory, visceral, and mental', and to make their representations powerful by doing so.[3]

From cinema's outset in the 1890s, film makers attempted to capture the wonders and attractions of urban modernity of which cinema was itself a product. Early film makers and their audiences were fascinated by the way that cinema could show the frantic pace and disjointed rhythms of modern urban life. They used cameras placed on forms of urban transport or rooftops to bring new street-level or panoramic perspectives on the city. Cinema thereby came to reflect visual and, after the introduction of sound, aural human experiences of urban life, while providing evidence of contemporary social attitudes to particular places, or the urban in general.

Whether visitors or residents, most of those making films in South Africa in the 1890s and 1900s were fascinated by the country's rapidly growing cities.[4] One of the first films shot in South Africa was a one-minute actuality piece featuring Cape Town in 1898 made by a touring Irish film maker. It depicted an electric tram, a form of urban transport only introduced to the city in 1896, moving through a central thoroughfare.[5] Soon – and in keeping with cinema elsewhere – cameras were placed on other varieties of urban transport like trains and cars. The resulting pieces, like *Train Ride from Cape Town to Simonstown*, provided urban spectacle in keeping with the global contemporary formula for 'Cinema of Attractions'.[6] These short films could be understood by local inhabitants or those in Britain to be celebrating British Imperial achievement in bringing about urban modernity, thereby further confirming British identity for some. Residents of South Africa's main cities were able to view them as part of theatrical variety shows and, from around 1908 onwards, in custom-built cinemas dubbed 'Bioscopes'.[7]

---

[2] Shiel and Fitzmaurice (eds), *Cinema and the City*, 1.   [3] Alter, *Imagined Cities*, x.

[4] For but one of many works that deals with Early Cinema around the world, see Geoffrey Nowell-Smith, *The Oxford History of World Cinema* (Oxford: Oxford University Press, 1999).

[5] British Film Institute (BFI): R.A. Mitchell (dir.), *Adderley Street, Cape Town*, (Great Britain, 1898).

[6] The term commonly used by film historians to refer to the nature of Early Cinema's actuality films.

[7] Gutsche, *Motion Pictures*. Gutsche remains by far the best guide to the full range of early films made in, or viewed in, South Africa, including early films that feature Cape Town, Durban and Johannesburg. British films include BFI: Anon (dir.), *Train Ride from Cape Town to Simonstown* (Great Britain: Co-Operative Cinematograph, 1911); and BFI: Anon (dir.)., *Scenes in and Around Cape Town* (Great Britain: Butcher and Sons, 1911). See also BFI: Anon (dir.), *Durban and Its Environs* (France: Production company unknown, 1914). Bruno, *Atlas of Emotion*, 18–20.

Local and international depictions along these lines subsequently included newsreels made by American immigrant I.W. Schlesinger's African Film Productions company (Johannesburg, 1913) and foreign companies, such as Britain's Gaumont Graphic.[8]

Yet not all observers were convinced, nor all portrayals of cities celebratory. Despite attempts to create thoroughly British South African cities, widespread concern was frequently expressed in anglophone middle-class circles and beyond about the nature and consequences of South African urbanisation. The nature of dissent was similar to that voiced in European and North American cities. Confidence in urban progress was challenged by perceived urban ills like immorality, disease and disorder.[9]

Always present to some degree from the Mineral Revolution onwards, there were nonetheless periods thereafter of greater and lesser anxiety, as there were of optimism. Frequently commentators offered a mixture of negative and positive perceptions, rarely entirely one or the other. Perceptions were related to contemporary realities. During the early decades of accelerated urbanisation, from the 1880s to the 1920s, these included economic recession, disease, a disproportionate number of young males in the urban population (especially in Johannesburg and Durban) and social disorder. In combination they were seen as grave threats from the perspective of many among urban elites during a period of political uncertainty in the form of conflict between Boers, British and Africans: most notably the Boer War of 1899 to 1902, the Bambatha rebellion of 1906, and an Afrikaner nationalist rebellion in 1914.

The outbreak of the Boer War in October, for example, meant the immediate interruption of gold production and ongoing problems in this respect after the British took the city in June 1900. It took a couple of years for output to regain pre-war levels.[10] The Boer War also meant that refugees from the Transvaal flooded into both the port cities, adding to urban problems like inadequate accommodation and the importation of gangsters and organised crime from the Rand. Disease was particularly rife before the provision of underground sewerage systems or reliable water supplies, and reflected extensive urban poverty and limitations in contemporary medical treatment. Smallpox decimated Cape Town in the 1880s. Bubonic Plague hit all three major cities in the early 1900s, and though mortality rates were low beyond those in overcrowded wartime Cape Town in 1901, the reputation of the disease terrified residents. The

---

[8] Many of the African Mirror newsreels can be viewed in the South African National Film, Video and Sound Archives (SANFVSA), Pretoria. Gaumont Graphic newsreels are also online (institutional or individual subscription access) at www.nfo.ac.uk.

[9] Lees, *Cities Perceived.* [10] Feinstein, *Economic History*, 105.

aftermath of the First World War brought the devastating Spanish flu pandemic of 1918.

Cities also experienced industrial strife, encouraged by the importation of trade union and socialist traditions from Britain and beyond and intermittently linked to broader political mobilisation. Strikes by White workers on the Rand were particularly violent in 1913–14 and 1922, the latter developing into the Rand Revolt aimed at delivering a White-controlled socialist South Africa. Black worker militancy on the Rand from 1918–20, and in Durban in the 1920s, included on occasion the involvement of members of the ANC.

Like writers before them, film makers found that many of these concerns translated into popular fictional and non-fictional productions, not least crime with its dramatic possibilities in terms of movement and moral issues. One of the earliest narrative dramas in American cinema was *The Great Train Robbery* (1903), emulated in what was probably South Africa's first fiction film, *The Great Kimberley Diamond Robbery* (1911).[11] Newsreels produced for Schlesinger's *African Mirror* and for those of overseas companies like Gaumont Graphic, Gaumont British Gazette and Pathé Gazette all contained actuality pieces about 'bandits' in Johannesburg in 1914.[12] These focused on the dramatic end that befell Johannesburg's murderous Foster gang robbers, who committed suicide when cornered by the police (and cameramen) in a cave in the suburb of Kensington.[13]

Perceptions of South African urbanism among the White middle classes often reflected reactions to readily perceivable sights, sounds and actions that seemed at odds with British traditions and values. This could be because they were 'unrespectable' or merely foreign, like 'the mono-tone of Abantu singing ... accompanied by the rhythmic beat of heavy feet stamping in unison' heard by Evans on Durban's Berea Ridge.[14] The existence of distinctly un-British traditions together with urban problems common to any city undergoing industrialisation implicitly put into ques-tion the extent of anglicisation and 'progress'.

---

[11] Edwin S. Porter (dir.), *The Great Train Robbery* (USA: Edison Manufacturing Company, 1903); BFI, Anon (dir.), *The Great Kimberley Diamond Robbery* (South Africa: Springbok Film Company, 1911).

[12] (British) Pathé Gazette footage is also online (open access) at www.Britishpathe.com. Gaumont British Gazette like Gaumont Graphic is online at www.nfo.ac.uk.

[13] See for instance *The Johannesburg Bandits*, Gaumont Graphic, 1 January 1914; SANFVSA, *Bandits on the Rand*, African Mirror (Johannesburg: African Film Productions, 1914). The gang robbed post offices and a bank and shot several of those who attempted to stop them.

[14] Evans, *Black and White in South East Africa*, 1–2.

Perceiving moral and physical dangers in city life

The moral and physical dangers of the city concerned many commentators. In 1863, the year in which wine flowed on Cape Town's Grand Parade to celebrate Prince Albert's wedding, *The Famous Trial of Dr Abstinence*, performed around Britain in the 1850s, had its first Cape Town performance. In the play, Dr Abstinence is prosecuted by those who advocate the sale of liquor, and defended by those in favour of temperance; the good doctor is duly acquitted.[15] Two decades later in 1889, with the temperance movement considerably stronger and no two-way debate deemed necessary in popular melodramas portraying the evils of alcohol like *Drink*, a Women's Christian Temperance Union (WCTU) was established. This signalled the acceptance of the cause by urban elites, the establishment of male temperance organisations, and the absence of free wine for the poor by the time of the 1897 Jubilee celebrations. Indeed the WCTU, which was formally advocating (White) female suffrage by 1895, was a significant pioneer of middle-class women's greatly enhanced public role in moral and political matters by 1910. Members subsequently played a major part in instigating enfranchisement societies in all the main cities and thereafter pro-Empire organisations like the Guild of Loyal Women and Victoria League.[16]

Women writers added their support to the WCTU's cause, particularly when depicting life in Johannesburg during Kruger's Republic, thereby also supporting British criticism of Boer rule. One of the most prominent female authors was Anna Comptesse de Bremont, born Anna Dunphy, an American singer and writer who adopted British nationality and toured South Africa around 1890. Her novel *The Gentleman Digger* (1890) provided 'studies and pictures of life in Johannesburg', with a particular focus on the evil consequences of selling alcohol to Africans, notably 'the cruel murder of an Englishman by five drunken natives' whose facts 'can be verified by the principal Johannesburg evening paper'.[17] 'The Curse of the Canteen', in *The Ragged Edge: Tales of the African Goldfields* (1895) pursued the same theme.[18]

---

[15] *Cape Argus*, 3 October 1863, 31 October 1863, 8 November 1863.

[16] *Evening Express*, 24 June 1880. Cherryl Walker, 'The Women's Suffrage Movement: The Politics of Gender, Race and Class', in Walker, *Women and Gender*, 313–45; Van Heyningen and Merrett, 'Guild of Loyal Women'.

[17] Anna, Comptesse de Bremont, *The Gentleman Digger: Being Studies and Pictures of Life in Johannesburg* (London: Greening and Co., 1899 [1890]). The unpaginated preface to the 1890 edition contained the quote.

[18] Anna, Comptesse de Bremont, *The Ragged Edge. Tales of the African Gold Fields* (London: Downey and Co., 1895), 189–210.

Men followed suit. A pioneering Cape 'holiday book' anthology of 1896 contained a short story, 'Lily you have broken my heart', about John, a young immigrant Englishman, almost ruined after leaving an eastern Cape farm for Johannesburg. John succumbs to alcohol and is only rescued from the gutter, and thereby able to marry Lily and return 'home' with her to England, thanks to a combination of Christian charity and the Good Templars.[19] The bars of Johannesburg and Pretoria, as well as the bad influence of a high-living remittance man, proved dangerous to another immigrant, Graham Wilmot, the young protagonist of *Richard Hartley, Prospector*. In this novel by British journalist and author Douglas Blackburn, a resident of the Rand and Natal between 1892 and 1908, Hartley also returns safely to England after many misadventures.[20]

Such perceptions mirrored reality in the early years of Johannesburg, where drunkenness, prostitution and crime were fuelled by the overwhelming preponderance of males on the Rand, only 12 per cent of whom were married in 1897. Large numbers of bars and brothels, situated in close proximity to the elite Rand Club and burgeoning Stock Exchange, formed the predominant 'entertainment'. Prostitutes were initially mainly Coloured women from the Cape, procured to work out of bars or 'canteens'. Around 1895, the time that deep-level mining ensured a foreseeably rich future for Johannesburg, White women began to be trafficked in considerable numbers from Europe, before the combination of post-Boer War economic depression and tighter state control meant that the majority of White prostitutes became poor Afrikaner women working out of brothels in Fordsburg and Vrededorp.

What contemporary media referred to as the 'White slave trade' reflected the emergence of the first international urban crime network spanning the Atlantic world. 'White slaves' were procured through a number of well-organised networks for Johannesburg and Cape Town brothels. Most were brought from continental Europe and London's East End, often under false pretences about the work they were expected to do, though some were also procured from as far afield as Japan, specifically to provide sexual services for Chinese labourers brought in by the Chamber of Mines to meet the post-Boer War labour crisis. A key role in all of this was played by a group of New York gangsters called the 'Bowery Brothers', controlled by the psychopathic Joe Silver. In emulation of British gentleman's clubs, the gang elected Silver as 'President' of its

[19] L. de Beer, *Half Hours of Leisure in South Africa: A Holiday Book* (Cape Town and Amsterdam: Jacques Dusseau, 1896). I have not as yet discovered the identity of L. de Beer, save that he describes himself as male in the preface.

[20] Douglas Blackburn, *Richard Hartley, Prospector* (Edinburgh: William Blackwood and Sons, 1905).

self-styled American Club, housed in hired premises in central Johannesburg, with Salus Budner, otherwise known as Joe Gold, as its 'Secretary'. So self-confident were members that they posed for photographs with their easily corrupted contacts in the Transvaal police.[21] The American Club forged ties with French international criminal George le Cuirassier and his associates, seemingly the major financier of the White slave trade, who ran brothels across the world, including in the United States, Manchuria, Mexico, Argentina and France. It was largely because of le Cuirassier's networks that central Johannesburg became known as Frenchfontein, a reference to the geographical origins of many of the working women and their *souteneurs*; of the ninety-seven identified brothels in central Johannesburg in October 1895, thirty-five were described as French.[22]

The informal naming of the city centre in this way presumably confirmed the idea for some middle-class observers that much behaviour there was foreign, not appropriately British. Paris and the French were international synonyms at the time in the British world and beyond for sexual adventure and lax morality. *The Standard and Diggers News*, one of the city's first English-language newspapers, was certainly shocked by the brazenness of Johannesburg prostitutes in the 1890s, some of whom accosted members of Kruger's *Volksraad* on a visit to Johannesburg; others took part in a working men's carnival parade and 'were cheered all along the line'. The newspaper talked of 'The Public Shame' of this, yet the size of crowds cheering the women suggest that most residents felt little shame, that 'the public' was not yet sufficiently respectable.[23]

Literary tales that featured British protagonists struggling in the city, and especially Johannesburg, were relatively rare. The British were generally associated with urban progress in the minds of White anglophone observers. Urban problems were associated with foreign or un-British local 'others', not implausibly given that immigrants from Britain generally had a clear advantage in terms of the capital, education, skills and networks necessary for urban success. So accounts from White authors that portrayed Africans and Afrikaners as imperilled by urban life and its Babylonian temptations were far more numerous up to the 1950s. In these stories the city was a place of alien and corrupting values and vices;

---

[21] Van Onselen, *New Babylon*, 109–34, which contains a copy of such a photograph; Charles Van Onselen, *The Fox and the Flies: The World of Joseph Silver, Racketeer and Psychopath* (London: Jonathan Cape, 2007). Given current concerns, there is a surprising lack of research that has revealed crime statistics for South African cities in the past.

[22] Van Onselen, *New Babylon*, 31, 112–13, 114–15, 147.

[23] *Standard and Diggers News*, 'Trades Carnival', 12 November 1896 and 'Public Shame', 22 July 1897.

the countryside was where Africans (in reserves) and Afrikaners (on the farm) really belonged, otherwise they would succumb to corruption or help convey it.

Novels and films with this message were particularly common between the 1930s and 1950s, but the message was of longer duration. The unsuitability of city life and 'civilisation' in general for those of African descent was a central concern of *Sitongo* (1884), seemingly the first novel written and published in southern Africa and one that therefore established what became known as the Jim-goes-to-Joburg (and struggles in the big city) theme in South African fiction. Its author, J.D. Ensor, had been secretary to the Cape Select Committee on 'Native Laws and Customs' (1883). Its report supported a growing anglophone ruling-class belief in the desirability of racial separation as the answer to most urban problems, whether disease, crime or disorder in general.

Many subsequent commissions that focused on urban Africans through to the Second World War came to much the same conclusion. Support for racial separation, or what became known by the early twentieth century as segregation, marked a move away from earlier, pre-1872 settler-controlled, Cape political philosophy. Associated most strongly with Governor Sir George Grey (1854–62), this had favoured a policy of assimilation towards Africans rather than the ideology of segregation in both town and countryside championed by Shepstone in Natal. Grey's policies, notably in terms of the franchise and education, had aimed at 'civilising' Africans through closer integration into Cape society, whether they wished this or not. An 1878 biography of Tiyo Soga, the first Black Presbyterian minister, hymn composer and translator of the gospel and Bunyan's *Pilgrim's Progress* into Xhosa, endorsed these policies and the missionary efforts that accompanied them. Written by a White fellow missionary, it recounted Soga's exemplary retention of personal dignity, integrity and Christian faith during a life that had taken him to town and countryside in the Cape and Britain; and the book was published in both places.[24]

In contrast, *Sitongo* and most subsequent novels up to the 1950s questioned the efficacy and worth of the 'civilising mission', and as a consequence whether Africans would ever be suited to city life, or would be too easily corrupted by European vices, a concern shared by many Christian African elites. Sitongo, the novel's eponymous hero, is the son of an African chief and the shipwrecked White wife of a ship's captain.

---

[24] J.A. Chalmers, *Tiyo Soga: A Page of South African Mission Work* (Edinburgh, London, Glasgow and Grahamstown, Cape Colony: Andrew Eliot, Hodder and Stoughton, David Bryce and Sons, and James Hay, 1878).

Sitongo's mission education enables him to travel and work in both Cape Town and London, but he ultimately succumbs to moral failings and decides to reject an urban way of life. In his first visit to Cape Town, Sitongo falls ill with typhoid, and epidemics are accurately described as regular occurrences in the town. In local newspaper and Medical Officer of Health reports they were often blamed on the supposedly unhygienic habits of Black inhabitants.[25]

Sitongo's initial lesson in 'White civilisation' consists only of encountering malevolent gossip in supposedly respectable White society. On moving to London and entering employment with a silk mercer on Oxford Street, Sitongo comes to believe that stealing items from employers is justified by meagre wages, is disrespectful to a 'handsome lady customer', and loses his job. With funds low, he is forced to move to lodgings in Seven Dials 'where I gradually became familiar with poverty and vice' and reaps 'the full reward of . . . folly and evil-doings'. Rescued from probable death on a London doorstep, Sitongo then works in a barber's shop until he meets Mr Thompson, a White trader whom he knew in South Africa and who helps Sitongo return to Cape Town. Arriving there, he masquerades as a German music professor, Herr von Lutz, but loses his good reputation after borrowing money from a pupil and leaving his lodgings without paying. Sitongo finally decides that 'though I had been petted and made much of . . . I was still a Kafir at heart'. Thus he 'renounced civilization . . . journeyed on until I could no longer detect traces of the onward march of Progress, and there my kraal was built'.[26]

The unsuitability not only of Africans but also of Afrikaners for urban life was a theme of several other early novels and plays by White authors. The work of Douglas Blackburn and a Cape Town playwright Stephen Black are particularly notable because of their contemporary popularity, hence their role in both reflecting and shaping popular opinion. In Blackburn's *Leaven*, probably written in the late 1890s but only published in London in 1908, a naive young missionary called David Hyslop is challenged by a worldly but decent goldmine compound manager with the question: 'Can you honestly say that you have ever met a kafir in this country who was a better creature for having been in contact with whites?'

[25] A smallpox epidemic in 1882 literally decimated the city's population and played an important role in strengthening support for the Clean Party: Bickford-Smith, *Ethnic Pride and Racial Prejudice*, 56–8.

[26] J.D. Ensor, *Sitongo: A South African Story* (Cape Town: A. Richards and Sons, 1884). Olive Schreiner's far more famous novel, *The Story of a South African Farm*, appeared in 1883, but was written and published in London.

What happens to Bulalie, the African protagonist of the novel, provides the negative answer. Having been taught reading and writing on Hyslop's mission station, Bulalie uses these skills purely in pursuit of mammon. He becomes a smuggler of illegal liquor to African mine workers in Johannesburg with the connivance of an evil White compound manager. On his deathbed, Bulalie tells Hyslop to inform his 'brothers in the kraal' that he (Bulalie) 'has seen all the white men's works, and ... they are foolishness'.[27] Similarly in *Richard Hartley, Prospector*, the only 'manly' African is one who has not 'been got hold of by civilisers'.[28]

An Afrikaner in *Richard Hartley*, Johannes Smeer, is just as out of place in the city. On his first visit to Johannesburg, Smeer

slouched along with that lack-lustre look in his eye, and utter absence of interest in his novel surroundings, that marks the difference between the South African Boer and the rustic of other countries, whose wonder and gaucheries on his first visit to congested civilisation have formed the text for such merriment ... he kept a sharp eye open for the thieves and murderers who, according to famous Krugerian dictum, formed the bulk of the population of the Rand.[29]

Smeer feels uncomfortable staying in a lodging house and prefers boarding in overcrowded 'ten-by-ten mud-rooms' in *Veldschoendorp* (Veldshoes Village) in the south-west part of Johannesburg, with Afrikaners who were 'the flotsam and jetsom of the *veld*'.

This depiction of the uncomfortable Afrikaner in the city was not just an anglophone invention. It was equally present in early Dutch and Afrikaans literature in the first decades of the twentieth century. Poems by Totius, Jacob Lub's sketches in *Donker Johannesburg* ('Dark Johannesburg') and Andries Vry's novel *Somer* are but some examples. Totius's *Trekkerswee* ('Trekkers Melancholy') tells of Afrikaners leaving a Boer paradise in the countryside for sorrow in the city.[30] As Oom Frans, a character in *Somer*, puts it 'Everything is only one terrible, false lie in Johannesburg'. Another character in *Somer*, Wynand, exemplifies what happens. He mixes with the wrong people, gambles, becomes a drunkard and ends up in prison. In other novels, innocent young Afrikaner women lead superficial lives, or are forced into prostitution or, perhaps worst of all, are seduced by unattractive Englishmen. *Donker Johannesburg* takes its readers through a veritable odyssey of misery that encompasses the stifling nature of being deep underground in gold mines, a Salvation Army

[27] Douglas Blackburn, *Leaven: A Black and White Story* (Pietermaritzburg: University of Natal Press, 1991), quotations from 167, 193.
[28] Blackburn, *Richard Hartley*, 257.   [29] Ibid., 194.
[30] Ampie Coetzee, '"They All Went Down to Gomorrah": An Episode in the Demise of the Afrikaner', in C.N. Van der Merwe (ed.), *Strangely Familiar: South African Narratives on Town and Countryside* (Cape Town: Contentlot.com, 2001), 147.

shelter, rows of grey-brown houses in Fordsburg, police cells, drunk women, and men abusing their children. Well into the twentieth century, this literature and its successors argued that the Afrikaner's natural home was *op die plaas* (on the farm). Part of the city's depicted hellish nature was that Afrikaners had to take orders from arrogant Englishmen, work along-side 'Kafirs', and risk losing their cultural identity.[31]

The Afrikaners of Stephen Black's play *Helena's Hope Ltd* (1910) are the Von Knaaps. Like many Afrikaners in the aftermath of the Boer War, they move from a farm into 'the slums' of Johannesburg. There the Von Knaaps are thoroughly lampooned as ignorant country bumpkins who speak a 'franglais'-style combination of simple Afrikaans and bad English. The son, Hendrik, is only interested in dancing, rugby and popular music like 'The Lily of Laguna' and 'Daisy', which he plays on his piano. As his father Jacob puts it when deciding to return to the countryside: 'on der veld a Boer is a Boer, but in a town he's a blerry fool'. Hendrik agrees, as he tells his anglicised cousin Helena: 'Ja, it'll be nice to pull a cow's tits again, hey, Helena'. In another Black play, *Love and the Hyphen*, the character Gerald van Kalabas unconvincingly pretends to be a British swell, but cannot shake off his agricultural Afrikaner origins, and is a doltish figure of fun who remains 'on the fringes of [Cape Town British] society' in the original (1908) version of the play.[32]

In contrast, Xhosa Christian convert Jeremiah (played by Black him-self) in *Helena's Hope* adapts easily to the city having been 'educated most royally' by a British missionary. Tennis-racket and umbrella carrying, he tells his White employer, who sees farm life in idyllic terms, that 'Once you are urbanised, sir, you may not return to your charming rural inno-cence'. Jeremiah adds: 'while we Xhosas of a thoughtful kind do our level best to become so utterly Christianised, we cannot help noticing ... that our white brothers become progressively de-Christianised'. However his employer correctly supposes that 'as a good Christian ... [Jeremiah] went into the Illicit Liquor Trade' (like *Leaven*'s Bulalie) to make money; and near the end of the play, Jeremiah prefers to swear 'not by your bible, but the spirits of honourable men, my ancestors'. Both statements raise the question of the extent and nature of his acquired British 'civilisation'. Yet given how Stephen Black depicted other characters, they also suggest that the plays were promoting an inclusive South Africanism which

---

[31] Quotation cited in Coetzee, '"They All Went Down to Gomorrah"', 141. Coetzee's article contains bibliographical details of this early Afrikaans literature. See also J.M. Coetzee, *White Writing: On the Culture of Letters in South Africa* (New Haven, CT: Yale University Press, 1988), 63–114.

[32] Stephen Gray (ed.), *Stephen Black: Three Plays* (Johannesburg: Ad. Donker, 1984), 44, 179. This is a compendium reconstruction by the editor of Black's work.

acknowledged existing stereotypes but emphasised cultural creolisation and the capacity for social change.[33]

Blackburn and Black were relatively even-handed in their depictions of human failings across racial, ethnic, gender and national boundaries. But Blackburn's novels were far harsher in tone than Black's plays, whose gently mocking comedy was deployed irrespective of race or class distinctions. They allowed characters to have redeeming features despite obvious flaws, and proved to be hugely popular, even if the idea of an inclusive South African identity did not. Thus *Love and the Hyphen* may have poked fun at Afrikaner Capetonians, but it did not spare the social-climbing snobbery of some White English-speaking city-dwellers like Lady Mushroom of the Government House set and the (fraudulently self-styled) Captain Montague Hay-Whotte, of His Majesty's Muddlers. The play also criticised Coloured attempts to 'pass' for White, not uncommon in the city given the permeable colour line, in the persons of Frikkie the gardener's wife and daughter.[34] In the 1928 version of the play, and demonstrating Black's disillusion following Union governments' inability to embrace an inclusive South African identity, Frikkie, taunted by his wife for being of darker hue, is given the last line: 'You can all go to hell.'[35]

Few Whites in Blackburn's novels are depicted sympathetically, and the majority are portrayed as corrupt, brutal and racially bigoted, or all three. In this respect his depiction of South African society was not unlike *Zidji* (1911), a novel by the Swiss missionary, ethnologist and supporter of the extension of the non-racial Cape franchise to other parts of South Africa, Henri-Alexandre Junod.[36] *Zidji*, while relating the experiences of its eponymously named hero, also portrays many (but not all) Whites as racist. Johannesburg with its gold-mining industry comes across as a Gomorrah of greed, semi-slavery, illicit liquor and sodomy: male-rape is depicted as the fate of some miners in the compounds.[37] But the major contrast with Blackburn is that Junod's novel predictably supports the missionaries' civilising mission and applauds those, both White and

[33] Gray, *Stephen Black*, 151–2, 180–1.
[34] For a study of 'passing' in Cape Town in the late 1960s, see Graham Watson, *Passing for White: A Study of Racial Assimilation in a South African School* (London and New York: Tavistock, 1970).
[35] Ibid., 125.
[36] On Junod and other Swiss missionaries see Patrick Harries, *Butterflies and Barbarians: Swiss Missionaries and Systems of Knowledge in South-East Africa* (London: James Currey, 2007).
[37] Homosexuality was certainly commonplace among migrant workers in the mines, though the extent to which all younger male partners were willing partners has been difficult for historians to discern.

Black, who continued to work on its behalf despite extensive hostility within colonial society.[38] Zidji retains his Christian beliefs, and at the end of the book is on his way out of Johannesburg to take a job as a court interpreter in a small town to the north, hoping in time to edit a newspaper advocating Black rights and upliftment.[39]

An ongoing dilemma for missionaries like Junod was how to Christianise and civilise Africans while keeping them safe from urban vice. Another dilemma, one shared by mining magnates more worried about obtaining labour than proselytising, was what to do about the tenacity with which most Africans still clung to their own non-Christian traditions that intimately linked them to a still viable rural existence, despite colonial conquest, diminishing access to adequate land, state taxation and capitalist market forces. The apparent answer, explicitly argued by government commissions and increasingly practised by urban employers, was to combine migrant labour with residential segregation: in mine compounds, labourers' barracks, locations or, the case for most domestic workers, on employers' property.

Yet in Christian liberal minds across racial divides, this still did not make Africans entirely safe from 'immorality', let alone lead to Christian conversion, or guarantee decent living conditions and the possibility of respectable existence. Instead, the migrant labour system itself helped sustain 'pagan' traditions, some of which could be easily noticed on the streets of the main cities, confirm missionary and broader middle-class concerns, and help to explain pessimistic urban perceptions. Concerns along these lines were expressed across potential racial divides. In 1923 William Scully, an author and magistrate who had emigrated from Ireland to South Africa, published *Daniel Vavanda: The Life Story of a Human Being*.[40] This novel portrayed the eponymous protagonist's downward moral and physical journey through the slums of Port Elizabeth and Johannesburg to eventual death, after being wrongly accused of stock theft and tortured by the police in the eastern Cape. Scully wrote that the majority of merchants who created Port Elizabeth's 'beautiful and substantial buildings ... accepted the miserable slums on the city's outskirts' built of tin and old paraffin cans where 'immorality, with its concomitant disease, was rife'. After struggling there, Daniel

---

[38] Black South Africans may well have played the dominant role in such efforts, see Neil Parsons, 'Towards a Broader Southern African History: Backwards, Sideways and Upside-Down', South African Historical Journal 66, 2 (2014), 223.

[39] H.A. Junod, *Zidji, etude de moers Sud-Africaines* (Saint Blaise: Foyer Solidariste, 1911). See also Harries, *Butterflies and Barbarians*; Bronwyn Strydom, 'Belonging to Fiction? A Reconsideration of H.A. Junod in the Light of His Novel *Zidji*', *African Historical Review* 40, 1 (2008), 101–20.

[40] William Charles Scully, *Daniel Vavanda: The Life Story of a Human Being* (Cape Town: Juta, 1923).

becomes a miner in Johannesburg, but the compounds offer little beyond gambling, 'nameless vices' (a reference to homosexuality among Black mine workers) and brandy. In the city itself there are 'native marauders' known as the 'Ama-foxes' and brothels where the 'Ama-French' made 'a speciality of the Native trade'. Dying eventually of miners' pthisis, Daniel's soul yearns for the 'Umbashe' valley. Back there in the eastern Cape, though, it was only by 'sending forth their youth wholesale to the corrupting Rand that they could hope to win the means of bare existence, to say nothing of paying the taxes imposed by government'.[41]

Members of Black elites, while also pointing out appalling living conditions and lack of amenities in cities, frequently denounced perceived moral failings among the Black poor more stridently than White commentators. Rolfes Dhlomo said that his *An African Tragedy* (1928), credited as being the first published novel by a Black South African, aimed at stemming 'the decline of Native life in large cities', by drawing attention to the 'grim struggle for existence in this tumultuous city of Johannesburg'. Of barely novella length, it told the *Daniel Vavanda*-style story of Robert Zulu's unsuccessful struggle to resist temptations like 'morally depraved women ... with uncovered bosoms', drink and gambling. Prospect Township was described as 'a revolting immoral place ... where strong and violent drinks are brewed in broad daylight'. Dhlomo condemned the music played there 'on an organ hammered by a drunken youth' while couples sang 'wildly to this barbaric time', and wondered whether 'people who have the welfare of our nation at heart ever visit these dark places'. Eventually Zulu, now 'fashionably dressed', returns to the countryside but brings his sins with him in the form of the 'violent disease from loose women' he contracted in the city.[42]

Corrupting influences that produced 'uncivilised' or unrespectable African behaviour were thus demonstrably present in the cities from the perspective of both Black and White middle-class commentators. Such behaviour was not confined to the Black poor, nor urban pessimism to the middle classes. Stories, drinking songs and poems shared among White Diggers, individual prospectors attempting to make their fortune from gold in the early days of Johannesburg, commonly about 'luck, chance, and gross coincidence' that could make a man's fortune, also reflected Digger traditions of heavy drinking. Thus 'Nat Donnel's Dream' was about an Irishman on the Rand unable to fulfil his promise to St Patrick to give up alcohol:

[41] Ibid., 174–8, 191–2, 195–8, 216, 218.
[42] R.R.R. Dhlomo, *An African Tragedy: A Novel in English by a Zulu Writer*, (Alice: Lovedale Press, 1928), quotations from preface, 5, 6, 26, 38. Sol Plaatje's historical novel *Mhudi* was published after *An African Tragedy* albeit written before it.

There's a moral Oi think to my story;
The practice, Oi'd have ye to thry;
'Twixt fortune and us there is whisky;
Fill up Bhoys! Let's drink this show dhry.[43]

Such drinking songs promoted either optimistic Digger bravado or wry fatalism about the constant pursuit of hidden treasure. Poems and stories gradually became more pessimistic, reflecting the reality that low-grade ore and the buying of claims by mining companies were beginning to make them redundant. Many eventually concluded that working in Johannesburg meant death, a good enough reason for some to persist with hard drinking.[44]

Black working-class culture and the challenge to British respectability

Large numbers of African men working at the docks of the port cities or in the mines of Kimberley and the Rand also arrived with a mixture of bravado and trepidation. Shared identity and traditions that helped maintain it were demonstrably strong. Often in sizeable groups led by a local headman, they were further bound together by migrant associations and kinship relationships that linked them to particular villages and regions. Also important in creating a strong sense of common identity once in the city were shared accommodation, communal eating and drinking, and mutual financial support. Shared traditions, with adapted or newly invented elements, played an important additional role here: whether they were mutually held supernatural beliefs, or shared participation in story-telling, songs and dance. Embarking on migrant work itself became a rite of passage, one that could include rituals practised while travelling, older men taking younger ones as 'wives' while barracked together on mine compounds, or the acquisition of a city name like 'Jim', 'Shilling', 'Cape Smoke' or 'God Damn'. Along with sometimes garish western dress, these ostensibly demeaning names were seemingly appropriated by Mozambique migrants, perhaps because they did not fully understand their English meanings, to situate themselves within a new social context when at work as well as to serve 'as badges of self-worth and achievement' when back home in the countryside.[45]

Musical and dance traditions were adapted to urban experiences and conditions. Some songs offered direct commentary in this respect. One

---

[43] Cited in Isabel Hofmeyr, 'The Mad Poets: An Analysis of an Early Sub-Tradition of Johannesburg Literature and Its Subsequent Developments', in Belinda Bozzoli (ed.), *Labour, Township and Protest* (Johannesburg: Ravan Press, 1979), 127.
[44] Ibid., 128–32. [45] Harries, *Work, Culture, and Identity*, 60.

sung by Xhosa dockworkers in Cape Town in the early 1900s described 'the ringing of the six o'clock bell calling [them] to work at the "docksin" [Dock's Location] and ... the hard life of the native ... banished from home and comfort, and compelled to eat calves' heads and such poor food'.[46] Songs performed later by Bachopi comedians in Johannesburg satirised their employers, while poetical-musical compositions by Basotho migrants combined self-praise with commentary on suffering caused by unpleasant White supervisors and having to work for little reward.[47] Several songs of migrants from Mozambique in the 1920s and 1930s were assertive, celebrating the courage of miners, and exhorting them to dance in warlike fashion.[48] Others mirrored the Basotho compositions in criticisms of employers, while a number were simply disconsolate, telling of how migrants were trapped between starvation in the countryside and underground death on the Rand. In this vein, Junod overheard his own servant quietly reciting a poem about a central symbol of modernity, the train that took migrants to the city:

> The one who roars in the distance . . ..
> The one who crushes in pieces the braves and leaves them
> The one who debauches our wives.[49]

Dance became part of self-generated recreation for African migrants whether in the mines, at the docks or on the streets. The invented traditions involved with Sunday Mine Dance performances in Johannesburg compounds seemingly stemmed from similar occasions in Kimberley. The dances, music and stick fighting that accompanied them were adapted and creolised versions of rural forms, licensed by mine managers as a means of ethnic team building and to release tension. British sports like football and cricket were used in similar fashion. Mine dances began to attract attention from film makers, photographers and tourists, including the British rugby team of 1896, who demanded 'authentic dress' rather than blankets and Western clothes. Mine managers in Johannesburg encouraged 'ethnic and atavistic elements' such as ersatz versions of 'traditional' war dress.[50] From participants' perspectives, mine dances were in part licensed occasions for ethnic and masculine self-assertion also displayed in unlicensed violent clashes or 'faction fights' with workers perceived to be of other ethnicities. In both cases, the aim was often to protect the group's position in the employment market. This also fed on occasion into industrial action, sometimes

---

[46] *Cowley Evangelist*, 1903, 90, 'Native Acting Songs'.
[47] David Coplan, 'The Emergence of an African Working-Class Culture', in Marks and Rathbone, *Industrialisation and Social Change*, 358–75.
[48] Harries, *Work, Culture and Identity*, 201–11.   [49] Ibid., 230.   [50] Ibid., 75–6, 124–6.

involving cross-ethnic alliances, most notably in a strike by 70,000 Black Johannesburg mineworkers in 1920, and periodically among stevedores at the Cape Town and Durban docks.[51]

Not all African migrants came to the cities in large groups, or returned at regular intervals to the countryside, or were male. Nor did all migrants seek, find or remain in legal employment; and even some who did were involved with crime and disorderly behaviour. Thus many African women who arrived individually or in small groups in the early 1900s, when even occupations like domestic work and washing in Durban and Johannesburg were dominated by men, attempted to make a livelihood in whatever manner they could. Commonly this was through the illegal brewing of 'traditional' beer, or far stronger adulterated concoctions, and for some it was through prostitution. Such activities were associated with illegal canteens, soon dubbed 'shebeens', in inner city areas or sometimes in shacks on city outskirts. In the 'slumyards' of Doornfontein after the First World War, by now abandoned by wealthy Whites, as well as those of inner city 'Prospect Township' in Johannesburg, Sotho 'shebeen queens' attracted the attention of male patrons by performing the *Famo* dance, 'a rather wild form of choreographic striptease', and accompanying self-assertive laments. These spoke of the woman's

abandonment, loss of family ties, and home, and the general hardness of her lot, while criticising the bad character and anti-social behaviour of others and praising her own personal qualities and attractions.[52]

Famo dancers were undoubtedly in Dhlomo's mind when he wrote of loose women without 'moral or religious scruples ... in short, daring skirts' selling noxious Skokiaan alcohol and their own bodies in *African Tragedy*.[53]

A 'civic association'-style need for mutual support and sense of belonging, whose absence *Famo* songs lamented, combined with economic necessity or perceived opportunity, were undoubtedly factors in gang formation among young males in the cities. So were both adolescent rebellion against authority and the self-assertion of independent masculinity. Sizeable organised gangs developed in an urban world full of class and race prejudice, inequality and exclusion that frequently meted out

[51] Phil Bonner, 'The 1920 Black Mineworkers' Strike: A Preliminary Account', in Bozzoli, *Labour, Townships and Protest*, 273–97; Harries, *Work, Culture and Identity*; Bickford-Smith, *Ethnic Pride and Racial Prejudice*, 180–4; David Hemson, 'In the Eye of the Storm: Dock-Workers in Durban', in Maylam and Edwards, *The People's City: African Life in Twentieth Century Durban*, 145–73.
[52] Coplan, 'African Working-Class Culture', 363–4.   [53] Dhlomo, *African Tragedy*, 8.

demeaning experiences to the less powerful. Many gangsters in both Johannesburg and Durban were drawn from the ranks of male domestic servants or 'houseboys', usually youths between 12 and 20 whose rural elders had determined that this was age appropriate.

Like respectable British civic associations, gangs had their own invented traditions, many of them complex and in some cases highly visible. Of major pioneering importance in terms of African gang formation in Johannesburg was 'The Regiment of the Hills', otherwise known as 'The Ninevites' because members saw themselves as rebelling against the Lord. It was formed by an ex-houseboy, who called himself Jan Note or Nongoloza ('he of the piercing eyes'). After working as a houseboy in Jeppie, Note moved to higher paid employment in Turffontein. His four employers turned out to be highway robbers, preying on White travellers and African migrants alike, who enlisted Note in their activities. Having learnt something of their trade, Note formed a gang of his own consisting of Zulu-speaking bandits living in the Klipriversberg hills to the south of the city.

The organisation of the Regiment of the Hills, as described by Note himself, demonstrated something of the creolised nature of migrant culture in the cities, allied in this case with unlicensed ritual inversion. Note styled himself *Inkoos Nkula* or King and appointed a Governor-General or *Induna Inkulu*. 'Government' members of his gang were given numbers, from one to four, while a 'judge' and '*landrost*' administered justice. A general modelled on a 'Boer *vecht generaal*' as well as colonels, captains, sergeant-majors and sergeants controlled his 'Amasoja', or soldiers. Note's followers greeted him with 'Bayete', the salute usually reserved for Royalty.

After the Boer War, Ninevite activity moved into Johannesburg itself, with gang members operating in and from mine compounds. This continued even after Note received a life sentence in Pretoria Central Prison, because he introduced the Ninevite military-style gang structure there as well, with only senior Ninevites having the right to take younger males as 'wives', and a complex communication system with outside members.[54] Brutal punishment faced anyone who defied the authority of gang leaders. Note's endeavours have proved to be a model for prison gangs in South Africa's cities ever since.[55]

---

[54] Charles Van Onselen, 'The Regiment of the Hills – Umkosi Wezintaba: The Witwatersrand's lumpenproletarian Army, 1890–1920', in *Studies in the Social and Economic History of the Witwatersrand, 1886–1914, Vol. 2 New Nineveh* (Harlow: Longman, 1982), 171–201.

[55] This is certainly the argument of one modern account of South African prison gangs: see Johnny Steinberg, *The Number* (Cape Town: Jonathan Ball, 2004).

The Ninevites seem to have played a part in the rise of Amalaita gangs of houseboys in Johannesburg and Durban. Having been a houseboy himself, it would seem that in the 1890s Note offered violent Ninevite assistance to Zulu-speaking houseboys in disputes against their employers.[56] Some of these houseboys left for Durban during the general refugee exodus during the Boer War, where they paraded through the streets by day and night (thereby brazenly defying the 9pm curfew) in groups of fourteen to twenty, noisily playing harmonicas and challenging rival groups to fights. By 1903, these gangs, predominantly of houseboys (males constituted 7,590 out of 8,944 domestic workers in Durban as late as 1921), were being referred to as 'Amalaita'. This was seemingly a creolised English term that derived from victims being told to 'light' the way of gang members by handing over money.[57] In similar fashion to the Ninevites, Amalaitas gave themselves military ranks. Significantly, 'Nongoloza' became a term used to describe their leaders.[58]

Connections between small groups of houseboys were facilitated by 'homeboy' migrant associations and kinship links to particular rural areas, as was the case with the large groups of miners and many other urban African workers. Apart from by their youth, Amalaita were highly noticeable in city streets because of their dress and music. For some in Durban in 1907, dress consisted of wearing hats on the side of heads, broad trousers, heeled boots, beads hanging from their clothes and *ebusengi* (wire rings) on upper arms, lower legs and wrists. During the First World War, different gangs were distinguished by a range of headgear: *umshokobezi* or ox-tails tied round the head in Zulu warrior tradition, black-ribboned hats, ground hornbill feathers or red-ribboned headbands, the latter similar to those worn by participants in the Bambatha rebellion.[59] In Johannesburg, where Pedi migrants came to dominate large Amalaita gangs of some fifty to one hundred members of both sexes who paraded the streets in military style, men wore red cloth badges and knickerbocker trousers while women sported pleated tartan skirts ('Scots rokkies'), black stockings and high-heeled shoes.[60] In 1920s Cape Town, Coloured gangsters wore caps back to front and trousers at

---

[56] Van Onselen, 'Regiment of the Hills', 176.
[57] Charles Van Onselen, 'The Witches of Suburbia: Domestic Service on the Witwatersrand, 1890–1914', in *New Nineveh*, 56. Paul La Hausse, '"The Cows of Nongoloza": Youth, Crime and Amalaita Gangs in Durban, 1900–36', *Journal of Southern African Studies* 16, 1 (1990), 79–111; Paul La Hausse, '"Mayihlome": Towards an Understanding of Amalaita Gangs in Durban, c.1900–1930', in Stephen Clingman (ed.), *Regions and Repertoires: Topics in South African Politics and Culture* (Johannesburg: Ravan Press, 1991), 30–59.
[58] La Hausse, "Cows of Nongoloza", 90, 98.   [59] Ibid., 91, 94, 99, 105.
[60] Van Onselen, 'The Witches of Suburbia', 57–9.

half-mast that clearly identified them as unrespectable 'skollies' (scavengers) to respectable observers.[61]

Gangster clothing in all three cities became a sub-cultural bricolage of old and newly invented traditions. It achieved defiant distinction from both typical working clothes and respectable British Sunday best. An emerging 'tsotsi taal', or gangster slang, had much the same effect in marking its speaker as unrespectable. Some sartorial and linguistic elements, like *ebusengi* or the rural metaphors used by Ninevites, bore witness to ongoing rural ties; others spoke loudly of adaptation or invention in the city, indeed of urban belonging.[62] By the 1920s, and perhaps pioneered by Pedi migrant Amalaita in Johannesburg, the appearance of some gangsters, like Durban's Abaqhafi, who rejected both Zulu tradition and Christianity, was unambiguously and fashionably urban: 'wide open shirts, coloured scarves and Oxford bags tied below their knees'.[63]

There was a satirical element to disrespect for authority and British notions of respectability demonstrated in gangster dress and behaviour, as there could be to gang language and names. Hence two Cape Town gangs in the 1900s were known as 'The Steal Club', which met outside a hotel where members worked as musicians, and 'the Hanover Street Burglar's Club' operating out of District Six. As the latter's name suggests, and several reports of trials of gangsters appear to confirm, there was also an emerging neighbourhood territorial dimension to gangster identity and activity in Cape Town, as there was also in Durban, perhaps because of the growing size of both towns.[64]

The reports of magistrates, municipal policemen and local newspapers reflected ongoing concern and occasional high panic not just about gang activity but crime in general. In keeping with their racial thinking about the poor and the reality of growing numbers of Black rural migrants in cities, Whites worried about the urban danger posed especially by Black males. For instance, following the violent mugging of an English carpenter, John Anderson, and the high profile trial that followed in 1880s Cape Town, the prosecutor of Anderson's assailants claimed that 'since Cape Town had been flooded with Kafirs there was no safety in walking out after dark'.[65] Similarly Durban's Superintendent of Police Richard

---

[61] George Manuel, *I Remember Cape Town* (Cape Town: Don Nelson, 1977), 56–7.

[62] Dick Hebdige, *Subculture: The Meaning of Style* (London and New York: Routledge, 1979). Van Onselen, 'Regiment of the Hills', 194.

[63] La Hausse, "Cows of Nongoloza", 105.

[64] This was reported on from the 1870s onwards for Cape Town, see *Cape Times*, 23 November 1876, 25 December 1876, 5 January 1878, 9 January 1878, 11 January 1897, 22 January 1897, 11 August 1897, 6 December 1905; See also, *Cape Argus*, 7 September 1893. For Durban, see La Hausse, "'Cows of Nongoloza'", 95–7.

[65] *Cape Times*, 20 July 1881.

Alexander, a former sergeant in the British Army, wrote in 1898 that there were '10,000 able bodied [male] Natives' in Durban, and that 'an evil-minded, barefooted black man on a dark night is a dangerous character to be at large'.[66]

Alexander worried about the 'temptations for liquor and other vices [*sic*]' facing Africans in Durban's inner city.[67] Such temptations existed despite the fact that colonial governments had introduced laws prohibiting the sale of alcohol to Africans in all South Africa's major cities by 1901. Indeed Natal had led the way in 1863. Concerns about the relationship between African drunkenness and criminality voiced for Johannesburg by the likes of de Bremont had seemingly been answered; if in the Transvaal largely because mine owners were concerned by alcohol's effect on African mineworker productivity.[68]

Prohibition merely gave birth to a brisk illegal liquor trade, as it did in the United States. This provided considerable urban employment opportunities to both White and Coloured go-betweens, whose racial classification allowed them to buy alcohol legally and who then sold it on at a profit to African customers, as well as to African women home brewers. Police reported that '112 [illegal] beer dens employing 200 people and producing 4,000 gallons a weekend' existed in Durban in 1908. It was also common knowledge that brewing of 'traditional' maize or sorghum beer was frequently adulterated with more potent ingredients.[69]

The further solution arrived at by Superintendent Alexander, one in keeping with parliamentary commission reports on Africans in towns, was residential segregation. Alexander wanted all Africans in Durban to be controlled by enforced segregation at night in a superior form of mine compound. The provision of adequate and improving amenities there would allow for respectable and orderly existence.[70]

In reality, the divide between respectable and unrespectable living was far from rigid. One case that came before Cape Town's resident magistrate in 1897 revealed that football club members also belonged to gangs, just as obedient houseboys during the day could become Amalaita at night. Equally gangsters were able to participate in an annual communal celebration hugely enjoyed by even the most respectable among the Coloured working class, the two-day New Year Carnival. The Carnival

---

[66] Richard Alexander, 'Police Report', *Durban Mayor's Minutes*, cited in Maynard Swanson, '"The Durban System": Roots of Urban Apartheid in Colonial Natal', *African Studies* 35, 3–4 (1976), 164.

[67] Swanson, '"The Durban System"'.

[68] See Charles Van Onselen, 'Randlords and Rotgut, 1886–1903', *New Babylon*, 44–102 for the complicated history of prohibition and its limitations in Johannesburg; Bickford-Smith, *Ethnic Pride and Racial Prejudice*.

[69] Swanson, '"The Durban System"', 174.   [70] Ibid., 164.

probably had its origins in licensed celebrations of temporary 'freedom' by the bonded during slavery. By the 1870s, participants were formed into singing and sporting clubs distinguished by different costumes and were noticed by White journalists. By the mid-1880s, New Year street-parading was reported in detail for the first time:

> The frivolous coloured inhabitants of Cape Town ... [went] ... about in large bodies dressed most fantastically, carrying 'guys', and headed by blowers of wind and players of stringed instruments ... At night time these people added further inflictions ... in the shape of vocalisations, singing selections taken from 'Rule Britannia' and the 'Old Hundreth' ... They also carried Chinese lanterns ... [when] the strange glinting of the street lamps and the lanterns fell upon their dark faces, they seemed like so many uncanny spirits broken loose from – say the adamantine chains of the Nether World.[71]

The nature of New Year Carnival demonstrated a variety of influences over time, not least the interaction of elite and popular cultural forms.[72] The fact that troupes paraded through the streets led by 'captains' suggests, as with gang traditions and organisation, a satirical emulation of British army ranks and military reviews. Dressing 'most fantastically' and public parading were features of many theatrical and festive occasions that accompanied British colonialism and that allowed elite and popular participation, whether circuses or the Royal wedding celebrations of 1863. The fete held in the Government Gardens in 1865, for instance, was attended by 'all classes and creeds' and 'bands of [White upper-class] masqueraders paraded among the crowd', dressed as policemen and beggars.[73] The following year, 5,000 adults – out of Cape Town's total population of 27,000 – attended in fancy dress or false noses while watching performances by White Christy Minstrels in black-face make-up.[74] It is hardly surprising, then, that employees of Mr Cole, a leading baker, dressed all in white and with their faces painted 'black, red, and every conceivable colour' featured in Victoria's Golden Jubilee parade of 1887, or 'Malay gim cracks', presumably New Year carnival troupes, in the Diamond Jubilee parade ten years later.[75]

---

[71] *Cape Argus*, 4 January 1886.

[72] From twentieth century evidence, the ability to wear elaborate costumes was facilitated by the central involvement of tailoring families. Costume purchase could be financed by a set-aside system of saving during the preceding months: Shamil Jeppie, 'Aspects of Popular Culture and Class Expression in Inner Cape Town, c.1939–1959', (MA thesis, University of Cape Town, 1991).

[73] *Cape Argus*, 2 December 1865. Such fetes appear to have been annual events in the late 1860s.

[74] *Cape Argus*, 1 December 1866, 4 December 1866. Cape Town population estimate comes from Cape Archive (CA) Cape Parliamentary papers (CPP), G20–1866, 'Cape Census for 1866'.

[75] *Cape Argus*, 22 June 1887; *Cape Times*, 3 January 1888.

The ingredients of disguise, parody and self-mockery in American minstrelsy were particularly influential in the long term in shaping the nature of New Year Carnival. White minstrels first came to Cape Town in the persons of Joe Brown's Band of Brothers in 1848.[76] The most successful proved to be the Harvey-Leslie Christy Minstrels who toured in 1862 and 1865. They performed 'nigger' part-songs, jigs and mocking caricatures of American slaves in a variety of venues to all classes. According to the *Cape Argus*, 'even at the Cape where the nigger character is so well understood, the caricature created a furore'.[77] The enjoyment of such sketches may have been confined largely to Whites, and visiting minstrelsy spawned local White imitators like those at the Gardens' fete in 1866. But Cape Town's slave descendants and other Black South Africans appear to have found resonance in Christy Minstrel songs like 'Massie's in the Cold Ground' and 'Hard Time'. The music proved popular even, or perhaps especially, with those who did not understand the lyrics, possibly because this spared them from the cruder racism of the sketches.[78]

The almost five years that African-American Orpheus M. McAdoo Virginia Jubilee Singers spent in South Africa between 1890 and 1898 ensured that American minstrelsy and 'Negro' spirituals became part of Black urban musical repertoire.[79] Three of the Jubilee singers stayed in Cape Town and linked up with the Dantu family, who ran the Cape of Good Hope Sports Club. This combination formed the Original Jubilee Singers, the first 'Cape Coon' troupe, with miniature top hats and blue tailcoats.[80] The names of Carnival troupes in 1907 testified to such influence: 'The Jolly Coon Masquerade Troupe', 'The Jolly Coons', 'The White Noses', 'The White Eyes' and 'The Diamond Eyes'. Within a couple of years, and demonstrating the growing influence of cinema, some names and costumes had become more exotic and international. The 1909 Carnival featured 'The Spanish Cavaliers', 'The King's Messengers' and the 'The Prince of Benin's Escorts'.[81]

British or American songs sung by Carnival participants were learnt at mission schools, concerts, the circus or music halls: 'the latest success of the concert-room is reproduced immediately on the streets of the Malay

---

[76] R.W. Murray, *South African Reminiscences* (Cape Town: J.C. Juta, 1894), 207.
[77] *Cape Argus*, 20 November 1862, 23 November 1865.
[78] *Cape Argus*, 26 August 1852, 30 November 1865. See also Erlmann, *African Stars*, for a detailed discussion of the attractions of minstrelsy for Black South Africans.
[79] Erlmann, *African Stars*, 21–53.
[80] Denis-Constant Martin, *Sounding the Cape: Music, Identity and Politics in South Africa* (Cape Town: African Minds, 2013), 84. See also Denis-Constant Martin, *Coon Carnival, New Year in Cape Town, Past and Present* (Cape Town: David Philip, 1999).
[81] *South African News*, 3 January 1907, 5 January 1909.

Quarter'.[82] They were also picked up from White street performances, whether by military bands or the Salvation Army. Late nineteenth century hits among both White and Black Capetonians included 'My Grandfather's Clock', 'Ta-ra-ra-boom-de-ay', 'Daisy' and 'After the Ball was Over'.[83] Older 'traditional' songs were also performed during Carnival, at festive season picnics on Camp's Bay beach, and on summer evenings in the city by 'Malay' men 'who strolled up and down . . . singing the most sentimental Dutch songs in perfect time and harmony.'[84] These were *Moppies* or *Ghoemaliedjies* (drum songs), originally slave songs, and their performance formed part of Carnival tradition. Some *Ghoemaliedjies* were indeed gentle and sentimental; others could be satirical and lewd, lampooning female employers or those who attempted to 'pass for white'. Some parodied 'respectable' Dutch or Afrikaner folk songs, or the mock-submissive behaviour towards judges or others in authority: 'Oe la, my master, what did I do? Then they give me nine months in Roeland Street (gaol)'.[85] For some of the more 'unrespectable' participants, parading through the main streets was presumably a defiant act aimed at the White middle classes, as was the case for many in Luanda's carnival.[86] Some *ghoemaliedjie* lyrics were equally defiant. One version of 'Rule Britannia' contained the lyrics 'Come Britannia, the civilising one, Make the Nations into slaves . . . O foggy Isle, What a lot of Crazy rogues you have by the hand'.[87] Perhaps as in all Carnivals, despite their many ambivalent ingredients, participation and spectatorship by kin and neighbours promoted a broader community consciousness: as another *ghoemaliedjie* put it, 'Listen to what the people are saying, the people of Canal Town [Kanal Dorp, another name for District Six in the nineteenth century]'.[88]

---

[82] David Kennedy, *Kennedy at the Cape: A Professional Tour Through the Cape Colony, Orange Free State, Diamond Fields and Natal* (Edinburgh: Edinburgh Publishing Company, 1879), 14–15.

[83] *Cape Times*, 28 October 1896; University of Cape Town (UCT), Special Collections, BC230, Martin Leendertz, 'The Vanished City' (Unpublished memoir, 1953), 17–18. Eric Rosenthal, *Fishorns and Hansom Cabs* (Johannesburg: A.D. Donker, 1977), 106.

[84] D.P. Faure, *My Life and Times* (Cape Town: Juta, 1907), 12.

[85] Chris Winberg, 'The "*Ghoemalidjies*" of the Cape Muslims: Remnants of a Slave Culture' (Unpublished paper, English Department Seminar, UCT, 1991), 30. This paper, available in UCT's African Studies library, contains many examples of these songs and Winberg's translations of them into English.

[86] David Birmingham, 'Carnival at Luanda', *Journal of African History* 29, 1 (1988), 93–103.

[87] Winberg, 'Remnants of a Slave Culture', 25–6.

[88] Ibid., 'Remnants of a Slave Culture', 18; see also Chris Winberg, 'Satire, Slavery and the Ghoemaliedjies of the Cape Muslims', *New Contrast* 19, 4 (1991), 78–96.

'Ancient Nineveh and Babylon have been revived'

There were certainly un-British urban sights and sounds aplenty to alarm Junod and many other observers. Johannesburg loomed particularly large in terms of Babylonian comparisons. Junod's denunciation of the city as suffused with greed and wealth born of semi-slavery echoed the heroine Ariadne's nightmare in de Bremont's *Gentleman Digger*. She sees a golden deity bloodily lashing the humans who pull his chariot, dreadful scenes of debauchery, and eventually a raging 'river of Famine, Fever, and Death' that sweeps away 'the garments of Sin and Greed' that clothe Johannesburg.[89] This apocalyptic vision presaged others that charac- terised twentieth century urban dystopias, most famously machine- turned-Moloch in Fritz Lang's film *Metropolis* (1927).

Other denunciations closely mirrored northern hemisphere accounts that condemned dramatic economic inequalities or overly lavish displays of wealth.[90] Lines written by John Noble, Clerk to Parliament in the Cape and cited in de Beer's anthology, expressed this straightforwardly: 'Everywhere a love of gold, Nowhere pity for the poor, Everywhere mistrust disguise, Pride, hypocrisy, and show.'[91] William Scully's non- fiction book *Ridge of White Waters* (1912) dismissed Durban's new town hall (see Illustration 2.2) as mere 'civic arrogance', condemned the Durban Club for exuding 'superfluous superiority from every pore', and the Rand Club as 'a megalomaniac's dream realised; it is barbaric, Titanic'.

Scully contrasted the latter's opulence with the poverty he found in working-class areas like Vrededorp, and which he described over many pages, in slum literature fashion typical of the wider anglophone world, as a place of undesirable racial mixing, crime, drink, drugs, promiscuity and 'warrens' of galvanised iron.[92] 'Most' of the latter were, according to Scully, owned by 'foreign Jews', and he reported seeing a 'Hoggenheimer' (a derogatory epithet for wealthy Jews) driving past in a 'fancy car'.[93] Indeed what Scully, Black, Blackburn and Junod all had in common was their anti-Semitic portrayals of Jewish South Africans as greedy and unprincipled. Scully concluded that life in Johannesburg was

---

[89] De Bremont, *Gentleman Digger*, 48–52.
[90] Lees, *Cities Perceived*, 106–35. Apart from the many depictions of poverty and slums in Hugo, Dickens and Engels onwards, there were writers like Daniel Kirwan who particu- larly focused on sharply contrasting urban wealth and poverty, as the title of his book *Palace and Hovel* (Hartford, CT: Belknap and Bliss, 1870) proclaims.
[91] De Beer, *Holiday Book*, 127.   [92] As argued by Mayne, *The Imagined Slum*.
[93] Mendelsohn and Shain, *The Jews in South Africa*, 62. For an extended account of South African anti-Semitism in this period, see Milton Shain, *The Roots of Anti-Semitism in South Africa* (Charlottesville: University Press of Virginia, 1994).

'demoralising', that 'no ideals could survive' and somewhat bizarrely that 'divorces are nearly as common there as Dakota'.[94]

Ambrose Pratt, a journalist who visited South Africa to attend the Union celebrations as part of an official Australian delegation in 1910, was another critic of Johannesburg, though he did appreciate many municipal efforts elsewhere in South Africa. Pratt declared after touring the Rand that 'Ancient Nineveh and Babylon have been revived. Johannesburg is their twentieth century prototype. It is a city of unbridled squander and unfathomable squalor'.[95] Pratt offered similar slumland portrayals to Scully in his description of the 'quarter of the "poor whites", wretched victims of the Kaffirs' monopoly of the unskilled labour market, who derive an infamous living by the . . . prostitution of their daughters, and by selling liquor in secret to the native hordes.' Meanwhile White children were 'scattered through this murk playing in the gutters, picking up the words and vices of the coloured scum'.[96]

Scully and Pratt, in expressing fears about racial mixing, were clearly both reflecting and giving sustenance to contemporary ideologies of racial difference, racism, discrimination and segregation. These racialised middle-class attitudes towards the urban poor in Britain by commonly distinguishing in South Africa between deserving 'White' poverty and an undeserving and dangerous 'Black' residuum that might bring about White 'degeneration'. The 'discovery' of this urban problem received extensive newspaper coverage in Cape Town during the economic depression of the 1880s. The argument largely accepted by local and central governments over subsequent decades was that Whites should be rescued through charity or state intervention.[97] This view was encouraged by the very visible and sometime violent demands for special treatment emanating from the majority of White workers and their trade unions, and ultimately the (Whites-only beyond the Cape) South African Labour Party (1910), in the first two decades of the twentieth century.[98] It was given further impetus by the findings of the highly

[94] W.C. Scully, *The Ridge of White Waters* (London: Stanley Paul & Co., 1912), 23, 78, 79, 171–4, 208, 211, 262. See also Shain, *The Roots of Antisemitism in South Africa*, 19–77.
[95] Ambrose Pratt, *The Real South Africa* (Milton Keynes: General Books, [1912] 2010), 56.
[96] Pratt, *The Real South Africa*, 51.
[97] Bickford-Smith, *Ethnic Pride and Racial Prejudice*. This argument draws on middle-class attitudes to the poor explored in Stedman Jones, *Outcast London*.
[98] Vivian Bickford-Smith, 'Protest, Organisation and Ethnicity among Cape Town Workers, 1891–1902', *Studies in the History of Cape Town* 6 (1994), 84–108; Jonathan Hyslop, 'The Imperial Working Class Makes Itself "White": White Labour in Britain. Australia, and South Africa before the First World War', *Journal of Historical Sociology* 12, 4 (1999), 398–421; Van Onselen, *New Babylon* and *New Nineveh*; Jeremy Krikler, *White Rising: The 1922 Insurrection and Racial Killing in South Africa* (Manchester: Manchester University Press, 2005). Bickford-Smith, 'Cape Town Workers' demonstrates that some

influential Transvaal Indigency Commission of 1906–8, which despite determining that some Whites were considerably more deserving than others, nonetheless concluded that unless White workers in general overcame African competition, South Africa would be 'owned and governed, but not peopled by the white races'.[99] Its immediate recommendation, one that resonated with pessimistic literary depictions of Afrikaners in the city, was that the White poor (almost synonymous with Afrikaners) should be sent back to the land, to farm colonies like the one established at Kakamas by the Dutch Reformed Church (DRC); if this failed, they could be employed by the government on relief work projects, as had already happened in the nineteenth century, or on the railways.[100]

Certainly both Pratt and Scully were very sympathetic to White labour. Pratt was noted for this in Australia, where he also displayed a concomitant stance against Asian immigration. In South Africa, he condemned exploitative mine-owners while recording the suffering of White miners and poor Whites generally. Pratt's plea was for would-be White working-class immigrants to boycott South Africa: 'Miners of England and Australia, however poor may be your lot, however dark your present prospects, let no man tempt you to South Africa.'[101] Scully's sympathies were not dissimilar, and like Pratt he publicised alarming mortality rates among miners wrought by phthisis.[102]

White working-class militancy and Afrikaner nationalism

Both of their books were published before the outbreak of major violent strikes by White workers on the Rand in 1913–14, and the internationally sensational Rand or Red Revolt of 1922. Leadership of the Revolt was

White workers believed in organising along non-racial lines, notably members of the Social Democratic Federation. Recently some studies have focused on the small but non-racial Syndicalist tradition among immigrant workers. See for instance, Lucien van der Walt, 'Revolutionary Syndicalism, Communism and the National Question in South African Socialism', in Steven Hirsch and Lucien van der Walt (eds), *Anarchism and Syndicalism in the Colonial and Postcolonial World, 1870–1940* (Leiden: Brill, 2010), 33–94. For a less optimistic view of the impact of non-racialism among White South African workers, even supposedly more enlightened Scottish ones, see Jonathan Hyslop, 'Scottish Labour, Race, and Southern African Empire c.1880–1922: A Reply to Kenefick', *International Review of Social History* 55 (2010), 63–81.

[99] Government (T.G.) 11–1908, *Transvaal Indigency Commission, 1906–1908*, 51. See also Lis Lange, *White, Poor and Angry: White Working-Class Families in Johannesburg* (Aldershot: Ashgate, 2003); Edward-John Bottomley, *Poor White* (Cape Town: Tafelberg, 2012).

[100] Bottomley, *Poor White*, 111, 169.   [101] Pratt, *The Real South Africa*, 56.

[102] For details of the pthisis mortality rates on the Rand, see G. Burke and P. Richardson, 'The Profit of Death: A Comparative Study of Miners' Phthisis in Cornwall and the Transvaal, 1876–1918', *Journal of Southern African Studies* 4, 2 (1978), 147–71.

unsurprisingly provided by socialists, including members of the recently formed Communist Party of South Africa (CPSA, 1921). It involved around 25,000 industrial workers, the vast majority of them miners, fighting fierce battles with police and soldiers, and temporarily seizing control of working-class areas like Fordsburg in south-western Johannesburg. Indeed, strikers' ability to resist was intimately connected to the nature of the community networks and alliances they had created in such places where they were 'socially embedded'. Here was where White racial and working-class identities, themselves informed by workplace divisions of labour that put Whites in better paid (often supervisory) jobs than Blacks, were reinforced by a sense of urban territoriality.[103]

Participants in the Rand Revolt marched under banners proclaiming 'Workers of the World, Fight and Unite for a White South Africa', and leaders went to the scaffold singing the Red Flag. Although immigrants from Britain were heavily involved, with some in leading positions, the influence of anti-British nationalism was also in evidence, including Irish and Afrikaner manifestations. Fordsburg strikers had a detachment called the Sinn Fein Commando, complete with green rosettes and flags. Appeals to Afrikaner nationalism were more significant, though. Several speeches evoked legends of heroic leaders of the *Groot Trek*. One, given to 3,000 workers in Jeppe, referring to the Chamber of Mines' replacement of Whites by cheaper Black migrant workers, exhorted the audience to stand unanimously behind 'the victory of the Voortrekkers over Dingaan in 1838'. Similarly Jopie Fourie, executed in 1914 for his involvement in an abortive Afrikaner rebellion against South African participation in the First World War, was invoked as a man prepared to die for his beliefs and his *volk*. The Union Jack was denounced by some as a '*vuile vadoek*' or dirty dishcloth, and hope given of a time when the Traansvaal *Vierkleur* would return. *Die Volkslied* was frequently sung by groups of strikers.[104]

The extent of Afrikaner nationalist sentiment among miners doubtless resulted in part from experiences expressed in oral traditions hostile to British Imperialism; the Boer War with Kitchener's scorched earth tactics and concentration camps was chronologically not far distant after all. Yet Afrikaner nationalism also reflected more recent middle-class inculcation or 'invention' of Afrikaner tradition among the poor. By 1922, this was taking place on several fronts, including the domestic. The *Zuid-Afrikaansche Vrouwe Vereneeging* (South African Women's Society) was organised by middle-class women with strong connections to the DRC in

---

[103] The term used by Krikler, *White Rising*, 30, in his magisterial history of the Revolt. See also Van Onselen, *New Babylon* and *New Nineveh*.
[104] Krikler, *White Rising*, 103–5.

1904. Its constitution urged members to promote 'Taal en Volk', now threatened by (mainly British) foreigners and their alien traditions. In 1907, the organisation had changed the first word in its title from Zuid-Afrikaansche to Afrikaansche, and the whole name was later translated from Dutch into Afrikaans as the *Afrikaanse Christelike Vroue Vereeneging* (ACVV). The ACVV was similar to the Guild of Loyal Women in its combination of politics, culture and philanthropy, and organised meetings in private homes and local DRC halls, as well as public events, in pursuit of its aims. These included conveying an idealised *volksmoeder* (mother of the nation) ideology and what it meant in general to be a true Afrikaner in terms of history, religion, language and domestic material culture.[105]

To be a proper Afrikaner came to require appropriate understanding and observance of 16 December, the anniversary of Boer victory over the Zulus at the Battle of Blood River in 1838, known as Dingaan's Day (after the Zulu chief Dingane) or the Day of the Vow because of the Boer pledge to God before the battle. Dingaan's Day was made a national holiday along with Empire Day and the King's Birthday by the Union government in 1910.[106] The fact that this happened was also the result of the efforts of men like Gustav Preller, a civil servant turned historian and journalist. His hagiographical articles on Piet Retief duly appeared in *De Volkstem* in the days leading up to 16 December, and were then published in book form, selling over 15,000 copies.

Preller was involved in the movement to get Afrikaans rather than Dutch accepted as the language of the *volk*, and published a magazine, *Die Brandwag* (from 1910), as a statement of this intent. Together with the unveiling of a *Vrouemonument* in Bloemfontein on 16 December 1913, to commemorate Afrikaner women's suffering in the Boer War, the formation of the (Afrikaner) National Party by the Boer War general J.B.M. Hertzog in 1914 (also in Bloemfontein), and the popular canonisation of Jopie Fourie after his 'martyrdom' in the rebellion of the same year, Afrikaner nationalism gradually developed a range of institutions and traditions, rediscovered, invented or popularised, that promoted an alternative to Britishness. The establishment of *Nationale Pers* in Cape Town in 1915, and the newspapers, magazines and books that it published, such

---

[105] Elsabe Brink, 'Man-Made Women: Gender, Class and the Ideology of the Volksmoeder', in Walker, *Women and Gender*, 273–92; Marijke du Toit, 'The Domesticity of Afrikaner Nationalism: Volksmoeders and the ACVV, 1904–1929', *Journal of Southern African Studies* 29, 1 (2003), 155–76.

[106] Dingaan's Day subsequently became the Day of the Covenant (1952), and then the Day of the Vow (1979), more directly conveying an Afrikaner nationalist sense of divine mission, before transforming into the Day of Reconciliation with the coming of democracy in the mid-1990s.

as Cape Town's *De Burger* (1915; *Die Burger* from 1922, as Dutch gave way to Afrikaans) and *De Huisgenoot* (The Family Companion, 1916), as well as Mabel Malherbe's women's magazine *Die Boerevrou* (1919), all helped ensure that traditions were transmitted by more than word of mouth. So did film, with Preller heavily involved in the making of the historical epic *De Voortrekkers*, an early product of Johannesburg's African Film Productions Company (1913), with its iconic mis-en-scène of ox-wagons traversing the veld, laagers from which Afrikaners fought off African warriors, and Afrikaner women in 'traditional' bonnet (*doek*) and long dress.[107]

In addition, an Afrikaner *Broederbond* (Brother's League) was formed in 1919 by Henning Klopper and others who met in the parsonage of William Nicol, the DRC minister for Johannesburg East. Its aim was to unite 'serious-minded Afrikaners' and 'to arouse Afrikaner national self-consciousness ... and to further every concern of the Afrikaner nation'. This was because, as Nicol later recalled, 'numerous households which still tried at the beginning of the [First World] War to be as English as possible found by the end ... that they had a unique future which they must seek and ensure for the sake of posterity'.[108] It may also have been a result of Afrikaans speakers being clustered in particular parts of the city, like the south-west, in sufficient numbers that promoted thinking in this ethno-national fashion. The *Broederbond* organised 16 December *Geloftedag* (Day of the Vow) celebrations on the Rand until 1922, when it became an underground organisation with secret initiation rites while extending its influence to other parts of the country.[109]

This development followed the crushing of the Rand Revolt in March of that year.[110] To this end, Prime Minister Jan Smuts had been willing to use overwhelming military might, including artillery and aircraft that strafed and bombed the strikers. Both South African and British news-reels captured this dramatic conflict.[111] Demonstrating the impact the strike had in terms of popular consciousness across the Empire, connected to transnational ruling class fears of Bolshevik revolution, the

---

[107] Isabel Hofmeyr, 'Building a Nation from Words: Afrikaans Language, Literature and Ethnic Identity, 1902–1924', in Shula Marks and Stanley Trapido (eds), *The Politics of Race, Class and Nationalism in Twentieth Century South Africa* (Harlow: Longman, 1987), 95–123; Hermann Giliomee, *The Afrikaners* (Cape Town: Tafelberg, 2003), 355–402.

[108] T. Dunbar Moodie, *The Rise of Afrikanerdom: Power, Apartheid, and the Afrikaner Civil Religion* (Berkeley, CA: University of California Press, 1975), 49–50.

[109] Moodie, *Afrikanerdom*, 96–115.

[110] Though this is not clear from Moodie's account of the early years of the Broederbond.

[111] See for instance *The Johannesburg Revolution and Rand Riots: General Smuts and the Bombardment of Fordsburg*, Gaumont Graphic, 24 April 1922. Smuts also deployed a tank. His ability to deploy such military power was the result of an effective Union defensive force from 1913 onwards, tried and tested in the First World War.

Revolt was referred to in one of Agatha Christie's early novels, *The Man in the Brown Suit*. Its villain, the arms dealer Sir Eustace Pedler, muses:

We are all living on the edge of a volcano. Bands of strikers ... patrol the streets and scowl at one in murderous fashion. They are picking out the bloated capitalist ready for when the massacres begin, I suppose.[112]

As Sir Eustace's remarks might suggest, the dominant symbol of White worker militancy during the strike had not been the Afrikaner nationalist *Vierkleur* but socialist red: banners, rosettes, ribbons, red flags and the anthem that celebrated them. These symbols of international working-class solidarity united White strikers in Johannesburg across potential ethnic or national divides. The violent suppression of the Rand Revolt dealt an all-but-fatal blow to mass White worker militancy. Only a remnant survived in the mixture of socialism and Afrikaner nationalism evident among White women of the Garment Workers' Union up to the Second World War, who came to see themselves as 'honest workers ... [whose] labour is for the benefit of our country and our *volk*'.[113]

> No beard grows upon my cheeks
> But in my heart I carry a sword
> The battle sword for bread and honour
> Against the poverty which pains my mother heart [sic].[114]

But for two decades White worker radicalism had been a major factor in both city and national politics. The history of socialist organisation in South Africa stretched back to the formation of an offshoot of the British Social Democratic Federation (SDF) in Cape Town in 1903. Wilfrid Harrison, ex-Coldstream Guardsman and Boer War veteran, was a founder member of what became an eclectic mixture of socialists and anarcho-syndicalists. The opening sentence of his vivid memoirs declared: 'Socialism had its beginnings as a propaganda force from the plinth of Van Riebeeck's Statue, Adderley Street, Cape Town, when it stood at the bottom of Dock Road in the latter months of 1903'.[115] Harrison

---

[112] Agatha Christie, *The Man in the Brown Suit* (London: John Lane and the Bodley Head Ltd., 1924), 249. A substantial part of the novel, more a thriller than a whodunit, is set in South Africa.

[113] H. Cornelius, 'Ons Werkers in Agterbuurtes en Waroom?', *Die Klerewerker* (October 1938), 3, cited in Louise Vincent, 'Bread and Honour: White Working Class Women and Afrikaner Nationalism in the 1930s', *Journal of Southern African Studies* 26, 1 (2000), 68.

[114] *Die Kerkweter* (October 1938) 9, translated and cited in Vincent, 'Bread and Honour', 61.

[115] Wilfrid H. Harrison, *Memoirs of a Socialist in South Africa, 1903–1947* (Cape Town: Stewart Printing Company, 1947).

described how some British traditions, including socialism and free speech, helped challenge the idea of a capitalist Empire.

Van Riebeeck's statue briefly became Cape Town's equivalent of Speaker's Corner in Hyde Park, London, as Harrison recalled, with speakers free to address almost any topic. It was here that Harrison encountered J.L. Page (see Illustration 3.1), a sculptor and French polisher working on the new town hall, telling the crowd: 'And so we sing "Rule, Britannia, Britons never shall be slaves". The British worker ought to know that he has never been anything else.'[116] Shortly afterwards, Harrison met another Van Riebeeck statue speaker called Blagburn, ex-member of the SDF in London, and they agreed to hold socialist meetings at the venue every Sunday morning. These were publicised by Jack Erasmus, a socialist reporter on a rare pro-Boer local paper sympathetic to criticisms of British Imperialism, the *South African News*.

The three decided to form an SDF branch in the city. With it came social activities and invented traditions that helped build a sense of socialist community: recreational outings to Camp's Bay, music and a choir in the 'spacious' Socialist Hall in Buitankant Street, and (for some at least) dedication services. These were intended as atheist alternatives to christenings, with anointment by the red flag replacing holy water, and the SDF 'became quite a religious institution'.[117] In 1908, Harrison placed his own child on his wife's lap while reciting 'In the name of liberty, equality and fraternity I now dedicate my son to the cause of international socialism'.[118]

The SDF grew in size and public impact in Cape Town. Harrison and others were invited to speak at informal gatherings called the Stone meetings, named for the circle of stones in District Six where they took place. These meetings had been organised by John Tobin, son of a slave-descendant and an Irish immigrant, who always began proceedings by saying 'Kom na die Klip' (Come to the Stone).[119] Tobin's own ideology was more redolent of the Black Atlantic than its White counterpart.[120] He stated at one gathering in 1903: 'The black man who is ashamed of his race is still a slave', and the anniversary of slave emancipation was duly commemorated on 1 December at the Stone. But Tobin's belief that 'the black man' would advance through 'honest toil, clean living, education, reading [and] . . . intellectual discourse', combined with British colonial governments' general adherence to freedom of speech, led to the Stone becoming a platform for politicians of all kinds.[121]

[116] Ibid., 2.   [117] Ibid., 10.   [118] Ibid., 16.   [119] Ibid., 22.
[120] Paul Gilroy, *The Black Atlantic* (London: Verso, 1993).
[121] *South African News*, 28 November 1903.

Early Beginnings

3

J. L. Page, speaking at the Jan van Riebeeck statue in 1903
when it stood at the bottom of Riebeeck Street in the centre of
Adderley Street, where Van Riebeeck landed at the Cape.

Illustration 3.1: J.L. Page of the SDF speaking at Van Riebeeck's statue,
Adderley Street, Cape Town in 1903 (From Wilfrid Harrison, *Memoirs
of a Socialist*, British Library)

The SDF gained widespread publicity and much criticism for the role it played in what became known as the Hunger Riots of 1906, which took place at the lowest point in the post-Boer War economic depression. In July of that year, and against the backdrop of a wet and windy Cape winter, the SDF called a 'Monster Meeting of the Unemployed' at its Barrack Street premises that was packed to overflowing. Several further gatherings followed on the Grand Parade, attended by as many as 6,000. At one addressed by SDF speaker Abraham Needham on 2 August, the crowd was told:

We look to you to give EXTREME PRESSURE to make the rich disgorge the wealth that they have taken from the country and which has been given to them by the men who have built the railways and the harbours, who dig in the mines and till the fields. [*Cape Times* emphasis] [122]

At a subsequent meeting at the same venue four days later, J.H. Howard, SDF secretary, declared that in his organisation 'there was no distinction ... whether white or coloured, and no class and no creed'; if those present got no satisfactory response to their demands for assistance 'It will be up to you what to do with the government'. Whereupon a one-eyed German socialist called Otto Meyer shouted 'Bring arms and plenty of ammunition'. When SDF leaders brought back a promise from Prime Minister Leander Starr Jameson (he of Raid infamy) that the government would help with food, housing and clothes, Meyer told the crowd not to be content with this, urging them to 'thieve and steal the same as they do in the Argentine'. About 1,000 in the crowd followed his instructions, with 'the coloured women screaming the loudest, leading the crowds, shouting out imprecations and generally urging on the men and boys to attack and plunder houses'. [123]

The Hooligan riots ended with thirty-five men and one woman receiving sentences that included a deportation but that were otherwise relatively mild, ranging from twelve months' hard labour to fines. The demonstrations and riots marked one of the last occasions before the 1980s that a substantial number of both White and Black South Africans took to city streets together in a radical cause. That this was so had much to do with White worker racism and the gradual extension of social and residential segregation. By the 1920s, socialist speakers at Van Riebeeck's statue had been replaced by wreaths laid by Afrikaner nationalists. [124] The Grand Parade became the new Speaker's corner

[122] *Cape Times*, 3 August 1906.
[123] *Cape Times*, 7 August 1906. For a more detailed account and analysis of the riots see Robin Hallett, 'The Hooligan Riots: Cape Town August 1906', *Studies in the History of Cape Town* 1 (1979), 42–87.
[124] Witz, *Apartheid's Festival*, 48.

and favoured place of demonstrations, and violent though predominantly racially distinct strike action continued; only most dramatically, before the Second Wold War, with the Rand Revolt.

Black Peril panics and fears of miscegenation

Much of what has been described rightly suggests that of the main cities Johannesburg was most commonly denounced as South Africa's new Babylon, even if it only reminded Churchill of Oldham when he viewed the city in 1900. Smuts labelled Johannesburg simply 'the Mecca of the hooligan'.[125] But Cape Town and Durban did not entirely escape opprobrium. Durban was a rare setting for South African city novels or films, yet under the unflattering pseudonym of Mosquito Town it appeared in George Hardy's *Black Peril*. Published in 1914, *Black Peril* acknowledged Durban's topographical beauty and the colourful cosmopolitanism of its streets with 'dozens and dozens of picturesque rickshaw boys, smiling and laughing and showing their white and gleaming teeth', but suggested that Africans would be morally better off in the countryside. Equally, in the spirit of Scully and Pratt, Hardy wrote that the Natal Governor's summer residence on the Berea was 'architecturally impossible, vulgar, and very red', and he contrasted it with humble shanties on the inland side of the ridge as well as an area of central Durban, presumably around Grey Street, where 'many filthy, wretched little buildings and shops' were inhabited by Indians.

A major difference, though, is that Hardy offers sympathy for Black as well as White poverty. Displaying socialist sympathies, he was especially scornful of Durban's elite of 'grocers, drapers and tea merchants', who lived on the Berea 'in all their pomp and glory', for building their fortunes from Black labour that was 'practically in a state of slavery'. *Black Peril*'s main protagonists, journalist Richard Chesterfield of the *Mosquito Argonaut* and Mary Roseberry, a Christian socialist recently arrived from England, criticise local Whites for their contemptuous treatment of Blacks and champion the idea of 'justice for all, including blacks'. Chesterfield believes in extending the Cape franchise northwards, and that Blacks should be allowed to sit in the Union parliament, although the thought of South Africa once again becoming a Black man's country makes him shudder.[126]

---

[125] Hyslop, *Notorious Syndicalist*, 105, 212.
[126] G.W. Hardy, *The Black Peril* (London: Holden and Hardingham, 1914), quotations from pages 18–20, 45.

Hardy, perhaps surprisingly, deemed Johannesburg 'a wonderful town now', though before the South African war it had been 'a human cesspool' in which one of *Black Peril*'s characters, the fat and ugly Isidore Hoggenheimer had once exploitatively resided. Clearly this echoes anti-Semitism in previous city novels, though Hardy allowed that there were 'very many fine' Jewish men.[127] However Hardy's book, as suggested by its title and plot, which has Mary narrowly escaping the sexual attentions of a male Zulu servant, is that White South Africans needed to recognise that cross-racial sexual encounters and miscegenation were undesirable and dangerous.

The 'Black Peril' of Hardy's title was a popular White term used in this period for the threat of rape that Black men supposedly posed to White women. 'Black Peril' anxiety characterised by moments of urban panic was reflected in the existence of several other novels with this theme, as well as numerous newspaper articles and correspondence. In *Leaven*, Blackburn had referred disparagingly to such panic in Natal's capital Pietermaritzburg, suggesting that sensational headlines about invented 'Kafir Outrages' sold newspapers.[128]

The Union government disagreed, and in 1913 appointed a commission 'to enquire into assaults on women'. More than 90 per cent of its report considered assaults by Black men on White women, even though accompanying statistics (see Table 3.1) showed that by far the greatest number were by Black men on Black women (mostly attributed to 'Native' culture), and that for White women attacks by White men were almost as frequent as those by Black men: around forty-two cases brought to court per annum compared to fifty-four.[129]

For the commissioners, 'the evidence seems conclusive that the natives who perpetrate sexual offences against women, are generally either unemployed ... or those engaged in domestic service or in stores and similar occupations'.[130] Factors that made 'Native' assaults more likely were then given. One was the continuing availability of strong alcohol, obtained despite its legislated prohibition. Another was that 'the Native' had been wrenched away 'from his customary mode of life'.[131] This was related to African contact with 'Undesirable Europeans', including criminals and prostitutes, and 'the evils of civilization' in general, including the availability of pornographic photographs and films, all most evident in cities:

[127] Hardy, *Black Peril*, 14, 51–2.
[128] Blackburn, *Leaven*, 70–1. Bulalie is wrongly accused of being the perpetrator in Pietermaritzburg of an 'Outrage on White Woman' as the local newspaper puts it. No assault in fact took place.
[129] U.G. 39–1913, *Report of the Commission Appointed to Enquire into Assaults on Women* (Cape Town: Cape Times Ltd. Government Printers, 1913).
[130] Ibid., 15.   [131] Ibid., 23.

Table 3.1: *Sexual assaults in South Africa, 1901–1912, according to contemporary racial categories*

	Total charges	Annual average charges	Total convictions	Annual average convictions
White man/White woman	508	42.3	201	16.8
Black man/Black woman	7,005	583.8	3,754	312.8
White man/Black woman	341	28.4	92	7.7
Black man/White woman	648	54	464	38.6

U.G.39–1913, *Report of the Commission Appointed to Enquire into Assaults on Women* (Cape Town: Cape Times Ltd Government Printers, 1913). The Commission uses the term 'Coloured' for all those it defines as not White, but to avoid confusion this has been changed in the table to 'Black'. The term 'Sexual Assault' encompassed rape, attempted rape and indecent assault although the term itself was not used in criminal charges in South Africa until the 1970s.

There are numerous factors in the social life of towns which conduce to the loss of the respect, and almost awe, in which at one time the white race was held by the native. By closer contact with the white race in towns the natives have learned that very often white people lead immoral lives, and that even finely dressed white women make a traffic of their persons. The ricksha boy has many a time conveyed his fare to a house of ill-fame, or has taken home persons in a state of intoxication. From such facts, from his contact with or observation of the actions of the white criminal classes and other experiences, the native's estimate of the European's virtue has suffered, and from these experiences he probably forms an exaggerated and distorted idea of the vices and profligacy of the white man, and especially of the frailty of the white woman. According to the testimony of a gentleman of great authority and experience: 'When first it became possible even in thought for a native to have connection with a white woman, that was the first beginning of the evil'.[132]

White women should therefore avoid mixing socially with Black men, not become overly familiar with them in domestic or work situations, or ever 'wander about alone' in the city, whose streets and open spaces were unsafe for them.[133] Equally, Whites should not be forced to live in 'close association' with Blacks, because this 'engendered' vice; Blacks had learnt how to form their own criminal gangs by emulating Whites. The employment of African men as domestic servants, hitherto common practice in

[132] Ibid., 21.   [133] Ibid., 12.

Johannesburg and Durban, should be avoided in favour of employing women: 'the house boy system is alleged by a very large number of witnesses to be at the root of the evil'.[134] The solution recommended by the commission was social and residential segregation, and particularly 'in his own interests' the housing of Africans in locations. This should be under 'clean, healthy and decent conditions of family and social life' in 'fairly decent houses', not 'miserable hovels and shanties', with gardens and trees, and medical and recreational facilities. In other words, 'the locations should be modelled on the examples of a modern town as far as the income derived from the natives themselves will allow'.[135]

Black Peril anxiety may have stemmed in part from White male desire to reserve White women for themselves in towns where the latter were in short supply, and where Black urban migrancy was still predominantly male. It is probable that Black Peril, or *Swart Gevaar*, developed into a political slogan because it expressed general White minority insecurity, possibly at its height in times of economic recession and industrial strife.[136] There were brutal rapes of White women by Black men. Two happened in the space of two years in Johannesburg: one of a White governess cycling in Orange Grove in 1911, the other of a Mrs W. Harrison in her home in Turffontein the following year. This led to thousands of White vigilantes patrolling the southern suburbs and hanging an African in effigy. The *Rand Daily Mail* organised a petition signed by 50,000 demanding action on the 'black peril', and this led to the appointment of the government commission.[137] Yet several other cases revealed that false accusations were made either by White women employers attempting to defraud servants of their wages, as the commission acknowledged, or by relationships between a White woman (employer or servant) and a Black servant being later regretted by the former.[138] Scully's *Daniel Vavanda* duly had its protagonist, who becomes a domestic servant in Johannesburg after leaving the mines, having to evade the advances of the young negligée-clad wife of his employer.[139]

Popular and official disapproval of over-familiarity between White and Black that might lead to sexual liaisons and 'miscegenation' was influenced by Social Darwinist ideas of degeneration.[140] English-language

---

[134] Ibid., 11.   [135] Ibid., 14.
[136] G. Cornwell, 'George Webb Hardy's *The Black Peril* and the Social Meaning of "Black Peril" in Early Twentieth Century South Africa', *Journal of Southern African Studies* 22, 3 (1996), 441–53. Cornwell mentions two other novels beyond Webb's that dealt with the Black Peril theme.
[137] Van Onselen, 'Witches of Suburbia', 49–50.   [138] Ibid., 51–3.
[139] Scully, *Daniel Vavanda*, 201–5.
[140] For a detailed account of pseudo-scientific racial thought in South Africa, and how the ideological content of racism changed over time, see Saul Dubow, *Scientific Racism in Modern South Africa* (Cambridge: Cambridge University Press, 1995).

Cape Town newspapers by the 1890s were full of vicious invectives against 'half-breeds'. Even Olive Schreiner, the novelist who became known for her socialist and anti-Imperialist sympathies, succumbed to such rhetoric. She wrote that 'half-castes' filled the gaols and brothels of the Colony, that they 'unite the vices of all races' and were particularly licentious, hated their own 'blood', and that Africans looked down on them.[141]

A book called *Of European Descent*, published in Cape Town in 1909, continued the attack, citing Schreiner as an expert on the topic. It provided what the authors declared were accounts of 'true' life histories that served as warnings against the 'insidious danger' of cross-racial liaisons in the city. The book advocated a ban on 'mixed' marriages and sexual intercourse, the careful supervision of White female servants, and thorough racial social segregation from school onwards.[142] Such views were still very much current throughout the British world up to the Second World War, and even beyond. One of the writers most responsible for ensuring that they were was Sarah Gertrude Millin, who had been part of the wave of Lithuanian Jewish immigration to South Africa. The dust-jacket of her best-selling and (to modern minds) deeply unpleasant *God's Step-Children* proclaimed, as late as the London and New York edition of 1951, that as Millin 'grew to young womanhood, the endless, self-repeating tragedy of mixed blood took horrified hold of her imagination'.[143] Like Emile Zola's *Les Rougon-Macquart* novels, 'blood' and heredity in *God's Step-Children* determines character. The fate of the progeny of cross-race sexual liaisons would be tragedy, and over many generations. At the end of the novel Barry, of 'mixed descent', refuses to leave for Britain with his White English wife and their son because of 'what had come down to me, and what I was handing on to others'. Instead he decides to work among 'my brown people', and 'for my sin in begetting him, I am not to see my child'.[144]

For Pratt, the consequences of such 'sins' were Cape Town's main problem. The city was the 'most civilized' place in South Africa, with a 'spirit of antiquity', and each suburb was 'a fairyland of restful beauty', but 'the evils of miscegenation' were greatest there. Miscegenation produced 'lazy and insolent . . . mongrels . . . [who] serve and hate the whites'

---

[141] *Cape Times*, 24 July 1896.

[142] Mary Frances Whalley and A. Eames-Perkins, *Of European Descent* (Cape Town: J.C. Juta, 1909). The declaration and warning was given at the outset in a 'Note to Readers'.

[143] S.G. Millin, *God's Step-Children* (London and New York: Constable and Co. and Boni and Liveright, 1924; Johannesburg: Central News Agency, 1951), the quotation is from the dustjacket of the 1951 edition; Coetzee, *White Writing*, 136–62 focuses on the theme of 'Blood, Taint, Flaw and Degeneration' in Millin's novels and makes the point that Millin's ideas were based on contemporary biological science.

[144] Millin, *God's Step-Children*, 306.

and who were barred from skilled jobs.[145] A similarly negative and racist depiction of the city characterised *Sold to the Malays* (1915), a cinematic melodrama from African Film Productions about 'white slavery'.[146] The film reflected genuine concern about the White slave trade in White colonial South African society. Court cases had revealed details of the international networks established in the country by the likes of the Bowery Boys.[147] Yet the sensationalism of films purportedly dealing with moral issues was one way that silent cinema throughout the world frequently sought to attract audiences before the introduction of stricter censorship and self-regulation.[148] The same went for literature, with newspapers, novelists and non-fiction writers often featuring the topic around the turn of the century, and the publication of the findings of an international congress on 'The White Slave Trade' held in London in 1899.[149] Both *Helena's Hope* and *Love and the Hyphen* referred to White slavery, with the suggestion that people only read about it in yellow-back novels for salacious purposes; a tea-room owner confiscates a book called *Maria Monk, or the White Slaves of Woodstock* from a waitress and denounces it as 'trash'.[150] As one historian of cinema in South Africa put it: 'Suggestiveness and indecency now [during the First World War] masqueraded as meritorious exposures of the "White Slave Traffic", as warnings to young girls of the dangers of city life, as anti-drink campaigns ... etc.'[151]

Commercial possibilities were surely in the minds of the makers of *Sold to the Malays*, whose plot had many popular ingredients along these lines. Yet to what extent, if at all, it was shown in South African cinemas is unclear. It is probable that the film fell foul of increased local and

[145] Pratt, *The Real South Africa*, 48–50.

[146] British Film Institute (BFI): *Sold to the Malays* (South Africa: African Film Production Company, c.1915). Seemingly the sole extant copy of this film is in the BFI, London. The single copy that survives confirms that it was made by African Film Productions, but it has thus far proved difficult to find details of its production circumstances or screening history. The copy in the BFI collection has several sequences out of logical narrative order or repeated, which may indicate that this at least was an unused version or versions. The BFI catalogue has dated the film at 1915, but there is no corroborating information on the print itself. To what extent it was shown in South Africa is unclear. There is no mention of the film in Gutsche, *Motion Pictures in South Africa*, which investigates a wide range of local (and foreign) films shown in South Africa up to the Second World War, and it might have fallen foul of tighter censorship.

[147] Van Onselen, *New Babylon*, 103–62; Van Onselen, *The Fox and the Flies*; Worden et al., *Cape Town: The Making of a City*, 234–7.

[148] Gutsche, *Motion Pictures in South Africa*, 291–4.

[149] National Vigilance Association, *The White Slave Trade: Transactions of the International Congress on the White Slave Trade* (London: Office of the National Vigilance Association, 1899). M.P. Botha (ed.), *Marginal Lives and Painful Presents: Cinema after Apartheid* (Cape Town: Genugtig, 2007).

[150] Gray, *Stephen Black*, 155.   [151] Ibid., 141.

international hostility to the distribution of 'improper' visual material in the mid-1910s, hostility expressed in the commission report on assaults on women, as well as at numerous public meetings and in letters to newspapers. This took legislative form in a Cape Provincial censorship ordinance in 1917 that prohibited the portrayal of 'White Slave Traffic' and 'Vampire Women' (vamps), as well as 'the Drug Habit' and 'improper impersonation of the King'.[152]

Whether screened or not, *Sold to the Malays* reflected commonly held contemporary White middle-class prejudices and 'Black Peril' anxieties in terms of race, nationality and gender. Remarkably, given that it was a product of the limited technology of early cinema, much of it contains what appear to be genuine exterior location shots of different parts of Cape Town. As a little known pioneer of the city film in South Africa, it merits some detailed description.[153] The opening sequence shows Cape Town's harbour and modern city centre, complete with trams and hansom cabs, in positive fashion; but once the heroine falls prey to White slavers, much greater attention is given to what is described in an intertitle as 'the Coloured quarter' and, to a lesser extent, a small Black shanty settlement. The former is depicted as a place of dirty alleys where inhabitants are shown living in shoddily furnished houses; the latter as somewhere of shabby poverty on the periphery of the city.

The melodramatic plot relates how a young English gentle-woman, Patricia Grey (of 'The Rectory, Baford') is tricked into coming to the Cape by a fake advertisement for a governess placed by an exotically non-British European couple called Mr and Mrs Torrandi. According to an inter-title, 'Patricia, noticing an objectionable picture [in the Torrandi house], begins to become suspicious'. But before she can escape, she is sold by the Torrandis to a lecherous and wealthy 'Malay' called Hadje Lalie Arend who wants to make her his wife.[154] Several other Malay characters, including the Torrandi henchmen 'Tiger' and '*Slang*' (snake) are portrayed in highly negative fashion: they kill a fisherman to whom Patricia had smuggled a message requesting help; they then hide Patricia with Coloured flower-sellers in the 'Coloured Quarter', though not before she has written another message, in her own blood, on the sole of a shoe thrown from her window.

---

[152] Gutsche, *Motion Pictures in South Africa*, 129–31, 283–305; quotations from pages 293–5.

[153] These other novels are referred to in Cornwell, 'George Webb Hardy's *The Black Peril*', 441–53.

[154] See Bickford-Smith, *Ethnic Pride and Racial Prejudice* for details of the 'Malays' and the ethnic complexity more generally of this port city.

Patricia is kept captive pending her submission to Arend's will, and beaten by her flower-seller captors. With her ability to resist evaporating, and in the process of being dressed in preparation for a Malay wedding, Patricia is only rescued at the last minute thanks to the alertness of two boy scouts, who find the shoe, and a plucky detective called Murray. In Sherlock Holmes manner, Murray dons various disguises (a drunk, a tramp) to bring this off. He and Patricia subsequently marry.

If anyone in the putative audience still wondered about the film's central message, a long inter-title near the end states:

The Malays have a passion for white girls, and will pay any amount of money for them, provided they are young and virtuous. A flourishing trade is done by anyone who will supply young European brides to this coloured race.[155]

The film's heroes were all British 'kith-and-kin'. So *Sold to the Malays'* narrative resolution clearly symbolises the triumph of those with such identity over 'others' who lived in un-British urban spaces, whether the Torrandi household with its lewd paintings, the 'Coloured Quarter' or a shanty settlement. Absent from the film are depictions of the way that many members of Cape Town's Black population, especially its elite, lived respectable lives as 'black British'.[156] This included APO leader and city councillor Dr Abdullah Abdurahman, whose first wife Helen Potter was the daughter of a Glaswegian solicitor.[157]

There are some significant similarities between *Sold to the Malays* and another melodramatic film, set partly in Durban, called *The Man Who Was Afraid* (1920). A little more is known about its production circumstances and screening history, although there appears to be no extant copy.[158] The film was shown in both South Africa and Britain, and the numerous reviews provide plot summaries.[159] One in the British press commented on the appeal of the Durban locale, mentioning like Hardy the presence of fantastically clad 'rickshaw boys' in wildly beaded and be-feathered versions of Zulu dress.[160]

The Man Who Was Afraid's plot has Sir Francis Tawse joining an international Secret Society in Britain that requires him to commit

[155] BFI, *Sold to the Malays*.   [156] Bickford-Smith, 'Betrayal of Creole Elites', 194–227.
[157] Mohamed Adhikari (ed.), *Dr. Abdurahman: A Biographical Memoir by J.H. Raynard* (Cape Town: Friends of the National Library of South Africa in Association with District Museum, 2002).
[158] Joseph Albrecht (dir.), *The Man Who Was Afraid* (South Africa: African Film Productions, 1920). It is mentioned in Gutsche and in several contemporary reviews. My thanks to Neil Parsons for generously providing me with his notes on this film.
[159] For instance, *South Africa Pictorial Stage and Cinema*, 14 August 1920; *The Bioscope*, 2 September 1920; *Daily Telegraph*, 2 September 1920; *Film Renter*, 3 September 1920; *Pall Mall Gazette*, 4 September 1920.
[160] *The Bioscope*, 2 September 1920.

murder. To avoid this, he escapes by ship to Durban. On arrival in the city he is immediately jeered and jostled by 'Indian urchins' at the Docks.[161] Tawse is then tortured by other Indians when he accidentally walks into 'an oriental prayer meeting' in an Indian area of the city, which results in his losing his memory and forgetting his identity.[162] As with *Sold to the Malays*, the existence of local Black Britishness is ignored. Rescued by a retired sea captain, Tawse marries the man's daughter and regains his memory. Seemingly safe on a farm in Natal, he is nonetheless tracked down by the Italian head of the Secret Society, who is defeated in a dramatic fight with Tawse on sea-swept rocks near Durban.[163]

Hence in both of these cinematic urban melodramas someone newly arrived from Britain is imperilled by unwitting encounters with people portrayed as decidedly un-British and dangerous, until these newcomers are rescued by local British White men. The message is clearly that danger stems from physically distinct and thus un-British locals, whose urban territory it would be folly to enter, as well as from continental Europeans, perhaps an unsurprising element of films made during or just after the First World War. Safety can only be achieved, appropriate social order gained or restored, by maintaining White British racial solidarity and avoiding social or residential mixing.

The Sanitation Syndrome and segregation

Disease was another cause for concern among urban residents. It was seldom dealt with by South African films before the Second World War, though an educational documentary was commissioned by the Chamber of Mines, *The Dust that Kills* (1921), which warned Johannesburg miners about phthisis.[164] Local newspapers became the main forum for popular concern, helping in the process to support Clean party-style expenditure on additional water supply and drainage and sewerage schemes. But editorials were commonly most strident on the topic only after an epidemic broke out, as with smallpox in 1881, Bubonic Plague in the early 1900s or Spanish flu in 1918.[165]

---

[161] *Film Renter*, 4 September 1920.   [162] *Trade Show Critic*, 17 September 1920.
[163] *The Bioscope*, 2 September 1920.
[164] Dr A.J. Orenstein (dir.), *The Dust that Kills* (South Africa: African Film Productions, 1921). See Gutsche, *Motion Pictures in South Africa*, 321. Dr Orenstein was Chief Medical Officer to Rand Mines Ltd. and a member of the Industrial Hygiene Committee. The film was regularly shown to miners through the agency of the Prevention of Accident Committee of the Rand Mutual Assurance Company.
[165] Swanson, 'Sanitation Syndrome'; E. Van Heyningen, 'Public Health and Society in Cape Town, 1880–1910' (PhD thesis, University of Cape Town, 1989); Howard Phillips, *Black October: The Impact of the Spanish Influenza Epidemic of 1918 on South*

Literature also worried about disease. One Digger poem described Johannesburg in 1889 as an 'unlovely town of iron and brick and wood, where the germ-laden wind swirls death and disease in alley, street, and square'.[166] Disease is also mentioned in de Bremont's Johannesburg stories set in the 1890s, and in Scully's *Daniel Vananda*, in which the protagonist dies of phthisis. Dhlomo's *An African Tragedy* alludes to venereal disease, contracted in cities from prostitutes and transmitted to the countryside, a result of the moral failings of men and women alike.

One novella put disease even more prominently centre stage. Published in Cape Town in 1902, *The Mysteries of the Secret Phial* was set during an imagined Bubonic Plague outbreak in the city in 1907.[167] Ostensibly about British secret agents protecting South Africa from Boer spies and their German allies, considerable attention was given to both the causes and consequences of the plague and descriptions of living conditions in the city. The somewhat mysterious author was a German immigrant called Albert Heyer. Heyer had been involved with SDF protests in Germany in the 1880s, and supposedly served in the Transvaal Secret Service in the 1890s before settling in Cape Town and opening a private detective agency in the southern suburbs by the time of the Boer War.[168]

Heyer's descriptions of the putative plague outbreak evidently drew on his close observations of what actually happened during its outbreak in Cape Town in 1901. This infected some 800 Capetonians of all races, almost half of whom died.[169] What was unusual about Heyer's writing about urban disease is that he made no use of morality or race to explain it, so did not scapegoat any racial group for its devastations. The plague, for Heyer, was simply the natural result of Cape Town being 'Slumtown' or 'the "Dirtiest City in the World"'. Disease was the consequence of 'vile slums, filthy streets and lanes, evil-smelling thoroughfares and insanitary houses and passages' in the 'east of the city, the "Whitechapel of the South"' (a reference to District Six).[170] It was not the result of social

---

Africa (Pretoria: Government Printer, 1990); Howard Phillips, 'Locating the Location of a South African Location: The Paradoxical Pre-History of Soweto', *Urban History* 41, 2 (2014), 311–32.

[166] C. Wilson-Moore and A.P. Wilson-Moore, *Diggers; Doggerel Poems of the Veld and Mine* (Cape Town: Argus Co., 1890), 90–1; also cited in Hofmeyr, 'The Mad Poets', 129–30.

[167] Albert E. Heyer, *The Mysteries of the Secret Phial: An Original South African Story of Afrikander Sedition, Rebellion, and Continental Conspiracy Against the Paramountcy of Great Britain in South Africa; Including Startling Disclosures Concerning a Bubonic Plague Camp in the Cape Division* (Cape Town: C. Heyer, 1902).

[168] Elizabeth Van Heyningen, 'The Mysteries of the Secret Phial: Spies and Plague in Cape Town in 1907', *Quarterly Bulletin of the South African Library* 34, 2 (December 1979), 53–8.

[169] Swanson, 'Sanitation Syndrome', 394.

[170] Heyer, *Mysteries of the Secret Phial*, 11.

habits of particular residents. On the other hand Heyer criticised colonial and municipal officials, and particularly their shoddy running of a plague isolation camp on the outskirts of the city, a thinly disguised version of events in 1901 when a camp of this kind was established.

Unfortunately officials dealing with the 1901 outbreak, which spread to Port Elizabeth, Durban and Johannesburg, did create scapegoats. Cape Town's Medical Officer of Health, Bernard Fuller, had previously promoted the idea that Africans lived in 'scattered nests of filth' in the city that made urban epidemics likely. Reflecting on the plague outbreak, he wrote:

> Rest the blame where it may, these uncontrolled Kafir hordes were at the root of the aggravation of Capetown slumdom brought to light when the plague broke out ... [Because of them] it was absolutely impossible to keep the slums of the city in satisfactory condition.[171]

The majority of White city journalists, doctors and municipal Medical Officers of Health like Fuller wrote in this fashion at the time. In doing so, they propogated 'Sanitation Syndrome' ideology that advocated racial separation as part of combating disease, and where metaphors like 'scattered nests of filth' were often employed to imply further moral or physical threats.[172]

This transcontinental ideology had been developed by networks of colonial officials representing different European colonial governments across Asia and Africa in the nineteenth century. Notable among them had been James Martin, a surgeon working in Calcutta. Martin arrived in the city in the middle of a cholera outbreak in 1817, and his *Medical Topography of Calcutta* (1837) combined contemporary British concerns about the dangerous social habits of the poor with eighteenth century theories about the divisibility of humankind into 'races'. One of Martin's conclusions was that because of racial customs and superstitions, Hindu-inhabited areas of Calcutta threatened the health of European residents. This logic was seized upon by the designers of British hill station cities like Simla and Ootacamund, where European residential areas called cantonments were set well apart from their Indian counterparts.[173]

---

[171] Swanson, 'Sanitation Syndrome', 392.
[172] This is the argument of not only Swanson's 'Sanitation Syndrome' article, but other pieces by the same author such as '"The Durban System"', cited above, and '"The Asiatic Menace"', 401–21; Bickford-Smith, *Ethnic Pride and Racial Prejudice*, 91–125; 158–63.
[173] Carl H. Nightingale, *Segregation: A Global History of Divided Cities* (Chicago and London: University of Chicago Press, 2012), 92–5.

For most White opinion and policy makers, Sanitation Syndrome ideology was a key element of a broader 'doctrine' that offered the panacea of segregation as a cure for all urban problems, and a blueprint for South African town planning.[174] In this doctrine, segregation provided the answer to the Native Question and what Maurice Evans termed its 'Asiatic and Coloured Sub-Problems'. It also offered the possibility of urban order and improvement. Segregation met White 'experts'' desire 'to prevent race deterioration, to preserve race integrity, and to give both [Black and White] opportunity to build and develop their race life'.[175] It solved the conundrum of how to 'provide for the mutual access of black labourers and white employers ... without having to pay the heavy social costs of urbanization or losing the dominance of white over black', a solution already suggested by the mine compounds of Kimberley and Johannesburg as well as rural reserves.[176]

Spatial division of cities along lines of perceived difference of nation, colour and race had a long history. Nineteenth century European colonialism drew on ideas about how to divide cities in this way borrowed across time and place.[177] The 'wild Irish' had been kept 'beyond the Pale' of earthwork barricades in English colonised Dublin in the fifteenth century. Native Americans were restricted to the other side of a wall (hence Wall Street) in Peter Stuyvesant's New Amsterdam (New York) in the seventeenth century. In eighteenth century Madras and Calcutta, where British trading posts and forts were placed next to existing indigenous settlements, DEIC officials demarcated a fortified White Town distinct from an unfortified Black Town. This colour-coding had been indirectly influenced by the Atlantic slave trade.[178]

The establishment of peri-urban 'Native Locations' by the 1840s for Port Elizabeth and East London, British immigrant settlements planted on the mobile and frequently violent frontier between the Cape Colony and the Xhosa, were in this European colonial tradition.[179] So was the Shepstonian system of establishing African reserves within walking distance of Durban, coupled with town curfews, like Native Americans told not to 'tarry ... during the night' in New Amsterdam.[180] The desire for control over 'barbarians' was also evident in the Transvaal Volksraad's

---

[174] Evans, *Black and White in South East Africa*, 216, 275–7. The doctrine of segregation is listed as such in his index on page 339.

[175] Evans, *Black and White in South East Africa*, 310. 'Asiatic and Coloured Sub-Problems' was the title of chapter ten of this book.

[176] Swanson, 'Sanitation Syndrome', 394.

[177] This is the argument of Nightingale, *Segregation*, which nonetheless acknowledges that it is not always easy, especially for pre-modern times, to demonstrate precisely how such borrowing occurred.

[178] Nightingale, *Segregation*, 67.   [179] Ibid., 31, 69–71.   [180] Ibid., 52.

decree of 1844 that no Africans could settle near towns without official permission.[181]

One difference between British colonies and Boer republics was that locations in the former allowed Christian evangelism. Port Elizabeth's Native Stranger's Location, established by Lutherans in 1847, was similar in this way to Native American 'mission' or 'prayer towns' placed adjacent to French and British settlements in seventeenth century North America.[182] So the establishment of locations in British South Africa incorporated the idea that they could be places of both spiritual and physical improvement, in keeping with the Imperial civilising mission. This optimistic vision was present in Evans' writing and in evidence given to successive commissions on Native affairs. It informed the views of two Africans interviewed by the Cape Native Location Commission of 1900. Both the Rev. Elijah Mdolomba and William Sipika believed that a Cape Town location would mean better housing and living conditions generally, even if this involved forced removals of thousands from inner city areas.[183] These views were in keeping with the intention of the Housing of the Working Classes Act (1890) in Britain, which made provision for the forced relocation of residents of 'slum' dwellings, and the destruction of the latter.[184] African elites could more easily support removals of this kind, or not offer great opposition, when they themselves were exempt and still able to purchase or rent decent property outside of locations.

Ideological and material reasons for wanting segregation were often mutually reinforcing. For mine owners in Johannesburg, compounds provided greater control over their labour force.[185] Labourers' barracks could provide a similar function from the perspective of municipal and government employers in all three cities. More thorough residential separation of all Black South Africans was desired by many White shopkeepers in Durban and Cape Town because it would remove competition, particularly from Indian retailers. In the meantime devices such as tougher building regulations, restriction on immigration and reduction in trading licences were deployed to this end.[186]

---

[181] David Welsh, 'The Growth of Towns', in Monica Wilson and Leonard Thompson (eds), *The Oxford History of South Africa*, vol. 2 (Oxford: Oxford University Press, 1971), 186.

[182] Nightingale, *Segregation*, 51–2.

[183] Bickford-Smith, *Ethnic Pride and Racial Prejudice*, 158–9.

[184] Nightingale, *Segregation*, 162.

[185] Maylam, 'Explaining the Apartheid City', gives both ideological and material reasons for segregation, leaning towards the latter as more important. However, given that the concept of race was at the heart of this process in South Africa and itself had to be imagined, it is perhaps difficult to ascribe primary determination to the economic, the more so when the *longue durée* global history of segregation, tackled by Nightingale, is brought into additional consideration.

[186] Swanson, '"Asiatic Menace"'; Bickford-Smith, *Ethnic Pride and Racial Prejudice*, 147–8.

Segregation in the thinking of most urban Whites would allow them 'to have the fruits of the growing city and tame its threats too'.[187] Most of these threats were recounted by Evans in *Black and White in South East Africa* as part of arguing for the desirability of urban segregation: Black criminality including Black Peril attacks; outbreaks of disease; immorality, miscegenation and the racial degeneration of Whites in the 'slums'. But segregation could also be promoted as protecting Africans from the contaminating influence of European vices, and accompanying temptations like strong alcohol and prostitution, and enabling better living conditions than in the 'slums'.[188]

These problems of urban disorder were raised by the Cape Native Location Commission of 1900. The commission consisted of Walter Stanford, head of the Cape Native Affairs Department, and three men whose jobs directly involved countering urban ills. Bernard Fuller as the Municipal Officer of Health was one of them. Dr John Gregory, the Colonial Medical Officer of Health, and Captain Jenner, Cape Town's Chief of Police, completed the trio.[189] Their joint recommendation was the residential segregation of urban Africans.

The South African Native Affairs Commission (SANAC) of 1903–5 came to the same conclusion. It was instigated by the British Transvaal government after the Boer War.[190] Much of the evidence it took concerned rural areas. Three officials chosen to give specialist evidence on conditions in cities were Major T.E. Mavrogordato, head of the Transvaal's Criminal Investigation Department (CID), Neason Adams Lowe, Superintendent of Cape Town's Dock's Location, and Superintendent of Durban Police Richard Alexander. Mavrogordato asserted that 'Johannesburg is undoubtedly the educational centre for crime for Natives … [that] flows through the towns of South Africa'.[191] White prostitutes with African pimps and clients conveyed the idea in African minds that every White woman was a 'whore', which encouraged Black peril outrages. Lowe thought that Coloured prostitutes and brandy were the 'demoralising influences' on African men in Cape Town.[192] All agreed that residential segregation would help solve such problems. Alexander wanted locations that could be 'towns of their own' for Africans, well away from city centres: 'There would be really no crime

---

[187] Nightingale, *Segregation*, 10.   [188] Ibid., 216–36.
[189] Cape Archives, Cape Native Affairs Department (NA) 457, 'Native Location Commission', 1900.
[190] South African Native Affairs Commission, *South African Native Affairs Commission* (Cape Town: Cape Times, 1905).
[191] *SANAC*, vol. 4, 862.   [192] *SANAC*, vol. 2, 120.

worth speaking of ... The men would be away enjoying themselves in their own town, and we should know nothing about it.'[193]

A major factor in restraining municipalities from instigating more rapid and substantial residential segregation remained the question of cost. Another was that the majority of employers worried that locations placed on the outskirts of the city might adversely affect their supply of labour. As Durban's municipal police commander Richard Alexander complained:

The moment it is found that the white employer must sacrifice something for the public good you will be told that you are attempting to interfere with the freedom of the subject and with the labour market.[194]

Most employers in industry, commerce, services and building industries preferred to house employees on their property, or nearby, as did most employers of domestic workers, like their counterparts in cities across the world at this time. In Durban, the cost of barrack accommodation made it unpopular with employees. Even when the lodging fee was dropped, available barrack accommodation was still but a fraction of the city's total African population. In Johannesburg, mining companies favoured housing its migrant employees in compounds. But employers involved in manufacturing industries colluded with the city council and landlords to allow Africans to live outside designated locations in the first two decades of the twentieth century. Ignoring Whites-only clauses in title deeds where they existed, Africans were accommodated in overcrowded back-yards in places like Doornfontein and City and Suburban near the city centre, as well as in the 'Malay location', better known as Malay Camp.[195]

Even when the municipality publically reversed its policy after the First World War, and built two new locations on the east and west edges of the city, it took many years before they removed substantial numbers of Africans from some areas such as Doornfontein. Africans remained in Malay Camp and the freehold townships to the west of the city like Sophiatown until the 1950s. In the same decade, some had returned to the east of the city centre, living in a shanty area dubbed Bottle Bar Township (see Illustration 5.1).

The advent of the global Bubonic Plague pandemic in 1894 did spur colonial authorities across Africa and Asia into some action, overcoming financial reservations and employer hesitations, and translated

[193] SANAC, vol. 3, 648–9.
[194] Swanson, '"The Durban System"', 165. For the opposition of many employers in Cape Town to residential segregation for Africans away from the city centre, see Bickford-Smith, Ethnic Pride and Racial Prejudice, 158–9.
[195] Susan Parnell, 'Race, Power and Urban Control: Johannesburg's Inner City Slum-Yards, 1910–1923', Journal of Southern African Studies 29, 3 (September 2003), 619–37.

segregation doctrine into at least somewhat greater practice. The pandemic started in Hong Kong and spread to cities across the Pacific, Asia and sub-Saharan Africa, prompting colonial officials to use the term 'segregation' for racial separation. Africans, Indians and Chinese were made scapegoats for outbreaks in different cities, with European experts arguing that segregation was essential to protect Whites from the disease. W.J. Simpson, Medical Officer of Health in Calcutta when plague hit India in 1896 and subsequently co-founder of the London School of Tropical Medicine, travelled extensively to cities affected by both plague and malaria, including Accra and Nairobi. His advice to colonial authorities was:

It is absolutely essential that ... town planning should provide well defined and separate quarters or wards for Europeans, Asiatics and Africans ... and that there should be a neutral belt of open unoccupied country at least 300 yards in width between the European residences and those of the Asiatic and Africa.[196]

'Plague emergency' action in Cape Town in 1901, taken by the Cape government rather than the municipality, followed this advice. It led to the establishment of two locations: one at the Docks, the other at Ndabeni on the outskirts of Cape Town. Their establishment was ratified *post facto* by legislation in the form of the Native Reserve Location Act of 1902, despite opposition from Ndabeni residents to paying train fares and location rents. The same Act gave legal sanction to further urban forced removals when plague hit Port Elizabeth and Africans were relocated to New Brighton location in 1903.[197]

In Johannesburg's case, as soon as plague had been discovered in the inner city 'Coolie Location', troops surrounded the area, its African, Indian and Coloured residents were evacuated, and their houses burnt down in a 'cleansing' method similar to that deployed by American officials following a plague outbreak in Honolulu in 1899.[198] Two weeks later, the Johannesburg city fire brigade completed the job. They surrounded six street blocks with a corrugated-iron fence, poured paraffin over what remained of its buildings, and set the whole area alight. Some 1,600 buildings were destroyed and 3,000 residents taken by ox-wagon sixteen kilometres south-west of the city centre to Klipspruit. Legislation only required Africans to remain there, though some absconded and joined Indians and Coloureds back in inner city areas like 'Malay Camp'. Those Africans who

[196] Nightingale, *Segregation*, 181.
[197] Swanson, 'Sanitation Syndrome'; Christopher Saunders, 'The Creation of Ndabeni: Urban Segregation and African Resistance in Cape Town', *Studies in the History of Cape Town* 1 (1979), 165–93.
[198] Nightingale, *Segregation*, 170–1.

remained found themselves neighbours to a city sewerage scheme, and ravaged by the likes of gastro-enteritis. Nonetheless, Klipspruit formed the beginnings of what became a cluster of south-western locations, later dubbed 'townships', explaining why the cluster was officially named South-Western Township or Soweto by the 1960s.[199]

In Durban, the visitation of plague in 1903 produced less immediate dramatic results beyond a Natal Native Locations Act the following year. Through this legislation, the Natal government gave the power of creating urban locations and concomitant costs to municipalities. But Durban officials were unwilling to take on the expense of housing all of its 18,000 African residents, given that they knew Cape Town's location for 6,000 people had cost some £100,000. So instead Durban's *togt* system of barrack accommodation was extended by only around 1,800 beds.[200]

The plague-induced flurry of forced removals and location construction in the end produced limited results. Most Africans who were affected wished to live near to their places of employment in city centres, so they voted with their feet and moved back there. Africans who qualified for the vote in the Cape and Natal were exempt from location legislation; Indians and Coloureds were not subject to it. Several individuals who gave evidence to SANAC made the point that new locations like Ndabeni and New Brighton in Port Elizabeth had not led to improvement in African accommodation: wretched living conditions and lawlessness continued, a further reason for residents' absconding.[201]

Most of the urban threats perceived by middle-class observers remained in the immediate post-First World War period. Yet from around the mid-1920s through to the late 1940s, pessimistic literary and visual representations of South African city life became less dominant. They did not disappear, but were outnumbered and their impact reduced by far more positive, sometimes utopian, urban depictions. This was partly the result of changing realities. Extended state power at central and local government level enabled both in combination to assert greater control over elements of urban disorder in inner city areas. More effective segregation of Africans was one of the results. So too were official efforts aimed at moralising the leisure time of the labouring classes. But more positive representations of the city were also the product of influential private and state place-selling efforts actively aimed at promoting Cape Town, Durban and Johannesburg as sunlit Utopias, both within southern Africa and internationally.

---

[199] Swanson, 'Sanitation Syndrome'; Beavon, *Johannesburg*, 75–8; Phillips, 'Locating the Location'.
[200] Swanson, '"The Durban System"', 170, 172.   [201] Ibid., 173.

4   Selling sunlit Utopias

A city of dignity and beauty seated at the foot of a blue mountain where
two oceans meet, and washed by a magic light that should make of men
poets, artists, and philosophers . . . here also are those things of the mind,
art and literature, interest in the past and love of tradition, without which
a city, no matter how fine, is just a body of buildings without a spirit.[1]

H.V. Morton, famous for his many travel books on Britain and the Holy
Land, visited South Africa in 1946 and published his impressions of the
country two years later. His comments on Cape Town, which he likened
to Athens, are nothing short of a eulogy. Though not quite as effusive
about South Africa's other two leading cities, Morton's judgements were
still overwhelmingly positive.

Durban reminded Morton of Miami. It was a 'delightful mixture of
business and fun' even if there was 'an air of musical comedy or a film set'
about the place. In Johannesburg, a local taxi driver warned the eminent
author that 'there's a murder a day in this place . . . shocking isn't it? Yes,
natives. We call them Amalayita [sic], which means toughs. Don't go
wandering about at night Guv'nor. Knock you on the head as soon as
look at you.' However, Morton described the taxi driver as a 'cruel and
destructive critic' of the city of gold and wrote that its suburbs possessed
'Californian luxuriance'. Johannesburg was a man-made wonder, 'a big
modern city with skyscrapers [where] only sixty years ago there was
nothing to be seen but a bare, treeless ridge and a few tents'. In addition
Morton wondered 'whether a more cosmopolitan population has filled
the streets of a city since the days of ancient Rome'.[2]

Morton's *In Search of South Africa* was well received by city governments, though his favourable opinions would hardly have come as a
surprise, for his travels had been subsidised by the South African
Railways and Harbours (SAR&H) department. In 1919 the SAR&H

---

[1] H.V. Morton, *In Search of South Africa* (London: Methuen and Co. Ltd, 1948), 11, 19.
[2] Ibid., 18–19, 209, 299–302. The taxi driver was obviously referring to Amalaita gangs,
   discussed in Chapter 3.

130

had established a publicity section that promoted tourism.[3] From 1927 onwards, the SAR&H had met with municipal publicity associations at annual National Publicity Association (NPA) conferences out of which came the South African Tourism Corporation (Satour) in 1938 to promote the country overseas. With NPA conferences suspended between 1939 and 1945, Satour came into greater effect after the war. Helping to arrange tours by potentially sympathetic foreign writers, travel industry experts and journalists became one of its functions.

Both Satour and the SAR&H facilitated Morton's visit. NPA minutes for 1946 reported that no effort was spared in ensuring that his visit would be 'successful', since its value to South Africa was 'enormous'. At the 1948 conference, the General Manager of SAR&H reported that *In Search of South Africa* 'would be on sale soon ... [and] be a very valuable contribution to our overseas publicity in even wider spheres than that of tourism'. The advent of a National Party apartheid government earlier in the year had made this task both more urgent and more difficult.[4] Nonetheless, the fact that the book ran to four editions suggests that money spent on Morton was not entirely wasted.

The Morton affair begins to illustrate how place-selling propaganda played a key role in the debate about South African urbanism. Publicity departments and local businesses moulded perceptions of South African cities, even if they could not do so entirely in circumstances of their own choosing. The pioneer department was the Cape Peninsula Publicity Association (CPPA) in 1909. After the First World War and the Rand Revolt, publicity associations were also set up for Durban (1922) and Johannesburg (1925).

Place-sellers like publicity association officials worked with inherited and often well-established views about the attractions and problems of particular cities, even if new attractions could be created or new problems discovered.[5] They had to consider current international opinion as well as contemporary realities and past representations of a city. In the event, South African city boosters often indicated an acute awareness of how

---

[3] Foster, *Washed with Sun*, 200–6. Foster explains that establishing a publicity arm of what was initially only the South African Railways department was first mooted in 1914 but postponed until after the First World War. The acquisition of a small merchant fleet and port expansion after the war led to 'Harbours' becoming part of this department in 1922.

[4] National Archives Repository Pretoria, SAB MGT 2/3/1/268, *Minutes of South African National Publicity Association Conference Bloemfontein 5&6 November 1946* (Pretoria: Government Printer, 1946); *Minutes of South African National Publicity Association Conference Lourenço Marques 15& 16 September 1948* (Pretoria: Government Printers, 1948).

[5] Kolb, *Tourism Marketing for Cities and Towns*, xv. See also Vivian Bickford-Smith, 'Creating a City of the Tourist Imagination: The Case of Cape Town, "The Fairest Cape of Them All"', *Urban Studies* 46, 9 (August 2009), 1763–85.

visitors, immigrants or investors might judge their cities.[6] By the 1920s, they were responsible for ensuring that a continual flow of positive literary and visual depictions of South African urbanism were in national and international circulation.

More positive representations of South African cities were also the result of changing historical circumstances. The media throughout the anglophone world was dominated by middle-class Whites, few of whom yet questioned racial discrimination or colonialism. The crushing of the Rand Revolt and absence of further major pandemics such as the Spanish flu formed part of these circumstances. So did better economic prospects for South Africa, despite a short hiatus between 1929 and 1932 created by the Great Depression. The immediate future of the gold mining industry was secured with the suppression of the Rand Revolt. Output of gold recovered strongly, from 7 million fine ounces in 1922 to more than 10 million two years later, as did gold's value. Exports showed similar improvement.[7]

Predominantly positive representations of cities reflected the self-confidence of anglophile urban elites within the country as well as observers elsewhere in the British world. The fact that South Africa remained within the Empire helped greatly, even after the pro-Imperial Smuts government was defeated in 1924 by a coalition of the Afrikaner National Party and (as junior partner) the Labour Party. Despite its composition, what was dubbed the Pact government under General Hertzog did not undermine either anglophone commercial ascendancy or Imperial ties. Hertzog wrote that he wished 'every citizen of the Union was a capitalist'.[8] City elites could continue to make money while remaining part of a British world and the networks that helped bind it together.

The South African media, clustered in the cities, continued to strengthen ties by making the British world part of everyday urban sensibilities. Local newspapers contained numerous reports and photographs of British scenery, events and issues: Trafalgar square, Queen Charlotte's Hospital or the Serpentine in London; Princess Elizabeth visiting a West End theatre; unusually heavy snow falls in the countryside; the launching of the Queen Mary; or how Britain was tackling its housing problem.[9]

---

[6] For an account of how towns and cities were promoted over a 150-year period in Europe and North America, see Ward, *Selling Places*.
[7] Feinstein, *Economic History*, 102, 105.
[8] Cited in Bill Freund, 'South Africa: The Union Years, 1910–1948' in Ross et al. (eds), *Cambridge History of South Africa*, 226.
[9] John Lambert, '"The Thinking Is Done in London": South Africa's English Language Press and Imperialism', in C. Kaul (ed.), *Media and the Empire* (London: Palgrave Macmillan, 2006), 37–54. Histories of local city newspapers, which give a good sense of their content, include: Wilks, *For the Love of Natal*; Gerald Shaw, *The Cape Times: An Informal History*

British books and periodicals, plentifully available in South African cities, also told of 'snow, babbling brooks, yuletide fare ... London and the Lake District' or the thoughts of Dickens on the urban poor in Victorian Britain.[10] British feature films may have been challenged by more popular Hollywood products, but they too taught many things British as well as sanitised versions of the Imperial civilising mission itself in *Livingstone* (1925), *Sanders of the River* (1935) and *Rhodes of Africa* (1936), to name but three.[11]

So too did British newsreels, screened regularly alongside their *African Mirror* counterparts in South African cinemas. Many editions of *African Mirror* before the 1950s also contained pieces that promoted British South African identity, including the two world wars and Trafalgar Day commemorations, visits by British warships and celebrities, and ceremonies accompanying the arrival and departure of British Governor-Generals. Some demonstrated connections between Britishness and material and moral progress by showing Governor-Generals or their wives review Boy Scout and Girl Guide parades, or opening buildings like the Johannesburg Public Library in 1936.[12] From 1930, British radio news and entertainment was relayed as part of South African broadcasting programmes; two years later it was independently available through the Empire (later Overseas) service of the BBC. Newsreels and radio

(Cape Town: David Philip, 1999); Michael Morris, *Paging Through History: 150 Years of the Cape Argus* (Cape Town: Jonathan Ball, 2007); *Today's News Today* (Cape Town; Argus, 1956); James Clarke (ed.), *Like It Was: The Star 100 Years in Johannesburg* (Johannesburg: Argus Printing Company, 1987); Benjamin Pogrund, *Sheer Cussedness: A History of the 'Rand Daily Mail'* (Cape Town: David Philip, 2003).

[10] Hirson, *Rebel Pity*, 39.

[11] M.A. Wetherell (dir.), *Livingstone* (UK: Butcher's Film Service, 1925); Zoltan Korda (dir.), *Sanders of the River* (UK: London Film Productions, 1935); Berthold Viertel (dir.), *Rhodes of Africa* (UK: Gaumont British Picture Corporation, 1936).

[12] For instance, SANFVSA: FA 140, *African Mirror* 485 (1920), 'Cape Town, Trafalgar Day: Display at Rosebank by Crews from HMS Dublin and Lowstoft'; FA 141, *African Mirror* 365 (1920), 'Sir Harry Lauder Visits the Rhodes Memorial, Groote Schuur, Cape Town, Empire Builder's Memorial'; FA 140, FA 23, *African Mirror* 446 (1921), 'HRH Prince Arthur Unveils Headstone of Memorial Chapel, St Mary's Church'; 'The Two Minute Pause: Service in Memory of Armistice Day'; FA 106, *African Mirror* 432 (1921), 'A Royal Rally: Princess Arthur of Connaught Inspecting Girl Guides at Albert Park, Durban'; 'Cape Town: Funeral Cortege of the Late Captain Proctor, V.C., Passing up Adderley Street'; FA 13, *African Mirror* 480 (1922), 'Pretoria: Delville Wood Memorial Service, Service and Parade on Church Square'; FA 1215 *African Mirror* 665 (1925), 'Johannesburg: Governor-General Takes the Salute at an Annual Scout Rally'; 'Cape Town: Ceremony Marks the Celebration of Armistice Day'; 'The English Team Arrives in Cape Town'; FA 257, *African Mirror* 850 (1929), 'The Men Who Fought and Won'; 'Wreath Laid on Cape Town Memorial in Memory of Old Comrades'; FA 164 *African Mirror* 164 (1935), 'Prince George Arrives in Cape Town'; FA 142, *African Mirror* 334 (1945), 'Naval Base and Fete, Simonstown, Docks Thrown Open for "Thank You Britain Week"'.

transmitted British traditions new and old, whether those associated with sporting events like the FA Cup and the Boat Race or with royalty; the monarch's Christmas speech was broadcast live across the Empire from 1932.[13] Even in Johannesburg mine compounds, Black workers were shown 'King George ... [opening] Parliament in his curious equipage', as part of free open-air cinema shows organised by ABM missionary Ray Phillips.[14] All of this exposure may explain the highly personal expressions of loyalty, huge crowds and seemingly genuine enthusiasm that accompanied Royal Tours of South African cities in the first half of the twentieth century. Many who turned up presumably felt that they already knew the Royal visitor involved, whether Edward, Prince of Wales who visited in 1925, Prince George in 1934 or Princess Elizabeth and her family in 1947.[15]

For White South Africans, the fact that per capita income was gradually rising in the inter-war period also boosted optimism.[16] Hertzog's government helped the White poor in this respect by building on earlier policies of state intervention that favoured White employment over Black and higher wages for Whites. These policies gave Whites easier access to artisan apprenticeships, extended welfare benefits and created land re-settlement schemes. In one analysis, such measures along with industrial arbitration mechanisms produced a working class united with employers in mutual pursuit of White supremacy.[17]

Government initiatives along these lines were given moral support in 1932 by an independent commission into White poverty funded by the Carnegie Corporation, motivated on its part by concern for poor Whites in the American South. Published in five volumes, the commission report argued that Whites went to large cities like Johannesburg for better employment prospects and the possibility of charitable relief; factory employment for women was specifically mentioned as helping family income. The Witwatersrand drew unemployed Whites from all over the Union, while Cape Town and Port Elizabeth were major destinations for those within the Cape Province. Because they arrived as adults with few technical skills and little English, Afrikaners often struggled when 'forced into permanent competition with the non-European unskilled labourer with a low standard of living who is prepared to work at very low

---

[13] Eric Rosenthal, *You Have Been Listening: A History of the Early Days of Radio Transmission in South Africa*, (Cape Town: Purnell & Sons, 1974); Sean Street, *A Concise History of British Radio, 1922–2002* (Tiverton: Kelly Publications, 2005).
[14] See Ray E. Phillips, *The Bantu Are Coming: Phases of South Africa's Race Problem* (London: Student Christian Movement Press, 1930), 142.
[15] Sapire, 'Royal Tour'.   [16] Feinstein, *Economic History*, 11.
[17] Stanley E. Greenberg, *Race and State in Capitalist Development: South Africa in Comparative Perspective* (New Haven: Yale University Press, 1980).

wages.[18,] Part of Johannesburg's attraction was that its municipality offered preferential employment to hundreds of poor Whites, which cost it £90,000 more than if only Africans had been hired.[19]

State employment patronage for poor Whites was further aided by the formal requirement that government employees should be bilingual in Afrikaans and English. Employment possibilities were boosted by the extension of harbour and railway infrastructure and the establishment of parastatal industries like the Electricity Supply Commission (ESCOM) and Iron and Steel Industrial Corporation (ISCOR). On the railways, for instance, the proportion of unskilled White workers rose under the Pact government from around 10 per cent in 1924 to nearly 40 per cent by 1933. Schooling that was subsidised at a far higher rate than for Blacks remained a key factor in pulling Whites out of poverty in the long term.[20]

Apart from helping poor Whites, the Pact government asserted Afrikaner nationalist interests by having Afrikaans recognised as an official language, introducing a South African flag alongside the Union Jack, and obtaining full Dominion powers for South Africa. The alternative Afrikaner national anthem for South Africa, *Die Stem*, was now sometimes sung on public occasions.[21] But the new flag still incorporated a Union Jack and South Africa was only emulating the likes of Australia or Canada in becoming a Dominion. The British monarch remained head of state, the British national anthem was retained; in 1933 Smuts returned to government as part of a new coalition, albeit Hertzog remained the prime minister.

This development stemmed from the political and economic problems wrought by the Great Depression between 1929 and 1932, and Pact's concomitant waning popularity. In 1932 South Africa was forced to abandon the gold standard, which linked its pound to the price of gold. The following year, Smuts' South African Party agreed to join Hertzog's National Party in coalition, and in 1934 the parties merged as the United

---

[18] Carnegie Commission, *The Poor White Problem in South Africa: Report of the Carnegie Commission* (Stellenbosch: Ecclesia, 1932), xxiii. This was the joint findings and recommendations gleaned from all five volumes, and published at the beginning of each of them by way of introduction. The five volumes were divided into separate economic, psychological, educational, health and sociological reports whose main focus was rural rather than urban but still included comments on the cities.

[19] Carnegie Commission, *The Poor White Problem*, ix, xx–xxiv; J.W.F. Grosskopf, *Economic Report: Rural Impoverishment and Rural Exodus, Carnegie Commission*, vol. 1 (Stellenbosch: Ecclesia, 1932).

[20] Nicola Nattrass and Jeremy Seekings, 'The Economy and Poverty in the Twentieth Century', in Ross et al. (eds), *Cambridge History of South Africa*, 531–3. See also Freund, 'South Africa: The Union Years', 227–30.

[21] H. Saker, *The South African Flag Controversy*, 1925–8 (Cape Town: Oxford University Press, 1980).

(South African National) Party. Only a small rump of Afrikaner MPs under D.F. Malan consequently split away to form the *Gesuiwerde Nasionale Party* (GNP, Purified National Party), ultimately victorious in the 1948 elections. The price of gold and with it the country's economic fortunes recovered rapidly, and the period between 1933 and 1945 was one of economic boom.[22]

Participation in the war brought approval and glowing representations of South Africa and its cities in Allied media. Smuts returned as prime minister, after Hertzog lost the parliamentary vote on participation and left the United Party, and became an iconic wartime leader. He was given the rank of Field Marshal in the British Army, and made a member of Churchill's Imperial War Cabinet. The United Party went on to win a convincing victory in a general election in 1943, helped by the war turning in favour of the Allies. Once the war had ended, the Royal Tour of 1947 gave renewed energy to British identity within South Africa while ensuring positive coverage of all its cities in both the domestic and British world media.

For White anglophone elites within South Africa, more positive perceptions of their cities required not just the continued sense of belonging that Royal Tours enhanced but also the taming of threats to urban order. As elsewhere in the world, the extension of electric street lighting in and around city centres was welcomed as promoting night-time security.[23] However, two broader processes were more important. One was the improved capacity of the local and central state to monitor, regulate and finance solutions to urban problems, aided by advances in technology that strengthened earlier methods of documenting and controlling citizens.[24] The other involved efforts by the state and civil society to dissuade Black elites from participation in radical politics and to continue propagating respectable British values among urban Blacks in general.

---

[22] Freund, 'South Africa: The Union Years'; Nattrass and Seekings, 'The Economy and Poverty'.

[23] David Nasaw, *Going Out: The Rise and Fall of Public Amusements* (Boston, MA: Harvard University Press, 1999), 7–9.

[24] This is still a history under-written for South Africa, apart from the considerable body of work on Native Affairs Administration, if particularly 'influx control' pass regulation. Much of this is referred to in Ivan Evans, *Bureaucracy and Race: Native Administration in South Africa* (Berkeley: University of California Press, 1997). See also Keith Breckenridge, 'No Will to Know: The Rise and Fall of African Civil Registration in 20th Century South Africa', in Keith Breckenridge and Simon Szreter (eds), *Registration and Recognition: Documenting the Person in World History* (Oxford: Oxford University Press, 2012). A pathbreaking work that explores the acquisition of 'knowledge' by the state in an even broader sense and that is suggestive for future possibilities in South African research is C.A. Bayly, *Empire and Information: Intelligence Gathering and Social Communication, 1780–1870* (Cambridge: Cambridge University Press, 1999).

Both processes observably reinforced one another in the period between the two world wars. Political and economic reconstruction under British suzerainty after the Boer War had led to the Union of South Africa in 1910. The impact of this major step in the reorganisation and expansion of central state power in the region took a while to be realised through national policies to improve urban conditions. Additionally, labour difficulties, rebellion and the First World War occupied much of the Union government's attention until 1918.

Consequently the response of government to the findings of a 1914 report on tuberculosis in South African cities, particularly extensive in overcrowded and predominantly Black residential areas, was delayed.[25] Both Durban and Cape Town municipalities had to set up their own Tuberculosis Bureaus to tackle the disease. Only the Spanish flu outbreak at the end of the war prodded central government into action. The Public Health Act in 1919 made notification of infectious diseases and combating epidemics the responsibility of municipalities, but stipulated that central government would refund 66 per cent (raised later to 80 per cent) of costs involved. Local officials had successfully argued that cities were 'becoming the dumping ground' for sufferers of tuberculosis and other infectious diseases from further afield, as the Medical Officer of Health for Cape Town testified.[26]

The Act gave local health officers the task of producing annual reports on housing conditions to guide the Public Health Department in terms of potential policy interventions. One result was that from 1920, central government loans were offered to municipalities for eradicating inadequate housing and providing alternative accommodation. Only limited use was made of the offer. Local authorities struggled to get legal permission to demolish 'slum nuisances', and dilapidated buildings were simply reoccupied. Local ratepayers (predominantly White) also baulked at paying any costs involved, especially for Black housing. Only the passing of a Slums Act in 1934 gave a municipality clear legal authority to declare properties as 'slums' that could be demolished without compensation.[27]

[25] UG SC 35–1914, *Report of the Select Committee on Tuberculosis* (Cape Town: Cape Times Ltd, Government Printers, 1914).

[26] UG SC 3–1919, *Report of the Select Committee on the Public Health Bill* (Cape Town: Cape Times Ltd, Government Printers, 1919), 61.

[27] UG SC 17–1934, *Report of the Select Committee on the Subject of the Slums Bill* (Cape Town: Cape Times Ltd, Government Printers, 1934), 5–8, 11, 13–14, 31–2.

The Durban system and the extension of African residential segregation

African barracks, compounds and locations were specifically excluded from the provisions of the Slums Act. Instead, providing better accommodation for Africans was tied to the implementation of residential segregation, now the responsibility of municipalities and linked to notions of urban improvement. Debate remained on an acceptable way to pay for this. The kernel of a Union-wide solution, one subsequently emulated by cities beyond South Africa in British sub-Saharan colonies like Dar es Salaam, came through the passing of the Natal Beer Act in 1908.[28] Despite protests from White and Black temperance groups, the Beer Act allowed Durban municipality to establish a monopoly on the production and sale of 'traditional' beer. This was sold in beer halls under their control, while domestic brewing by African women remained illegal. Proceeds from municipal beer sales together with fines, rental and licence payments by Africans were sufficient by 1916 for Durban to form its own Native Affairs Department and begin to extend African accommodation in the city.[29] Already by 1912, beer revenues were bringing in four times the revenue of the *togt* licensing system.

The Durban system provided a way of paying for African administration that included segregated housing. It promised a future in which this could be made compulsory for all urban Africans without burdening White ratepayers with the cost. Extended housing in Durban in the first two decades after implementation of the Beer Act was still mainly for single men, whether in the original municipal barracks in Bell Street or in the Baumanville and Somtseu compounds. But limited provision was now made for married couples, and a hostel added for single women. Larger locations further from the city centre with family housing as hoped for by Chief Police Alexander only followed in the 1930s, in the form of developments like Lamontville. The Union government also, if reluctantly, allowed a Clermont Township (Pty) Ltd syndicate to develop a more central freehold suburb for Africans on ex-Berlin Mission land. Clermont had the support of both the Durban Town Council and

---

[28] Justin Willis, 'Unpretentious Bars: Municipal Monopoly and Independent Drinking in Colonial Dar es Salaam', in James R. Brennan, Andrew Burton and Yousuf Lawi (eds), *Dar es Salaam: Histories from an Emerging African Metropolis* (Dar es Salaam and Nairobi: Mkuki na Nyota Publishers and The British Institute in Eastern Africa, 2007), 157–74.

[29] Willis, 'Unpretentious Bars', 174–6. See also, La Hausse, 'The Struggle for the City: Alcohol, the Ematsheni and Popular Culture in Durban, 1902–36', in Maylam and Edwards (eds), *The People' City*, 33–66.

prominent local Africans, including John Dube and King Solomon of the Zulus.[30]

However it was municipal-controlled provision of segregated housing financed by the Durban system that became central to Union-wide policy after the First World War, even if debate continued on the precise form and purpose of accommodation. Two government reports in 1922 presented contrasting recommendations. The Godley Commission supported the principle of allowing a permanent, Western-educated African urban population of skilled workers and traders alongside unskilled rural migrant labourers, with the two categories requiring different housing. The Stallard Commission rejected this differentiation because 'If the Native is . . . a permanent element in municipal areas . . . there can be no grounds for basing his exclusion from the franchise on the simple ground of colour'.[31] Africans should only be allowed in towns on a temporary basis for work purposes. Their proper homes were in the reserves. Complete segregation of Black and White in town and countryside should remain the aim of Union African policy.

When a Natives (Urban Areas) Act was eventually passed in 1923 it was a compromise between the two views, if leaning towards the Stallard Commission's perspective. The 1923 Act formed the lynchpin of government policy on urban Africans up to the 1960s. In keeping with the more liberal ideas of the Godley Commission, it did retain the idea that municipalities could build 'Native Villages' with decent amenities for settled African family life, paid for out of money raised from Africans themselves. But demonstrating Stallardist influence, these villages would not allow freehold ownership still obtainable in inner city areas like Sophiatown, Johannesburg. Forced removals of Africans from any such areas could only take place if alternative accommodation was available.

Individual municipalities were allowed to determine when to introduce the Act. They were then obliged to open Native revenue accounts administered separately from the rest of their budgets. African accommodation and amenities were to be paid for in the way the Durban system had pioneered. All African men would have to seek documented municipal permission to look for work. Once obtained, the employment contract had to be registered, and the municipality could remove 'idle, dissolute or disorderly' Africans from the city. These restrictive elements of the 1923 Act were extended to apply to African women in 1930. A further amendment in 1937 stipulated that municipalities had to exercise a monopoly on

---

[30] Louise Torr, 'Lamontville: A History, 1930–1960', in Maylam and Edwards (eds), *The People's City*, 245–73; Maynard Swanson, 'The Joy of Proximity: The Rise of Clermont', in Maylam and Edwards (eds), *The People's City*, 274–98.
[31] Cited in Welsh, 'Growth of Towns', 228; Worden, *Making of Modern South Africa*, 43–4.

beer production and distribution or otherwise allow domestic beer brewing.[32]

Further attempts at taming the disorderly city

The combination of White electoral control, increased tax revenues and stronger law and order agencies encouraged central and local governments to introduce further legislation aimed at producing urban order. This included municipal by-laws against various kinds of urban 'nuisances' from building regulations to night-time noise. But after the suppression of the Rand Revolt, government officials associated urban order particularly with controlling Africans. This often involved brutal policing methods no longer used on Whites, in raids for Africans without passes, or illegal beer brewers, or non-payers of tax. In Johannesburg, the police even deployed large trucks around the city to accelerate the processing of pass offenders, doubtless contributing to the Transvaal accounting for 90 per cent of 40,000 Africans arrested in this category in the early 1930s.[33]

New legislation was introduced in the inter-war period aimed at increasing government powers over Africans, and making resistance more difficult. The Native Administration Act of 1927 made the Governor-General Supreme Chief over every African in the Union, which meant almost unrestricted executive powers over movement of individuals, appointment of chiefs, judicial procedure, the carrying of passes and censorship.[34] A new Riotous Assembly Act of 1930 gave the Minister of Justice the power without trial to 'banish, ban or prohibit any person, public meeting or book, if in his opinion there was reason to believe that they would cause hostility between whites and other people'.[35]

Enforcing laws to control Africans, like other legislation aimed at urban order, required well trained and efficient national military and police forces. Creating consolidated, technologically modern agencies of law and order took time, even if it was a legislative priority for the Union government. The South African army, for instance, was brought into being by the Defence Act of 1912. This gave it a policing function within the country, just as members of the police could be deployed within the

[32] Welsh, 'The Growth of Towns', 197–9.
[33] Edgar H. Brookes, *The Colour Problems of South Africa: Being the Phelps-Stokes Lectures, 1933, Delivered at the University of Cape Town* (London and Alice: Kegan Paul, Trench, Trubner, & Co., Ltd, and Lovedale Press, 1933), 97.
[34] Davenport, *Modern History*, 266–7.
[35] Jack Simons and Ray Simons, *Class and Colour in South Africa* (London: International Defence and Aid Fund, 1983), 430.

defence force. A paramilitary element typical of colonial policing consequently became part of the Union government's attempts to maintain law and order, especially when dealing with Black South Africans.[36] However, the Union Defence Force (UDF) 'was a marriage of British and Boer traditions ... [that] did not have an easy time of it between the sheets'; hardly surprising given that the Boer War was so recent.[37] The UDF's first commander was an ex-Transvaal general frequently at odds with more enthusiastically pro-Empire officers. Disputes included Afrikaner antipathy to the wearing of British khaki, the lack of bilingualism and British insistence that soldiers needed short haircuts and had to be clean shaven. When South Africa entered the First World War on the side of Britain, a number of ex-Boer officers led the Afrikaner rebellion of 1914.[38] But the army demonstrated its effectiveness by suppressing the rebellion and defeating the Rand Revolt eight years later.

The merging of pre-existing police forces into the South African Police (SAP) and South African Mounted Rifles (for rural areas), inauspiciously set to take effect on 1 April 1913, posed many similar problems. British South Africans remained over-represented at officer level, while Afrikaners increasingly dominated the White rank and file. Matters were made more complicated by the fact that British colonial cities like Durban and Cape Town had their own municipal forces, while Johannesburg mine compounds were unofficially policed by men drawn from the ranks of mineworkers.[39] The quality of recruits to the SAP as well as manpower levels also fell short of expectations over the first decade or so.

By the second half of the 1920s the creation of a modern national police force was well underway. Numbers and educational levels of recruits rose, as did the average time they spent in the force, producing a corps of more experienced officers. The organisation of a national CID was an important part of modernisation. Before this, there had been separate CIDs for the major cities, the first of these established in Durban in 1894. By the mid-1920s, the SAP controlled a centralised CID service with branches in all the main cities. Plainclothes detectives and informants were deployed against professional criminals or those deemed to be political subversives. African 'Trap Boys' were used as bait in catching Whites

---

[36] David Anderson and David Killingray (eds), *Policing the Empire* (Manchester: Manchester University Press, 1991).

[37] Bill Nasson, *Springboks on the Somme: South Africa in the Great War, 1914–1918* (Johannesburg: Penguin, 2007), 38. For the policing function accorded the South African defence force, see John D. Brewer, *Black and Blue: Policing in South Africa* (Oxford: Clarendon Press, 1994), 38.

[38] Nasson, *Springboks on the Somme*, 38–45.   [39] Brewer, *Black and Blue*, 1–104.

selling liquor to Africans.[40] The Criminal Bureau of the national CID housed tens of thousands of fingerprints, photographs and drawings used to identify suspects. These were but a few of many technologies added to an ever extending array at the disposal of the police in monitoring and regulating urban populations. By the late 1920s, the telephone, radio, police cars and pick-up vans supplemented foot, bicycle and horse patrols. Hand-guns, rifles, machine-guns and teargas were additions to police weaponry. By the mid-1930s, a small number of police cars were equipped with radio communication.[41]

The state needed strong armed forces. If White workers became more submissive after 1922, Black workers and some among Black elites did not. Objection to the pass laws and general dismay at White racism remained a major issue for all Black urban residents. So for most did the high cost of rented accommodation and transport as well as police raids, whether for passes, tax collection or the suppression of home brewing by African women.

These discontents were given a unified voice by political organisations and trade unions in the aftermath of the First World War. Resentment at White racism, low wages, poor housing and rising living costs persuaded members of the small Black educated elite within the Transvaal branch of the ANC to make brief common cause with workers. Some among this elite were influenced in doing so by a strong sense of mutual Zulu identity, though most withdrew from militancy after the violent suppression of the 1920 strike.[42]

The post-war cross-class militancy among Durban's Black elite stemmed from similar motives, although lasting somewhat longer. It was fashioned by John Dube's Natal branch of the ANC and the ICU under the local leadership of A.G. Champion. ICU membership grew to a peak of some 100,000 members countrywide by 1927, before falling into decline. In addition, the CPSA transferred its attention from White to Black workers after the failed Rand Revolt. Although the CPSA only had a meagre 1,750 members by 1928, most were Black, and its message could reach beyond paid-up members. Both the ICU and CPSA used

---

[40] For Johannesburg's mixed success in some early efforts in this respect see Charles Van Onselen, *Studies in the Social and Economic History of the Witwatersrand, 1886–1914, Vol. 2 New Nineveh* (Harlow: Longman, 1982), 103–62.

[41] Brewer, *Black and Blue*, 56–168. Brewer provides detailed statistics on the likes of police finances, manpower levels, wastage, racially differentiated salaries and proportion of police to civilians.

[42] Phil Bonner, 'The Transvaal Native Congress, 1917–1920: The Radicalisation of the Black Petty Bourgeois on the Rand', in Marks and Rathbone (eds), *Industrialisation and Social Change*, 270–313; Paul La Hausse, '"Death Is Not the End": Zulu Cosmopolitanism and the Politics of the Zulu Cultural Revival', in Benedict Carton, John Laband and Jabulani Sithole, *Zulu Identities: Being Zulu, Past and Present* (Pietermartizburg: University of KwaZulu-Natal Press, 2008), 256–71.

confrontational language while advocating more direct action. As future Western Cape ANC leader James Thaele put it in the ICU's paper, *The Workers Herald*, in 1923:

We are fed up with the white man's camouflage, his hypocrisy, his policy of pinpricks in the land of our forefathers ... when those in authority become so unreasonable ... disregard that authority, be blind and damn the consequences.

ICU leader Clements Kadalie's pithy comment was, 'There is no native problem, but a European problem of weakness, greed and robbery'.[43]

The fact that some among the ANC's leadership became temporarily more radical in the late 1920s was partly a reaction to Union government plans to introduce a number of 'Native Bills'. One of these threatened to destroy any lingering hope of the extension of the Cape franchise north-wards by removing Africans from it even in that province. For a few leaders, it also stemmed from their exposure to Communist or Garveyite 'Africa for the Africans' rhetoric. The CPSA encouraged such thought by flirting with the idea of a 'Native Republic' as a stage on the road to the construction of a peasants' and workers' state.[44]

The ICU, CPSA and ANC briefly came together within a 'League of African Rights' in 1929. All condemned a new and more stringent Riotous Assembly Act aimed at curbing their political activism. The League wanted to collect a million signatures in favour of protecting freedom to protest and other civic rights, and provocatively chose 16 December, the Afrikaner nationalist holiday of Dingaan's Day, to hold pass demonstrations.[45]

Several songs became popular across class divides by the late 1920s, and suggest that political activists were tapping into widespread frustration with hardships and state interference in African city life. The lyrics of the League's anthem '*Mayibuye i Afrika*' (Let Africa Return), sung to the tune of My Darling Clementine, went in part:

> We, the Black Race, cry for freedom!
> Africa, our Mother Land,
> Was taken from our fathers
> When the darkness hemmed them round.
>
> Give it back now! Give it back now!
> Give us back our Africa!
> Let us break our chains – the passes.
> Rightly striving to be free.[46]

---

[43] Cited in Tom Lodge, *Black Politics in South Africa since 1945* (Johannesburg: Ravan Press, 1987), 6.
[44] Ibid., 8–9.   [45] Simons and Simons, *Class and Colour*, 416–18.
[46] Cited in Ibid., 418.

Another song was '*Sixotshwa Emsebenzini*' (We Are Being Expelled from Work), which criticised mid-1920s legislation favouring White employment.

> A serious problem is facing the black nation.
> Whites are expelling us from work.
> They only employ whites.
> We have been working for them for many years, without any problems.
> But now blacks are excluded from work
> In Durban and Johannesburg . . .
> What are we going to do, people?[47]

Some songs were less overtly political but still made mention of urban difficulties facing Africans. Two mentioned the possibility of arrest for infringing liquor legislation. In '*Ingoduso*' (Fiancée), a man is arrested after his enemies put alcohol in his room and then call the police:

> They got to his house at night and beat him up,
> And drove away saying he is a bandit who sells liquor . . .
> He started thinking about his fiancée and his home.
> When they arrested him and took him to jail
> At Marshall Square [police station],
> He was handcuffed to detectives.[48]

Similarly, three lines of '*UBunghca*' (People who wear Oxford Bags) are:

> How is Johannesburg?
> How is the liquor in Johannesburg?
> They are being arrested for concoctions brewed in their homes.[49]

Songs about problems in a particular city gained local popularity. One was '*Idiphu eThekwini*' (The Dipping in Durban) about the compulsory de-lousing of Black work-seekers entering that city. Some of its lines urged African solidarity behind the local ANC leadership:

> What are you people saying about the dipping in Durban?
> What is chasing people away from Durban?
> You fellow countrymen, long live the black nation.
> Talk on our behalf, Mafukuzela! [John Dube, leader of the ANC in Natal].[50]

The composer of the last two songs was Reuben Caluza, a graduate of Dube's Ohlange Institute who contributed to the development of musical traditions there. His songs demonstrated that members of Black elites anxious to retain their social status could be driven to oppose Union government policies that imperilled their aspirations.

---

[47] Cited in Erlmann, *African Stars*, 133–4. The following short extracts are Erlmann's translation from the original Zulu compositions.
[48] Erlmann, *African Stars*, 128.   [49] Ibid., 130.   [50] Ibid., 133.

But for some, including Caluza, this did not mean complete abandonment of Black Britishness.[51] Union government legislation and police
action could still be rationalised as White settler betrayals of British
Imperial promises, which permitted millenarian-style hope for positive
Royal intercession. Cultural anglicisation gradually evolved into a more
assertive 'New African' identity for many, which was eventually understood in unequivocally African nationalist and anti-Imperialist fashion.
When this happened, the British element of a British Black identity
among Africans would disappear. But this was a lengthy and ambivalent
process.[52]

The 1925 Royal Tour, for instance, came in the middle of a decade of
ICU radicalism that culminated in a violent riot involving White vigilantes and Africans in June 1929 in Durban that left more than a hundred
wounded and eight dead. The ICU had initially been formed among
dockworkers in Cape Town, but by the mid-1920s was most active in
Natal, and especially in Durban. White communists like Sydney Bunting
addressed ICU members, telling any who still thought that the British
monarchy might protect them that the Imperial government had been
'largely responsible for your exploitation'.[53] However, the call for a boycott was largely ineffectual, and numerous ANC leaders took prominent
parts in mass receptions in town and countryside, pledging their continued loyalty to the British crown. Some in Johannesburg openly expressed
the hope that Edward would further their efforts to 'improve our positions
... along accepted paths of European civilisation'.[54] In Durban, Caluza
wrote '*Bayete*' in the Prince's honour:

> We salute your majesty,
> Your children are saluting you.
> Rule us, your children!
> Salute, your majesty.[55]

At the time of the Royal Tour of 1947, there were more boycott calls by the
ANC Youth League, the Indian Passive Resistance Movement (inspired by
the protest methods employed by Gandhi), the Communist Party and
Trotskyite leaders of the Non-European Unity Movement (NEUM).
These calls were also largely ignored. Hundreds of thousands of Black

---

[51] Ibid., 66–8.
[52] Hilary Sapire, 'Ambiguities of Loyalism: The Prince of Wales in India and Africa, 1921–2 and 1925', *History Workshop Journal* 73 (July 2011), 37–58; Sapire, 'African Loyalism'.
[53] *Indian Opinion* 24 April 1925 cited in Sapire, 'Ambiguities of Loyalism', 54.
[54] This was part of a petition by the Transvaal Native Mine Clerks Association, cited in Sapire, 'Ambiguities of Loyalism', 56–7.
[55] Cited in Erlmann, *African Stars*, 121.

Illustration 4.1: The British Royal family visiting Orlando,
Johannesburg, 1947 (Mary Evans Picture Gallery)

South Africans turned up to meet the royal visitor, 100,000 alone in
Orlando, birthplace of the Youth League (see Illustration 4.1). Herbert
Dhlomo, ANC member, occasional Durban city poet and denouncer of
White discrimination, penned this poem to the Royal family:

> Your Presence here we take as sign prophetic
> Of greater things to come; of a new birth
> Of freedom, righteousness and peace; when worth,
> Not race, will be the standard and the law.[56]

The apparent absence of any persuasive alternative in the face of state
power encouraged this position, even after the Representation of Natives
Act in 1936 removed African men from the common voters' roll in the
Cape. The sop to African elites was continued parliamentary representation by three White MPs elected on a separate voters' roll, and the
establishment of a purely advisory Natives Representative Council.

---

[56] Nick Visser and Tim Couzens (eds), *H.I.E. Dhlomo: Collected Works* (Johannesburg:
Raven, 1986), 378.

Africans were prevented from purchasing any further property in cities by a Native Trust and Land Act in 1937.[57]

Meanwhile, the Pact government's response to the threat of Dingaan's Day protests in 1929 took the form of an intimidating display of state power in Durban, site of the violent June riots.[58] Oswald Pirow, the Minister of Justice, himself led a contingent of 700 policemen on tax-gathering raids aimed at the city's African population on 14 December. Not only were the police armed with fixed bayonets and machine-guns; the occasion saw the first use of teargas in South Africa against supposedly 'riotous assemblies'.[59]

This particular moment of threatened urban insurgency passed, the CPSA, ICU, ANC alliance broke apart, and ANC leadership fell back into relative quiescence. A more radical younger generation of political leaders, uninfluenced by British promises or personal expectations of pre-Union days, did emerge in organisations like the National Liberation League in the late 1930s. But this generation was split along lines of ideology and personality. Different racial categorisation also proved divisive: identity as Indian, African or Coloured frequently meant distinct political priorities.[60]

The inclusion of many among the Western-educated elite in cross-racial consultative boards, welfare societies and recreational organisations also contributed to moderating Black politics throughout the inter-war period. Frequently initiated by White anglophone liberals, cross-racial associations encouraged among their Black participants a consciousness of elite status, hope of 'greater things to come', and thereby retention for a while longer of a Black British identity.

ABM missionary Ray Phillips initiated several of these associations. As with others involved, Phillips had pragmatic and principled reasons for doing so. He recognised that cross-racial co-operation was essential to assuage Black political alienation, counter violence and promote urban order for all. Yet as a Christian evangelist who specialised in social service courses during his time at Yale Divinity School, Phillips was genuinely convinced of the need for moral and material upliftment for all in the brotherhood of man and saw cross-racial co-operation as a prerequisite

---

[57] Through the Natives Law Amendment Act of 1937.
[58] La Hausse, 'The Struggle for the City', 54–6.
[59] Simons and Simons, *Class and Colour*, 419–20.
[60] N. Worden, *The Making of Modern South Africa* (Oxford: Wiley-Blackwell, 2000); W. Beinart, *Twentieth Century South Africa* (Oxford: Oxford University Press, 2001).

for this.[61] As a South African anthropologist put it in 1970, such missionary 'conviction [was] matched since 1918 only by communists'.[62]

Moralising urban leisure time

Phillips and other White Christian liberals made no secret of their desire to thwart such ungodly activism while reassuring Black South Africans that there was still substance to the British civilising mission. Shortly after arriving in Johannesburg in 1918, and aware of cross-class Black unrest on the Rand, Phillips 'tried to gain the confidence of . . . embittered native leaders'.

> They said to us, 'You are not wanted here . . . There's not a white man in South Africa who cares the snap of his fingers for the black man. Peaceful measures have failed. We are being forced to try violence!'[63]

Yet Phillips persisted. He organised a 'Gamma Sigma' – named from the first letters of the Greek for 'know thyself' – debating and literary club for Africans in Doornfontein, which White leaders and opinion makers attended.[64] Their number included city councillors, academics, labour leaders, businessmen and the Director of Native Labour on the Witwatersrand. Discussions were held on topics like the necessity and functions of government and 'Native Affairs' in general. Eight more clubs of this kind followed, and attracted several thousand Africans.

The Gamma Sigma initiative led to the establishment of a Johannesburg Joint Council of Europeans and Natives (an organisation with twenty-five Whites and twenty-five Africans) in the early 1920s. Its brief was to present African views on proposed legislation to government, publicise such views in White newspapers and organise sub-committees and conferences on issues affecting urban Africans, like passes and housing. Joint Councils were soon set up in other cities, and in 1929 Phillips co-founded the South African Institute of Race Relations, which collated information from organisations like these involved with Black social conditions.

Phillips' parallel strategy was tackling 'the whole great problem of moralizing . . . leisure time . . . [because] the Devil . . . is in full charge of the leisure activities of the majority of the native people in Johannesburg and other South African towns'.[65] Such thoughts were shared by many

---

[61] Alan Gregor Cobley, *The Rules of the Game: Struggles in Black Recreation and Social Welfare Policy in South Africa* (Westport, CT: Greenwood Press, 1997), 123–4.
[62] Monica Wilson, 'Co-operation and Conflict: The Eastern Cape Frontier', in Wilson and Thompson (eds), *Oxford History of South Africa*, 239.
[63] Phillips, *The Bantu are Coming*, 118.   [64] Ibid., 118–20.
[65] Phillips, *The Bantu are Coming*, 58, 124. The details of Phillips' initiatives that follow are drawn from this book and from another by the same author, Ray E. Phillips, *The Bantu in*

involved in importing British institutions and traditions into southern African cities, if not limited to worrying only about the morality of Africans. As we have seen, their institutions, from schools to scouting, contributed to the anglicisation of cities that was meant to include the inculcation of respectability by both White and Black elites among urban residents of all races. Imported British traditions included middle-class women's involvement in this process through teaching and social welfare, which facilitated the participation of Black women in the same fields.

The importation of over 4,000 British women for domestic service formed part of the accelerated anglicisation of South Africa planned by the Imperial government during and after the Boer War. This was organised by the South African Expansion Committee (known as SAX) of the British Woman's Emigration Association. Great care was taken by SAX to ensure that immigrants retained their respectability en route to employment in South Africa. SAX matrons travelled with each group. Sections of the ships in which the women sailed were sealed off to deter contact with male passengers. On arriving in Cape Town, groups were met by the port chaplain. Those women destined for Johannesburg travelled on a chartered train. On arrival, they were accommodated in two hostels funded by a mining company.[66]

This concern for the morals of young British women arriving in Johannesburg and other cities was extended to African migrants. The first of several hostels for African women was opened by Anglican Cowley evangelists in Doornfontein in 1908. A second, called the Helping Hand Club and instigated by ABM missionaries, was established in Fairview to the south-east of the city centre in 1919. Both offered training in domestic skills and, like SAX, aimed to provide respectable recruits for domestic service. By the 1930s, the hostels housed single women in a range of employment, from factory to social work.[67]

The moralising of leisure time became a cross-racial enterprise, not just something Whites imposed on Blacks in a particular colonial urban context, even if most Whites in the inter-war period retained a sense of race as well as class superiority. Respectability was enthusiastically propagated by Black journalists who professed loyalty to Britain and preached morality in their publications. Francis Peregrino, a pan-Africanist born in

the City (Alice: Lovedale Press, 1939). See also, Tim Couzens, '"Moralizing Leisure Time": The Transatlantic Connection and Black Johannesburg 1918–36', in Marks and Rathbone (eds), Industrialisation and Social Change, 314–37.

[66] Jean-Jacques Van-Helten and Keith Williams, '"The Crying Need of South Africa": The Emigration of Single British Women to the Transvaal, 1901–10', Journal of Southern African Studies 10, 1 (1983), 17–38.

[67] Cobley, The Rules of the Game, 85–9.

Accra, established in 1900 one of the earliest of several newspapers aimed at a Black urban readership, *The South African Spectator*. Peregrino stressed in its columns 'the need for black probity'. He argued that Blacks had to break White stereotyping to achieve 'civilised' status, and thus gain the franchise throughout South Africa. Abdurahman's APO, aimed particularly at Coloureds, took a similar line. The APO's eponymously named journal, launched in 1909, campaigned relentlessly against drugs, alcohol and prostitution and in favour of education and sensible recreation. The need for respectability was also the message to Africans of John Dube's *Ilanga Lase Natal*, initiated in Durban in 1903. Enthused with the spirit of improving Christianity, Dube also addressed girls at the Inanda Seminary on 'what our sisters do in public in cities and town, and cautioned us to lead upright lives'.[68]

Charlotte Maxeke, who founded the Bantu Women's League (later the ANC's Women's League) in 1918, was equally concerned about the particular moral dangers women faced in the city and the breakdown of family life.[69] In 1928 she was appointed as a Native probation officer attached to the Johannesburg Magistrate's Court, becoming the first Black woman officially employed as a social worker. After her retirement, Maxeke became the inaugural president of the National Council for African Women (NCAW) in 1935, the initiative of a group of African women in Kimberley who wanted to 'care for Non-European welfare'.[70]

Nimrod Makhanya, a graduate of Marianhill and the Ohlange Institute, popularised such elite concerns through song. 'Ndiyi Traveller' was about drunken vagrant George: 'I am neither a minister nor a teacher, I am just a "thing that drinks"'.[71] Another, *'Ikhiwane Elihle'*, went in part:

> Girls and young men, you are needed at your homes.
> You are swallowed up by Durban . . .
> O, the vanity of worshiping liquor.[72]

Respectable recreation was deemed desirable by urban elites irrespective of race, as was the case with their counterparts in northern hemisphere cities. The difference was that segregation along lines of race as well as class and gender was applied to its provision in South Africa. Take the example of forms of scouting. In 1915, seven years after an official scouting movement for White boys had been established in South Africa, African boys at Lovedale School in the Eastern Cape applied to form their own troop. Their application was turned down by the official

---

[68] Cited in Hughes, 'Inanda Seminary', 215.
[69] Walker, 'The Women's Suffrage Movement', 329.
[70] Cobley, *The Rules of the Game*, 76.   [71] Erlmann, *African Stars*, 66–8.   [72] Ibid., 82.

organisation, as were similar requests for a Coloured troop in Cape Town in 1916 and an African troop in Johannesburg three years later. Organised both by Black elites and White liberals, Black scout-like organisations had to adopt different names such as 'Braves', 'Paladins', 'Trackers' and 'Pathfinders'.

White scouting authorities were persuaded by White liberals to take the African Pathfinders under their auspices in 1924, but still insisted that their uniforms were distinct from those of proper Boy Scouts. Pathfinders had to omit the Scout belt, scarves were replaced by ties, Stetsons by peaked caps, and fleur-de-lis badges by a triangle around the letter P, which stood for Pathfinder, Progress, Peace and Prosperity. Only in 1936 were Africans (still as Pathfinders) as well as Coloured and Indian troops given full scout status, though in parallel segregated units to Whites, and each with its distinguishing uniforms. Gender segregation was also applied, with White girls organised as Girl Guides in 1916 and their African counterparts as Wayfarers in 1925. What all of these parallel units had in common was the link to an institution of Imperial Britain. Consequently Afrikaner middle-class nationalists reacted by establishing *Voortrekkers* as a rival organisation for inculcating respectability among Afrikaner boys.[73]

Whether as part of ethnic mobilisation or not, clergy and teachers played a leading role in transmitting appropriate leisure time activities; so too did major employers of labour like gold mining companies and municipalities, who were able to allocate urban space and appropriate amenities for the purpose. Working-class recipients had varied reactions. Despite some success by temperance organisations, the majority continued to drink alcohol, often in large quantities. Equally, many African women persisted with domestic beer brewing and its adulterated off-shoots, despite official prohibition, because they had few money-making alternatives. Working-class Whites on the Rand, Afrikaners to the fore, resented the abolition of greyhound racing in 1947 due to middle-class disapproval of potentially ruinous gambling that went with it. Participants had enjoyed the festive atmosphere at the Wanderers' track, and had no desire to be saved from 'going to the dogs'.[74]

Yet much respectable leisure activity was greeted with enthusiasm, especially the many sports imported from Britain beyond greyhound racing. The most popular for men proved to be soccer, the British version

---

[73] Parsons, *Boy Scout Movement*, 72–112. White and Coloured Guides and African 'Wayfarers' were nominally in one united movement rather than the parallel arrangement for scouts.

[74] Albert Grundlingh, *Potent Pastimes: Sport and Leisure Practises in Modern Afrikaner History* (Pretoria: Protea Book House, 2013).

of earlier, rougher and less regulated kinds of football, adapted and codified to meet the constraints of time and space in the industrial metropolis.[75] Several forms of pre-industrial leisure activity in South Africa like New Year Carnival in Cape Town and African 'tribal' dancing in Durban and Johannesburg followed a similar trajectory. Local authorities ensured that they were removed partly or completely from the streets into (municipal or mining compound) grounds and stadiums. The timing could be related directly to concerns about urban unruliness as in Carnival being moved to the Green Point stadium in 1907, after the Hooligan Riots of 1906; or Ingoma dancing to the Somtseu municipal recreation grounds in Durban in 1932, after a disorderly decade that culminated in the riots of 1929. Once in these venues, performances took place at fixed times and were of limited duration. Participants competed for prizes presented by members of urban elites, or as part of paid exhibitions for tourists. Street-parading remained an important element of Carnival, but times and routes became subject to municipal licensing and regulation. Municipal by-laws against the carrying of sticks in all three cities diminished stick-fighting.[76]

Phillips was involved in numerous initiatives aimed at moralising leisure time. Like many others involved, White and Black, he saw these as part of welfare provision, not just in terms of social control, in similar fashion to members of the *Vrouefederasie* or DRC working only among the Afrikaner poor. Throughout the 1930s, Phillips was on a co-ordinating council of Johannesburg's welfare organisations, and in 1941 he became the director of the Jan Hofmeyr School, South Africa's first training centre for Black social workers.[77] His Gamma Sigma club initiative that encouraged reading and debating was an early example of how moralising leisure time was combined with social welfare. Another was his introduction into mine compounds of games like Hunt the Thimble, football and volleyball and the provision of more 'suitable' films than what he saw as the morally

---

[75] Peter Alegi, *Laduma! Soccer, Politics and Society in South Africa* (Scottsville: University of KwaZulu-Natal Press, 2004); John Nauright, *Sport, Cultures and Identities in South Africa* (Cape Town: David Philip, 1997); Christopher Merrett, *Sport, Space and Segregation: Politics and Society in Pietermaritzburg* (Scottsville: University of KwaZulu-Natal Press, 2009).

[76] La Hausse, '"Cows of Nongoloza"'; La Hausse, 'The Struggle for the City'; Bickford-Smith, 'Leisure and Social Identity in Cape Town', 125–6; Veit Erlmann, 'But Hope Does Not Kill: Black Popular Music in Durban, 1913–1939', in Maylam and Edwards (eds), *The People's City*, 70–99, especially 88–9; Cecile Badenhorst and Charles Mather, 'Tribal Recreation and Recreating Tribalism: Culture, Leisure and Social Control on South Africa's Gold Mines, 1940–1950', *Journal of Southern African Studies* 23, 3 (1997), 473–89.

[77] Phillips, *The Bantu in the City*; Couzens, '"Moralizing Leisure Time"'; Cobley, *The Rules of the Game*.

dubious offerings available in the four Johannesburg bioscopes open to Africans in the inter-war years. Even after the introduction of a Union Board of Censors in 1931, these screened films supposedly banned for 'exhibition to Natives' including *King Kong, Frozen Justice, One Night at Susie's, Too Many Women* and *The Cheat*. Several passed by the censors, like *Blonde Venus, The Ghoul, Doctors' Wives, Sin Ship* and *Love Me To-night*' also worried Phillips: 'the titles are sufficient to suggest . . . [they do not] convey an elevating or ennobling picture of Western Civilised Life'.[78]

Phillips' solution was to provide alternative viewing through a mobile cinema circuit. He had persuaded the Chamber of Mines to start funding this in the early 1920s, with £1,500 for machinery and £5,000 for annual running costs. Soon it reached mine compounds, city centre venues and institutions like reformatories, gaols and orphanages on the Rand. Phillips sent its films to other parts of the country, including African areas of Durban. He wrote of an early mining compound screening:

With amazed delight the happy crowds went off on trips on the modern magic carpet to other lands; saw the surf riders of Honolulu, the explorers in the Arctic, the reindeer of Lapland, and the potter's wheel in India . . . they shook their heads at pictures of mining in England and America, showing white men at work with pick and shovel and drill: 'Ai kona! Mfundisi is fooling us here! No white man works like that. Only black men!'[79]

Charlie Chaplin gained particular popularity among African miners, who nicknamed him 'SiDakwa [or] little drunken man'. When some at the New Primrose compound were about to retaliate against attacks by White strikers, Phillips claimed that his screening of a Chaplin film restored calm.[80]

Attacks on Blacks by White strikers were indirectly responsible for the opening of a Bantu Men's Social Centre (BMSC) as a venue for respectable leisure activity in 1924, another initiative involving Phillips. White liberals had donated money to a fund for victims of these attacks. The funds' trustees, lawyers John Hardy and Howard Pim, used some of the money to purchase two pieces of land in central Johannesburg for what became the BMSC's club house and sports grounds. The club house soon incorporated a library and gym, and hosted concerts, debates, ballroom dancing and drama. A Rolfes Dhlomo play about the end to slavery in the United States was staged at the BMSC in 1934 to mark the centenary of emancipation. Herbert Dhlomo, Rolfes' brother, became the BMSC librarian in 1937. The success of the BMSC in Johannesburg led to its

[78] Phillips, *The Bantu in the City*, 323. See also, 316–23,
[79] Phillips, *The Bantu are Coming*, 141–2.   [80] Ibid., 147–50.

emulation by liberals in Durban, where a Bantu Social Centre was opened in 1933.[81]

Such developments gave White elites reason to believe that urban problems were being tackled on a broad front in the inter-war period. The growth of residential and social segregation played a major symbolic and practical role in that belief, offering both continued White political supremacy and greater urban social control. At the same time, new accommodation, even if segregated, was promoted as a form of urban improvement in keeping with working-class housing provision in the northern hemisphere. Its construction frequently accompanied slum clearance. Thanks mainly to the efforts of Christian missionaries and some enlightened compound managers, segregated accommodation in South Africa could be shown to allow moral as well as physical improvement.

As major providers of segregated accommodation, mine owners, central government and municipalities soon learnt from these early initiatives and emulated them. Once again, the motivation of those involved combined principled belief with the pragmatic sense that moralising leisure time was helpful in taming disorder. This was eminently the case in Durban. In the immediate wake of protest and riot the municipality appointed a Native Welfare Officer, began building Lamontville in 1930, added a Native Advisory Board the following year, and supported the development of Clermont as a freehold township. Simultaneously, Durban's NAD established a Bantu Recreational Grounds Association that oversaw the provision of facilities for both British sports and a confined version of Ingoma dancing.[82] Johannesburg had formed its own NAD in 1927, and under its manager Graham Ballenden invested in sports facilities in its own compounds and locations as well as financing those of the BMSC's Bantu Sports Club from 1931. Key to the considerable success of these initiatives was the appointment of Solomon G. Senaoane as its 'native sports organizer'. He founded the Johannesburg's Bantu Football Association in 1931, sponsored by the Council, who did the same for the Bantu Lawn Tennis Association, formed the same year. The Chamber of Mines financed African cricket, initially played on municipal grounds, as well as other sports and mine dancing on its own land.[83]

---

[81] La Hausse, 'The Struggle for the City', 58.
[82] La Hausse, 'The Struggle for the City', 57–8; Erlmann, 'But Hope Does Not Kill', 88–90.
[83] Cobley, *The Rules of the Game*, 25–32; Alegi, *Laduma!*, 39–47.

Planning cities beautiful

In considering how to achieve greater urban order and improvement, municipalities constantly drew on ideas and practices from abroad. These informed initiatives like provision of recreational space, extending water supplies or underground drainage schemes, producing more efficient fire brigades and introducing the latest forms of urban transport like trams or motorised buses. Outside expert advice was sought when needed, as in dealing with new problems when encountered, like traffic congestion.[84]

International opinion was influential in determining South African views on what would create cities that were more beautiful and cultured, in which greater social harmony would therefore prevail. One influence was Ebenezer Howard's Garden City idea of combining the best of town and countryside. This was put into practice with the construction of Letchworth and Welwyn Garden cities in Britain before and after the First World War.[85] The Cape Town suburb of Pinelands was developed in 1919 by a Garden City Trust championed by local businessman Richard Stuttaford, who had visited Letchworth in 1917, and served as a model for much further suburban development in South Africa.[86] The Cape Town municipality's Maitland Garden City was just one modest version of the Howard ideal. Some White liberals and African elites hoped the Garden City movement might inform the design of 'Native Villages' too, as with Ndabeni's replacement, Langa. The reality fell far short though of Howard's dream, the more so when the accommodation provided in African townships increasingly failed to keep pace with demand in the course of the Second World War.[87]

Fashioning city centres in British metropolitan style had been intended to inculcate not just loyalty but order. The inclusion of museums, art galleries and educational institutions was meant to be intellectually and morally improving. But from around the 1890s onwards, the American City Beautiful movement became important in communicating such ideas while arguing in particular that the nature of the urban built environment could affect social behaviour. Correct urban design itself could help create less dangerous cities.

The American movement built not just on British views in this respect, but on those of Europe, such as Haussmann's refashioning of Paris. The City Beautiful concept was particularly associated with architect Daniel Burnham's World Columbian Exposition (Chicago, 1893) and his plans

---

[84] As described in Chapter 3.   [85] Howard, *Garden Cities of Tomorrow*.
[86] Mabin and Smit, 'Reconstructing South African Cities', 193–223.
[87] Bickford-Smith et al., *Cape Town in the Twentieth Century*, 144–5.

for Washington DC and Chicago. Influential in transmitting City Beautiful principles were the publications of Charles Mulford Robinson, who became Professor of Civic Design at the University of Illinois.[88] The message was enthusiastically pursued by South African municipalities in the early twentieth century. City centres should be beautified with parks, squares, fountains, monuments and neo-classical public buildings. Unsightly and potentially dangerous slums should be removed, and municipalities were given greater ability to do this by the Slums Act of 1934.

More comprehensive international models of town planning exercised by trained professionals were applied at the same time. Ordinances passed in all the provinces gave municipalities powers to control the zoning of land use and density, and the positioning and size of buildings. Longstreth Thompson, of the British firm Adams, Thompson and Fry, was made regional planner for a number of Witwatersrand municipalities from 1935 to 1939 and devised the first land zoning scheme for Johannesburg in that period. Cape Town devised its own zoning scheme in 1941. Three years earlier, Witwatersrand University hosted an inter-disciplinary colloquium at which the international modernist ideas of Le Corbusier and others were popularised among architects and planners in South Africa. One of the prominent results was the development of modernist plans in the early 1940s to reconstruct central Cape Town. This involved land reclaimed from Table Bay, substantial enlargement of the harbour and arterial roads that would cut through working-class housing in areas like District Six. Much of the plan was realised over the next two decades.[89]

The question of what to retain in the process of re-designing and improving South African cities was similarly affected by international trends in urban design. The architectural preservation movement in Britain, and notably William Morris' Society for the Preservation of Ancient Buildings, was already influential in this respect by the late 1870s when the fate of Cape Town's Castle was unsure, demolition a possibility.[90] Trollope wrote in the Castle's defence that though 'ugly and almost useless' its destruction would mean the loss of 'the most conspicuous relic' of early settlement. Trollope's judgement influenced local

---

[88] They included an illustrated report on Burnham's Chicago exposition. See also C.M. Robinson, *Modern Civic Art or the City Made Beautiful* (New York: Putnam's, 1903); C. M. Robinson, *The Improvement of Towns and Cities*. Robinson was the first professor of Civic Design at the University of Illinois at Urbana-Champaign.

[89] Mabin and Smit, 'Reconstructing South African Cities', 193–223; Bickford-Smith et al., *Cape Town in the Twentieth Century*, 145–52.

[90] This helped produce the Ancient Monuments Protection Act of 1882.

opinion. The *Cape Argus* argued in favour of retaining the Castle when the
Imperial government planned to replace it with modern military barracks:

We pleaded ... for the preservation of the Town House, ugly and insignificant as it
is, simply because we have so few buildings of any age to impress colonists with the
idea that the country they live in has a history. We hope that the Castle, whether it
is required for military purposes or not, will always remain to redeem Cape Town
from the rawness of most colonial towns.[91]

The Castle duly survived to become a tourist attraction with the addi-
tional support of the political movement of Cape Afrikaners, the *Afrikaner
Bond*. It was to woo Afrikaner support that Rhodes donated the statue of
Van Riebeeck to Cape Town, unveiled in 1899 and soon frequented by
SDF speakers.[92]

Nonetheless, there was a constant pursuit by city authorities and local
entrepreneurs of new attractions and amenities for tourists and residents
alike. The timing of their introduction, as in the case of Cape Town's pier
in 1913, was largely determined by a combination of financial considerations, international taste, and available technology. Electricity, wrought
iron, steel-frame skyscraper building, plate glass and elevators were introduced in the first instance as part of practical urban improvement and
design. Their use within the architectural design of public buildings,
places of entertainment, office blocks and suburban homes was influenced in the inter-war period by international movements like art deco
and modernism.[93] New technologies contributed not just to innovation in
individual urban entertainment but to the production of entire cityscapes,
including nightscapes, which became attractions in themselves.[94]

Electricity, for instance, facilitated entertainments like cinemas, cable
car rides up Table Mountain (1929) and the illumination of Durban's
Victoria Embankment. But it was also reshaping the South African city at
night, like its American counterpart, 'into a fairyland of illuminated
shapes, sights, and brightly coloured, sometimes animated, messages
and images – forty-foot green pickles, gigantic pieces of chewing gum,
Racing chariots on top of a hotel ... a new landscape of modernity'.[95]
After sunset, city nightscapes became a dramatic chiaroscuro canvas that

[91] Cited in Lawrence G. Green, *Growing Lovely, Growing Old* (Cape Town: Howard
Timmins, 1975), 21–2.
[92] Picard, *Grand Parade*, 102.
[93] Clive M. Chipkin, *Johannesburg Style: Architecture and Society 1880s–1960s* (Cape Town:
David Philip, 1993).
[94] This is apparent in the many descriptions in South African city literature. See Chapter 5
for examples of this in terms of Black South African writing.
[95] Nasaw, *Going Out*, 8. See also Richard Dennis, *Cities in Modernity: Representations and
Productions of Metropolitan Space, 1840-1930* (Cambridge: Cambridge University Press,
2008), 278–80.

highlighted this modernity while throwing 'everything unsightly into an impenetrable darkness'.[96] Nelson Mandela remembered his arrival in Johannesburg in the early 1940s:

At about ten o'clock that evening, we saw before us, glinting in the distance, a maze of lights that seemed to stretch in all directions. Electricity has always been to me a novelty and a luxury, and here was a vast landscape of electricity, a city of light.[97]

Cable cars, aircraft and motor cars provided new perspectives from which cities could be viewed. The ascent of Table Mountain was hugely simplified by the opening of a cable car in 1929, an event soon popularised by a travelogue made for the Fox-Hearst Corporation.[98] Motor transport offered the possibility of promoting day excursions to enlarged city hinterlands which could be added to place-selling attractions: the Stellenbosch wine lands for Cape Town perhaps, or the Valley of a Thousand Hills for Durban. Such possibilities were aided by new road building. The hitherto relatively inaccessible Cape Point was brought more readily within the tourist's ambit by a road that was built for strategic reasons during the First World War. Shortly afterwards, the CPPA published *The Cape Peninsula* (c.1920) with Bartolomeu Dias on its cover, and Francis Drake's comments about the Fairest Cape. It obviously made greater sense to promote Cape Town and its surrounds in this way now that it was considerably easier to get to the Cape, and a Cape Point Nature Reserve was opened in 1939. Similarly, Chapman's Peak Drive, built with convict labour, was opened in 1922, and soon CPPA material compared it to the route between Sorrento and Amalfi, well known to British tourists, at whom the material was aimed. By 1936, a CPPA publication *With Your Car at the Cape* was able to describe the drive down the west coast of the peninsula, to Cape Point, and back via the east coast. The book also detailed possible drives inland, like to the wine lands.[99]

Promoting the 'unique' identity of South African cities

Efforts like these contributed to very positive national and international depictions of South African cities between the late 1920s and late 1940s. The publicity associations established for the Cape Peninsula in 1909, Durban in 1922 and Johannesburg in 1925 used all the multimedia possibilities at their disposal to promote tourism, investment and White

[96] David E. Nye, *Electrifying America: Social Meaning of a New Technology, 1880–1940* (Boston: Massachussets Institute of Technology Press, 1992), 60.
[97] Mandela, *Long Walk to Freedom*, 56.   [98] Gutsche, *Motion Pictures*, 332.
[99] H. Hope, *With Your Car at the Cape* (Cape Town: CPPA, 1936).

residence.[100] A central role here was played by the comparatively new technologies of photography and film. Both appeared to break down the distinction between artistic image and reality and to reproduce reality directly. As such, they seemingly offered a more trustworthy claim than verbal language in depicting the objective nature of a place.

Visual, literary and electronic media worked together in conveying ideas about South African cities. Guidebooks, brochures and official city histories were richly endowed with photographs, often deployed to contrast humble pasts with metropolitan presents and thereby demonstrate progress. City histories offered highly detailed accounts of how such progress had come about. In the case of Johannesburg, where photography was available from its mining camp birth, this was particularly dramatic and effective.

Films conveyed this message to a far larger audience. More powerfully than illustrated literature, film could 'show' many elements of South African modernity in a few short sequences. These were commonly juxtaposed with the retrogressive 'traditional', often a matter of White contrasted with Black, and urban spaces allotted to each. Inter-titles, then voice-over narration, provided didactic instruction to viewers.[101]

The development of cinema coincided with innovations in transport in the late nineteenth century that facilitated the growth of mass long-distance travel. Travelogues offered a beguiling mixture of spectacle and education. In doing so, they drew on a long European tradition of representing cities in which literary descriptions were gradually being greatly supplemented by art and photography in the course of the nineteenth century: 'the tongue was giving way to the eye'.[102]

Photography and, yet more viscerally, cinema offered a form of virtual tourism that could promote the real thing. Both could also promote immigration and commercial investment. The two technologies deployed in combination in publicity material offered enticing examples of what a sociologist has described as tourist 'gazes' (static, associated with painting or photography) and 'glances' (mobile, as if filmed through a vehicle window): sights worth experiencing when arriving in a particular city.[103] Frequently they did so by building on earlier notions of the city's

[100] Bickford-Smith, 'Creating a City of the Tourist Imagination', 1763–85.
[101] Robert A. Rosenstone, *Visions of the Past: The Challenge of Film to Our Idea of History* (Cambridge, MA: Harvard University Press, 1995) offered an early comparison of cinematic and written history 'information loads', suggesting the strengths and weaknesses of each.
[102] Bruno, *Atlas of Emotion*, 191.
[103] John Urry, *The Tourist Gaze* (London: Sage Publications, 2002). For a demonstration of Urry's theory about gazes and glances in terms of Naples, see Bruno, 'City Views', 45–58.

attractions that had been affirmed by prominent visitors, artists, travel writers and residents.

With its seventeenth-century foundation, Cape Town had a long history of place description and promotion before the establishment of an official publicity association, as was the case for cities in Britain.[104] Many of these descriptions were significant in establishing twentieth-century tourist sites and gazes. In keeping with the discovery of the Romantic Movement in Europe and North America, they included published accounts by travellers like Trollope and Twain who extolled the topographical beauty of the Cape Peninsula, as well as others who made the pilgrimage up the north (city centre) face of Table Mountain.[105] There were also countless paintings and sketches of the city nestled beneath the mountain, the perspective of those on board European ships approaching Table Bay.[106]

Two nineteenth-century Cape Town painters, Thomas Bowler and Thomas Baines, were most influential in popularising this iconic portrayal of the city.[107] Bowler seemingly never tired of painting the scene, probably because in Baines' experience it never failed to find a buyer.[108] From the mid-nineteenth century onwards, photographers such as Arthur Green and Frederick York made *carte-de-visite* reproductions of these paintings. They also sold photographic studies of their own, whether panoramas of the city from Signal Hill or views of important buildings and streets. A set of Green's photographs was published in 1862 by the *Cape Argus* as *Murray's Views of the Cape*.[109] Arthur Elliott was a prolific photographer of the city between the 1870s and 1930s. He promoted through his exhibitions two further attractions of Cape Town mentioned in travellers' accounts: Cape Dutch buildings (notably farmhouses) and 'Cape Malays', particularly Malay weddings and the Malay Quarter.[110]

---

[104] Ward, *Selling Places*, 31–2.

[105] Urry, *Tourist Gaze*, 20; L. Van Sittert, 'The Bourgeois Eye Aloft: Table Mountain in the Anglo Urban Middle Class Imagination, c.1891–1952', *Kronos: Journal of Cape History* 29 (2003), 161–90.

[106] N. Vergunst, *Hoerikwaggo: Images of Table Mountain* (Cape Town: South African National Gallery, 2002).

[107] Although they were not the first; just some of the many earlier depictions in this vein include those by E.V. Stade in 1710, Johanne Rach in 1762 and Thomas Whitcombe in 1817.

[108] C. Pama, *Bowler's Cape Town: Life at the Cape in Early Victorian Times 1834–1868* (Cape Town: Tafelberg, 1977), 16–17; J.P.R. Wallis, *Thomas Baines: His Life and Explorations in South Africa, Rhodesia and Australia, 1820–1875* (Cape Town: A.A. Balkema, 1976), 5.

[109] M. Bull and J. Denfield, *Secure the Shadow: The Story of Cape Photography from Its Beginnings to the End of 1870* (Cape Town: Terence McNally, 1970).

[110] H. Fransen, *A Cape Camera* (Cape Town: A.D. Donker, 1993), 7–16, 47–51.

The attention given to Malays was an example of 'local colour', or the 'customs, manner of speech, and dress' of local inhabitants, being used alongside history, nature, architecture, high culture and entertainments in the promotion of cities.[111] White anglophone interest in Malay culture in Cape Town was an extension of Orientalism, Imperial British fascination with romanticised perceptions of eastern cultures.[112] Depictions of Malays as local colour were also portraying the 'popular in its place'. This was the term used by Gareth Stedman Jones to describe British middle-class representations of working-class Londoners as cheery Cockney costermongers, harmless and humorous people of the market-place, in implicit comparison to the more threatening industrial working class of cities like Manchester.[113] Depicting Black inhabitants as 'local colour' in this way became part of promoting a South African city's distinctiveness similar to place-selling in Europe; Cockney Pearly Kings and Queens for London perhaps, or gondoliers for Venice.

It was not physical difference alone – such as dark skin – that warranted the attention of White observers of South African cities but outward appearance that went beyond the anatomical: flamboyant dress, appendages, behaviour and tastes. These served to obscure physical differences as the main external signifier of group identity. It was these cultural elements that made their bearers sufficiently 'exotic' to include as local colour, endlessly captured as such by the new technologies of photography and cinema in the Imperial age, despite the fact that they were often the consequence of (transnational) cultural creolisation.[114]

As with other city attractions, what merited inclusion as local colour was commonly determined by important visitors. David Kennedy, a professional singer who toured the Cape in the 1870s, wrote that Malay men wore

large broad-brimmed hats of basket-work, and many have coloured handkerchiefs tied round their heads. The women flaunt gay head-dresses, and when a wedding or a feast takes place, the streets are ablaze with colour.[115]

[111] 'Local Colour', entry in the *Oxford Dictionary of English* (Oxford: Oxford University Press, 2003), 1028.
[112] Edward W. Said, *Orientalism* (New York: Vintage Books, 1978).
[113] G. Stedman Jones, 'The "Cockney" and the Nation, 1780–1988', in D. Feldman and G. Stedman Jones (eds), *Metropolis London: Histories and Representations since 1800* (London and New York: Routledge, 1989), 301, 315–16.
[114] Bruno, *Atlas of Emotion*, 77–9. On photography, see E. Edwards (ed.), *Anthropogy and Photography, 1860–1920* (New Haven: Yale University Press, 1992); P.S. Landau, 'With Camera and Gun in Southern Africa: Inventing the Image of the Bushmen c.1880 to 1935', in P. Skotness (ed.), *Miscast: Negotiating the Presence of the Bushmen* (Cape Town: University of Cape Town Press, 1996); J.R. Ryan, *Picturing Empire: Visualization in the British Empire* (Chicago: University of Chicago Press, 1997).
[115] Kennedy, *Kennedy at the Cape*, 14–15.

Kennedy's description of Malays as local colour was just one of many in the nineteenth century; other notable contributions were made by the likes of George Angas' lithograph 'Malay Boy of Cape Town' published in London, J.S. Mayson's *The Malays of Cape Town* and Lady Duff Gordon's *Letters from the Cape*.[116]

Detailed portrayals of Cape Town itself, still small, untidy and 'foreign' in appearance, were rare compared to panoramas before the 1890s, despite efforts by Bowler to represent its streets and buildings in ordered and picturesque fashion. When Cape Town featured in the pages of the *Illustrated London News* (*ILN*), this was mainly in portrayals of political or commercial events like Prince Alfred's tour in 1860 rather than in a focus on the town itself.[117] Where buildings appear they are not foregrounded, save in the single case of a Cape Dutch-style farmstead, an architectural attraction praised by Lady Anne Barnard.[118]

The Mineral Revolution encouraged a variety of urban place-selling initiatives. It quickened urban growth and increased municipal revenues that allowed expenditure on improvements. Economic growth and immigration also gave rise to a potentially profitable domestic publishing market. South African cities were vying for further development as resorts, entrepôts, financial and industrial centres. Place-selling strategies were devised to attract tourists and residents at a time when improvements in transport and communication were making travel from Europe to southern Africa and within the region easier. As elsewhere, the rise of South African tourism accompanied the transport revolution associated with harbour development, railways and steamships.[119]

Harbour improvements were essential for the promotion of tourism. As late as 1865, a devastating gale destroyed scores of ships in Table Bay. The first stage of Cape Town's harbour was only completed in 1870. In Durban's case, shifting sand bars, the Durban 'Bar', blocked access to the Bay of Natal. Passengers and cargo had to be offloaded and taken to shore by smaller vessels, a serious impediment to trade and an unnerving experience for many travellers, including Anthony Trollope. Extensive dredging was necessary before sizeable ships were able by the 1890s to enter the Bay and dock in the harbour itself.[120] In 1888, the British and

---

[116] G.F. Angas, *Kafirs Illustrated* (London: J. Hogarth, 1849); J.S. Mayson, *The Malays of Cape Town* (Manchester: Cave and Sever, 1855); Lady Duff Gordon, *Letters from the Cape* (Cape Town: Maskew Miller, 1925). Arthur Elliott's photographs are in the Cape Archives, Cape Town, but have also been used to illustrate numerous histories of Cape Town. A selection of Elliott's photographs form the subject of Fransen, *A Cape Camera*.

[117] See for instance *Illustrated London News*, 25 August 1849, 20 October 1860, 5 March 1864, 28 September 1867.

[118] *Illustrated London News*, 5 March 1864.

[119] Urry, *Tourist Gaze*; Ward, *Selling Places*.   [120] See Trollope, *South Africa*, 193–4.

Cape governments negotiated a mail contract with the Union and Castle lines (amalgamated in 1900). This stipulated that the voyage between Britain and Cape Town should be no longer than twenty days. Ships then continued up the coast to Durban. By the 1890s, liners from these companies capable of carrying 500 passengers could complete the journey to Cape Town in only fifteen days. The Natal Direct Line's smaller ships were able to enter Durban harbour within twenty-four days of leaving London, and connected Durban to India and Indian Ocean islands.[121]

Railways linked all major South African cities by the early 1890s, which opened the way to Durban and Cape Town becoming internal destinations for up-country tourists. Muizenberg, on Cape Town's warm-watered if windy False Bay coast, developed as a fashionable resort for wealthy families from Kimberley and Johannesburg, and several besides Cecil Rhodes built cottages there.[122] Luxury 'terminus' hotels in European style, like the Grand and Mount Nelson in the recently anglicised city centre, now accommodated wealthy visitors from inland and overseas. The luxurious Mount Nelson had 150 rooms, a 20,000-bottle wine-cellar, and a grand salon complete with a bust of the famous admiral carved out of oak from the HMS *Victory*, and was soon favoured by British 'swallows', visitors staying for several months to escape the northern hemisphere winter.[123] The Boer War interrupted such tourism, though the fact that high-ranking British officers stayed at the Mount Nelson during the conflict along with war correspondents like Winston Churchill and Arthur Conan Doyle enhanced its reputation. Durban had several 'first-class' hotels of its own. One was the Royal, so named because Prince Alfred had stayed there in its modest early years; another was the Ocean View on the Berea: 'throughout fitted with electric light, and every modern convenience … a bus will meet any train by appointment'.[124] Accounts of the Boer War in Britain publicised the sun-washed South African landscape, as did those of numerous post-war pilgrims to the graves of British soldiers, and Union under the British flag in 1910.[125]

All these developments encouraged the production of greater amounts of literary and visual material for potential tourists or residents of South African cities, including maps (see Illustration 4.2). An early offering was the *Descriptive Handbook of the Cape* in 1875, compiled by the clerk of the Cape Parliament, which waxed lyrical about Cape Town's beautiful

[121] Ingram and Sams, *Story of an African Seaport*, 163–7.
[122] Worden et al., *Cape Town: The Making of a City*, 250–1.
[123] E.H. Bolsmann, *The Mount Nelson* (Pretoria and Cape Town: Haum, 1978).
[124] Ingram and Sams, *Story of an African Seaport*, 175–5, 182. Quotation from 175.
[125] Foster, *Washed with Sun*, 116.

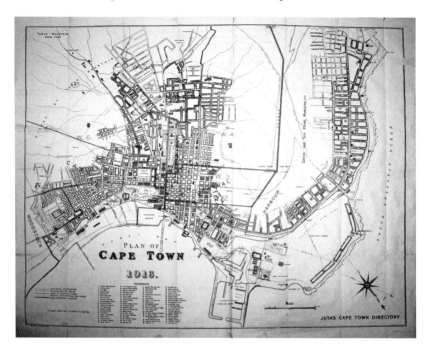

Illustration 4.2: Asserting order through cartography: a map of central
Cape Town published in 1918
(African Studies Library, UCT)

setting, sylvan suburbs, significant buildings and 'useful' local labour.
Malays, for instance, were described as 'very serviceable not only in
household occupations, but in various mechanical employments'.[126]
Glanville's *Guide to South Africa*, published in London in 1878, reassured
travellers that Cape Town's docks were now 'fine and convenient'.[127]

   As transport networks improved, global travel writing grew as a commercial enterprise. Nineteenth-century predecessors of Morton helped
determine worthy South African city attractions. Their views, as well as
those communicated orally by famous visitors over the years, mattered
and were often cited in local tourist material and city histories. Two of the
most famous were Trollope and Twain, who visited in the late 1870s and
1890s respectively. Their accounts served as report cards to local

---

[126] Noble, *Descriptive Handbook of the Cape*, 44.
[127] Richard Glanville, *Glanville's Guide to South Africa: Being a Cheap Hand-Book to the
South African Colonies* (London: Richards, Glanville and Co., 1878), 32.

authorities and place-sellers alike in determining their city's strengths and shortcomings.

Trollope acknowledged that he had 'always heard that the entrance into Capetown ... was one of the most picturesque things to be seen on the face of the earth', and, once there, that Lion's Head put him in mind of Landseer. He thought the Castle the 'most striking building in Cape Town' and Constantia 'well known in England for the name of its wine'. Twain also noticed such 'fine old Dutch mansions'.[128] Yet in keeping with British metropolitan taste, Trollope deemed Cape Town's cultural riches lacking in the capacity to deliver a civilising agenda, and its sanitary state woefully deficient.[129] Both writers praised what Twain described as 'the beautiful sea-girt drives that wind about the mountains'.[130]

Promotional material for Cape Town took note of these and other outsider judgements about the city's local colour, and grew in tandem with increased immigration and tourism in the decade before the Boer War. For instance, a souvenir photographic album produced by local publisher J.C. Juta featured a 'Malay Man and Woman'.[131] Local-colour depictions of Malays also appeared in unofficial guides, pictorial collections and accounts by British visitors.[132]

Malays were less conspicuous in official publications between the 1880s and 1920s. This may have been because of 'The Revolt of the Malays' in 1886, riotous protests against Clean Party sanitation policies that closed Muslim cemeteries within the municipal area. The popular was only put back in its place after a call-up of White volunteer regiments.[133] Changes in 'traditional' dress also made Malays less colourful. One guidebook complained in the 1920s that 'the Malay men ... are refusing to wear even the distinctive red and black fez, while their women have nearly given up their picturesque wide skirts'.[134]

Many who wanted to promote Cape Town did so instead in terms of European modernity, topography and climate. The lengthy *Guide to Cape Town* of 1890 was overtly aimed at potential 'Colonial residents' and emphasised urban progress under British rule. Much had been done to

---

[128] Twain, *Following the Equator*, 711.
[129] Trollope, *South Africa*, 52, 53, 56, 62. Ward, *Selling Places*, 27.
[130] Twain, *Following the Equator*, 710–11.
[131] Anon, *Souvenir of Cape Town* (Cape Town: J.C. Juta & Co., 1889)
[132] For instance: Eleanor Tyrell, *South African Snapshots for English Girls* (London: Gay and Hancock, 1910), 118; Anon, *Cape Town and the Picturesque Peninsula* (Cape Town: *Cape Times*, 1912); Dorothea Fairbridge, *Along Cape Roads: The Wanderings of a Stranger at the Cape of Good Hope* (Cape Town: Maskew Miller Ltd, 1928).
[133] Van Heyningen, 'Public Health'.
[134] Cecil Lewis and Gertrude Edwards, *Cape Town: Treasures of the Mother City* (Cape Town: Speciality Press of South Africa, 1927), 165.

'beautify' the city and give it a 'more modernized' appearance, thanks to the removal of Dutch *stoeps*, levelling of roads, creation of footpaths, and a 'well organised police force' and Fire Brigade whose members wore the same uniforms as their counterpart in London. Thanks to Mr Pritchard, sanitary engineer for Birmingham and London, a comprehensive water and sanitation scheme was on its way.[135] Structures built during British colonial times were singled out for praise, like the recently completed Houses of Parliament. Thanks to Trollope the Castle received mention as a 'landmark reminder of an extraordinary history', but one marked by executions and slavery; equally, the Dutch Town House was 'far from being a credit to the city'.[136] Only oblique reference was made to Malays in a reference to the 'interesting' sight of 'women [some of whom would have been Muslim] taking washing backwards and forwards' to the Platteklip wash-house. In terms of Cape Town's uniqueness, the emphasis instead was on Cape Town's topographical splendour and climate, with cooling south-easterly winds producing the dramatic 'table-cloth' cloud effect over Table Mountain. In addition, 'no city has such pleasant suburbs'.[137]

Overall, the guide was meant as a testament to British achievement. This was a sentiment shared by a short guidebook produced by the Queen's Hotel, Sea Point, in 1897: 'old flat-roofed houses of bygone days' were now 'standing side by side with fine new buildings which would do credit to the streets of any modern city'.[138] This association of progress with British rule came to characterise promotional material for Durban as well. Before the 1880s, the city had fared poorly in most external depictions. The insubstantial frontier nature of the place was captured in several sketches and articles in the *ILN* in the 1850s.[139] Two decades later, Trollope noted that Durban had a 'reputation for heat' and mosquitoes, and warned his readers against going there in summer. Having crossed the Bar himself, Trollope believed Durban had the worst harbour in South Africa. The city's one redeeming feature was the beauty of the flora, fauna and vistas of the Berea, to which 'the visitor is taken . . . as the first among the sights of the place'.[140]

By the 1880s, municipal improvements along British lines were applauded in the local anglophone press and began to produce more flattering external reports. The *ILN* referred approvingly to a *Mercury*

[135] Anon, *The Guide to Cape Town: with Information Covering Kimberley and Johannesburg* (Cape Town and Johannesburg: J.C. Juta, 1890), 11, 13, 70.
[136] Ibid., 67, 84.   [137] Ibid., 13, 98.
[138] *A Nutshell Guide to Cape Town* (Cape Town: Queen's Hotel, 1997), 4.
[139] *Illustrated London News*, 16 March 1850, 'Emigration to Natal'; 6 November 1852, 'Entrance of the First Steamer into Port Natal'; 6 January 1855, 'West Street in D'urban: From an Original Sketch'; 27 June 1857, 'West-Street D'urban, Natal'.
[140] Quotation from Trollope, *South Africa*, 202–3; other comments from 193 to 203.

special issue of 1885 on the opening of Durban's first town hall. This boldly declared that the city had at last 'reached the age of architecture'. Paraphrasing much from the *Mercury*, the *ILN* spoke of 'that spirited colonial municipality', gave lengthy details of the building and its tower clock made by a Croydon company, and concluded that the opening celebrations had passed off very well.[141] Mark Twain's favourable judgement reflected the more substantially changed town he encountered a decade later. He thought that Durban was a 'neat and clean town. One notices that without having his attention drawn to it.'[142] Increased municipal revenues had enabled much further tidying of the city centre. Steamers of considerable size could now pass the Bar and dock alongside the wharfs.[143] Like Trollope, Twain praised the Berea. However, what really caught his attention were rickshaws 'drawn by splendidly built black Zulus, so overflowing with strength, seemingly, that it is a pleasure, not a pain, to see them snatch a rickshaw along'.[144]

Twain had identified what subsequently became the leading local-colour element in Durban's place description and promotion for the next eighty years. Rickshaws had only made their appearance in Durban in 1893, a few years before his visit. The first vehicles had been imported from Japan; thereafter they were manufactured locally. To attract custom, especially the custom of tourists, some rickshaw pullers adopted eye-catching headgear and other adornments that grew increasingly elaborate.[145] Rickshaw pullers duly found their way into Joseph Ingram's *The Story of an African Seaport* of 1899, in a photograph and separate comment that they had become 'an important feature in every street scene ... [a few years ago] to ride in a handcart drawn by a feather-bedecked barbarian would have been regarded by respectable burgesses as preposterous'.[146]

African Seaport was an officially sanctioned history, the first of its kind for a South African city. Its appearance reflected the increased market for such publications and was but one of several books by Ingram on Natal's history. In compiling his material, Ingram had the full co-operation of

---

[141] *Natal Mercury*, 28 October 1885 cited in the *Illustrated London News*, 16 January 1886
[142] Twain, *Following the Equator*, 644.
[143] Ingram and Sams, *Story of an African Seaport*, 62–91.
[144] Twain, *Following the Equator*, 644.
[145] Ingram and Sams, *Story of an African Seaport*, 109 (illustration on opposite page); Henderson, *Durban*, 341; R. Posel, 'The Ricksha-pullers of Durban', in P. Maylam and I. Edwards (eds), *The People's City: African Life in Twentieth Century Durban* (Pietermaritzburg and Portsmouth, NH: University of Natal Press and Heinemann, 1996), 202–21.
[146] Ingram and Sams, *Story of an African Seaport*, 27, 109; the illustration of a rickshaw puller is opposite page 109.

port, railway and Town Council officials in a collaboration that formed part of South African place-selling efforts up to the 1960s. A collage of photographs of past mayors of Durban formed his frontispiece and set the tone for what followed. Ingram provided extensive details on municipal development, explained how urban beautification was financed from a Public Improvement Account and the port had become 'an entrepot to the vast trade resources of the sub-continent of Africa'.[147] A short final section focused on contemporary Durban and highlighted services offered by local businesses, hotels and the newly constructed Beach Tea Room.

Like almost all South African city histories before the 1970s, Ingram's book told a story of progress. It was also a particular testament to British colonial achievement serving as promotional material, and a passage asserted 'British Rights to the Seaport'. Ingram proudly described Durban as the most British of South African cities, with magnificent new buildings that were the product of the nation's mercantile enterprise. Ingram concluded that the city had 'a certain and brilliant future'.[148]

George Russell's *Old Durban*, an unofficial history by an early settler, contained the same promotional patriotic sentiments. Both books were published in 1899 on the eve of the Boer War. Russell revelled in the story of Dick King's ride to lift the Boer siege of Durban and denounced the 'cowardly' tactics of the Boers who had 'wanted the country for themselves'. He argued that Durban had been 'squarely traded, bought and paid for' by the British in a deal with Zulu king Shaka, and likened the arrival of British immigrants in the 1840s and 1850s to Romans splashing ashore in ancient Britain. An immigrant sense of Britishness was kept alive by celebrations of Royal occasions like the Queen's birthday. Russell hoped that 'the old British stock' would never be diluted and engender a 'whitey-brown people, subjects of some greater Britain, speaking the language of Volapuk, and ruling the destinies of the borough'. Nonetheless he conceded that there were some in Durban who could be deemed a 'civilized "coloured citizen"'.

Old Durban was a record of 'the struggles, the difficulties, and the victories of those early days', of 'labours achieved and hardships overcome' that would demonstrate to future generations to whom they owed 'the prosperity of the beautiful town which is their heritage'.[149] Russell glorified Durban further by linking its history to classical times,

[147] Ibid., Preface.   [148] Ibid., 27–8.
[149] G. Russell, *The History of Old Durban and Reminiscences of an Emigrant of 1850* (Durban: P. Davis and Sons, 1899). Quotations given are from xiv, 6, 18, 38, 511. Volapuk was an attempt at constructing an international language by a German Roman Catholic priest, Johann Schleyer, in its ambition a forerunner of other such attempts such as Esperanto.

suggesting that the Phoenicians may have visited the Bay of Natal area. This connection to classical times was a device typical of many eighteenth-century histories of British towns, as well as a suggestion that occurs in histories of Cape Town and Johannesburg.[150] For Russell, Durban had become 'the most progressive seaport town of South Africa, a fitting replica of the Carthage of the North'.[151]

W.P.M. Henderson's *Durban: Fifty Years' Municipal History* promoted the city in similar patriotic fashion after the Boer War, when the creation of South Africa under the British flag had become an imminent possibility. Durban was competing with Cape Town to be its major port and seaside resort. All the major cities were seeking immigrants and investment. Henderson provided a minutely detailed chronology of municipal meetings, decisions and progress in transforming 'a few wooden huts and shanties ... sandy tracks ... and primitively sunk wells ... on an unhealthy, sand-swept flat into the most beautiful South African seaport town' replete with the amenities of a city in Britain. Illustrations of Durban's past and present reinforced the message. In what was an official history to mark the Town Council's golden anniversary, Henderson, like Ingram, featured portraits of large numbers of mayors, councillors and council officials, British immigrants or men of British descent, who contributed to this transformation, which would presumably have affirmed a sense of British identity among its likely readers.[152]

Given that the war was now over, Henderson gave more space than the earlier histories to the overt promotion of tourism. Rickshaw pullers featured again, but many other attractions of the 'most picturesque town' in South Africa, one with an 'incomparable climate during the Winter Season', were set out in detail. 'Mailships now enter the harbour directly', to a modern all-season resort. Everything possible had been done to preserve the 'picturesque' through its public buildings, the recently completed Victoria Embankment, 'which provides a magnificent promenade along the Bay side', the Town Gardens and other parks.[153] Endorsement came from Australian visitor Ambrose Pratt, denouncer of Johannesburg as New Babylon, who applauded municipal efforts in making Durban 'a beautiful city'.[154]

Durban by the Sea: Official Illustrated Handbook, the city's first guidebook published jointly by the Natal Railways and Durban Municipality in

---

[150] Rosemary Sweet, *The Writing of Urban Histories in Eighteenth-Century England* (Oxford: The Clarendon Press, 1997).

[151] Russell, *Old Durban*, 511.

[152] Henderson, *Fifty Years' Municipal History*; quotations from page 1 to 361.

[153] Henderson, *Fifty Years' Municipal History*, 360–74; the quotations are from page 360.

[154] Pratt, *The Real South Africa*, 46.

1908, indicated that tourism was increasing. Local colour loomed large in its description of Durban's attractions, along with sub-tropical flora and fauna and plentiful examples of modernity. 'Brightly-turbaned Indians' and rickshaw pullers 'fantastically adorned with plumes, curiously fashioned bracelets of copper wire, and necklaces of bead work; electric tramcars; the latest design in motors – all these give life to the streets.'[155] A guide produced by the Marine Hotel offered visitors the possibility of seeing similarly startling juxtapositions, such as an anthropology professor being pulled through the streets by a 'burly Zulu, decked out in all the gaudy trappings of barbarism'. Additionally, the Fitzsimons Snake Park was a unique local attraction with 'hundreds of deadly poisonous snakes from all parts of Africa.[156]

Both guidebooks depicted Durban as simultaneously modern, with its new town hall (Illustration 2.2) 'the most handsome structure on the continent', and enticingly exotic, demonstrating the way that promotional city material recycled and reinforced distinctive characteristics even if the tone varied. The Marine Hotel guide's description of cosmopolitanism was fanciful:

In the main streets a raw Kafir girl in beads and blankets, just in from the kraal, may be seen walking alongside her civilised sister, radiant in all the glory of a fashionable European gown, with picture hat and high-heeled shoes to match ... a mingling of the most primitive savagery and most advanced civilization ... all living in peace and comfort under the same laws, and the protection of the same flag.[157]

The *Illustrated Handbook*'s description, in contrast, was more restrained:

At every turn one is struck by the cosmopolitan air of the town, where the sons of three great continents, besides representatives of almost every civilised and uncivilised nation, live and work in harmony.[158]

The Marine Hotel guide's title, *Durban, the Brighton of South Africa*, reveals the way publicity material promoted the city in Mother Country fashion to the British as a seaside resort for health and recreation.[159] Although it acknowledged that the summer might be 'a little warm for the English constitution', winter weather was favourably compared to

---

[155] General Manager of Railways and Durban Corporation, *Durban by the Sea: Official Illustrated Handbook* (Durban: Durban Municipality and Natal Railways, 1908), 5–6. Both this early publicity material and post-1922 Durban Publicity Association publications are available in the Durban Municipality, Don Collection, Durban.
[156] James J. McQuade, *Durban: The Brighton of South Africa, a Souvenir from the Marine Hotel* (Durban: Marine Hotel, c.1910), 2, 17, 18.
[157] Ibid., 3.
[158] General Manager of Railways and Durban Corporation, *Durban by the Sea*, 6.
[159] Ward, *Selling Places*, 31–82; Urry, *Tourist Gaze*, 20, 155.

that of the renowned Karoo.[160] Statistics were used to support the claim that Durban's death rate was now 'the lowest in the world', around 5 per 1,000 in some monthly returns, 'in spite of a large native and Asiatic population'.[161] This had been achieved through filtered water supply, the 'almost complete' sewerage system and the elimination of malaria and other infectious diseases.[162]

Pratt's *Real South Africa* was one traveller's account that acknowledged the Marine Hotel's line of promotion by also calling Durban 'the Brighton of South Africa'.[163] This angle remained a feature of Durban publicity material after Union. The *Durban Guide* of 1915 boasted that the city had a 'complete sewerage system', no 'dust, fog, mist or mud' and even that it was 'free of slums'. An official visitor's room and enquiry bureau had now been set up opposite the town hall, itself 'lasting proof' of the municipality's effort to 'beautify Durban'. Amenities compared well with the best resorts in England: an enclosure for (Whites-only) mixed gender bathing; a zoo with 'almost all' African animals and even polar bears; the Victoria Embankment and sea front; and excellent schools, cinemas, theatres and concert halls. As well as rickshaw pullers, local colour was provided by the Indian market's 'truly oriental atmosphere'. Patriotic Britishness predictably remained part of a guide produced during the First World War. It contained photographs of Dick King, mention of the memorial to those who died for queen and country during the Boer War, and comment that the Old Fort 'teems with memories of the early pioneers who fought for liberty'.[164]

Compared to the two port cities, there was little promotional material for Johannesburg before the 1920s. The existence of gold had been lure enough for prospectors and businessmen. Artisans, labourers and the self-employed followed, driven there through desire for material betterment or by poverty, taxes and insufficient land. Brief descriptions in early travellers' accounts and guides were far from enticing, even if less melodramatically off-putting than those of De Bremont's or Blackburn's novels. Juta's *Cape Town Guide* of 1890, which provided some information on Johannesburg, listed some positive developments like the (first) Rand Club, banks, the stock exchange, skating rink, circus and theatres. However, Johannesburg was still described as unprepossessing, with

[160] General Manager of Railways and Durban Corporation, *Durban by the Sea*, 4, 8, 9.
[161] Ibid., 8. McQuade, *Durban. The Brighton of South Africa*, 4.
[162] General Manager, South African Railways and Durban Corporation, *Durban. The White City. Official Illustrated Handbook* (Durban: South African Railways and Durban Corporation, n.d. [c.1914]), 15–16.
[163] Pratt, *The Real South Africa*, 46.
[164] Anon, *Durban Guide* (Durban: P. Davis and Sons Ltd, 1915), 8, 10, 21.

many living in shacks or under canvas. Similar comments were made in *The Transvaal and How To Reach It*, also published in 1890, whose author could find no distinguishing 'characteristic, such as tall towers, chimney stacks, or graceful church steeples, which would break the severe monotony of the vast amount of galvanized iron roofing'.[165]

Yet one characteristic mentioned in passing by the two early guides was seized on by the *ILN* in 1895 as a matter of positive distinction, namely Johannesburg's 'shock city' rapid growth.[166] From then on most books about Johannesburg featured photos of a few tents amid open veldt in 1886 juxtaposed with skyscrapers of 'today', whenever today happened to be. As Johannesburg historian L.E. Neame put it in 1959, this was proof that 'No town in the world has grown more rapidly than Johannesburg' into a modern metropolis.[167]

Other positive distinctions were discovered around the time of Union. Scully's predominantly negative account of 1911 contained two when he described the Rand as 'the most frenzied centre of physical energy in the world', and suggested that mine dumps were its 'Swiss Alps'. Emile Lauste, a French cinematographer, thought another worth filming. His short travelogue, *Sunday Morning Scenes, Kaffir Compound, Johannesburg*, captured what an inter-title described as 'the Kafir Boys prepare for their usual Sunday morning occupation: dancing.'[168] In time, mine dancing became Johannesburg's principal element of local colour, its promotional equivalent of Durban's rickshaw pullers or Cape Town's New Year minstrels. The ersatz 'traditional' dress of mine dancers stressed a rural migrant identity distinct from that of thoroughly urbanised industrial workers, even if miners were clearly not people of the market-place.

The first official Johannesburg publicity material, published after the crushing of the Rand Revolt, initially ignored the possible use of mine dancers as local colour. It focused instead on Johannesburg's shock city achievement of European modernity and the health-giving qualities of its climate, like much port city material. A guide published jointly between the municipality and the SAR&H in 1924 took this approach despite acknowledging that Johannesburg had no river, sea, mountain or major lake. Instead Johannesburg's appeal was to be found in its modernity, epitomised in a photograph of the 'irresistibly fascinating' Munro Drive.

---

[165] Dennis Edwards, *The Transvaal and How to Reach It* (Cape Town: Dennis Edwards and Co., 1890), 27.
[166] Anon, *The Guide to Cape Town*; Edwards, *The Transvaal and How to Reach It*; *Illustrated London News*, 24 August 1895.
[167] Neame, *City Built on Gold*, 238.
[168] BFI, Emile Lauste (dir.), *Sunday Morning Scenes, Kaffir Compound, Johannesburg* (Britain: W. Butcher and Sons Production Company, 1911).

Borrowing ideas from Scully, the guide also spoke of Johannesburg as a 'vital force that is as irresistible as it is unique ... an atmosphere so charged with electricity and life and animation that the very memory of it makes the blood tingle and your heart beat more quickly'. Aimed at potential residents as much as (perhaps more than) tourists, the guide included photographs of white mine dumps and what it described as 'ceaseless and reverberating' mine batteries, adding that for returning South Africans they 'tell of home'. The guide also waxed lyrical about the city's northern suburbs:

In delightful valleys, out of sight and sound of the busy industrial area, the red roofs of thousands of handsome and even palatial residences besprinkle the verdure of the plantations which abound ... the houses present a pleasing appearance of individuality and architectural craft.[169]

In a sole exception to the air-brushing out of an African presence in Johannesburg, the guide mentioned here that 'native houseboys and maids are easily obtainable'.[170]

City publicity associations

When a Johannesburg Publicity Association (JPA) was established in November 1925, on Rotary Club initiative, early distinguishing characteristics discovered for the city featured in its publicity material. Considerable strategic continuity was provided by the fact that the JPA's first director, H.J. Crocker, served in this capacity until 1953. His guiding mantra was that promotional material should be about 'making accessible what we have to show and what we have to sell'. The JPA soon did so through further guidebooks, a Johannesburg history published in London aimed at a popular market, and sponsoring elaborate celebrations to mark Johannesburg's decennial anniversaries starting in 1926.[171]

Hedley Chilvers' *Out of the Crucible* was the JPA-sponsored history dedicated 'to those pioneers of the Witwatersrand whose faith and tenacity made the miracle of our goldfields possible'. It provided a racy Dark Tourism foray into what its readers could understand to be a stormy past no longer present, full of colourful characters, hard living, disasters, death and revolution: the title of one chapter was 'Karl Marx comes to town'.[172]

---

[169] Johannesburg Municipality and SAR&H, *Johannesburg, South Africa* (Johannesburg: Johannesburg Municipality and SAR&H, 1924), 7.
[170] Ibid., 40.
[171] Crocker cited in Felix Stark, *Johannesburg: Seventy Golden Years, 1886–1956* (Johannesburg: Felstar Publishing, 1956), 31.
[172] John Lennon and Malcolm Foley, *Dark Tourism: The Attraction of Death and Disaster* (New York and London: Continuum, 2000).

A lengthy account of the Rand Revolt preceded a concluding account of the pageant held to celebrate the city's fortieth anniversary held on 22 September 1926 that suggested traumatic events were a thing of the past.[173] Chilvers' book concluded with the assertion that Johannesburg continued 'to stand, assertive, solid, and enduring through the nights and dawns of the crowded years'.[174]

Organised by the JPA, the 1926 pageant was intended to be 'a picturesque endorsement of historical achievement' with triumphal arches, numerous floats of pioneers and aeroplanes dropping leaflets with celebratory greetings. The pageant also featured Black mine workers as local colour, with miners grouped on different floats according to perceived ethnicity, and music supplied by a Chope band. Only a month later, and proving the success of this promotional tactic, the *ILN* featured a vividly coloured painting of a mine dance against the backdrop of mine dump and battery. The heading was 'Where visitors to South Africa can watch real barbaric "jazz": A Native War Dance on the Rand' (Illustration 4.3). Details were provided of how arrangements could be made to see this 'regular weekly' event through South Africa's High Commission in Trafalgar Square.

Cape Town had pioneered organised city promotion through the Cape Peninsula Publicity Association (CPPA) in 1909, presumably influenced by similar initiatives by British cities. Unlike municipalities in Britain, for whom restrictive government legislation meant that publicity efforts had to be surreptitious, the Cape Town City Council could play an open and central role.[175] The CPPA's origins lay in events of 1908. A municipal council committee, chaired by Mayor William Duncan Baxter, a leading merchant, organised a Grand Gala season to attract South African and overseas visitors to the city over the summer months. The wide array of activities included 'Fancy-Dress' cricket, kite-flying, daily concerts by military bands, nightly performances by naval cadets under torch-light, a 'Water carnival', bicycle procession and regatta in Table Bay. Cecil Rhodes' estate, Groote Schuur, was opened to the public, as were British warships. A guidebook listed events, recommended suitable hotels and boarding houses, and described Cape Town as a 'glorious … warm-hearted Tavern of the Oceans'.

The CPPA was meant to maintain the momentum gained by the Grand Gala and take advantage of promotional possibilities enhanced by South African Union. In more American than British fashion, it interleaved city boosterism with nation-selling.[176] Distancing both city and nation from

---

[173] *ILN*, 23 October 1926.
[174] H.A. Chilvers, *Out of the Crucible: Being the Romantic Story of the Witwatersrand Goldfields and the Great City Which Arose in Their Midst* (London: Cassell, 1929), Dedication, 231.
[175] Ward, *Selling Places*, 37.   [176] Ward, *Selling Places*, 5.

Illustration 4.3: The use of local colour in promoting cities 1: mine dance, Johannesburg, first published in 1926 (Mary Evans Picture Gallery).

the horrors of the Boer War, the CPPA's inaugural guidebook featured the contribution of both Dutch and British in bringing 'civilisation' to Africa, and promoted Cape Town as the 'Mother City' of a White British South African nation. This concept was reinforced by the pageant held in the city to celebrate the birth of this nation in 1910.

The guidebook's stated aim was to make 'the attractions of the Mother City of South Africa better known to the travelling public'. Approving comments of notable British visitors to the Cape were listed by way of endorsement, from Sir Francis Drakes's 'the fairest Cape we saw in the whole circumference of the world' to Lord Curzon's assertion that of all South Africa's cities Cape Town was 'richest in historical association'. Randolph Churchill was invoked to suggest that the Cape 'brought into mind successively Gibraltar, the Riviera, and the Bay of Palermo', though British travellers would not find 'foreigners' but 'people of their own race, speaking their own language', alongside beautiful scenery and sunshine. Confirmation that the guide was aimed at British tourists or immigrants was the inclusion of Milner's doubtless reassuring view that the city was an 'outpost of British power' as well as a 'home of European culture'.[177]

---

[177] J.R. Finch, *Cape of Good Hope: Being the Official Handbook of the City of Cape Town* (Cape Town: CPPA, 1909), 5–9.

Over a further 200 pages, the guidebook went beyond eulogies of Cape landscape, climate, flora and fauna to provide a Baedeker-style compilation of information about notable buildings, monuments, cultural institutions, historical associations, recreational possibilities and suggested excursions. The CPPA opened a visitor's bureau in Adderley Street and produced hundreds of brochures, guides, posters and films over subsequent decades, continuing to promote the city as both the Tavern of the Oceans (or Seas) and the Mother City of South Africa. Its promotional efforts were aided by those of local newspapers, with the *Cape Times* having series like 'Cape Town and the Picturesque Peninsula', 'Sights of Cape Town' or a 'Visitors Daily Page' running intermittently in the summer season from Union to the 1950s.[178]

Portrayals of its picturesque setting remained central to Cape Town's promotion. As *The Land of the Golden South* put it, 'few of the great enterprises of nations have found their origins in an environment more striking and beautiful'.[179] Also much used was Cape Town's claim to being 'the oldest civilised part of the sub-continent' that had 'historical associations which can be claimed by no other part of South Africa'.[180] 'Discovery of the past' in twentieth-century South Africa became part of popularising urban attractions as it had done in eighteenth-century Britain.[181]

The CPPA and unofficial guides like *Cape Town: Treasures of the Mother City of South Africa* featured sites with historical associations related to a grand narrative of White South African history established in the nineteenth-century accounts by Wilmot and Theal.[182] Several sites, like the Castle or Groot Constantia, reflected the Dutch colonial period. Others were creations of the British colonial period intended to create a common White identity for British and Dutch settlers, like the South African Library, Houses of Parliament and the South African Museum. Their inclusion nonetheless implied that British colonialism was crucial in ensuring that Cape Town, *pace* Trollope, was not without its improving cultural riches.[183]

---

[178] CPPA pamphlets are in the University of Cape Town Library, Special Collections/ African Studies Library. CPPA, *Cape Town for Health and Pleasure* (Cape Town: CPPA, 1913); Ward, *Selling Places*, 30–82.

[179] CPPA, *The Land of the Golden South* (Cape Town: CPPA, 1927), 3.

[180] CPPA, *Cape Town for Health and Pleasure*, 4.

[181] Rosemary Sweet, *Antiquaries: the Discovery of the Past in Eighteenth-Century Britain*, (London: Hambledon, 2004), 309–43.

[182] Lewis and Edwards, *Treasures of the Mother City*. Apart from much other CPPA material, the Finch guide of 1909 was also revised and reissued in a new edition in 1926.

[183] Saul Dubow, *A Commonwealth of Knowledge: Science, Sensibility and White South Africa, 1820–2000* (Oxford: Oxford University Press, 2006).

Several sites more overtly reinforced a British or Dutch/Afrikaner ethno-nationalism. Many were associated with leading proponent of a British South Africa Cecil Rhodes, a man 'who never spared himself in the service of the country' as one among many CPPA pamphlets put it: the cottage where he died at Muizenberg, his Groote Schuur estate and Rhodes Memorial.[184] In contrast, Koopmans De Wet House had Afrikaner associations not simply because it was an example of a Dutch colonial townhouse, but because it was used as a clothing depot for Boer prisoners during the South African War. The national botanical gardens at Kirstenbosch were opened in 1913, in the wake of Union, to counter potential divisiveness and suggest a sense of shared White South African heritage.[185]

Some popular Cape histories had a similar intention, motivated by didactic and commercial considerations. Several women authors targeted a female readership. *South African Yesterdays* featured a gallery of famous women and had sections on gossip of by-gone days, old-time shopping, servant problems in the 1850s and the question of whether women came to the Cape in search of husbands.[186] Ex-Guild of Loyal Women member Dorothea Fairbridge's history of *Lady Anne Barnard at the Cape* was overtly about a woman who had attempted to reconcile Dutch colonists to British rule.[187]

Fairbridge wanted similar unity under the British flag. Two other books by her, *Historic Houses* and *Gardens of South Africa*, included examples from cities to suggest that White South African national identity within the British Empire consisted of equally valuable Dutch and British contributions.[188] She praised both indigenous and British flora, advising that though you might have to plant roses in pots in Durban because of the 'ravages of white ants', they 'grew to perfection in the Transvaal'.[189] In Fairbridge's view, those of British origins had to love South Africa as much as they did the Mother Country. This was the position taken by her fictional protagonist, Rosetta Moore, in her informal guidebook, *Along Cape Roads*. Moore opts to settle in the Cape rather than return to Britain.[190]

---

[184] CPPA, *The Cape Peninsula* (Cape Town: CPPA, c.1920), 5.
[185] Bickford-Smith et al., *Cape Town in the Twentieth Century*, 42.
[186] Annette Joelson, *South African Yesterdays* (Cape Town: Unie-Volkspers Beperk, 1940); Apart from Dorothea Fairbridge's work cited below, another woman writer was Gertrude Edwards, co-author of *Cape Town: Treasures of the Mother City*.
[187] Fairbridge, *Lady Anne Barnard at the Cape of Good Hope*.
[188] Dorothea Fairbridge, *Historic Houses of South Africa* (Cape Town: Maskew Miller, 1922); Dorothea Fairbridge, *Gardens of South Africa* (London: A. & C. Black Ltd, 1924).
[189] Fairbridge, *Gardens*, 25, 32.   [190] Fairbridge, *Along Cape Roads*.

Percy Laidler, author of several books on Cape history, probably had men more in mind when writing *A Tavern of the Ocean*, 'a history of Cape Town and its white inhabitants from the people's point of view'.

It is a drunken, roistering history, for the Cape was not the home of the merchant princes of the East India Company, but merely the sordid workshop in which many employees drank their wages, died, and were sometimes eaten by dogs.[191]

Like Chilvers for Johannesburg, Laidler was providing a dark historical tour of the past, the better to attest to progress in the present. In Laidler's account this was achieved 'step by step' under British rule.[192]

From its inauguration through to the Second World War, CPPA material, like Durban place-selling, advocated *Cape Town for Health and Pleasure*, as one title it put it.[193] Cape Town was presented as if it were a European seaside, spa or mountain town with equivalent facilities. CPPA publications continued to be aimed at the metropolitan British, who were urged to 'follow the example of the swallows' and 'escape the European winter', and contained advertisements for the Mount Nelson and International Hotels.[194] Views of the gardens and sea in Camp's Bay, with its warm sea-water swimming pool, were again like Durban compared to a more sunlit Brighton or Hove. Outdoor activities in a splendid climate were lauded for the physically and spiritually improving qualities they afforded.[195] An early CPPA publication, *The Summit*, listed seventy different routes up Table Mountain to indulge in the South African equivalent of Alpine pleasure.[196]

What distinguished CPPA material from its Durban equivalent from the 1890s to late 1920s was the CPPA's emphasis on the European nature of Cape Town's attractions and almost complete omission of local colour. Pratt had denounced the 'evils of miscegenation' he perceived in the 'lazy and insolent ... mongrels' of the city in 1910, and the CPPA wished rather to promote his view that Cape Town was the Union's 'most civilized town' by making little mention of its 'mixed-race' inhabitants.[197] Cape Town was not advertised as a cosmopolitan African destination, as in much Durban place promotion, but as *The Riviera of the South*, with the

[191] P.W. Laidler, *A Tavern of the Ocean* (Cape Town: Maskew Miller, 1926), Preface.
[192] Ibid., 176.   [193] See footnote 103.
[194] CPPA, Bulletin No. 63, *The Climate of South Africa* (Cape Town: CPPA, undated c.1920), 9, 20.
[195] CPPA, Bulletin No. 62, *The Call of the Camp's Bay Coast* (Cape Town: CPPA, c.1920); Ward, *Selling Places*, 31–82; Urry, *Tourist Gaze*, 20, 155.
[196] CPPA, *The Summit* (Cape Town: CPPA, 1913). Clearly material here as elsewhere was almost endlessly recycled: see CPPA Bulletin 66, *Table Mountain: Some Easy Ways to the Summit* (Cape Town: CPPA, 1914).
[197] Pratt, *The Real South Africa*, 48.

view from its pier surpassing any in Naples.[198] This was a similar strategy to initial JPA Union government publicity material like *Urban Residence in the Union of South Africa* (1929), which showed Black South Africans only as domestic servants amid its panoramas of scenic beauty and urban modernity.[199]

A rare exception in CPPA material was made in the relatively un-exotic and unthreatening case of Coloured women flower-sellers outside the Post Office in Adderley Street (Illustration 4.4). Through the CPPA's agency, photographs of flower-sellers by a Mrs Caleb Keen first made their appearance on Cape Town postcards in 1910. After the First World War, postcards produced by Central News Agency bookstores also featured Cape Town flower-sellers. One much photographed was a Mrs Susan Ferreira, who also appeared on chocolate box covers.[200] CPPA guidebooks featured flower-sellers by 1927.[201] In 1937, flower-sellers achieved central government tourist authority recognition in an official SAR&H guide to South Africa.[202] Thereafter they featured not only in guides but also city histories, souvenir photograph collections and film travelogues.[203]

The Durban Publicity Association (DPA), inaugurated in 1922, continued to make extensive use of local colour in Durban place promotion, far more so than the CPPA in the 1920s. In 1926 the DPA's *Delightful Durban* insisted the city was as diverse in terms of race, speech and dress as London, Paris and New York. West Street was 'at once [Durban's] ... Oxford Street and ... Cheapside'. Cosmopolitan juxtapositions followed as in earlier Durban guidebooks. One addition was a passage expressing confidence in the city's racially stratified police force:

to round off the varied kaleidoscope of Durban life, here are Native and Indian policemen, supplementing the European ... The Bantu policemen, garbed in neat knickerbockers uniform, carry the native sticks and knobkerries which ... they can use with unerring aim and skill; ... the Indian police officer is dressed much in the

[198] CPPA, *The Riviera of the South* (Cape Town: CPPA, 1929). J.R. Finch, *Cape of Good Hope: Being the Official Handbook of the City of Cape Town* (Cape Town: CPPA, [1909] 1926), 126. A revised edition of the original guide.

[199] SAR&H, *Urban Residence in the Union of South Africa* (Pretoria: SAR&H, 1929).

[200] Lawrence Green, *A Taste of South-Easter* (Cape Town: Howard Timmins, 1971), 103.

[201] See for instance CPPA, *The Land of the Golden South*; Fairbridge, *Along Cape Roads*, 4; Lewis and Edwards, *Treasures of the Mother City*, 14–15.

[202] Anon, *Six Thousand Miles of Sunshine Travel over the South African Railways* (Pretoria: South African Harbours and Railways, 1937), 19–20.

[203] Katherine L. Simms, *Springbok in Sunshine* (London: Hutchinson and Company, 1946), 19–24; A. Mehrtens, *Cape Town: 50 Photographs* (Cape Town: A.A. Balkema, 1950), photograph 11; H.C. Weaver (dir.), *South Africa: A Preview* (Johannesburg: South African Tourist Corporation (producers), 1954); Alfred H. Honikman, *Cape Town: City of Good Hope* (Cape Town: Howard Timmins, 1966), 9.

Illustration 4.4: The use of local colour in promoting cities 2: flower-sellers, Adderley Street, Cape Town in the late 1920s (Mary Evans Picture Gallery).

manner of the European constable save that a peaked cap takes the place of the familiar helmet.[204]

Delightful Durban was one attempt to give the Natal Port a sobriquet in response to Cape Town's Tavern of the Seas or Mother City. Another, not seen as at odds with cosmopolitanism, was 'The Most British of all South African Towns'.

Its people, its buildings, its thoroughfares and parks, its manners and customs, are so inherently British that its very atmosphere seems redolent of the Old Country … it is no foreign or alien city … but a distant branch of 'Home', a bit of Britain dumped down amid the splendid, sub-tropical environment of the coastal region of Natal.[205]

Both the DPA and JPA appear to have realised more swiftly than the CPPA that overseas visitors would rank local colour high among unique attractions of British South African cities. By the 1930s, the CPPA was

[204] Durban Publicity Association (DPA) and SAR&H, *Delightful Durban. Sunny South Africa's Seaside Resort* (Durban: DPA, 1926), 3, 4, 49.
[205] DPA and SAR&H, *Delightful Durban* (Durban: DPA, c. mid-1920s), 3. This had much similar material to the 1926 guide, but also new sections including the one cited.

embracing its potential more enthusiastically. The lessening threat of major urban unrest in an economically more prosperous and politically quiescent decade may help explain why this happened. Another may have been that the CPPA, for all its protestations to the contrary, realised that colonial cities like Cape Town could not easily compete with northern counterparts in terms of modernity alone, and needed to be judged by different criteria as well.

Urban Residence in the Union implicitly acknowledged as much when mentioning the 'superior joys of London and such places' while suggesting that 'for those who can separate themselves from the Strand and Oxford Street there should be no difficulty in finding contentment in a South African town selected with discrimination'.[206] Contentment would be delivered by a more congenial climate, splendid topography and 'easier' domestic circumstances than those in inter-war Britain.

Servants are much more plentiful to-day throughout South Africa than in most countries ... [and] ... the Bantus are on the whole a docile race, respectful and amenable to discipline when in the hand of competent employers ... the drawback of employing males ... is not nearly as disconcerting as the general drawbacks in the servant position in Britain.[207]

That South African cities should be judged by different criteria, in this case the relative absence of urban congestion, was also evident in a poem called 'London Traffic', contained within a South African anthology of the 1930s:

> A bus in Oxford Street, and he and I within it,
> Held up by press
> Of traffic. 'So this is London! Here' said I,
> 'Must be the central stream.' In his reply
> Compassion for Colonials spoke: ...
> 'At Hyde Park Corner pass,'
> Said he, 'a hundred vehicles a minute
> For twelve hours every day; and where Trafalgar's hero, in Trafalgar
>   Square
> Salutes South Africa, tis little less –
> ...
> What think you now of Adderley Street, old boy?
> And where's Johannesburg? And Durban? Pity
> That more Colonials cannot see a city!'
> –But the 'old boy',
> Not willing to destroy

---

[206] SAR&H, *Urban Residence*, 16.
[207] Ibid., 44. Six pages are devoted to the availability and average wages of domestic servants in towns of the Union.

His eager friend's exuberance of patriotic joy,
Withheld retort.
Why damp such fervid eloquence by telling what I thought![208]

A further reason for South African publicity associations to embrace local colour was the close relationship between the development of cinema and the growth of mass tourism. Cinema offered a form of virtual tourism, a spectacle of movement along with information, for which mine dances, rickshaw pulling and New Year carnival parades were perfect subjects. By the 1930s, the possible addition of sound and colour made them even more appealing, at a time when film was playing an ever increasing role in shaping transnational perceptions.[209]

Film, photography and local colour

From 1910 the SAR&H, the department of central government responsible for promoting tourism, made extensive use of both photography and film in South African place promotion, as government-owned railways did in other countries.[210] Many travelogues were made for the SAR&H by Schlesinger's African Film Productions (AFP) company; indeed the latter's patronage helped to sustain South Africa's often faltering film industry before a state subsidy system was introduced in the 1950s. Even then the state information office continued to help finance numerous travelogues.[211]

Early SAR&H films focused on the country's landscape of wide open spaces and wild animals, as did its photography. This iconography of emptiness in a landscape washed with sunshine was also portrayed in SAR&H posters and brochures.[212] Cape Town was the city that featured more than most thanks to its dramatic geographical setting, making brief appearances in *The Beautiful Cape Peninsula* (1915), *The Cape of Good Hope* (1932), *The Sea* (1935) and *The Day Awakens* (1936). By the 1930s, the CPPA gave Cape Town greater prominence in films it commissioned AFP to make, like *Cape Town: A Tavern of the Ocean* (1936) and *Cape Town: Gateway to a Continent* (1940), to 'lend to passenger liners' on the Cape route, and to exchange with similar films in the possession of 'overseas publicity associations'.[213]

[208] Arthur Vine Hall, 'London Traffic', in *Poems of South Africa* (London: Longmans, Green and Co., 1935), 62–3.
[209] Bruno, *Atlas of Emotion*, 191.
[210] Ward, *Selling Places*, 41–4; Foster, *Washed with Sun*, 200–37.
[211] On the introduction of a state subsidy system see K. Tomaselli, *The Cinema of Apartheid* (New York: Lake View Press, 1988).
[212] Foster, *Washed with Sun*.   [213] Gutsche, *Motion Pictures*, 312–54.

Of the SAR&H films, *The Cape of Good Hope* gave most screen time to Cape Town itself, and did so with foreign tourists much in mind. An opening sequence featured a map of Africa and the tip of the Cape Peninsula, accompanied by the commentary that this was rounded by Bartholmew Diaz in the 1480s. Panoramas of the Peninsula's mountain chain followed by shots of the 'Mother City's' harbour inform the viewer that this is the 'Gateway to Africa', thereby adding another sobriquet to Cape Town's list. Aspects of the city's built environment that feature are in keeping with CPPA guides: the Castle, Groot Constantia and Rhodes Memorial, in 'illustrious memory of a great patriot'.

Local colour was offered as a further distinctive Cape Town trait in a sequence that begins with the voice-over narration 'Just a moment, here come the Cape Coloured Coons', and has minstrels wearing satin costumes, playing violins and banjos, and singing American negro spirituals strolling past electric trams.[214] The likely reason for this inclusion was that Britain's Topical Film Company had already produced *Coloured Folks Carnival* in 1928, in which New Year minstrels were introduced by the inter-title: 'grotesquely attired grown-ups and piccanins celebrate New Year's Day with procession and war-dance through the streets of Cape Town'. Groups parading up Adderley Street included 'Red Indians'; a troupe seemingly dressed as cowboys was shown on the pier. The eminently cinematic Coon Carnival had received outsider endorsement as a unique South African city attraction, as had happened with rickshaw pullers and mine dances.[215] All were making regular appearances in both local and overseas newsreels, travelogues and photography as well as publicity association material and city histories by the 1930s.

Local-colour depictions of New Year minstrels were further additions to South African portrayals of the popular in its place, with Coloured Capetonians referred to as the Cockneys of the Cape by anglophone authors like Sarah Gertrude Millin.[216] As novelist Joy Packer put it in the 1960s, 'the Cape Coloureds are a gay, good natured people ... their ready humour is as quick and individual as the cockney'.[217] Coloureds, like Cockneys, were represented as people of wit, cheerfulness and

[214] SANFVSA: Publicity Department, SARH, *The Cape of Good Hope* (South Africa: African Film Productions Company, 1932).
[215] BFI: Anon (dir.), *Coloured Folks Carnival* (Britain: Topical Film Company, 1928). Further information on the Topical Film Company can be obtained from the British Film Institute website.
[216] Sarah Gertrude Millin, *The South Africans* (New York: Boni & Liveright, [1927] 1928), 215; A.W. Wells, *South Africa* (London: John Dent & Sons, [1939] 1947), 43.
[217] Joy Packer in *Apes and Ivory* cited in John A. Stokesbury, *Apartheid, Liberalism and Romance: A Critical Investigation of the Writing of Joy Packer* (Umea: Umea University Press, 1996), 123.

picturesque display. They were prone to 'clownish fancy dress', whether as 'Coon' or 'Pearly', and musical 'knees-ups', and depicted as people of distinct dialects and residential areas whose interests seldom extended beyond their immediate locale.[218]

South Africans as local colour continued to be juxtaposed with examples of modern architecture, technology and material progress in literary and visual representations of all three cities, an intentional contrast between un-progressive Black tradition and White modernity. Africans as local colour particularly emphasised rural cultural links, confining the more obviously Westernised among them to the background if shown at all, implying that Africans were not fully part of the city at all.

Such juxtaposition of tradition and modernity was evident in the SAR&H travelogue *On Tour in South Africa: Land of Sunshine and Romance* (1936). This interweaved sequences of Durban's Indian Market, rickshaw pullers and 'mine workers doing their war dances' with Durban's City Hall and Johannesburg's gold mining technology.[219] City histories were narratives of progress from the primitive past to the technologically sophisticated present. A chapter of *Durban: Past and Present* (1936), an officially sanctioned history by Allister Macmillan to mark the acquisition of city status in 1935, was simply 'From Sandbank to Superport'. The book described in detail how this had come about thanks to British enterprise. Durban Indian contribution was that 'by their customs, processions, temples and gay apparel [they] impart to local life a colourful representation of the great land of their birth'. African local colour was more explicitly than ever the popular in its place, a sense conveyed that the unrest of the 1920s had been safely navigated:

From the happy, care-free and gaily decorated Ricksha Puller [*sic*] of the Beach to the head 'ringed' and dignified elder escorting his wives through the streets ... the Zulu race has come to earn itself pride of place as a servant and manual labourer ... he brings to the discharge of his duties a cheerful obedience to the orders of the white man.[220]

Throughout the book prose and photographs contrasted modest urban beginnings and unprogressive but cheerful local colour with European achievement. Such achievement included a lengthy section on what the Council was doing for African welfare, and the assertion that race relations were much improved since the 1920s.

[218] Stedman Jones, 'The "Cockney" and the Nation', 274, 278, 281, 306–7.
[219] SANFVSA: J. Albrecht (dir.), *On Tour in South Africa: Land of Sunshine and Romance* (South Africa: African Film Productions, 1936).
[220] Macmillan (ed.), *Durban Past and Present*, Preface, 83, 113.

Johannesburg's Golden Jubilee celebrations of 1936, and films that depicted it, were of the same ilk. A Pageant of Progress included near its beginning 'Natives' in 'traditional dress' pulling gold bars whose relative sizes contrasted output in 1886 with that of 1936. After floats featuring 'Medieval Knights' and a 'Medieval Castle', (implicitly White) progress took the form of further floats carrying a giant model telephone, a 'Modern House', miniature skyscrapers and tributes to gas power and electric light.[221] To borrow Walter Benjamin's phrase, this was 'modernity ... always quoting [supposedly] primeval history'.[222] One Johannesburg history-come-local-business-directory even speculated that Phoenicians obtained gold from the Rand, before embarking on the story of Johannesburg's transformation from mining camp to 'the vital centre, the very heart of South Africa'.[223]

'Progress' with urban problems

Up to the late 1940s, the representation of South African cities in the national and international media was overwhelmingly positive, helped by continued White middle-class control of the media and South African participation in the Second World War. A rare occasion when the negative opinion of an international visitor reached a substantial audience occurred when a public relations exercise backfired. This involved internationally renowned British playwright and socialist George Bernard Shaw. The CPPA and *Cape Times* persuaded the visiting Shaw in 1932 to ride the cable car up Table Mountain then fly in a Junker aircraft over the peninsula. When asked whether he enjoyed the experience, he merely replied that 'at my time of life you are ... only ... pleased that nothing unpleasant is happening'. Nonetheless the newspaper used Shaw's presence in Cape Town to promote both the existence of the Cape's natural beauty and new ways of seeing it. On the eve of his departure, a reporter for the nascent South African radio service asked Shaw to say some 'nice

---

[221] SANFVSA: Anon (dir.), *Johannesburg Golden Jubilee* (South Africa: African Film Productions, 1936); Anon (dir.), *The Opening of the Empire Exhibition at Johannesburg* (South Africa: African Film Productions, 1936); see also www.Britishpathe.com: Anon (dir.), *News in a Nutshell: Johannesburg Celebrates Its Jubilee* (Britain: Pathe Gazette, 1936). For a detailed analysis of the Exhibition see J. Robinson, 'Johannesburg's 1936 Empire Exhibition: Interaction, Segregation and Modernity in a South African City', *Journal of Southern African Studies* 30, 3 (2003), 759–89.

[222] Walter Benjamin, *Reflections: Essays, Aphorisms, Autobiographical Writings* (New York: Shocken Books, 2007), 157.

[223] Theodore Reunert, *Forty Years of Progress* (Johannesburg and London: Reunert and Lenz Ltd and Albion Publishers, 1928). Reunert was an immigrant from Yorkshire who was co-founder of the Johannesburg Library and on the council of the University of the Witawtersrand.

things' about his visit. His response was that Cape Town 'deserves to be destroyed by fire from heaven' because of its slums.[224]

But Shaw's denunciation of South African slums was nothing new. Commentators across the political spectrum in the anglophone world condemned their existence. Municipalities were publically committed to their erosion, and the Union government introduced the Slums Act of 1934 to hasten the process. Anglophone local newspapers were to the fore in publishing their own 'slum' descriptions.

These newspapers reported extensively on the findings of government commissions, conferences and academic surveys into the living conditions of the poor, publicising their statistics and those of censuses. They pressed for action. An editorial in Johannesburg's *The Star* stated in 1935 that Africans 'herded into slums such as in many South African towns mock our claims to civic progress'.[225] The *Rand Daily Mail* declared the same year that slum 'Plague Spots Must Go', and singled out the likes of Newclare, Malay Camp and Sophiatown as examples. In January 1936, the *Cape Times*, reporting on a housing conference convened by J.H. Hofmeyr (Minister of Public Health) in the city, claimed that Cape Town's housing crisis was the worst in the Union, and the Union housing problem worse than Britain's. Yet the paper acknowledged that some dilapidated parts of District Six had been replaced by flats 'which offer slum dwellers decent accommodation at practically the same rate'.[226] Ndabeni had finally been closed down and replaced by 'fine homes' in Langa, where the 'Native eating house' was supplied with electricity, though even more needed to be done with central government help.[227] Hofmeyr responded by making £1 million of government money available for sub-economic housing.[228]

Books by missionaries and liberals further publicised 'slum' conditions and what was being done to tackle them. Phillips' *The Bantu in the City* of 1939 provided a virtual compendium of inter-war investigation, accompanied by much statistical information on income, cost of living, employment, crime, education and health to show the dire circumstances of Africans in Johannesburg. Phillips reproduced statistics from the Johannesburg Medical Officer of Health between 1923 and 1936 to show that the annual White death-rate was steady at around ten per thousand, whereas for Africans the number had fluctuated between seventeen and twenty-three; this for a population that had a far higher proportion of youthful temporary residents. Yet Phillips stated

---

[224] Cited in Shaw, *The Cape Times*, 86.   [225] *The Star*, 28 October 1935,
[226] *Cape Times*, 9 January 1936.
[227] *Cape Times*, 7–10 January 1936, 16 January 1936.
[228] *Cape Times*, 9 January 1936; *Natal Mercury*, 17 January 1936.

approvingly that 'the gradual elimination of slums from the cities ... is removing the greatest single breeding ground for disease'. The greatest problems remained in the case of premises owned by employers in parts of the Black freehold areas (like Sophiatown and Malay Camp). Remedial action was underway in municipal locations.[229]

Other non-fiction accounts took a similar position, highlighting the need for greater efforts to eradicate slums while acknowledging that much was already being done. *The Christ Visits the World's Wonder City*, published in 1936 and described by its author 'C. Valentine' as a 'reverie', imagined how Jesus would respond on visiting Johannesburg, particularly to the gulf between rich 'social butterflies', who dress extravagantly and leave all domestic work to 'Jim', and the poor in the 'mighty, pulsating, ultra-modern city ... the world's most prosperous'. The reader is guided around Johannesburg's 'poorer haunts ... [characterised by] sordid environment ... [and] sickening dreariness'. Valentine's message was that even the 'lowliest' inhabitants were individuals capable of redemption; immorality and domestic violence were products of social conditions, not the result of any inherent racial characteristics. South Africa should therefore follow Britain's example and pledge sufficient funds to eradicate slums completely, albeit Johannesburg's municipality was trying to do so. Meanwhile all its residents needed to become more Christian, and the rich should contribute generously to charities including Christmas funds sponsored by the *Rand Daily Mail* and *Sunday Times*.[230]

Most non-fiction literature on South African cities argued that progress was possible and happening even if more needed to be done, especially about slum eradication. This was the overall finding of a lengthy exploration into city government in Johannesburg in the late 1930s. It was written by John Maud, later Baron Redcliffe-Maud and the chairman of a British parliamentary investigation into local government in the 1960s that bore his name. Maud's tome was commissioned by the Johannesburg municipality as a review of its history, successes and failures. Maud was given the task because of his experience on Oxford's Town Council. His book was generally complimentary, albeit stating that 'in the sphere of culture the municipality has not been adventurous'. Here Maud noted Johannesburg's relative slowness in creating an art gallery (only in 1912) and public library (in 1924), as

---

[229] Phillips, *The Bantu in the City*, 111–16 for information on mortality rates and incidents of disease.

[230] C. Valentine, *The Christ Visits the World's Wonder City: The Home of a Thousand Witcheries* (Johannesburg: C.L.D. [Pty] Ltd, 1936), 7, 8, 16, 19, 40, 42, 49, 57, 94.

well as the absence of a municipal orchestra, present in Cape Town and Durban.[231]

Maud spent only ten of 400 pages discussing the situation of Africans in Johannesburg. He attributed relative municipal neglect of their welfare to the fact that Africans lacked the municipal franchise and thereby could not directly influence Council decisions. Consequently he found that there were still inadequate transport, roads, lights, sewerage and schools in Black residential areas. Equally, there were almost no amenities in White areas beyond the Zoo and Zoo Lake that Africans could use. Maud's suggested solution for local political reform was what he saw as a variation of Soviet style cultural autonomy for Black 'minorities' in Johannesburg, combined with federal municipal government.

Maud also mentioned slums, but as with the makers of *My Song Goes Forth* was optimistic that these were receiving adequate attention. Orlando was being developed as a 'model township' with post office, public hall, schools, police station and shopping centre. The 1934 Slums Act would speed up necessary clearances. His main criticism of racial segregation was its economic inefficiency.[232]

A.W. Wells' *South Africa*, first published in London in 1939 and running to several editions over the next decade, drew attention to Cape Town's 'notorious slum', namely District Six: 'Hundreds of coloured families lived in single rooms and disease and crime grew apace'. However, 'six million pounds were being spent in banishing the old and putting up twelve thousand new houses', which would solve the problem. The grandiose foreshore reclamation scheme would also help transform Cape Town, allowing the building of a new railway station, civic centre, skyscrapers for offices and shops, and underground cinemas. Wells concluded that soon no city in the world was likely to be 'more changed than Cape Town at the end of the next ten years'.[233]

Several social realist novels by White liberals in the mid-1930s were more stridently critical of urban conditions and White racism than non-fiction accounts. Their criticisms demonstrated the influence of academic surveys and government commissions. Yet each remained within the overall 'Jim Goes to Joburg' narrative trajectory that had marked city novels from Ensor's *Sitongo* of 1884 through to Rolfes Dhlomo's *African Tragedy* in 1928. Hence the overall message was still that Africans

---

[231] John Maud, *City Government: The Johannesburg Experiment* (Oxford: Clarendon Press, 1938), 185.
[232] Maud, *The Johannesburg Experiment*, 123–4, 135, 142, 150, 172, 209–10, 357–8.
[233] Wells, *South Africa*, 50–3.

struggled to adapt to city life and were better off living in the countryside.[234]

When problems were raised in foreign depictions of South African cities, these, like local non-fiction accounts, were placed within an overall message that was optimistic, as with the documentary *My Song Goes Forth* (1937); one of its alternative titles, *Africa Looks Up*, suggests as much.[235] This missionary-sponsored British film focuses on Johannesburg and Durban, with an introduction and musical contribution from Paul Robeson, the famous African-American singer, actor and political activist. The film discussed many of the unique characteristics and achievements of both cities already featured in books, travelogues and newsreels. Johannesburg had become a large modern city in only a few decades, had its own (Witwatersrand) University, 'some of the most beautiful cinemas in the world', and a well-organised mine industry. In the mine compounds, most Black mineworkers are 'splendid types of all kinds of South-East Africans', and we are shown mine dancers and marimba players. Similarly, Durban had arisen from 'dense bush and scrub' to become an industrial centre and the 'Riviera of South Africa'; and the screen is filled by rickshaw pullers decked out in the 'most fantastic fashions ... who don't seem to mind the work'.

We are then shown what are described as 'really squalid slums'. Immediately, though, the narration states that new locations with modern sanitation and schools are being built, and the camera pans across their 'quite decent bungalows'. This reflected both the reality of Durban municipal efforts to expand African family accommodation in the 1930s as well as place-selling contributions like Macmillan's history of Durban that had recently discussed them. The film concludes that Africans are adapting well to modern city life and want 'civilization ... [so] Africa marches on from jungle, kraal and hut to towns and cities'.

A British Pathé Gazette piece, *Slum Clearance in Johannesburg*, had a very similar message. It began with sombre music accompanying shots of a bulldozer demolishing buildings, then narration:

Johannesburg likes to think of itself as the cleanest city in the world. But for many years a place called Prospect Town has been a blot on Joburg's pride, a place

---

[234] Baptist R. Hernekin (pseudonym of Ethelreda Lewis), *Wild Deer* (London: Faber, 1933); Laurens Van der Post, *In a Province* (London: L. and V. Woolf, 1934); J. Grenfell Williams and Henry John May, *I am Black: The Story of Shabala* (Johannesburg: Juta, 1935).

[235] J. Best (dir.), *My Song Goes Forth* (UK: Gilbert Church Production Company, 1937). This film can be viewed in the British Film Institute archives or the African Studies Library at the University of Cape Town.

where seven thousand natives lived in squalor, a place where there was robbery and even murder.

But the viewer is told that the problem is being addressed as inhabitants and their possessions are being moved – we are shown this – to a 'new estate outside the city' (Orlando township, not shown). The piece concludes with more shots of buildings reduced to rubble and the final line 'South Africa's Golden City marches on'.[236]

Even detailed notes on South African cities made by Africa-American visitor Ralph Bunche between September 1937 and January 1938 included positive comments amid his overall view that the country was 'riven with race prejudice' and discrimination. Bunche was only allowed into South Africa after intercession by the liberal Minister of the Interior, Jan Hofmeyr, on condition that he promised to be cautious and not make speeches. Bunche was the first African-American to gain a PhD in Political Studies, had occupied the Chair in that discipline at Howard University, and also recently co-founded the National Negro Congress.[237]

Bunche's notes were meant to be turned into a book, but this was never completed. They reveal that Bunche was unconvinced by local-colour representations of content Black South Africans. He saw the antiques and adornments of rickshaw pullers as a purely commercial exercise. He noticed that the ersatz costumes of mine-dancers included kilts and that mine workers did not look happy. He was present when a Coloured group sang Coon songs in a Cape Town radio studio. They had to be deferential to Whites there, who called them boys or lads.

Bunche noted the extensive social and residential segregation that existed in each of the major cities and affected many beaches, hotels, night clubs and most public transport. As Evans had noticed two decades earlier, segregation in Johannesburg and Durban was greater than in Cape Town. Africans had to use the goods lift in Johannesburg's new Escom skyscraper, there were separate turnstiles for Blacks and Whites at the 1936 Empire Exhibition, and even the main reading room at Witwatersrand University's library was reserved for Whites. Likewise there were 'European' and 'Non-European' signs all over Durban, including at post-office counters and on some rickshaws. But there were

---

[236] www.britishpathe.com: Anon (dir.), *Slum Clearance in Johannesburg* (Britain: British Pathe Gazette, 1937).
[237] Compared to the more moderate National Association for the Advancement of Coloured People. For more information on Ralph Bunche and his South African journey see Robert Edgar's introduction in Robert R. Edgar (ed.), *An African American in South Africa: The Travel Notes of Ralphe J. Bunche* (Johannesburg: Witwatersrand University Press, 1992).

Illustration 4.5: Johannesburg as modern metropolis in the 1930s: a view of Commissioner Street (Mary Evans Picture Gallery)

some positive surprises. Bunche noted the considerable freedom of speech allowed throughout the country, not least the often radical soap box oratory on Cape Town's Grand Parade. Left-leaning books were available to both White and Black politicians and writers. In some private commercial enterprises, even in Johannesburg's Barclays Bank, Whites queued up behind Blacks. In Durban, Albert Park was open to all. Bunche thought the park better than anything on offer in the way of amenities for African-Americans in Washington DC.

That was the point. Ralph Bunche was perfectly aware that White South African racism and segregation was the rule in anglophone countries rather than the increasingly dramatic exception it became after the Second World War. He even thought it much easier for a Black man to travel around South Africa than the American South. Bunche had 'no really unpleasant experiences, though some that might be described as humorous or ludicrous'.[238] He came to the conclusion that anglophone White South Africans were like yankees, Afrikaners the equivalent of American rednecks, perhaps because most English-speakers he met were from the left-liberal minority.

In short, Bunche believed that material progress and Black self-betterment was still possible, as did many middle-class Black South Africans, including some in the ANC, APO and NIC, and liberal Whites. Bunche was appalled by conditions in some of the older inner city Black areas he visited, but unlike most Whites he also found liveliness there as well as some decent housing. He felt that Prospect Township was unlamented and that new locations, though dull, were better than the old 'slums' and permitted the possibility of individual houses being beautified by flowers or statues. Bokmakirie and especially Garden Village (Maitland), Council-subsidised projects in Cape Town, were a 'vast' improvement 'over the crowded living conditions in the Colored sections in town' or shanties on the Cape Flats. Even the municipal married quarters for Black workers in Durban were 'not too bad' and he reported favourably on the early phases of Lamontville's development.[239]

There was as yet little Black writing critical of South African cities. As Bunche had learnt on his travels, Black writers found it hard to get their work published. Publishing and film production was largely under White control, even if some newspapers were edited by Black South Africans, like the Durban journal *Ilanga*. Black editors were generally cautious, either because of their own career and status considerations or due to their religious or political beliefs and continued hopes of gradual progress.

---

[238] Edgar, *The Travel Notes of Ralphe J. Bunche*, 313.   [239] Ibid., 67, 296–7, 301.

Whispers of more bitter and unequivocal denunciations to come were present in some poems by Herbert Dhlomo. His more strident protestations were mostly published in *Ilanga* when he assisted his brother Rolfes in editing the paper (1943–56), and after the National Party won the general election of 1948. Anglophone publishers were then more willing to indulge anti-government pieces. Yet he wrote several poems at the beginning of the 1940s that echoed earlier White condemnations of Babylonian Johannesburg and expressed his own moments of despair in semi-biblical language. One was 'On Munro Ridge, Johannesburg', which went in part:

> Jerusalem can boast no better sight,
> For here the veld with glorious scenes is dight.
> O sweet miniature Edens of the north!
> O glorious homes! Is gold but all your worth? . . .
> How can you rest content so near the hells
> Of poverty where Moloch fierce still dwells;
> Where children die of hunger and neglect,
> While City Fathers boast suburbs select.

The other published piece was a sonnet, 'Evening Falls on the Berea Hills [Durban]'. It began:

> I'm weary of myself. I'm dejected.
> I stand and gaze and feel – and marvel! Is
> This then the great city that has planted
> Despair in me? What contrasts jolt in this
> Strange Hive: souls kind and hard; pure Good; great Sins!

Both poems were in keeping with the thinking of a Phillips or Valentine. Yet the second poem's ending was a celebration of modernity not unlike passages in Durban publicity material.

> I've been with God! I'm back content! I look
> Where Nature's work and Man's mingle or flight –
> Up sprout Man's flowers! Electric Lights! 'Tis night!

'On Munro Ridge' finished in almost identical fashion, the poet lifting his eyes beyond the ridge and declaring "'Tis hope, I thrill!'.[240] It was with hope that Dhlomo subsequently penned his poem 'The Royal Visit, 1947'.[241]

Favourable depictions of South African cities as places of modernity with local colour, sun, sea and young women, often in beach attire,

---

[240] Both poems are included in Nick Visser and Tim Couzens (eds), *H.I.E. Dhlomo Collected Works* (Jonannesburg: Ravan Press, 1985), 364–5. For details on dates of publication see 290.

[241] Visser and Couzens, *H.I.E. Dhlomo Collected Works*, 377.

dominated local and foreign media coverage up to 1947. South Africa's participation in the Second World War ensured positive international coverage of the country and its cities in the Allied media. The approving tone of British newsreels was to be expected, given the strategic importance of her ports. Little mention if any was made of urban problems, protests or *Ossewabrandweg* sabotage.

For instance, BBC radio's programmes for British schoolchildren depicted Cape Town, Johannesburg and Durban, complete with local colour, as each city's publicity associations would have wished.[242] From 1942, Cyril Watling's 'News From South Africa' from BBC studios gave Springbok forces fighting in North Africa and Europe news of 'back home': the war effort, Cape Town's South-Easters, enthusiasm for Smuts and re-employment schemes and rent control to help returning servicemen were some of the topics covered. One programme focused on the spectacular 'Liberty Cavalcade' of armed strength in Johannesburg in June 1942.[243]

The Second World War did mean a hiatus in South African place-selling initiatives. They returned in its immediate aftermath in cinematic form through SAR&H-sponsored travelogues like *Land of the Springboks* and *Harbours of History*.[244] The latter film built on the glowing wartime reputations of Cape Town and Durban in accounts of visiting Allied servicemen. As Evelyn Waugh recalled of arriving in Cape Town:

> After weeks at sea with blackened portholes we found a town alight, but much more than this we found what seemed to be the whole population extended to welcome us, the whole quay lined with cars to take us into the country.[245]

Between 1945 and 1947, the task of selling South African cities to the rest of the anglophone world was easy. Enthusiastic accounts similar to Evelyn Waugh's had already been transmitted through word-of-mouth by hundreds of thousands of visiting troops. Both these cities received glowing praise for the welcome and hospitality they offered. BBC radio's Women's

---

[242] BBC WAC School Scripts 27 January 1944: 'British Africa: Cities of the Rand' by Grenfell Williams. Williams, co-author of *I am Black*, gave the tin shack to modern city history of Johannesburg; BBC WAC School Scripts 17 March 1944: 'Ports of Call' by South African Marjorie Juta, a CPPA-style description of Cape Town and the Peninsula; BBC WAC School Scripts 10 March 1944: 'Ports of Call', for Juta's similarly place-selling account of Durban, complete with description of rickshaw pullers.

[243] BBC WAC: News From South Africa with Cyril Watling, 26 June 1942 on Johannesburg's Liberty Cavalcade; see also for example 6 March 1942, 15 April 1942, 25 April 1945, 7 June 1945, 11 October 1945.

[244] BFI: SAR&H, *Harbours of History* (Johannesburg: African Film Productions Company, 1946); SAR&H, *Land of the Springboks* (Johannesburg: African Film Productions Company, 1945).

[245] Evelyn Waugh, *A Tourist in Africa* (London: Chapman & Hall, 1960), 161–2.

Hour programme paid tribute to Durban's 'Lady in White', Perle Siedle Gibson, who was also interviewed for an Across the Line programme.[246] The British government lent practical and moral support to Smuts' post-war drive to recruit immigrants from Britain. The Royal Tour of 1947 was accompanied by unequivocally positive daily coverage in the Imperial media, in which sunlit South African cities stood in stark contrast to bomb-blasted counterparts in chilly Britain.[247]

Whispered warnings

Morton's Satour-sponsored visit might have been an unnecessary expense if Smuts had won the election of 1948. Instead, it presaged decades of far more difficult place-selling to come. This is evident even in *South of Suez*, an account of South Africa written by Douglas Reed, a British writer and post-war immigrant to Durban, published soon after Morton's. Reed was famous for *Insanity Fair*, his 1938 denunciation of Hitler's megalomania, but became internationally controversial in the 1940s for his anti-Zionism.

South of Suez gave a far less flattering portrayal of South African cities than Morton's. His observations on local colour in the form of New Year Carnival combined fascination with closer scrutiny than that of most previous White commentators. Reed detected both Carnival's assertion of rights to the city, not just the popular always happy to stay in its place, as well as an element of dismay at lot in life amid the festivities:

Each group wore an especial uniform, secretly devised and saved for during the old year and sprung upon the public on this great day . . .; the gangs of District Six shimmied and shook with lolling heads and rolling eyes to the dirges of Tin Pan Alley. Some paraded as Christy Minstrels . . . faces already dark were daubed with blacking . . . It was the carnival of the world which is neither all white or all black, and it debauched from its native mean streets to claim right of way in the central broad ones . . . There were the gipsy [*sic*] violinist's song of homelessness and the Styrian peasant's song of home, the . . . melancholy of the negro spiritual . . . and familiar melodies . . . 'All the world is waiting for the sunrise . . .' [it was] A lament in quickstep, past the Old Slave Tree.[248]

Reed wrote about the sense of fear among White British residents he encountered in the cities, which stemmed from political uncertainty surrounding South Africa's future and everyday worries about Black crime, poverty and numbers. Reed reported that Whites would not walk

---

[246] BBC WAC: Women's Hour 23 January 1946: 'The Lady in White' by John Whitehouse; BBC WAC: Across the Line 24 January 1950: 'Interview with Perla Siedle Gibson'.
[247] Not least in numerous AFP and British Pathé Gazette newsreels.
[248] Douglas Reed, *Somewhere South of Suez* (London: Jonathan Cape, 1950), 153–5.

in Johannesburg after dark, while White Durban was a 'beleaguered city' surrounded by Indians and Zulus. Cape Town had District Six near its centre, 'where the police go in pairs, and only if they must; that is where the *skollies* live, the roughs or hoodlums'. Meanwhile other Black Capetonians lived 'almost like wild men among the bush and scrub of the Cape Flats, their *pondokkies* [shanties] often hidden from view'.[249]

South of Suez contained many of Reed's own idiosyncratic views. Yet the fact that he chose to view *pondokkies* on the Cape Flats, and said what he did about South African cities, reflected the influence of recent opinions given by local writers. Two that Reed cited in his book were the dystopian urban visions of Arthur Keppel-Jones and Alan Paton, and it is to these, as well as contrasting and innovative Black responses, that we now turn.[250]

[249] Ibid., 163, 265.   [250] Ibid., 51, 119–20 for Reed's citing of these two authors.

5   Bitter cries and Black Baudelaires

> The slaughter at Orlando [a Johannesburg township] made perhaps a greater impression on the outside world than any other event of the war ... The description of what followed by the official bulletin and the republican Press differs very greatly from that given by eye-witnesses who were able to cross the border. According to the latter, great numbers of the inhabitants ... tried to get out of the town as the flames began to envelop it, and these were mown down by the machine-guns. Horrifying accounts of babies bleeding to death beside the corpses of their mothers, of screams of pain and terror audible in the din of battle, reached the Press of the world.[1]

So wrote Arthur Keppel-Jones, senior lecturer in history at the University of the Witwatersrand (Wits) in *When Smuts Goes*, one of the two dystopian visions of South Africa read by Douglas Reed. Published in London by Victor Gollancz in 1947, the book's subtitle was 'A History of South Africa from 1952 to 2010, First Published in 2015'. More than 80 per cent of its first edition's print run of just under 10,000 was taken up by the Left Book Club in Britain, and was that association's last publication.[2] The book went into several further editions and received considerable attention in both the South African and British press.

The passage above is Keppel-Jones' prediction that an urban uprising by Black South Africans would engulf Johannesburg and Cape Town in 1972. The uprising is brutally suppressed by the armed forces of an Afrikaner Nationalist government. The African elite becomes increasingly frustrated and radical, and all Africans subject to harsher restrictions on movement and pitiful living conditions. This brings United Nations military intervention that leads to democratic elections and the coming to power of a multi-racial Progressive Party in 1988 under the seemingly wise leadership of Prime Minister Mfundisi. But economic difficulties

---

[1] Arthur Keppel-Jones, *When Smuts Goes: A History of South Africa from 1952 to 2010, First Published in 2015* (London: Victor Gollancz, 1947), 108–9.

[2] Victor Gollancz Archive, Modern Records Collection, Warwick University MSS 318/2/1/15 'Production Book 1945–8'.

Table 5.1: *The percentage of those urbanised in South Africa, 1911–1960, according to racial categories used in government censuses*

	1911	1921	1936	1946	1951	1960
Whites	51.6	55.8	65.2	74.5	78.5	83.6
Africans	12.6	12.5	17.3	23.7	27.2	31.8
Coloureds	46	45.8	53.9	60.9	64.7	68.3
Indians	46	50.9	66.3	71.3	77.5	83.2
Total	24.7	25.1	31.4	38.4	42.6	47

An extended version is given in Walsh, 'Growth of Towns', 173.

and skills shortages are worsened by White emigration, which results in Mfundisi's assassination and his replacement by unscrupulous 'African National Party' leaders. The first is President Funamali, or 'Want-Money', who comes to power in another uprising that follows the stoning of a Whites-only bus in Orlando and the killing and mutilation of its passengers.

Funamali is succeeded by President Bulalazonke, or 'Kill-All'. South Africa and its cities fall into sharp decline and decay. Johannesburg, now called Erautini, is but a shabby shadow of the old golden city. Durban is once again ravaged by plague and malaria. Health conditions in all the cities worsen because of the government-sanctioned influence of witch-doctors and disparagement of Western medical knowledge.

Keppel-Jones was clearly near the mark with his prediction of a Black urban revolt in the 1970s. The Soweto uprising took place in 1976 and led to intermittent low-level civil war in both cities. But the contemporary significance of *When Smuts Goes* was that it was part of intense multimedia debate on South Africa's future in the aftermath of the Second World War. Much of this debate focused on what was happening, and might yet happen, in South African cities. To reiterate the point once more, in most industrial societies a common image of the future is an image of cities.[3]

A key question was the matter of appropriate policy responses to the acceleration in urbanisation during the Second World War (evident in Table 5.1). Of particular concern to White commentators was the numbers of Africans now involved, even if a far lower percentage of Africans as a whole were urbanised than other 'race groups'.

As with the First World War, industrialisation had been boosted by wartime import substitution. For Africans, movement to the cities was facilitated by temporary relaxation of the pass laws in 1942 to ensure an

---

[3] Williams, *The Country and the City*, 297.

Table 5.2: *Populations of Cape Town, Durban and Johannesburg, 1921–1946, according to racial categories used in the census of 1946*

| | Cape Town | | | Durban | | | Johannesburg | | |
	1921	1936	1946	1921	1936	1946	1921	1936	1946
Europeans	117,027	173,412	220,398	61,098	96,804	130,143	153,544	260,747	332,026
Coloureds	92,101	152,911	208,451	4,079	7,753	11,409	11,757	23,216	30,222
Indians	2,481	3,740	6,865	57,386	89,469	117,065	6,243	10,184	16,034
Africans	8,893	14,160	35,197	46,180	70,531	113,612	118,652	231,889	387,175
Total	220,502	344,223	470,911	168,743	264,557	372,269	290,196	526,036	765,457

Again these figures must be used as guide lines, and are liable to have undercounted the poor and particularly 'illegal' Africans.

adequate industrial labour supply. Black employment in industry that included a high percentage of Africans rose from around 105,000 in 1932–3 to 207,000 on the eve of the Second World War, with a further doubling to around 440,000 by 1948–9.[4] Ongoing rural push factors added to urban numbers, with African reserves unable to sustain an ever-increasing population. In addition, the mechanisation of White agriculture hastened the expulsion of Afrikaner *bywoners* and African tenants from White farms. The calculation by struggling rural dwellers across the racial spectrum was that economic opportunities would be more abundant in the cities. Official statistics, ever liable to undercount illegal African migrants, still registered an increase in African urban residents from less than 600,000 in 1921 to close to 2 million by 1946. Around 540,000 of this number lived in the three main municipalities, according to the government census of 1946, including just over 180,000 women (see Table 5.2).[5]

Black inner city areas and locations became overcrowded as rural migrants poured in from a countryside that could no longer sustain them. As housing shortages and rents increased, substantial shanty towns appeared on the outskirts of major cities, as observed by Reed when he visited those *pondokkies* on Cape Town's Cape Flats. In 1944, the *Sofasonke* ('We die together') squatter movement on the Rand led by James Mpanza set up shacks on the Orlando commonage, levied rates from their inhabitants, sold trading rights and deployed guards to keep order through fines and beatings. The Johannesburg municipality was forced to set up emergency camps with government help.[6]

[4] Feinstein, *Economic History*, 122.   [5] *Government Census 1946*, 78–81.
[6] Lodge, *Black Politics*, 12–20; Davenport, *Modern History*, 307–9.

Illustration 5.1: Visual bitter cries? Stephen Madumo from Pretoria photographed in 'Bottle Bar' shanty on the fringes of central Johannesburg in 1956 (Mary Evans Picture Gallery)

It was apparent to White observers that an African presence in the cities was substantial, increasing and permanent. What was also more apparent than ever before was the extent of Black poverty, because the spread of shanty towns made it more dramatically visible and shaming. With the end of the Second World War, city newspapers turned their attention more squarely to this South African crisis, providing detailed illustrated reports of the local situation.[7] The Johannesburg-based *Bantu World* had

---

[7] See, for instance, *Cape Argus*, 21 August 1945, leader on distress on the Cape Flats or 23 August 1945, increasing cases of TB; *The Star* 5 April 1946 report that temporary housing would be needed 'for ten to fifteen years'.

numerous articles on the situation on the Rand, but tried a new tactic in June 1946 by featuring a photograph of neat housing for Africans built by the Salisbury municipality in Rhodesia, with the caption 'Perhaps the City Fathers of Johannesburg Will One Day Follow This Good Example'.[8] Four months later *Ilanga* commented in more confrontational fashion that Durban's council could find money for beach improvements but not for African housing.[9]

British newspapers like the *Daily Mirror* weighed in with reports on the 'squalid horror of District Six', 'Slum Town, the shame of Jo'burg' and 'Windermere ... the worst slum in the Empire'.[10] An epilogue to the 1948 edition of Chilvers' history of Johannesburg felt bound to mention the 'appalling "shanty towns" made of jute bags and packing cases, where thousands of Native men, women and children lived – and some died.[11]' Even the Johannesburg Publicity Association's (JPA's) commemorative film for the city's sixtieth anniversary admitted that much still needed to be done in terms of housing but that eradicating slums 'cannot be achieved overnight'.[12]

Recent African discontent on the Rand was difficult for even committed place-sellers to ignore. It was enhanced by rising transport costs leading to periodic bus boycotts and anti-pass demonstrations when pass laws were enforced again in 1943. Aided by White communists, African trade unionism grew and strikes became more frequent. In response to popular discontent, a number of younger ANC members such as Anton Lembede and Nelson Mandela formed the ANC Youth League at the BMSC in 1944. Most involved lived in cities, were educated at mission schools and universities, including Wits where Keppel-Jones was lecturing, and were influenced by the Atlantic Charter and European notions of ethnic nationalism. They were wary of political collaboration with Whites, including communists. Youth League members believed that the ANC should become a truly national movement with indigenous leadership aimed at African self-determination. To this end, they felt that the ANC should cease being an organisation that only defended the rights and interests of elites and instead represent 'popular aspirations and ideals'.[13]

Responding to developments but provoking further debate, Smuts appointed the Fagan Commission to make policy recommendations on

---

[8] *Bantu World*, 1 June 1946.   [9] *Ilanga*, 12 October 1946.

[10] *Daily Mirror*, 21 July 1947, 3 April 1948.

[11] Hedley A. Chilvers, *Out of the Crucible: Being the Romantic Story of the Witwatersrand Goldfields and the Great City Which Arose in Their Midst* (Cape Town: Juta and Company, [1929] 1948), 258.

[12] National Film Archives, Pretoria: Anon (dir.), *Sixty Years After* (South Africa: African Film Productions, 1947).

[13] Lodge, *Black Politics*.

the future of Africans in cities. Its task was made more urgent when a strike by 70,000 members of the African Mineworkers Union, violently suppressed by the police, led to the deaths of twelve strikers. ANC members of the Natives Representative Council first suspended its meetings then demanded direct African representation at all levels from municipalities to parliament.[14]

The Fagan Commission report was only published in February 1948. Stating that African urbanisation was an economic phenomenon that affected all races and was impossible to reverse, it favoured African family settlement in the cities, rather than a reliance on migrant labour. This would stabilise the industrial labour supply and reduce the need for squatting caused by migrants, otherwise confined to single-sex barracks, wanting their families with them in the city. The principle of residential segregation would be maintained, as in the short term would passes to control urban overcrowding, 'purposeless movement, squatting, vagrancy, and crime', even if 'no penalty should be imposed' merely for being unable to produce a pass.[15]

Albeit short on details, the Fagan report demonstrated some awareness of African grievances and willingness to address them: cities were where the 'relation between European and Native ... [was producing] explosive situations' that needed to be defused. Locations should be improved and become proper 'Native Villages', Africans should have greater powers of urban self-governance and passes might eventually be replaced by a voluntary identity card system. Whites and Africans were 'economically and territorially ... intertwined', and the 'destructive wars of Europe have shown that the total territorial separation of peoples is no guarantee whatever of peace'.[16]

These views challenged the 1922 Stallard Commission assertion that Africans should only be allowed in cities as temporary workers to serve the needs of White employers. The Stallard position was propounded with renewed vigour in the run-up to the general election of May 1948 by Afrikaner nationalist ideologues, such as Professor Gert Cronje of the University of Pretoria, and confirmed in the Herenigde (Reunited) Nasionale Party's (HNP) Sauer report, published on the eve of the election. This proposed comprehensive separate development of racial groups, or *apartheid*.

As with the Fagan report, details were limited, but the Sauer report's intention was that apartheid would reverse any tendencies towards racial assimilation in every aspect of life save the labour market.

---

[14] Davenport, *Modern History*, 309–13.
[15] U.G. 28–1948, *Report of the Native Laws Commission [Fagan Report], 1946–8* (Pretoria: Government Printer, 1948), 30, 50.
[16] Ibid., 50–1.

Coloured South Africans would be separated politically, residentially and socially from Whites, possibly in a completely separate territory. Indians were dismissed as *uitheemse* (alien) to South Africa, potentially subject to repatriation. The political and social future of Africans was to be in the reserves, and their education removed from ideologically suspect missionary bodies. Native Representative Councils and other African–White consultative bodies would be abolished, as would African representation by White members of the House of Assembly. A tightly controlled African presence in 'White' cities would be limited to migrant labour.

Afrikaner Bitter Cries

Not unlike their ANC Youth League counterparts, Afrikaner nationalists were responding to accelerated urbanisation and problems of urban poverty with ethno-national mobilisation. Afrikaner urbanisation rose from 29 per cent in 1910, to 50 per cent by 1936 and 75 per cent in 1960.[17] Apartheid proposals were intended to win votes from Afrikaners forced off the land into the cities. Cape Town and Johannesburg were favoured destinations, and in both cities Afrikaans speakers constituted 25 per cent of the White population by 1936. For many of the reasons disclosed by the Carnegie Commission, Afrikaners continued to struggle in anglophile-dominated big cities. In 1939, almost 40 per cent of male adult Afrikaners in Johannesburg were bricklayers, mine workers, railway workers or unskilled labourers. Afrikaners constituted a tiny proportion of urban White professionals, and only three commercial enterprises of any substance were Afrikaner-owned in the city in 1936.

D.F. Malan, leader of the HNP, encapsulated the view that Afrikaner urbanisation was akin to a second Great Trek in a speech during the centenary celebrations of the original migration in 1938:

> Your Blood River lies in the town … at that new Blood River of our people white and non-white meet each other in much closer contact and in a much tighter wrestling-hold than one hundred years ago when the circle of white-tented wagons protected the laager and the shotgun and assegai clashed against each other … Where he must stand in the breach for his people, the Afrikaner of the new Great Trek meets the non-white at his Blood River, half-armed or even completely unarmed, without a barricade, without a river between them, defence-less in the open plains of economic competition.[18]

Urban existence required *voortrekker* fortitude and ethnic solidarity for poor Afrikaners to survive and retain their identity. This message was

---

[17] Giliomee, *The Afrikaners*, 405.   [18] Cited in Welsh, 'Growth of Towns', 205.

collectively conveyed across a variety of Afrikaans media in the 1930s and 1940s. The foreword of F.W. Boonzaier's cheerily titled play *Die Stad Sodom* warned that urban poverty was forcing Afrikaner daughters into prostitution. P.W.S. Schuman's play *Hantie kom hans-toe* (Hantie Come Home) has its eponymous heroine working to uplift the poor Whites living precariously among Malays, 'Hottentots', Syrians and Greeks in a Cape shanty called *Lappiesdorp* (Patchwork Town).[19] D.P. Opperman's poem '*Ballade van die Grysland*' (Ballad of the Grey Land) has a farmer driven from the land by drought going insane in the city.[20] British contempt towards Afrikaners, commonly their employees in the city, was part of the problem. In S. Bruwer's novel *Bodemvas,* an Afrikaans-speaking farm girl who is married to an Englishman in that most British of cities, Durban, has to endure endless unpleasant taunts about fellow members of the *volk*. She eventually escapes back to her parents' farm.[21]

Nationalists like Malan believed that their kith and kin needed to be rescued from such perilous circumstances to strengthen the *volk*. The DRC endorsed this view in booklets written by the head of its Poor Relief Committee, J.R. Albertyn, and the report he co-authored on Afrikaner migration to major cities, *Kerk en Stad* (Church and City), published in 1947. *Kerk en Stad* argued that the DRC must be involved in working for better conditions for urban Afrikaners while recognising 'the divine providence in the current trek towards the cities'.[22] A *Volkskongress* on Afrikaner urbanisation followed in Johannesburg, addressed by DRC clergymen and Afrikaner academics, which came out in support of *rasse-apartheid* or complete racial separation.[23]

The extension of the DRC's religious and social outreach among Afrikaans-speaking migrants gathered in particular parts of the cities, like south-western Johannesburg or the emerging northern suburbs of Cape Town such as Bellville and Parow, further nurtured ethnic identity. Fostering this identity by suggesting that the Afrikaner poor should be protected from economic competition by racial separation, and perhaps

---

[19] F.W. Boonzaier, *Die Stad Sodom* (Cape Town: H.A.U.N., 1931); P.W.S. Schumann, *Hantie kom huis-toe* (Pretoria: J.L. van Schalk, 1933). These plays are mentioned in Johan Van Wyk, *Constructions of Identity and Difference in South African Literature* (Durban: C.S. A.L.L., 1995), 71–4.

[20] A.J. Coetzee, 'White South African Literature after World War 2 – Afrikaans', in Albert S. Gerard (ed.), *European-Language Writing in Sub-Saharan Africa* (Budapest: Akademiai Kiado, 1986), 217–29.

[21] Welsh, 'Growth of Towns', 203.

[22] J.R. Albertyn, P. Du Toit and H.S. Theron (eds), *Kerk en Stad: Verslag van Kommissie van Ondersoek oor Stadstoestande* (Stellenbosch: Pro Ecclesia, 1947), 70.

[23] Robert Vosloo, 'From a Farm Road to a Public Highway: The Dutch Reformed Church and Its Changing Views Regarding the City and Urbanisation in the First Half of the 20th Century (1916–47)' *Studia Historiae Ecclesiasticae* 39, 2 (December 2013), 19–32.

benefit from an urban employment quota system, was the intention behind the nationalists establishing *Die Transvaler* in Johannesburg in 1937. The newspaper was published by the *Voortrekkerpers* with the fiery Dr Hendrik Verwoerd as its editor. Those seen as enemies of the Afrikaner were denounced as liberals, communists, Jews, Freemasons and British Imperialists. After Hertzog resigned as prime minister in 1939, Johannesburg's other Afrikaans-language newspaper *Die Vaderland* (1936) rallied to the cause, as did *Die Burger* in Cape Town.[24]

The Great Trek centenary celebrations provided a major boost for Afrikaner ethnic mobilisation. Future HNP member and Hitler admirer Oswald Pirow, now the Railways and Harbours minister in the United Party government, used £70,000 of his department's publicity budget to sponsor a historical feature film that focused on Afrikaner achievement called *Die Bou van 'n Nasie* or *They Built a Nation*. The film was criticised for its bias in the English press, but greeted with considerable enthusiasm by Afrikaner audiences; when screened in special sessions to Afrikaner schoolchildren, *voortrekkers* were cheered and any British presence on screen was booed.[25]

Large numbers of Afrikaners in *voortrekker* dress gathered to observe commemorative ox-wagons passing through cities, as they did to observe the laying of the foundation stone of a Voortrekker Monument at the wagons' destination, a hill outside Pretoria, on 16 December (the Day of the Vow) 1938. Newsreels and photographs recorded and further celebrated these occasions in city cinemas. So did *'n Nasie Hou Koers* (A Nation Keeps on Course), a documentary about the 1938 ox-wagon treks, and special events that accompanied them, like the laying of plaques to commemorate *voortrekker* history, or group marriages and christenings with participants in *voortrekker* dress.[26]

Trek celebrations, followed so swiftly by South Africa's entry into the Second World War, accelerated the growth of pro-German Afrikaner organisations. Notable among them were the *Ossewabrandwag* (*OB*, Ox-wagon Sentinel) and its paramilitary wing, the *Stormjaers* (Assault Troops). Encouraged by German success in the early stages of the war, Ossewabrandwag members assaulted South African and Allied servicemen and participated in a full-scale riot in Johannesburg in 1941 that led to more than one hundred soldiers being seriously injured. Although a hidden

---

[24] Moodie, *Afrikanerdom*; Patrick J. Furlong, *Between Crown and Swastika: The Impact of the Radical Right on the Afrikaner Nationalist Movement in the Fascist Era* (Hanover, NH: Wesleyan University Press, 1991); Giliomee, *The Afrikaners*, 416–18.
[25] Joseph Albrecht (dir.), *Die Bou van 'n Nasie* (South Africa: African Film Productions, 1938); Gutsche, *Motion Pictures in South Africa*, 345–51. Pirow met Hitler in 1933.
[26] Maingard, *South African National Cinema*, 53–66.

Ossewabrandwag arms cache was discovered in Durban, the organisation was particularly active on the Rand. Damaging electric power stations and pylons, and cutting telephone lines, the Ossewabrandwag also planted bombs at post offices, cinemas, cafes and the Johannesburg offices of the *Bantu World*. One of several attacks on United Party meetings led to Harry Lawrence, Smuts' Minister of the Interior, being badly assaulted.[27] A failed German plot to assassinate Smuts with *Stormjaer* assistance involved former South African Olympic boxer turned German secret agent Robey Leibbrandt. Many Ossewabrandwag leaders were interned, including future prime minister John Vorster.[28]

Afrikaner nationalist leaders and supporters distanced themselves from paramilitary activities deemed to have aided Smuts' overwhelming election victory in 1943, and as the war turned against the Axis powers. By the time that Keppel-Jones was writing *When Smuts Goes*, Afrikaner nationalist fortunes were on the rise again, aided by post-war discontent associated with demobilisation, housing shortages and continuation of wartime food controls. Smuts' support for aided British immigration brought some 60,000 new immigrants in 1947–8, and could be portrayed by nationalists as a new Imperial attempt to swamp the Afrikaner. Apartheid, not the United Party's Fagan report acceptance of a permanent and threatening African urban presence, was the way to secure Afrikaner survival.[29]

When Smuts Goes reflected Keppel-Jones' view that South Africa and its cities were at a turning point in the late 1940s, and would be doomed if Afrikaner nationalists, associated in many anglophone minds with wartime support for the Nazis, came to power. The HNP would promote sectarian interests at the expense of all other South Africans, and do so in increasingly repressive fashion, leading inevitably to violent Black response. Yet in making this argument Keppel-Jones did not explore the nature of South African urbanisation in any detail, beyond pre-empting the Fagan report finding that it was creating 'explosive situations'.

Cry the Beloved Country

Attempting to explain why such situations were developing was Alan Paton's aim in *Cry the Beloved Country*, the second contribution to the debate on South Africa's future cited by Reed. It was published in New York and London in 1948 to critical and popular acclaim throughout the

---

[27] Brewer, *Black and Blue*, 155–62; Furlong, *Crown and Swastika*.
[28] Furlong, *Crown and Swastika*, 145–7.
[29] Davenport, *Modern History*, 320–1. Giliomee, *The Afrikaners*, argues that this was the most important reason for apartheid.

anglophone world.[30] Selling some 15 million copies by the 1970s, *Cry the Beloved Country* became one of the most widely read novels in the history of South African literature. A British film version, directed by Zoltan Korda and starring the American actors Canada Lee and the young Sidney Poitier, followed in 1951.[31] Both novel and its simplified screen adaptation were especially influential in terms of international perceptions of South Africa and its cities.

The novel in particular provided detailed information about harsh African living conditions in Johannesburg and the possible consequences of ignoring these. Urbanisation had been forced on Africans because they could no longer survive in the countryside, 'the soil can no longer keep them any more'.[32] Both novel and film tell of how a humble rural Natal priest, the Reverend Stephen Kumalo, goes to Johannesburg to look for his son Absalom. Absalom had not been in contact with his father since journeying himself to Johannesburg in search of his Aunt Gertrude, Stephen's sister. Stephen Kumalo is helped in his search for Absalom by Father Msimangu (played by Poitier in the film). Msimangu guides Kumalo, and thereby the reader and viewer, around a number of African areas of Johannesburg on this quest. Kumalo is shocked by the 'shabbiness and dirtiness, and the closeness of the houses, and the filth in its streets' in Claremont.[33] Here he finds Gertrude living as a prostitute and neglecting her child. The film version shows this happening in dilapidated parts of Sophiatown instead.

In the novel, while continuing the search for Absalom, Msimangu and Kumalo visit Alexandra, just outside municipal boundaries, and learn that inhabitants are boycotting the local bus service and walking to work because of fare increases. Msimangu tells Kumalo that African home-ownership is allowed in Alexandra, but its streets are not cared for and there are no street lights.[34] The place is overcrowded because owners have built additional rooms to sub-let to others, and many of these rooms have become hide-outs for thieves, prostitutes and illicit beer brewers as people have been forced into Johannesburg from the countryside:

---

[30] Alan Paton, *Cry the Beloved Country* (New York and London: Charles Scribner's Sons and Jonathan Cape, 1948).

[31] Zoltan Korda (dir.), *Cry the Beloved Country* (Great Britain: London Film Productions, 1951).

[32] The edition from which this and subsequent quotations are taken is Alan Paton, *Cry the Beloved Country* (Harmondsworth: Penguin, 1971), 8.

[33] Paton, *Cry the Beloved Country* (1971), 27–8.

[34] For a history of Alexandra that investigates the conditions and struggles of its inhabitants in great detail, see Phil Bonner and Noor Nieftagodien, *Alexandra: A History* (Johannesburg: Wits University Press, 2008).

All roads lead to Johannesburg . . . If the crops fail . . . If there are taxes to be paid, there is work in Johannesburg. If the farm is too small to be divided further, some must go to Johannesburg . . .[35]

Eventually Msimangu takes Kumalo to look for Absalom in Shanty Town, near Orlando to the south-west of Johannesburg in what became Soweto. Here Paton breaks up his narrative to offer a lengthy meditation on the origins and nature of this new kind of slum and the death through disease of an African child. Paton reveals that Shanty Town is now under intense scrutiny from the local press.[36]

Kumalo eventually learns that Absalom has joined a gang, and been responsible for the murder of a young man called Arthur Jarvis who is involved with African urban upliftment projects. Absalom is executed for his crime. Coincidentally, Arthur is the son of James Jarvis, a White farmer of illiberal racial views who lives near the Kumalos in Natal. After Arthur's death, James discovers his son's writings on South Africa. One piece reveals that Arthur's childhood innocence about his country stemmed in part from the propaganda efforts of those who promoted it:

I read when I was a boy, the brochures about lovely South Africa, that land of sun and beauty sheltered from the storms of the world . . . it is only as one grows up that one learns that there are other things here than sun and gold and oranges.[37]

James is especially moved by Arthur's desire to serve all South Africans. The novel ends with White and Black fathers united in grief, but with Jarvis senior building a new church for Kumalo's congregation in Natal.

Paton's overall argument was that Johannesburg consumed lost (because detribalised) African people forced into wretched living conditions, immorality and crime. The current state of Africans in the city threatened White urban existence. Though they had wanted Black labour in the cities, Whites had failed to replace the broken tribal system with appropriate new Christian traditions. Black South Africans needed to accept these traditions and be wary of potentially self-seeking and hypocritical African politicians like John Kumalo, Stephen's brother. John was right to want African advancement and say that African labour built Johannesburg, but neglected Christian morality in the way he lived and covered up his own son's role in Jarvis' murder.

White South Africans had for their part to discard racism, adopt Christian values and recognise the common humanity and fellow citizenship of their Black compatriots. Otherwise, in Father Msimangu's famous words, 'one day when they [Whites] are turned to loving, they will find we

---

[35] Paton, *Cry the Beloved Country* (1971), 48.   [36] Ibid., 57.   [37] Ibid., 150.

are turned to hating'. Implicitly, the results would mirror the predictions of *When Smuts Goes*.[38]

Cry the Beloved Country's argument was informed by Paton's Christian beliefs and personal experience of Johannesburg, where he worked as head of the Diepkloof reformatory for African boys. Paton had read Richard Wright's autobiographical account of moving from the American South to Chicago, *Black Boy* (1945), as well as Steinbeck's *Grapes of Wrath* (1939) and the work of theologian Reinhold Niebuhr. Paton had also been shocked by Smuts' violent suppression of the miners' strike in 1946.[39]

Paton's novel demonstrated the influence of pre-Second World War portrayals of urban African existence. One commonality was its denunciation of African residential areas in 'slumland' descriptions reminiscent of Victorian accounts like Mearns' *Bitter Cry of Outcast London*. This was true, for instance, of a survey into conditions in Doornfontein yards, published in academic journals before the war by Ellen Hellman, then a social anthropology research student at Wits, but only republished in booklet form in 1948. Hellman worried amongst other things about the 'unsavoury disorderliness of the yard', the 'apathetic indifference' and 'desultory efforts' of some of the inhabitants, and wondered how at night 'Rooiyard, dark and eerie and lit by the fitful gleam of candles and glowing coals in the brazier, is situated in the midst of a large and reputedly progressive city'.[40]

Rooiyard, in the guise of 'Swatyard', was described in similar fashion in an account of the life of one of its inhabitants, 'John Chavafambira', published as *Black Hamlet* in 1937, and republished in politically refashioned form more in keeping with the times as *Black Anger* in 1947. The biographical narrative was reconstructed by Johannesburg psychoanalyst Wulf Sachs through interviews he conducted with Chavafambira, having been introduced to him by Hellman, and contains many of Sachs' own opinions. Rooiyard is described as 'this disgraceful slum', where on Saturday nights 'Drunken men and women scream and sing and fight', disappearing for a while into the gloom to exchange 'intimacies' before returning to the 'orgy of drink and noise'.[41]

---

[38] Ibid., 38.
[39] Peter Alexander, *Alan Paton: A Biography* (Oxford and Cape Town: Oxford University Press, 1995), 187–214.
[40] Ellen Hellmann, *Rooiyard: A Sociological Survey of an Urban Native Slum Yard* (Cape Town: Oxford University Press), 9. Earlier versions of her investigation were published in *Africa* 8 (1935) and *Bantu Studies* 19 (1935).
[41] Wulf Sachs, *Black Hamlet* (Baltimore and London: John Hopkins University, [1937], 1996), 208, 220. This has useful analyses of Sachs' original version and its later incarnation, *Black Anger* by Saul Dubow and Jacqueline Rose.

'Disgraceful slum' depictions also typified Johannesburg novels of the 1930s. One that was first written in 1935 but also republished after the Second World War was *I am Black: the Story of Shabala*, co-authored by future BBC employee J. Grenfell Williams and writer Henry May. Here what was named only as the 'Big City of the white man' was 'full of angry mutterings and evil witchcraft', 'a monster, waiting to pounce'. Despite the 'wonders of the white man', Africans live in 'dirty, brick, tin-roofed hovels ... mean and dirty parts ... with foul-smelling passages ... and ... yards where women lived in rickety tin shacks and plied their trade'.[42]

Wild Deer, written under the pseudonym R. Hernekin Baptist by British immigrant Ethelreda Lewis, well known for her told-to-the-author life of Trader Horn, was published in 1933. It described the slums of otherwise exciting 'Goldburg' as worse than those in London and Glasgow. They were 'haunts of ... utter depravity, filth and hideousness', where the 'Dutch' suffered alongside African 'primitives' whose men were broken on 'the wheel of the machine' and whose women lived by beer brewing or prostitution. The only amusements were crude music, dagga, adulterated beer drinking and mixed-race brothels. Even in the compounds where more acceptable recreation was provided, men were forced into 'perversion'.[43]

The young Laurens van der Post's *In a Province* depicted similar misery in Port Benjamin, his pseudonym for Cape Town where he worked as a journalist on the *Cape Times* between 1929 and 1931. Like Scully writing on Johannesburg, van der Post's novel questions municipal spending priorities, though sympathising more with Black rather than White poverty: ratepayers prefer to raise a loan of £300,000 for an entertainment park and esplanade for visitors rather than £90,000 on African housing. *In a Province* seemingly contained autobiographical elements. The Afrikaner protagonist, van Bredepoel, listens to 'a negro baritone', presumably Paul Robeson, singing 'Ol' Man River' on fellow boarding-house resident Major Mustard's gramophone: 'What does he care if de man ain't free ... Ah'm tired of livin' an' scared of dying ...'. Van Bredepoel becomes interested in the problems besetting Kenon, an African migrant to the city. Both become disillusioned with Port Benjamin's 'pretentious' architecture and 'pretentious and carefully kept business thoroughfares ... [with] a quarter whose squalor was as unpicturesque as it was unexpected'.[44] What was evidently District Six appeared in several passages of typical 'slum-land' description.

---

[42] John Grenfell Williams and Henry John May, *I am Black: The Story of Shabala* (London: Cassell and Co., 1936), 57, 86–8.
[43] Baptist, *Wild Deer*, 77, 110–12, 115, 122, 178.
[44] Van der Post, *In a Province*, 13, 182, 197.

Everywhere there had been the same oppressive odour of rubbish and stopped drains, the same overcrowded rooms; Malays, Hindus, natives, half-castes, shabby white men sleeping with their heads in filth on broken and damp pavements. He remembered a room in which a woman was sleeping naked with two children in her arms, her body covered with festering sores.[45]

This 'blot on the escutcheon of our beautiful city' had to be removed.[46]

What *Cry the Beloved Country* also had in common with much 1930s writing was its warnings against African political activism. Paton's critical characterisation of John Kumalo was a muted form of the concern shown in these three earlier novels that urban Africans could be led dangerously astray by radical 'agitators'. Both Kenon, the would-be self-improving protagonist of *In a Province*, and streetwise Dimbu in *I am Black* are killed during protests. When Sachs pays a visit to Rooiyard in *Black Hamlet*, he describes 'moving slowly among the angry, drunken, frenzied crowd, ready to burst out in revolt at the slightest provocation'.[47]

Where *Cry the Beloved Country* differed from the message of earlier novels was in its acceptance that African urbanisation was inevitable and irreversible, the position also adopted by the Fagan Commission. Africans no longer had the option of being better off remaining in the countryside, as pre-Second World War novels, the Stallard commission or the Sauer report suggested they might be. Instead Paton was agreeing with Ray Phillips that complete segregation of Africans as residents of the reserves and only temporary visitors to the city was impossible. The idea was dishonest because only a tenth of the land was reserved for four-fifths of the people. An African presence in the city was permanent and therefore the intolerable urban conditions they experienced there had to be improved. Like Phillips, Paton's novel also challenged White assumptions about racial superiority by arguing that it was wrong to bar Blacks from acquiring skills (through civilised labour policies), or to split families through migrant labour. Racism prevented the application of universal Christian principles.

In making these points Phillips and – far more successfully in terms of extent of readership – Paton popularised arguments previously made in academic publications. The growth in number of such publications between the 1920s and 1940s came because universities – Wits in Johannesburg, the University of Cape Town (UCT), and the University of Natal with its main campus in Durban – were expanding in all three main cities. Each introduced 'Bantu Studies'. Their research activities as a whole reflected the development of international interest in areas such as social anthropology, economic history, urban poverty and social

---

[45] Ibid., 195.   [46] Ibid., 105.   [47] Sachs, *Black Hamlet*, 209.

delinquency. In conducting research into all these areas, academics were able to use the information contained in government reports and censuses and, like Hellman, produce their own surveys.[48]

Isaac Schapera, who taught briefly at Wits before moving to UCT, produced influential findings that questioned those who thought that at least migrancy from beyond South Africa's borders was still voluntary. His fieldwork was conducted among Kgatla migrants to Johannesburg and their families in Bechuanaland. Schapera demonstrated that this migrancy was essential for most household incomes, though enabling some to invest in improvements and meet new desires for European goods; pajamas, bloomers, contraceptives and gramophones were among the items mentioned by informants. It was also apparent that some migrants had come to see themselves as permanent urban dwellers. New economic and social forces in Africa, as in Europe, had consequently weakened family ties and contributed to what Schapera termed 'the revolt of modern youth'. As revealed in correspondence between rural residents and migrants cited by Schapera, this often had heart-rending consequences. This is part of what Paton was trying to capture in *Cry the Beloved Country*.[49]

Exposing the fallacy of segregation and racism

Several academic histories also made the argument that South African urbanisation was typical of industrialising societies throughout the world. In *Complex South Africa* (1930), William Macmillan, professor of history at Wits, wrote that to deny this made problems worse. Data compiled both by the state and civil institutions like Johannesburg's Poor Relief Committee proved that both Black and White were being forced off the land into the cities and that urban poverty was a cross-racial problem. It needed to be tackled as a whole, and not with preferential 'civilised labour' policies for Whites. South Africa 'must keep the idea of a complete civilization' for its entire population, which must also mean political inclusion and better opportunities for educated Africans.[50]

Macmillan's views in this respect were shared by Edgar Brookes, whose career included being president of the Institute of Race Relations,

---

[48] For histories of the two universities in this period see Bruce Murray, *Wits, the Early Years: A History of the University of the Witwatersrand, Johannesburg, and Its Precursors 1896–1939* (Johannesburg: Wits University Press, 1982); Howard Phillips, *The University of Cape Town 1918–1948: The Formative Years* (Cape Town: University of Cape Town Press, 1993).

[49] Isaac Schapera, *Married Life in an African Tribe* (London: Penguin, [1940] 1971).

[50] William Miller Macmillan, *Complex South Africa: An Economic Foot-Note to History* (London: Faber & Faber, 1930), 273.

headmaster of Adams College and professor of history and political science at the University of Natal. In a series of lectures he gave at UCT in 1933, Brookes cited Bernard Shaw, who had described South Africa as the 'worst kind of slave state' during his visit the previous year, to argue that neglecting the poor of any race was disastrous.[51] Complete segregation was 'impossible', a 'fallacy', and the country must be developed in terms of a single South Africa and South African identity. Brookes applauded those university students who shared this aim. He though that though they might 'occasionally ... speak the language of Johannesburg with the accent of Moscow',

It is right to remind ourselves that an indiscreet zeal for revolution is a higher quality than a mere ignoble content with things as they are in an unjust and inefficient society.[52]

Cornelis De Kiewiet, a London University-trained South African who became dean of the College of Arts and Sciences at Cornell, also drew heavily on statistical information to declare 'segregation a myth' in his *History of South Africa, Social and Economic*. It was first published in 1941, with an acknowledgment to Macmillan for reading the manuscript. De Kiewiet argued that

Every stroke of a hammer on an anvil, every thrust of a foot on a delivery bicycle, every pot that was scoured, took the natives farther from ancestral habits and closer to the habits of a new society.[53]

Information drawn from government commissions on wages allowed De Kiewiet to prove that Africans had to find work outside the reserves, even after these were extended in 1936. But they were unable to live healthily in the cities on what they currently earned, and civilised labour policies had contributed to keeping African wages artificially low. Through policies like these, cities had grown wealthy on the back of poverty in the countryside.

The white-walled houses of Cape Town, the flower-markets and fish pedlars of its streets; the jingling bells of the white-washed legs of Durban's rickshaw boys; the fine organ, the University, and the metropolitan din of Johannesburg accentuate

---

[51] For Bernard Shaw's comment see Shaw, *The Cape Time*, 87.
[52] His lectures were published as Edgar H. Brookes, *The Colour Problems of South Africa: Being the Phelp-Stokes Lectures, 1933, Delivered at the University of Cape Town* (Alice and London: Lovedale Press and Kegan Paul, Trench, Trubner, & Co., Ltd, 1934), 111.
[53] C.W. De Kiewiet, *A History of South Africa, Social and Economic* (London and New York: Oxford University Press, [1941] 1946), 233, 242. De Kiewiet made particular use of data contained in the government's Economic and Wage Commission of 1926 and Native Economic Commission of 1932. The other historian who read De Kiewiet's manuscript was UCT's Eric Walker.

the unusually great difference between town and country . . . Though the towns were expanded and beautified, and the amenities of modern life were introduced, the level of native payment advanced very little during the space of more than a generation.[54]

The publication of a major investigation into poverty in Cape Town demonstrated that Coloured poverty was also severe. Funded initially through two £1,000 grants from the Carnegie foundation and the South African government, it was led by UCT's Professor Edward Batson. The Social Survey of Cape Town calculated that 50 per cent of Coloured Capetonians were below the poverty datum line compared to around 5 per cent of Whites. It demonstrated that tuberculosis mortality rates were similarly uneven, at 123 per hundred thousand for 'Non-Europeans' compared to a figure of 41 for Whites, with a similar pattern in terms of infant mortality from the disease. These figures showed a significant improvement from those for 1900, though comparative statistics for England and Wales showed the adult mortality rate at 10 per 100,000, though the infant rate was 62. Between 1921 and 1937 Cape Town municipality had only built 1,000 houses for 'Europeans', with another 1,500 supplied through the efforts of a citizens' Utility League. The total provided for 'Non-Europeans', whose overall need was much greater, was 2,500. By 1937, so before accelerated wartime urbanisation, the housing shortage in Cape Town was estimated at 12,500. Local newspapers and a pamphlet by the Bishop of Cape Town, S.W. Lavis, called *Cape Town's Underworld* publicised these findings.[55]

What Paton learnt from some or all of these contributions was that South African unity and progress was held in check by contemporary notions of permanent racial and cultural difference. Brookes had implied as much by calling his book *The Colour Problems of South Africa*. Leonard Barnes, a future British Labour Party member and stringent critic of Empire, went further by calling the account he gave of predominant White South African attitudes in 1930 *Caliban in Africa: An Impression of Colour Madness*. Barnes, an ex-Colonial Office employee who had emigrated to South Africa in 1925, believed that within a couple of decades 'the solidity and compound mass of . . . colour prejudice' would lead to 'violent strife'.[56] In the

[54] De Kiewiet, *A History of South Africa, Social and Economic*, 208, 229. For further information on De Kiewiet, Macmillan and other historians of this period and beyond see Saunders, *The Making of the South African Past*.
[55] Anon, *Official Report of the Social Survey Conference*, Cape Town (Cape Town: Paul Koston, 1942), 33–4, 97, 103; S.W. Lavis, *Cape Town's Underworld* (Alice: Lovedale Press, 1943).
[56] Leonard Barnes, *Caliban in Africa: An Impression of Colour Madness* (London: Victor Gollancz Ltd, 1930), 241–2. For further information on Barnes see Anthony McAdam, 'Leonard Barnes and South Africa', *Social Dynamics* 3, 2 (1977), 41–53. Barnes had spent three years in the Flander trenches, and reflected that his radical ideas about

meantime, Africans he observed in the cities had been reduced to 'grimy thing of shreds and patches'. Only when taking in a 'little soap-box Communism on the [Grand] Parade at week-ends and on bank holidays' might an urban African become 'sub-aggressive and his gait jaunty – quaint emblems, perhaps, of his defiance and hope'.[57]

Strident public condemnation of White South African racism by other Whites, within or outside the country, was rare before the Second World War. So was casting doubt on the European civilising mission. Two friends of Barnes in South Africa, the writers William Plomer and Roy Campbell, were exceptional in expressing both. Plomer caused outrage with his novel *Turbott Wolfe* (1926), set in Natal, which was denounced throughout the mainstream South African press for its position on race. Plomer's novel praised African culture and beauty, while lampooning White men and their hypocrisy in having Black mistresses. Going to a fairground in the 'slums' of Durban, dubbed Dunnsport by Plomer, the eponymous hero witnesses a 'gross European' planting an unwanted kiss on a young Black woman to lascivious comments from the multi-racial crowd. Turbott Wolfe rejects 'our obscene civilization that conquers everything' and questions the view that scientific prowess necessarily means progress. He becomes a founder member of a small cross-racial Young Africa society that believes Africa does not belong to the White man, miscegenation is positive, and that members are pioneers of a future Coloured World.[58]

Poet Roy Campbell, who strongly defended Plomer's book in the Durban literary journal *Voorslag* (Whiplash), which he co-edited with Plomer and van der Post in 1926, longed himself for the day 'When the Rudyards cease from Kipling, And the Haggards Ride no more'.[59] Campbell's satirical poem *The Wayzgoose* (1928) mocked Durban's dullness, the narrow mental horizons of its White residents, which

appropriate social order had taken shape there. His friendship with Norman Leys, campaigner for African rights in Kenya, was influential in sowing doubts in his mind about British colonialism.

[57] Barnes, *Caliban in Africa*, 151.

[58] William Plomer, *Turbott Wolfe* (New York: William Morrow and Company Inc, [1926] 1965), 62–4, 89, 144. This 1965 edition has a foreword by van der Post that explains how the three writers met and contains his positive analysis of the book. Plomer presumably dubbed Durban 'Dunnsport' after hunter and trader John Robert Dunn. Dunn grew up in Durban when it was called Port Natal and eventually became an adviser to the Zulu king Cetwayo, and acquired numerous Zulu wives with whom he fathered over one hundred children. He also helped supply guns to the Zulus, but when war broke out in 1879 sided with the British.

[59] Roy Campbell, William Plomer and Laurens van der Post (eds), *Voorslag: A Magazine of South African Life and Art: Facsimile Reprint of Numbers 1, 2 and 3 (1926)*, (Durban and Pietermaritzburg: Killie Campbell Africana Library, University of Natal Press, 1985), 45.

stretched only 'from Berea to Bluff', and their misplaced sense of superiority:

> Is it the sign of a 'superior race'
> To whine to have 'the nigger kept in place'.[60]

A book-length indictment of racism in Durban was only published fourteen years later. Written by P.S. Joshi, *The Tyranny of Colour* drew particular attention to ways in which Indians were on the receiving end of White racism, including the introduction of new legislation aimed at limiting where they could purchase property.[61]

Plomer's and Campbell's views were ignored or roundly condemned by most South African Whites at the time. Campbell resigned his editorship of *Voorslag* when asked by its owners to moderate its views on race, and the magazine folded after a few issues. Within a few years, all three editors had left South Africa, as had Barnes and Macmillan, despairing of attempts to make any impact in changing White attitudes.

Two decades later, Paton's attack on racism in *Cry the Beloved Country* enjoyed critical acclaim and renown. The novel's success was due partly to its gentler tone, Christian message, absence of party politics and redemptive ending. Even D.F. Malan felt that it was possible and opportune to attend the première of the yet more sanitised cinematic adaptation.

Civilisation on trial in South Africa

But the timing of its publication best explains the extent of *Cry the Beloved Country*'s appeal. Against expectations, the HNP narrowly defeated Smuts in the election of 1948, gaining a crucial six seats in White working-class constituencies on the Rand. The new government ignored the findings of the Fagan Commission and set about implementing apartheid policies. Early legislation forced all South Africans to accept legal assignation to a particular racial group, White, Native (or Bantu), Coloured (with Malay being a subset of Coloured) and Asian, whether a person wished this or not. Once this Population Registration Act of 1949 had been passed, it paved the way for further laws aimed at promoting cradle to grave segregation. They included the Prohibition of Mixed Marriages

---

[60] Roy Campbell, *The Wayzgoose: A South African Satire* (London: Jonathan Cape, 1928), 24, 27. On *Voorslag* see Peter Alexander, 'Campbell, Plomer, Van der Post and *Voorslag*', *English in Africa* 7, 2 (September 1980), 50–9.

[61] P.S. Joshi, *The Tyranny of Colour* (Durban: EP and Commercial Printing Co., 1942). The legislation referred to was the Pegging Act, enacted in 1943, and the Indian Land Tenure and Representation Act, 1946.

Act in 1950 and Immorality Amendment Act the following year, aimed in combination at preventing all cross-racial sexual liaisons.

The Group Areas Act of 1950 envisaged the complete segregation of residential areas. Although there was already a close correlation between race and space in urban social geography, the aim of the Act was to make this absolute. When its officials saw anomalies, as in the substantial 'pockets' of Coloured residents who formed half of the population of Cape Town's southern suburbs, these were normally resolved by declaring the whole area for Whites only; Black residents were expelled. Group Areas planning had as a general principle the creation of an inner spatial ring for White commercial and residential purposes. Black residents within this circle, or in suburban areas beyond declared White, had to move to areas further afield, Africans usually furthest of all. Industrial areas, railway lines, major roads and open spaces acted as buffer zones between residential group areas designated according to the racial definitions of the Population Registration Act.[62]

The Reservation of Separate Amenities Act of 1953 aimed at equally thorough racial separation in social and recreational facilities. In 1952, the Natives (Abolition of Passes and Co-ordination of Documents) Act, in Orwellian fashion, strengthened pass laws by introducing photographs into identity documents. A year later the Bantu Education Act, while widening African access to schools, introduced a separate and inferior syllabus. By removing government subsidies, the National Party (a fusion of the HNP and its small ally the Afrikaner Party in 1951) forced most mission schools to close. Any lingering hope that the Cape system might still prevail was extinguished by the South Africa Act Amendment Act of 1956. First introduced five years earlier, this removed Coloured men from the common voters' roll in the Cape after government gerrymandering of the composition of the Senate and Supreme Court.

This gradual extension of more thorough discrimination in all aspects of urban life, sustained through to the 1980s, came at a time when the rest of the world was moving slowly in the opposite direction. Equally, in the British world, including anglophone South Africa, there was particular shock that Smuts had been defeated by a party that had favoured Germany in the Second World War. Whereas before the war foreign commentary on South African cities had been overwhelmingly positive, it was now more often equivocal or downright hostile. A high proportion of literary and visual engagements with urban South Africa in the decade

[62] Western, *Outcast Cape Town* explores these ideas and practices in detail. Bickford-Smith, 'Urban History in the New South Africa' provides references to much further work on how segregation and group areas were put into practice in the different cities.

after 1948, if especially those by outsiders, referred directly or indirectly to Paton's *Cry the Beloved Country*. Shortly after the novel came out, Britain's *Daily Mirror* attacked Morton's depiction of South Africa and advised its readers to believe Paton instead.[63]

One such engagement, a film of 1950 called *Civilisation on Trial in South Africa*, referred to Paton's view of Sophiatown in its narration.[64] It was made by Anglican clergyman Michael Scott in combination with a British editor and future commercial film director Clive Donner.[65] Scott's title also (consciously or otherwise) recalled Arnold Toynbee's collection of essays published in 1948, *Civilization on Trial*, which appealed for a unified world civilisation. Scott's film argued that civilisation in South Africa was for Europeans only, and that segregation was humiliating for Blacks. The film was shown unofficially to United Nations delegates and also distributed by the Africa Bureau in London, which Scott helped to found in 1952.[66]

Scott had been brought up in a working-class area of Southampton, where his father was a vicar. He ministered in London's East End before taking up work in African residential areas on the Rand, and held what could be described as Christian socialist political views; indeed at one stage he was close to becoming a committed communist.[67] The Sophiatown he portrayed on film, and which he warns is now under threat from the Group Areas Act, was similar to that shown in the film version of *Cry the Beloved Country*. Thus a long sequence filmed in Sophiatown lingered first on a naked child framed in a particularly humble dwelling, and then on dirty water lying in the street. There were also shots of tents in the shanty town of Tobruk, in which Scott worked for a time, and narrative comment that new municipal dwellings were drab and monotonous. The film also shows extraordinarily brutal Sunday fights between male African domestic workers in Pretoria, officially sanctioned by the municipality, with White spectators displaying interest rather than disgust, as if at a dog fight.

---

[63] *Daily Mirror*, 20 October 1948.

[64] BFI: Michael Scott and Clive Donner (dir.), *Civilisation on Trial in South Africa* (UK: Scott and Donner Production, 1950).

[65] Clive Donner went on to direct such films as *The Caretaker* (1963; with Harold Pinter's script) and *What's New Pussycat?* (1965), with Peter Sellers and Sophia Loren.

[66] A. Toynbee, *Civilization on Trial* (Oxford: Oxford University Press, 1948); Michael Scott, *A Time to Speak* (London: Faber & Faber, 1958); P. Calvocoressi, 'The Africa Bureau', *Journal of Modern African Studies* 2 (1964), 292–4.

[67] Scott, *A Time to Speak*; A. Yates and L. Chester, *The Troublemaker: A Biography of Michael Scott* (London: Aurum Press, 2006); R. Gordon, 'Not Quite Cricket: "Civilization on Trial in South Africa": A Note on the First Protest Film Made in South Africa', *History in Africa* 32 (2005), 457–66.

Where Scott differs from Paton's depiction of urban poverty is by blaming it overtly on the South African authorities rather than moral failings among the White population as a whole. Africans are described as 'these landless, voiceless people'. Much of Scott's film focused on the threat posed by South Africa to British protectorates and the African inhabitants of South West Africa, governed by South Africa under a League of Nations' mandate since the First World War. But its opening sequences provide a stinging indictment of conditions in South African cities.

Whether or not they shared Paton's beliefs, what visiting writers, film makers and photographers had in common was the desire to visit, describe, show and condemn South African slums. Because they were perceived to be both exotic and particularly appalling, shanties were of particular interest. The success of Paton's book did much to ensure that slumming became part of any investigative trip to South Africa in the 1950s, part of the proper traveller's experience.

Many visitors went to each of the main cities in search of slums. The Swedish political scientist Herbert Tingsten visited this 'scandal' every day as he toured round South Africa's main cities, mentioning Paton and (in contrast to Bunche's comments in the 1930s) arguing that segregation was now much sharper than in the American South.[68] Paton had proved there was a market for portraying slums. Part of the reason was international demand for critical insights into apartheid South Africa.

Henry Gibbs, a British writer and self-declared 'independent conservative' did well with his 1949 book, *Twilight in South Africa*. Running to eight editions within two years, it had an entire chapter called 'In Search of Kumalo'. Gibbs described his own wanderings through Johannesburg's shanty towns, including one named Tobruk after the North African 'fortress on the sand', and similar 'cesspools' he discovered outside Port Elizabeth and Durban. Gibbs proclaimed Durban's Cato Manor the worst 'slum' in South Africa, and indeed the world. He also visited District Six, Cape Town's 'crime corner' and found 'despair, poverty, overcrowding', and reported on the high TB rate in the peninsula. Gibbs found positive things to say about each city, and had been assisted during his visit by local publicity associations. But he described at some length the unease he particularly felt while in Johannesburg. An American tourist had been shot by armed bandits at Gibbs' hotel the previous year, and a notice in the corridor warned against leaving boots

---

[68] Herbert Tingsten, *The Problem of South Africa* (London: Victor Gollancz, 1955).

outside rooms to be cleaned in case they were stolen; he closely scruti-
nised the daily 'crime list' column in the *Rand Daily Mail*.[69]

The view of *Through Malan's Africa* (1954), by American journalist,
NBS broadcaster and writer, Robert St John, is that Paton – whom he
meets in Cape Town – has become more famous than the South African
prime minister. Like Gibbs, St John mixes a predominantly negative
account of politics, poverty and fear with some positive comments about
most of the cities: for instance, Johannesburg is a 'little' like New York,
though more like Newark, New Jersey. Black shanties and townships are
like a 'noose round the neck' of the city and 'all white Johannesburgers
know it'; and as many as thirty murders occur some weekends. District
Six is much like a slum in any big city, and St John enjoyed the New Year
Carnival. The Malay Quarter is 'picturesque', but there is garbage in the
streets, sores on childrens' faces and a 'stench of decay'. Cape Town's
real disgrace though can be found in shanty towns like Cook's Bush,
which St John is shown round by the warden of the Cape Flats Distress
Association (CAFDA), Oscar Wollheim. This has no facilities at all, and
the *pondokkies* are flooded for four months of the year. Despite the
comfortable life enjoyed by most Whites, 'fear is here [in Cape Town]
like a London fog'.[70]

There are also distinct overtones of Paton near the beginning of
famous American broadcaster Ed Murrow's two-part documentary
called *African Conflict* (1954), made for CBS but also shown in
Britain. Commentary tells the viewer that Africans have been 'sucked'
into the big city of Johannesburg from the 'jungles of many centuries ago
into concrete jungles', as shots are displayed of labour recruitment in
rural areas. There is substantial footage of poor housing for Africans in
the cities themselves, including Sophiatown. But one of those interviewed in the documentary is Trevor Huddleston, the anti-apartheid
Anglican priest working in Sophiatown. Huddleston argues against the
imminent removals facing its inhabitants as many were 'respectable' and
already had houses, and thus Sophiatown should not become a White
suburb as planned. One of those residents, ex-ANC leader Dr Alfred
Xuma, particularly lamented the loss of mission education. Both he and
Huddleston hint at forthcoming disaster for the country.[71]

---

[69] Henry Gibbs, *Twilight in South Africa* (London: Jarrolds Publishers, 1949), 25, 34, 36,
42, 66–74, 107.

[70] Robert St John, *Through Malan's Africa* (London: Victor Gollancz Ltd, 1954), 24, 66–7,
191–2.

[71] BFI: Howard Smith (dir.), *Ed Murrow's See It Now: African Conflict* (New York: CBS,
1954).

Illustration 5.2: Continued use of local colour in promoting cities beyond the Second World War: Durban rickshaw puller, 1954 (Durban Publicity Association Guidebook 1954, British Library)

Denouncing hardship but asserting creativity

These negative perceptions of South African urban life from the late 1940s did not go uncontested. Part of the challenge came from continued professional place-selling (see Illustration 5.2). What was less predictable was that a number of writers officially classified as 'Coloured' or 'Native' would celebrate elements of creativity and joy amid the hardships of Black urban existence. Their writing formed the first substantial wave of Black literature, and challenged Bitter Cry portrayals that lamented the breakdown of the African 'tribe' in the city, or depicted Blacks in general as victims of urban vice. The new Black literature also challenged local colour stereotypes of the popular in its place so common in White publicity association material, city histories and travelogues; likewise, the related way that urban Blacks were referred to by most Whites as Jim, 'Kafir', 'Hotnot', 'boy' or 'girl'.

The majority of Black writers grew up in or worked at some time in Johannesburg. They included Peter Abrahams, Henry Nxumalo, Can Themba, Lewis Nkosi, Todd Matshikiza, Casey Motsisi, Nat Nakasa and Bloke Modisane.[72] A smaller group came from Cape Town, notably Richard Rive, Alex La Guma, James Matthews and Peter Clarke.[73] In addition, Henry Dhlomo provided some comment on Durban.[74]

---

[72] See for instance, P. Abrahams, *Dark Testament* (London: Allen and Unwin, 1942); P. Abrahams, *Song of the City* (London: Dorothy Crisp, 1943); P. Abrahams, *Mine Boy* (London: Faber & Faber, 1946); P. Abrahams, *Tell Freedom* (London: Faber & Faber, 1954); P. Abrahams, *Return to Goli* (London: Faber & Faber, 1952); E. Mphahlele, *Down Second Avenue* (London: Faber & Faber, 1959); T. Matshikiza, *Chocolates for My Wife* (London: Hodder and Stoughton, 1961); Modisane, *Blame Me on History*; Nkosi, *Home and Exile*. Later anthologies or commentaries on these writers that contain short stories and non-fiction pieces published in Johannesburg journals and in some cases considerable additional information and analysis include: E. Patel (ed.), *The World of Nat Nakasa* (Johannesburg: Ravan Press, 1975); M. Mutloatse, *Casey and Co., Selected Writings of Casey 'Kid' Motsisi* (Johannesburg: Ravan Press, 1980); E. Patel (ed.), *The World of Can Themba* (Johannesburg: Ravan Press, 1985); T. Matshikiza and J. Matshikiza, *With the Lid Off* (Johannesburg: M & G Books, 2000); M. Chapman (ed.), *The Drum Decade* (Pietermaritzburg: University of Natal Press, 2001); M. Nicol, *A Good-Looking Corpse* (London: Secker & Warburg, 1991).

[73] See contributions by these authors in Chapman (ed.), *Drum Decade*; see also R. Rive, *Advance, Retreat: Selected Short Stories* (Cape Town: David Philip, 1983); R. Rive, *Emergency* (Cape Town: David Philip, [1964] 1988); A. La Guma, *A Walk in the Night and Other Stories* (Cape Town: David Philip, [1967] 1991); A. La Guma, *The Stone Country* (Cape Town: David Philip, [1967] 1991); A. Odendaal and R. Field (eds), *Liberation Chabalala: The World of Alex La Guma* (Cape Town: Mayibuye Centre, 1993); H. Willemse, *More than Brothers: Peter Clarke and James Matthews at Seventy* (Cape Town: Kwela Books, 2000).

[74] Visser and Couzens (eds), *Dhlomo Collected Works*. See also KCM 8290 'Herbert Isaac Eliot Dhlomo papers', Killie Campbell Library, University of KwaZulu-Natal.

The political ideology and engagement of these authors varied: from the committed communism and leading role in Congress alliance politics of La Guma, through the PAC sympathies of Modisane, to the self-professed ideological and organisational scepticism of Themba. What differed accordingly, but was additionally influenced in the case of African writers by the need to stake a right of urban belonging given apartheid policies, was the balance between the attention given to negative and positive elements of Black urban life.

What Black authors had in common was a Western education, often at esteemed institutions like Adams College near Durban, Trafalgar High School in Cape Town, and St Peter's in Rosettenville, Johannesburg. The British writer Anthony Sampson, editor of *Drum* in the early 1950s, noted that seven of the journal's twenty staff had attended St Peter's.[75] What Black writers also shared was a post-World War Two generational shift in political consciousness akin to that of the ANC Youth League's desire to expose and more stridently denounce White racism and discrimination. As Lewis Nkosi argued, Africans might have forgiven their great-grand-fathers for losing a country to the Whites, but not their parents' generation for continuing to put their trust in 'whites meaning us well'.[76]

A third common factor was that Black writers, because of racial segregation, were – unless they went into exile – trapped in residential areas called slums by outsiders which forced people of different class and degrees of respectability into close physical proximity. Much of what they wrote therefore offered 'moment-by-moment experience – sensory, visceral, and mental' of 'slums' by people who actually lived in them.[77] Part of what they reported on in their writing was the 'terrific disorientation of transition' that accompanied rapid urbanisation akin to that undergone in north-western Europe a century earlier. Most Black writers belonged to what Marx referred to as La Boheme, the precarious classes, seldom with much money, not infrequently in debt.[78] Because of tight financial circumstances, or the fact that many lived reasonably close to city centres in areas without access to reliable transport, Johannesburg writers in particular lived in what was for them often perforce a walking city, were flâneurs like Charles Baudelaire in Haussmann's Paris.

Black writers in South African cities were now more able to obtain paid outlets for work in metropolitan journals. White publishers and editors learnt that there was a market among Black city-dwellers for material that reflected their everyday interests and experiences. One such publisher,

[75] Sampson, *Drum*, 134.   [76] Nkosi, *Home and Exile*, 3.
[77] Alter, *Imagined Cities*, x–xii.
[78] Karl Marx, *The Eighteenth Brumaire of Louis Bonaparte* (Rockville, MD: Arc Manor, 2008 [1852]).

mining fortune heir Jim Bailey, had brought Anthony Sampson out from
Britain to edit the magazine he established in 1951 called *African Drum*.
When both visited the BMSC to test opinion they were told that what was
wanted was a proper Black paper:

Tribal Music! Tribal History! Chiefs! We don't care about chiefs! Give us jazz and
film stars, man! We want Duke Ellington, Satchmo, and hot dames! ... You can
cut out this junk about kraals and folk tales and Basutos in blankets – forget it!
You're just trying to keep us backward ... Tell us what's happening right here,
man, on the Reef![79]

Renamed *Drum*, Bailey's magazine employed Nxumalo, Themba,
Modisane and others who knew and could write about subjects like
these, as well as everyday city life that reflected their own and their readers' interests and experiences. As *Drum* became more successful, other
newspapers like *The Bantu World*, which changed its name to *The World* in
the mid-1950s, *Ilanga* and *Golden City Post* (established in 1955) emulated elements of its formula. In doing so, they provided further outlets for
Black writing about city life, as did the pro-communist *Guardian* and its
1954 successor, *New Age*, and some liberal newspapers like the *Rand
Daily Mail*.[80] Apartheid also brought international interest in South
African race relations at a time when the world was moving away from
official discrimination. This provided the opportunity for Black writers to
place novels and autobiographies with London publishers such as Faber
and Faber, or their short stories in international anthologies like Langston
Hughes' *An African Treasury*, Peggy Rutherfoord's *African Voices* and
Ezekiel Mphahlele's own *African Writing Today*.[81] In the process they
gained a cross-racial and international readership for their representations of South African cities.

African writers in particular emphasised a positive side to Black urban
life to challenge apartheid ideology that argued that Africans belonged in
the reserves. But all Black writers also bore witness to the poverty,
violence, crime, dirt and disease that accompanied or imperilled Black
urban experience, including their own. *Dark Testament*, the title of the
first published collection of short stories by a Black South African writer,
suggested as much. Its author was Peter Abrahams, who wrote the stories

[79] Sampson, *Drum*, 7.
[80] Sampson, *Drum*, xi, 7–9, 20, 146; Sylvetser Stein, *Who Killed Mr Drum?* (London: Corvo
Books, 2003), 47–9.
[81] L. Hughes (ed.), *An African Treasury: Article, Essays, Stories, Poems by Black Africans*
(London: Victor Gollancz Ltd, 1961); P. Rutherfoord (ed.), *African Voices: An Anthology
of Native African Writing* (New York: Grosset and Dunlop, 1958); E. Mphahlele (ed.),
African Writing Today (London: Harmondsworth, 1967).

when he was living in South Africa in the 1930s, though the collection was only published in 1942 after he had left the country.

Abrahams was born in Vrededorp in Johannesburg, the son of an Ethiopian father and 'Coloured' mother. He managed to get a place at St Peter's Rosettenville. He read voraciously, as did the other Black writers, from the established canon of great European literature as well as American authors whose work was available at the BMSC, notably that of Harlem Renaissance writer Langston Hughes.[82] Much of his writing described his early years in Johannesburg, or the return visit he made there from self-imposed exile in Britain in the early 1950s.[83] Many of the stories in *Dark Testament* spoke of the 'dirt, death, [and] stinking squalor' that faced the majority of South Africans. 'One of the Three' featured Tommy, a boy who wants to overcome poverty and earn enough to relieve his mother from heavy work; Johnny, another boy in the story, had a mother who had 'died of starvation' to keep him at school. Similarly, in 'Love' a woman develops a bad back from carrying heavy loads of washing but brings up her daughter's grandchild after the daughter dies in childbirth.[84]

The writing of other Black authors from the 1940s onwards reiterated such statements, often in more vivid or acerbic fashion. For instance, Ezekiel Mphahlele, an old boy of both St Peter's and Adams College and graduate of the University of South Africa, wrote a short story about life in Newclare, Johannesburg, published in *Drum* in 1957:

It was Saturday. The white man's work was suspended. And then someone beat his wife and children. A boy dug his knife into human flesh. A boy twisted the arm of a girl. The Zionists sang their half-pagan, half-Christian songs. All so brutally.[85]

Can Themba, graduate of Fort Hare University, had actuality pieces in *Drum* with titles such as 'Terror in the Trains', 'Why our Living is so Tough' and 'Our Hungry Children'. His *Drum* short story 'The Urchin' featured a character called Boy-Boy who 'looked like a social worker's explanation of "conditions in the slums": thin to malnourished, delinquent, undisciplined, dedicated to a future gallows'.[86]

---

[82] Abrahams, *Tell Freedom*; S. Graham and J. Walters (eds), *Langston Hughes and the South African Drum Generation: The Correspondence* (New York: Palgrave Macmillan, 2010).

[83] Abrahams, *Dark Testament*; Abrahams, *Song of the City*; Abrahams, *Mine Boy*; Abrahams, *Return to Goli*; Abrahams, *Tell Freedom*.

[84] Abrahams, *Dark Testament*, 12, 14, 22, 24, quotation from 58. See also Dora Taylor's review of *Dark Testament* in the South African journal *Trek* republished in *English in Africa*, 29, 2 (2002), 75–80.

[85] E. Mphahlele, 'Lesane', cited in Chapman (ed.), *Drum Decade*, 152.

[86] Patel, *The World of Can Themba*, 97–110; 111–15; 120–5; 140–3. The quotation is from 99 to 100.

Illustration 5.3: Can Themba (Mary Evans Picture Gallery)

Accounts of the Mother City, especially those by communist author Alex La Guma in his two novellas *A Walk in the Night* and *Stone Country*, were almost relentlessly grim. *A Walk in the Night*, whose plot features the accidental killing of an elderly White District Six resident by the unemployed and angry Michael Adonis, allows La Guma to muse at length on the living conditions of the poor. An extract gives some sense of the tone and prose poem form he produces while appealing to the reader's emotions through extensive use of sensory-laden description:

On the floors of the tenements the grime collected quickly . . . water was spilled or somebody urinated and left wet patches onto which the dust from the ceilings or the seams of clothes drifted and collected to leave dark patches as the moisture dried . . . in the dampness deadly life formed in decay and bacteria and mould, and in the heat and airlessness the rot appeared . . . so that things which once were whole or new withered or putrefied and the smells of their decay and putrefaction pervaded the tenements of the poor.[87]

[87] La Guma, *A Walk in the Night*, 34.

La Guma then proceeds to describe in some detail the 'insects and vermin' that flourished in the 'fetid heat and slippery dampness' in a fashion reminiscent of Baudelaire's 'A Carcass' in *The Flowers of Evil*.[88]

Black urban hardship and violence was now blamed squarely on government policies and economic circumstances. In an early edition of *Drum*, Henry Nxumalo's 'The Birth of a Tsotsi' ascribed the growth of gangs to poverty.[89] It was not the result of any inherent, racially-determined, problems of adaptation or ability as suggested in most Jim Comes to Joburg literature. As Lewis Nkosi put it:

We were made to understand that Jim's loss of place in the tightly woven tribal structure and the corresponding alternative of the elders' authority over him was the main cause rather than the result of the nation's tragedy.[90]

Nkosi went on to describe his experience of apartheid legislation as one of 'entrapment', as being 'like a Kafka novel' and mentioned the needs for passes to seek work in cities, night permits to move around urban areas after dark, and 'petty' police insults and persecution.[91] James Matthews followed the example of William Scully, Laurens van der Post and Herbert Dhlomo in blaming local government spending priorities for the extent of urban poverty and social delinquency. Dhlomo had written in his poem 'On Munro Ridge' that Johannesburg was 'Where children die of hunger and neglect, While City Fathers boast suburbs select'.[92] Matthews' short story 'Dead End!', about the death of a young car thief at the hands of the police, featured a Cape Town councillor's plea for more money to be spent on housing the poor:

In our tourist booklets we are apt to describe our city as fair but forget to add the hideous blot which mars its fairness. Gentlemen, Windermere [the shanty town on the Cape Flats] is our duty.

The councillor is howled down by colleagues who believe 'Our duty is to the city, to beautify it, to protect it, and not to the welfare of a pack of Natives!' Consequently the council proceeds with 'the plans regarding the foreshore'.[93] La Guma echoed Matthews' sentiments in a non-fiction piece for *New Era*: 'Vast sums have been spent on beautifying the

---

[88] Charles Baudelaire, *The Flowers of Evil* (Oxford: Oxford University Press, 2008), 59–63.
[89] H. Nxumalo, 'The Birth of a Tsotsi', *Drum*, November 1951, reproduced in Chapman (ed.), *Drum Decade*, 18–23.
[90] Nkosi, *Home and Exile*, 4–5.   [91] Ibid., 35–6, 44–5.
[92] H.I.E. Dhlomo, 'On Munro Ridge', in Visser and Couzens (eds), *Dhlomo Collected Works*, 365.
[93] J. Matthews, 'Dead End!', *Drum Magazine*, September 1954, also published in M. Chapman (ed.), *Drum Decade*, 60–5.

beachfront at Sea Point, so there can be no excuse that better housing cannot be provided.'[94]

An even more common refrain was racial discrimination that affected Black South Africans irrespective of class. One of Richard Rive's more powerful short stories involved a man determined to protest against apartheid, in Defiance Campaign fashion, by sitting on a 'whites only' bench at Cape Town railway station: the kind of story about 'intergroup problems' that Langston Hughes encouraged Rive to write.[95] Rive also wrote about the difficulties of cross-race sexual relationships, now prohibited by law. The point he and many other Black writers made, and that became a persistent theme from the 1950s in White liberal writing as well, was the absurdity and inhumanity of such prohibitions on love and, by extension, of all racial discrimination. South African journals also gave considerable attention to cases of 'love across the colour bar', including that of Seretse Khama's marriage to Englishwoman Ruth Williams in 1948.

Khama was *kgosi* or king of the Bamangwato people of Bechuanaland. Though later educated at Oxford and the Inner Temple, he had been an undergraduate at Fort Hare like Can Themba. Themba declared that 'I do not necessarily want to bed a white woman [though he and other Black writers certainly went to bed with some]; I merely insist on my right to want her'. Themba saw the legal prohibition on such desire as merely one part of an apartheid world that prevented Black South Africans from entering 'so many fields of human experience'.

It is a crepuscular, shadow life in which we wander as spectres seeking meaning for ourselves ... The whole atmosphere is charged with the white man's general disapproval, and where he does not have a law for it, he certainly has a grimace that cows you. This is the burden of the white man's crime against my personality that negatives all the brilliance of intellect and the genuine funds of goodwill so many individuals have. The whole bloody ethos still asphyxiates me.[96]

The fabulous decade

Despite such extensive White racism, the advent of apartheid policies and Black urban hardships, Lewis Nkosi called the 1950s 'the fabulous decade', a time of 'infinite hope and possibilities'.[97] Can Themba more equivocally quoted the entire opening paragraph of Dickens' *Tale of Two Cities*, which begins with the line 'It was the best of times, it was

---

[94] La Guma, 'Don't Sneeze', *New Era*, 8 November 1956.
[95] Graham and Walters (eds), *Langston Hughes*, 30.
[96] Themba, 'Crepescule', in *Requiem for Sophiatown*, 66, 72.
[97] Nkosi, *Home and Exile*, 25.

the worst of times'.[98] There were several reasons why Black writing contained as much optimism as it did. One stemmed from the fact that for them experience of urban life was flavoured by their relatively privileged status within Black society. Another, for African writers, was the need to reject the un-nuanced slum-land language of outsiders. This airbrushed out creative and hopeful elements of Black urban existence and justified forced removals and destruction of freehold property rights. Most Black writers accepted the appellation 'slum' as shorthand for the objectively densely populated, often dangerous and dirty neighbourhoods they inhabited. Some categorised as Coloured, like La Guma and Matthews, did so enthusiastically, as part of denouncing capitalism and contemporary priorities of local government spending, believing that places like District Six might be renovated, not destroyed. Those classified as Africans were more careful, given that apartheid principles challenged their very right to residence in the city.

A further reason for some optimism in Black city writing of the 1950s was that not all the apartheid legislation that accompanied National Party victory in 1948 was implemented thoroughly or with immediate effect. Substantial forced removals in contentious areas under the new Group Areas Act or amended Slums Act of 1934 only began in the second half of the decade, when the National Party had a more secure majority. Even then, Group Areas removals within a city were staggered over many years. Even in a single residential area like Sophiatown they began in 1955 but continued in piecemeal fashion through to the end of the decade. A similar pattern accompanied removals in District Six, declared to be a 'white group area' in 1966, and then demolished in stages into the late 1970s.[99]

Likewise the Separate Amenities Act did not instantly banish all possibilities of cross-racial socialising. Several restaurants and places of entertainment in major cities remained open to all throughout the 1950s and early 1960s, like Uncle Joel's or the Crescent restaurant in Fordsburg, or the Little and Maynardville theatres in Cape Town. The majority were in cross-racial residential areas like District Six, the Grey Street area (Durban) or the area to the immediate south-west of Johannesburg's city centre. These were places where boundaries between White and Black areas were still not clear up to the 1960s. From an African perspective, old western areas of Johannesburg like Sophiatown, Newclare, Vrederdorp and Malay Camp were un-monitored by White location supervisors. Visits by friends of other races, often themselves writers,

[98] Themba, 'Crepescule', in *Requiem for Sophiatown*, 69.
[99] Jeppie and Soudien (eds), *The Struggle for District Six*.

were easier than in fenced townships. Together with the possibility of freehold rights, social networks and shared institutions, this enabled some Africans to experience not just a sense of territorial belonging there, but pride of ownership.

In all three cities, mixed gatherings or parties in private homes were legal, albeit the serving of 'European' alcohol was not if 'Natives' were present. In addition, such encounters were possible in urban spaces beyond streets and shops. Zoo Lake in Johannesburg was one in which White teenagers sometimes danced 'side by side with black teenagers' to penny-whistle music. The botanical gardens in Durban and Cape Town, or the slopes of Table Mountain itself were others.[100]

Mass extra-parliamentary political opposition and demonstration was substantial and still legal. Hope for imminent peaceful political change remained plausible, though expectations of what this change might entail differed among members of ideologically diverse opposition movements. For a while, some Blacks as well as Whites could believe that the battle to retain what some still perceived as British South African liberties was not yet lost, and when some liberties were lost, like first the African then the Coloured component of the Cape franchise, that the war might still be won. Afrikaner republicanism was not yet decisively triumphant. Until the early 1960s, South Africa remained a monarchy within the British Commonwealth. Richard Rive remembered:

> those who used to live in District Six, those who lived in Caledon Street and Clifton Hill and busy Hanover Street. There are those who still remember the ripe warm days ... a decade after the end of the Second World War ... *in those red-white-and-blue days.*[101] [emphasis added]

In the early 1950s there was the possibility, for instance, that the National Party could be defeated at the polls. It had been elected on a considerable minority of White votes, and this happened again in 1953, because the constituency boundary system was weighted heavily in favour of rural constituencies. Almost all the seats in the major cities were still held by the United Party. National Party electoral weakness helps to explain the gradual rather than rapid implementation of apartheid policies. Only by the late 1950s had the National Party firmly entrenched its parliamentary position, partly through political gerrymandering.

The possibility endured that successful mass Black resistance to key elements of apartheid like the pass laws could force change upon the government. 'Communists' and the South African Communist Party

---

[100] Modisane, *Blame Me on History*, 173.
[101] Richard Rive, *'Buckingham Palace', District Six* (Cape Town: David Philip, 1986), 1.

itself were banned in 1950, and the government definition of 'communist' was sufficiently broad to include almost anyone who strongly opposed them. Yet the ANC and its smaller allies in the Congress movement – the South African Indian Congress, the Coloured Peoples' Congress and the (White) Congress of Democrats – as well as the breakaway Pan African Congress (PAC), formed in 1959, remained unbanned until 1960. So did the Trotskeyite Non-European Unity Movement, of particular importance among Coloured teachers and students in Cape Town. These organisations were able to organise openly and embark on protest actions in the 1950s. Worker and consumer strikes and boycotts were also possible.

The coming of apartheid encouraged the more radical orientation of the ANC, prompted by its Youth League and the launching of the Defiance Campaign in 1952. This meant defying apartheid laws in similar fashion to Gandhi's strategy of peaceful civil disobedience or *Satyagraha*. Peaceful Defiance Campaign protestors were arrested in the cities for flaunting segregation on trains, buses and public benches. The ANC's Freedom Charter, drawn up in Bloemfontein in 1955, stipulated that 'South Africa belongs to all who live in it, black and white' and that no government could rightly claim authority to rule unless it was based on the will of all the people.[102] In the following year, about 20,000 women, including some Whites, marched to the Union Buildings in Pretoria against the proposed extension of passes to African females.[103]

There was also extra-parliamentary White opposition to apartheid beyond the small numbers of mainly ex-CPSA members who joined the Congress of Democrats. Albeit many participants were motivated primarily by hostility to Afrikaner nationalism, a Torch Commando was formed in 1951 by White Second World War veterans. They protested in large numbers and dramatic fashion in the major cities against the proposed removal of Coloured men from the common voters' roll in the Cape. A White women's organisation, the Black Sash, staged its own protests outside parliament against National Party tampering with the constitution and evolved into a broadly-based civil rights organisation. Alan Paton co-founded the small non-racial Liberal Party in 1953. Although initially in favour of a Cape-style qualified franchise, it adopted a policy of universal franchise in the 1960s. Many White students and staff at UCT, Wits and the University of Natal (whose main campus was in Durban) took part in protests against the extension of apartheid to higher education in the late 1950s.

[102] Lodge, *Black Politics*, 71.   [103] Ibid., 142–6.

All of this was taking place in a global context of anti-colonial movements, closely followed by educated Black South Africans in the cities. India had already gained independence in 1947, while Ghana initiated sub-Saharan success in this respect in 1957. From 1955, civil rights activists in the United States employed tactics similar to the Defiance Campaign. Although Congress leaders were put on trial for treason in 1956, all the accused, who included some Whites, were eventually acquitted. The state security system was not yet as extensive, armed with almost limitless ability to ban and detain enemies of the state, as it was to become in the 1960s. As Lewis Nkosi later recalled of the previous decade, 'there was not as much torture'.[104]

These national and international developments were widely reported in English-language journals and read and written about by Black writers like Nkosi. *Drum*, the magazine that most worked for at some stage or another, was no exception. It also gave additional space to the achievements of African Americans.[105] It was in this context that Black writers felt able to celebrate creativity amidst misery, and in the process demonstrate their right to belong in the city and be seen as fellow citizens.

Creative elements they wrote about included African *stokvel* parties, occasions organised by women to raise funds for their families, the boisterous nature of cinema attendance, and street activities and spectacles. Many lines were spent describing the lively 'land of dope and glory' shebeen culture of convivial conversation, music and dancing in the old freehold areas of western Johannesburg like Sophiatown.[106] Nat Nakasa argued that the township jazz or penny-whistle playing that accompanied this could excite and enliven Black and White alike, and that this should not be dismissed by outsiders as 'cheerless, slum noises that nobody cared for'.[107]

The catalogue of inventive Black city culture in all the main cities extended to dress, manners and language, including the naming of homes and local places that gave a sense of urban territorial belonging. The names of Johannesburg shebeens were themselves a tribute to Black urban creativity: Little Heaven, Paradise, the Sanctuary, the Kind Lady, the Basement, Hell's Kitchen, Back-o'-the-Moon, the Thirty-Nine Steps, Cabin in the Sky and the Greenhouse. Can Themba named his own home in Sophiatown, venue for much philosophical discussion, 'The

---

[104] Nkosi, *Home and Exile*, 8.   [105] Chapman (ed.), *Drum Decade*, 194–7.
[106] The sobriquet of 'land of dope and glory' was the 1960 invention of Dan Chocho, according to Todd Matshikiza. See Matshikiza and Matshikiza, *With the Lid Off*, 60.
[107] Patel, *Nat Nakasa*, 117.

Illustration 5.4: Cross-racial patronage of a Johannesburg shebeen, possibly in Vrededorp, photographed for *Drum* magazine, 1956 (Mary Evans Picture Library)

House of Truth'; Bloke Modisane, inspired by Billy Wilder's Hollywood search for truth and beauty, called his 'Sunset Boulevard'.[108]

All Black authors celebrated elements of city life. Writing by those categorised as Coloured may have been bleaker, because unlike Africans their status as permanent city dwellers was not under any immediate threat; committed communist La Guma could afford to be more purely critical of Black urban conditions.[109] But even he wrote in humorous fashion about teenagers dancing in a Hanover Street (District Six) café to Elvis Presley and Little Richard, or the fact that a District Six pub offered similar enjoyments to those of its counterparts elsewhere in the world.[110] La Guma liked Johannesburg not just for its 'long line of bus boycotters' or warm working-class welcomes but because of

[108] Patel, *The World of Can Themba*, 160; See also Matshikiza, *Chocolates for My Wife*, 76, 110; Modisane, *Blame Me on History*, 8.
[109] Rive, 'Moon Over District Six', in *Advance, Retreat*, 4.
[110] La Guma, 'Me and "Cultcha"', *New Era*, 13 February 1958; La Guma, *A Walk in the Night*, 13.

the coffee stalls where you can buy a cup of steaming hot brew and two delicious flat-cakes for a sixpence, and chat idly with the friendly man behind the counter ... there is richness greater than gold in the penny-whistle man walking easily along Pritchard Street, playing his lively tunes ... There is beauty, too, in the welcoming smile of the shebeen queen, for the shebeen has become a place of relaxation, the local pub where pleasantries are exchanged and the chatter is quiet and meaningless.[111]

Themba added to the perception that Black urban experience was neither an unadulterated Bitter Cry nor unique by arguing like Macmillan and De Kiewiet against South African exceptionalism. What was happening in South African cities was merely another example of a world-wide and age old phenomenon: 'the city called and the peasants came'. He ridiculed White laments about 'the spoiling of the pure native', whose 'grasp of "civilisation" was purely "imitative", "superficial", "evanescent"' with the retort that urban Africans 'didn't give a damn'.[112]

Themba and his contemporaries avidly read the work of those who had experienced rapid urbanisation in other societies and at other times, the better to understand their own: 'Sometimes I think ... only Charles Dickens – or, perhaps, Victor Hugo – could have understood Sophiatown'.[113] Themba believed that he and his fellow writers were beyond any existing categorisation of Africans:

We were not the calm dignified Africans that the Church so admires (and fights for); nor the unspoiled rural African the Government so admires, for they tell no lies, they do not steal and, above all, they do not try to measure up to the white man. Neither were we 'tsotsis' in the classical sense of the term, though the tsotsis saw us as cousins.[114]

Similarly, Nat Nakasa declared 'I am just not a tribesman, whether I like it or not. I am, inescapably, a part of the city slums, the factory machines and our beloved shebeens'.[115]

Black Baudelaires

Black South African writers offered alternative literary snapshots that aimed to capture the beauty as well as the ugliness in African experience of the sharp juxtapositions modern metropolitan life produced. This is what Baudelaire had requested of 'Painters of Modern Life', and that he had practised himself in *Paris Spleen*. Black South African snapshots were

[111] La Guma, 'City of Gold', *New Era*, 27 April 1957.
[112] Themba, 'The Bottom of a Bottle', in *Requiem to Sophiatown*, 62–3.
[113] Themba, 'Crepescule', in *Requiem to Sophiatown*, 69.
[114] Themba, 'The Bottom of a Bottle', in *Requiem to Sophiatown*, 57.
[115] Patel, *Nat Nakasa*, 159.

in a variety of linguistic styles, influenced to varying degrees by Charles Dickens, Victor Hugo, Raymond Chandler, Damon Runyon, Friedrich Engels, Langston Hughes and Hollywood crime movies. Often featuring the author as protagonist, much of their work was in short stories or reports on genuine events and people, though the divide between the two in terms of style and extent of factual information was fluid. Both provided the opportunity for suitably rapid verbal sketches of the ephemeral, which often deployed inventive prose rhythms or individually stylised versions of English. Todd Matshikiza gave his name to a staccato and American urban detective fiction style that became known as Matshikese:

I loved the dingy lights of the club house. The smell of roast meat from the kitchen behind the stage. The people muttering through tobacco smoke and the rhythm pounding through my head . . . Snowy's soprano. Tutus's piano. Roast meat and jazz overpowered me and I fainted over the piano.[116]

Even in longer pieces like La Guma's *A Walk in the Night* or Peter Abrahams' *Song of the City*, there were passages of staccato sentences akin to prose poetry:

A voice broke into song. It was a woman's voice. It rose gently and rang out in clear silver notes that grew louder minute by minute. It was the 'Song of the City.' The Natives's consciousness of Johannesburg at night found voice in it. It was a tribute to that deep monotonous hum. The clear words filled the hall and the minds of the dancers.[117]

There was conscious intent here to capture 'the fullest expression of the bubbling life around us and the restless spirit within us' as Themba put it, whether beautiful and miraculous or brutal and disgusting.[118] Lewis Nkosi recollected in exile that it was 'generally assumed that one couldn't deal professionally [i.e. as writers] with urban African life unless one had descended to its very depths as well as climbed to its heights'.[119]

Themba occasionally mourned the loss of the psychological support once supplied by old 'tribal' traditions and beliefs. But this was his momentary reaction to being surrounded by what he viewed as the cold world of White urban prohibitions, and it was self-evident to African writers that, for better or for worse, they were part of a Western-educated, detribalised elite. Mphahlele made the point in his autobiography, *Down Second Avenue*: 'your tribal umbilical cord had long, oh so long, been severed and all the

---

[116] Matshikiza writing in *Drum*, 1957, cited in Nicol, *A Good-Looking Corpse*, 77.
[117] Abrahams, *Song of the City*, 74.   [118] Themba, *Requiem for Sophiatown*, 47.
[119] Nkosi, *Home and Exile*, 12.

The Emergence of the South African Metropolis

talk of Bantu culture and the Black man developing along his own lines was so much tommy rot'.[120]

The protagonists of Abrahams' pre-apartheid novels *Song of the City* and *Mine Boy* missed rural life. But one who retreated to the countryside is soon lured back to the city by its noise and bright lights; the other, once in the city, never leaves. *Song of the City*, as the book's title suggests, mentions the new and pulsating Marabi music. Marabi expressed 'the Natives's consciousness of Johannesburg at night' and enabled Africans to dance

away the seething bitterness that is attendant with repression! And like a stream the two-point rhythm washed away those nameless volcanoes so that on the morrow the house-boy would be a good and humble house-boy! And the kitchen maid too. And the mine boy. And the rickshaw boy ...[121]

Marabi was a fusion of African, European and American styles, a product of the nature of South African urbanisation. The novel's protagonist Nduli, who is given the city name 'Dick' by a policeman, listens with his girlfriend Daisy to lyrics that 'told of a young woman coming from the farms and finding work in the big city and being lonely ... [and of] a young man who had come to the big city and had been arrested and imprisoned for seven years'.[122] Near the end of the book, Daisy herself sings a song that laments the loss of rural ways but accepts that city life is permanent and with positive possibilities. It ends:

> For you are a son of the city
> And the song will lighten your pain;
> To-day there is pain – but to-morrow
> The song will be gay – rich with hope.[123]

Herbert Dhlomo, whose early work focused on rural themes within African oral tradition, like Zulu kings, or elements of nature, moved to urban themes with his 1940s poems published in *Ilanga*. Although many of these bitterly bemoan Black experience of discrimination and toil, in keeping with the Dhlomo brothers' more acerbic editorials, a few poems combine this with paeans to Durban's splendour and urban modernity. So 'Evening Falls on the Berea Hills' begins with Dhlomo's dejection about 'the great city that has planted Despair in me', but ends with 'I'm back content! I look Where Nature's work and Man's mingle or fight – Up sprout Man's flowers! Electric Lights! 'Tis night'. In 'Evening, Esplanade, Durban', Dhlomo writes of this place 'The pain and tears,

---

[120] Mphahlele, *Down Second Avenue*, 202–3.   [121] Abrahams, *Song of the City*, 73.
[122] Ibid., 74. See also David B. Coplan, *In Township Tonight: South Africa's Black City Music* (Johannesburg: Ravan Press, 1985).
[123] Abrahams, *Song of the City*, 174.

here seem to die! ... Here ... launches, boats, docked ships, soft lights! The whole Transfigured scene refutes "man is such stuff As dreams are made of" ...'[124] Dhlomo also wrote an unpublished short story that revelled in the nature of buses and experiences travelling on them in Durban:

I like buses. Unlike seas, mountains, cathedrals and beauty spots, they are familiar, human, fraternal. You need not go to them on special occasions, under certain moods. They refuse to be the sights and seats, the tabernacles and temples of meditation ... They are stages where now a comic scene is seen, anon a tragic one.

Dhlomo noted the way that buses changed pre-existing notions of distance and increased the circulation and penetration of 'visitors, influences and ideas'.[125]

Many African writers showed not even momentary nostalgia for old rural ways, either directly or through characters they created. Nat Nakasa wrote that he was depressed by the very sight of new 'raw' rural recruits for the mines who 'spoiled my image of Johannesburg as the throbbing giant which threw up sophisticated gangsters, brave politicians and intellectuals'.[126] Nkosi wrote enthusiastically of Johannesburg, despite its ugliness and his own occasional 'appalling loneliness':

In Johannesburg I loved the city noises, the home-bound crowds, the chaotic traffic ... my senses opened to that keen dry Johannesburg air that was so exhilarating; I was fascinated by the garish lights, by the colour and the rumble of the city.[127]

Johannesburg's African authors in particular revelled in elements of urban modernity: neon lights at night, displays in shop windows, caverns formed at street level by skyscrapers and forms of urban transport. Sensory recollections were part of recording this experience. Abrahams wrote of the feeling after rain fell in Johannesburg and 'heat mists rose from the macadamised streets ... curving highways ... and narrow slum streets. It was a strange new touch to a beautiful city. And the people of Johannesburg smiled and commented on it.'[128] Mphahlele gazed out of the dining-room window of his not-yet-electrified house in Orlando to 'contemplate the beauty of distant electric lights ... [that] blink and tease the spirit of the night: little sparkling fires, so unearthly, so inorganic'.[129]

[124] See 'Evening, Esplanade, Durban' and 'Evening Falls on the Berea Hills', in Visser and Couzens (eds), *Dhlomo Collected Works*, 360–4.
[125] Killie Cambell Africana Library, KCM 8290, H.I.E. Dhlomo manuscripts, 'Stopping the Bus'.
[126] Patel, *Nat Nakasa*, 5.   [127] Nkosi, *Home and Exile*, 16–17, 26.
[128] Abrahams, *Song of the City*, 138.   [129] Mphahlele, *Down Second Avenue*, 201–2.

In asserting their right to be part of metropolitan life, African writers presented themselves as divorced from the rural, and living the detribalised lives of the self-consciously modern man. They did so at least partly along lines defined by another French poet, Paul Verlaine:

Modern Man, made what he is by the refinements of excessive civilisation, modern man with his sharpened and vibrant senses, his painfully subtle mind, his brain saturated with tobacco, his blood poisoned by alcohol.[130]

As Lewis Nkosi put it, 'A *Drum* man took sex and alcohol in his stride'.[131]

Several of the writers, if only most thoroughly perhaps James Matthews and Can Themba, lived their lives in almost constant intoxication. Some of the titles of Themba's short stories such as 'Let the People Drink' and 'From the Bottom of the Bottle' recall Baudelaire's 'Get Drunk'.[132] Themba told British journalist and *Drum* editor Thomas Hopkinson that he was only happy when 'sinful'.[133]

This was in sharp contrast to the self-presentation of Black elites, and many among the working classes, who aspired to urban respectability, whether through religious observance, teetotalism, appropriate recreation or their inclusion in social pages established in *Ilanga* or *Bantu World*. Rolfes Dhlomo's *An African Tragedy* came from this milieu. Nkosi described writing of such kind as romantic, Christian and crusading and thought that its authors saw the new generation of Black writers as 'irresponsible, cynical, pleasure-loving, world-weary'. He acknowledged that there was much truth in the accusation, but preferred to describe the style of his generation of writers as 'urbane, ironic, morally tough and detached'.[134] In doing so, Nkosi was implying that Black writers of the 1950s displayed the morally ambivalent or even blasé attitudes that a Georg Simmel or Walter Benjamin thought appropriate for any individual facing life in a great metropolis. As Simmel put it:

The deepest problems of modern life flow from the attempt of the individual to maintain the independence and individuality of his existence against the sovereign powers of society, against the weight of the historical heritage and the external culture and technique of life.[135]

---

[130] Cited in J. Culler, 'Introduction', in Baudelaire, *The Flowers of Evil*, xxv.
[131] Nkosi, *Home and Exile*, 12.
[132] These can be found in Patel, *The World of Can Themba*, 158–66, 227–36; Charles Baudelaire, 'Get Drunk', in *Paris Spleen* (New York: New Directions, [1869] 1970), 74.
[133] Tom Hopkinson, *In the Fiery Continent* (London: Victor Gollancz, 1962), 146.
[134] Nkosi, *Home and Exile*, 4.
[135] G. Simmel, *On Individuality and Social Forms* (Chicago: University of Chicago Press, 1971), 324. This is the first line of Simmel's chapter on 'The Metropolis and Mental Life'.

Illustration 5.5: Casey Motsisi posing in top hat and tails in the 1950s
(Mary Evans Picture Gallery)

In the manner Simmel believed typical of the thoroughly urban personality, many in Johannesburg desired to be noticed. They performed in
often dramatic fashion in front of friends and strangers. Bloke Modisane
offered his visitors champagne and Mozart, and wore a cowboy hat at
parties. Nat Nakasa was prone to leaping up from the table to recite

Shakespeare. Casey Motsisi was not averse to clowning for the camera in top hat and tails.[136]

According to Nkosi, Can Themba was wont to meander down the street 'like Stephen Daedelus through Dublin' carrying the complete works of Oscar Wilde, or quoting from the Rubaiyat of Omar Khayyam:

> Oh Thou, who with Pitfall and with Gin,
> Beset the Road I was to wander in,
> Though wilt not with Predestined Round,
> Enmesh me, and Impute my fall to Sin.[137]

Having multiple female lovers, and among them White lovers, was another way of being noticed in a modern, amoral Baudelarian way. As Themba's White lover Jean Hart observed:

> He (Bloke Modisane) would have someone at the bottom of the garden at one point in the party, someone else in the shed, then he'd go upstairs and have somebody else in the bathroom.[138]

This behaviour did not necessarily signify solipsistic inability to feel concern for others, or a failure to empathise in particular with women's hardships and struggles. Having staccato relationships with women, being adulterous or applauding pin-up girls in *Drum* magazine may have demonstrated emotional callousness. Male violence to women, so common in the cities, was seldom dwelt on at any length in Black writing. It was downplayed in the numerous accounts, including a renowned musical staged in Johannesburg and London, of boxer Ezekiel Dhlamini, nicknamed King Kong, who murdered his girlfriend; instead the murder was portrayed as part of Dhlamini's own tragedy, like Othello's killing of Desdemona. In contrast, there are several stories by Maimane and Themba that focus on women who hire assassins to kill their male partners. Many women appear to be stereotyped as 'the helpless wife, the fickle lover, the alluring vamp' as they often were in American pulp fiction.[139]

On the other hand, Black city writing was full of real or fictional women who defied such stereotypes, and male violence toward women was on

---

[136] Nicol, *A Good-Looking Corpse*, 288–94, 341; Mphahlele, *Down Second Avenue*, 198–9.

[137] Nkosi, *Home and Exile*, 20, 29.

[138] Jean Hart, 'Can Themba's White Lover', cited in Nicol, *A Good-Looking Corpse*, 294 (see also 180).

[139] The musical was Todd Matshikiza, Pat Williams and Harry Bloom, *King Kong* (Johannesburg: Bernhardt Production, 1959). See also, for example, N. Nakasa, 'The Life and Death of King Kong', in Chapman (ed.), *Drum Decade*, 166–70; A. Mogale [A. Maimane], 'Crime for Sale', in Chapman (ed.), *Drum Decade*, 28–31; C. Themba, 'The Nice Time Girl', in Patel, *The World of Can Themba*, 53–60. The quotation on *Drum* stereotypes is from Nicol, *A Good-Looking Corpse*, 149.

Illustration 5.6: Johannesburg's Dolly Rathebe in *Drum* magazine, 1960 (Mary Evans Picture Gallery)

occasion portrayed as simply brutal. For instance, Themba's short story 'Marta' depicted a woman almost strangled by her adulterous husband who later kills a young man he wrongly believes to be her lover. Feisty women, whether mothers, shebeen queens, lovers, 'nice time' girls, wives, beer brewers or night club singers, were usually depicted as heroines of modern life. Women endure relationships with patently unpleasant men or give as good as they get. When Themba wrote a biographical piece about the glamorous singer, film actress and Johannesburg resident Dolly Rathebe, he appeared to see something of a female mirror image of himself:

It is true that she has had a tempestuous life. Men have floated in and out of it, some as gloomy spectres, some as rogues, some as vital, effervescent boilers. She has known and lived the violence and sordidness and stink of township life. She has drunk . . . and has found in vino veritas, the tot of truth. People have called her all sorts of names, those who thought they were entitled to cast the first stone. But somehow none of these things stuck . . . If she has been a she-devil, that's because she's a helluva woman![140]

[140] Patel, *The World of Can Themba*, 204.

Equally Mphahlele wrote about the very respectable ANC Women's League leader Lilian Ngoyi that 'it has required guts and granite to lead and inspire thousands of women who have now come to the front line in African politics'.[141] Whether naively or not, Nadine Gordimer believed that enjoyment of female pin-ups did not necessarily make Black writers working for *Drum* sexist:

The nice thing about the men on *Drum* is that they really loved women. I think when men really love women the idea of women being objects doesn't arise.[142]

More certainly, *Drum* writers invited recognition of the intoxications of urban life largely from a masculine perspective. Thus Casey Motsisi's 'On the Beat' column for *Drum* featured characters like Kid Hangover, Kid Booze and Kid Playboy. Motsisi's stories were full of common male township experiences, camaraderie, tricks and jokes, which drew on the author's lengthy fieldwork in numerous shebeens.[143]

Black writers undoubtedly saw themselves as distinct because of their education, White friends and literary connections. Apart from the fact that their work achieved international exposure, Abrahams, Rive, Mphahlele, Modisane and Matshikiza corresponded with the doyenne of the Harlem Renaissance, Langston Hughes.[144] Johannesburg writers like Ezekiel Maphlalele were equally at home listening to Vivaldi with Nadine Gordimer in her garden in Parktown as they were watching gangster films or Westerns in their own township fleapits.[145] Richard Rive, from a 'respectable' family in District Six, recalled introducing James Matthews, who was from a much rougher family background, to Beethoven.[146]

Living in the 'slums', Black writers were both at one with the crowd and able to observe the crowd, somewhere between respectable and unrespectable, flâneurs who sometimes walked the city simply to experience it and had their protagonists navigate the city in this fashion.[147] In the process, most seemed intent on encountering 'all the joys and all the sorrows that chance offers' of wine, women and song, both the beautiful and the bestial, in a world of rapid and dramatic urban juxtapositions.[148] Several writers recount walking far and wide across Johannesburg, including to the flatlands of Hillbrow and the northern suburbs. As Nat Nakasa wrote, 'while others made for their homes hurriedly at the end of

[141] E. Mphahlele, 'Guts and Granite!', *Drum*, March 1956, cited in Chapman (ed.), *Drum Decade*, 105–8.
[142] From an interview she gave for Nicol, *A Good-Looking Corpse*, 145.
[143] Mutloatse, *Casey and Co.*   [144] Graham and Walters (eds), *Langston Hughes*.
[145] Mphahlele, *Down Second Avenue*, 220.
[146] P. Abrahams, 'The Virgin', in *Dark Testament* (London: George Allen and Unwin, 1942), 141–59.
[147] Baudelaire, 'Crowds', 20–1.   [148] Ibid., 20–1.

the day, I took long leisurely strolls from one end of the city to another ...
I was especially fascinated by Johannesburg at night.'[149] Lewis Nkosi
'walked about the streets of the bustling noisy city with new English
words clicking like coins in the pockets of my mind; I tried them out on
each passing scene'.[150] Can Themba composed some of his stories while
walking up and down the streets of Sophiatown. His pieces featured
vignettes of characters and escapades that were in his words 'only high-
lights from the swarming, cacophonous, strutting, brawling, vibrating life
of Sophiatown', the part of Johannesburg he dubbed the 'little Paris of the
Transvaal', a place where 'you can't be bored'.[151]

In *Song of the City*, Abrahams had Dick walking the streets and remarking on the constant hum of mine headgears and the wonder of neon lights.
Xuma, Abrahams' protagonist in *Mine Boy*, pondered on the din of the
city, including the 'pulsating motion of Malay Camp at night', which was
'warm and intense and throbbing'. Here people sang, cried, fought,
loved; 'children played in the gutters, and picked up dirty orange peels
and ate them'; but there was also 'dancing on a street corner', and a
'woman singing in a beautiful voice ... singing ... poverty, prostitutes ...
but also warmth, living people, a stream of dark life'.[152]

The acquisition of personal honour in the diverse ways that people
struggled to exist in the modern metropolis, which lacked the more
predictable social structure and cultural coherence of rural life, was
acknowledged.[153] As Nat Nakasa put it of Soweto, 'It lives precariously,
sometimes dangerously, but with relentless will to survive.'[154] Elements
of respectable existence and the 'high-life' were juxtaposed in Black South
African writing with stories of the unrespectable, whether beggars, nice-
time girls, prostitutes or gangsters, often dealt with empathetically. Like
Baudelaire, Black writers found that the 'heroism of modern life' surrounded and pressed in on them.[155]

Challenging stereotypes

Black writers presented themselves and many of those around them as
modern, complex, individual and coping. This contrasted with

---

[149] Patel, *Nat Nakasa*, 4–5.   [150] Nkosi, *Home and Exile*, 10.
[151] Themba, *Requiem for Sophiatown*, ix, 51, 54.
[152] Abrahams, *Song of the City*; Abrahams, *Mine Boy*, 70–4.
[153] A path-breaking study of the concept of honour and its various manifestations in African history is J. Iliffe, *Honour in African History* (Cambridge: Cambridge University Press, 2004).
[154] Patel, *Nat Nakasa*, 25.
[155] See Marshall Berman, *All That Is Solid Melts into Air* (London: Penguin Books, 1988), 142–8 on Baudelaire and the heroism of modern life.

unadulterated Bitter Cry or Jim goes to Joburg portrayals of Black South
Africans disorientated and struggling in the city. Ezekiel Mphahlele dis-
liked what he dubbed 'Paton's sermon', and South African literature in
general that depicted Africans as 'frustrated creatures of the city'.[156]
Equally Black authors objected to White writing, including studies of
Black urbanisation emanating from South African universities, that por-
trayed Black South Africans only in group form as Africans, Indians or
Coloureds and apportioned them characteristics accordingly.[157]

Part of the failure to recognise Blacks as individuals was the ongoing
way in which Whites often referred to urban Africans in derogatory or
depersonalised ways as 'boys', 'girls', 'kafirs', 'Jims', 'Natives' or 'Bantus'.
As Mphahlele put it:

I had my share of troubles with whites and their superior airs. It was, 'yes, John'
here; 'yes, Jim', there; 'what do you want, boy' here . . . A few times I had white
lads chasing me . . . to 'put the Kafir in his place'.[158]

Bloke Modisane, Lewis Nkosi and Themba, playing themselves in a
shebeen scene in the docudrama *Come Back Africa* – a rich cinematic
documentation of harshness and creativity in African urban experience
filmed secretly in Johannesburg in the late 1950s – spoke disparagingly of
the deference shown to Whites by Paton's Reverend Khumalo.[159]
Writing his 'With the Lid Off' column for *Drum* from London, which he
was visiting in 1960 for the opening of his musical *Kong Kong* (about the
Johannesburg boxer), Matshikiza happily noted how many times he was
addressed as 'Sir'.[160]

Depictions of 'the popular in its place' as exotic local colour denied
individuality and questioned the extent to which Black South Africans
could be thoroughly urban, civilised or modern. This implicitly challenged their right to be considered equal citizens or to belong in the city
at all.[161] Black writers responded to this challenge. Herbert Dhlomo
wrote a poem in the 1940s about rickshaw pullers that began:

Hamba! Mwini! Kwela, [Go! Boy! Climb!] Ricksha, my boy!
Grin, shout and jump about; play pranks and clown!
And let them think you are their kaffir toy!

[156] Mphahlele, *Down Second Avenue*, 167, 196.
[157] *Nat Nakasa* made this exact point: Patel, *Nat Nakasa*, 155.
[158] Mphahlele, *Down Second Avenue*, 137.
[159] Lionel Rogosin (dir.), *Come Back Africa* (United States and South Africa: Lionel Rogosin Films, 1959).
[160] *Drum*, August 1960.
[161] Vivian Bickford-Smith, 'Providing Local Colour? "Cape Coloureds", Cockneys and the Identity of Cape Town from the Late Nineteenth Century to the 1970s', *Journal of Urban History* 38, 1 (January 2012), 133–51.

Yea, let them mock and cheat and kick you down!
How wounded, lacerated, shamed I feel
Each time I see a rickshaw passing by![162]

The Johannesburg rickshaw puller in Abrahams' *Song of the City* gets sick because of his work, at one stage spitting blood, and eventually dies. Rickshaw pullers attempt to dance away their bitterness along with 'the mine boy' in the Marabi dance.[163]

For his part, La Guma wrote a piece in 1957 on whether the New Year Carnival was degrading. In doing so, he was participating in an ongoing debate in Coloured elite circles. La Guma thought that carnival's 'lower standard of culture' simply demonstrated participants' lower standards of living. If the latter was raised, carnival would (implicitly should) 'die out'. Yet he liked the satirical touch of a 'coon with a picture of Herr Strijdom [D.F. Malan's successor as prime minister] sewed to the seat of his pants'.[164]

Many Johannesburg writers noted, a decade or more before Black Consciousness activist Steve Biko made the same point, that the 'smiling' of urban Black South Africans was commonly a strategy, not part of genetic cheerfulness. Nkosi drew on Langston Hughes' view of smiling among African Americans to argue that it was also a way of concealing anger.[165] The cheery outward appearance of working-class people around the world was commonly aimed at gaining employment or making sales.[166] In South Africa, as Bloke Modisane pointed out, along with unctuous flattery, smiling was seen as a method of disarming potentially difficult White employers and officials. Humour was also a way of dealing with the hardship and absurdity of so much Black South African experience. To illustrate the point, Modisane cited the example of a Johannesburg road board, 'Natives Cross Here', where some African wit had painted a 'very' between the first two words. This was a story that Henry Nxumalo also related to Anthony Sampson.[167]

Senses of urban place

But even though Black writers wished to be seen as individuals, racial legislation made it impossible to avoid thinking of oneself in racial terms much of the time. All had personal experiences of White racism, had

---

[162] Visser and Couzens (eds), *Dhlomo Collected Works*, 362.
[163] Abrahams, *Song of the City*, 15–16, 21, 171.
[164] 'The Coons', *New Era*, 5 December 1957 cited in Odendaal and Field (eds), *Liberation Chabalala*, 114.
[165] Nkosi, *Home and Exile*, 39.   [166] Stedman Jones, 'The "Cockneys" and the Nation'.
[167] Modisane, *Blame Me on History*, 88–91. Sampson, *Drum*, 18.

fictional characters encountering it, or wrote about it in their journalism. Residential and social segregation produced a powerful correlation between senses of urban place and race. There were frequent comparisons in Johannesburg writing between vibrant Black places and dull White ones. Mphahlele wrote:

While we shouted and laughed in our packed and stuffy trains, in our long, long weary bus queues, in the buses, they boarded their clean buses and separate platforms, and travelled to their separate suburbs – clean, quiet but either dead or neurotic. And at our end of life Black humanity, though plunged into a separate, overcrowded, violent and dark existence; still vibrant, robust, with no self-imposed repressions.[168]

Similarly, Lewis Nkosi felt that Whites with 'appalling empty lives' envied the 'vivid colour' of township life, and compared this to the 'self-consuming monotony and boredom' of parties in Parktown and Houghton.[169] In *Song of the City* Peter Abrahams gave a swift ethnic-racial social geography of Johannesburg:

Vrededorp, slum home of the dark-skinned thousands; . . . Parktown, home of the wealthy Europeans; . . . Berea, predominantly Jewish; . . . Forsdburg, melting pot of the poor whites.[170]

In keeping with such taxonomies, writers expressed senses of belonging associated with particular suburbs or townships. In Abrahams' *Mine Boy*, the novel's protagonist becomes 'a citizen of Malay Camp and people showed it in their eyes'; Malay Camp had 'air that is found nowhere else on earth except in the dark places of Johannesburg'.[171] In his autobiography, *Tell Freedom*, Abrahams recalled being 'reclaimed' by Vrededorp, where he was born, after a period of absence: 'people recognised me, and I them'.[172] Modisane's autobiography recalls people and landmarks in Sophiatown like Martha Maduma's shebeen, Aly's fish and chip shop, the Odin cinema and Good Street. An irony of residents' removal to Meadowlands was their belief that they needed to demonstrate extensive local knowledge to prove they were long-term residents of Sophiatown and thus be eligible for a house in Meadowlands, Soweto; otherwise they risked being removed from Johannesburg altogether. The rumour spread that to prove their status they might be asked questions like 'Who is the oldest Chinese woman in Sophiatown . . . [or] . . . where is the biggest rock'.[173]

---

[168] Mphahlele, *Down Second Avenue*, 174.   [169] Nkosi, *Home and Exile*, 31, 33, 56.
[170] Abrahams, *Song of the City*, 23.   [171] Abrahams, *Mine Boy*, 161, 169.
[172] Abrahams, *Tell Freedom*, 68.
[173] Modisane, *Blame Me on History*, 6, 110. These proved to be just that, rumours; as Modisane discovered when attending interviews conducted in the Pass Office in

In *Emergency*, Richard Rive's protagonist reminisced on 'the bother and the dirt and the rubble and the gaiety and sadness of District Six', and the characters, events like the New Year Carnival and landmarks he associated with it, fondly contrasting this with the slightly paler-skinned, more socially select and snobbish Walmer Estate:

Upper-class Coloureds with electric stoves, refrigerators and venetian blinds on their windows. As soon as a family established itself, it moved to Walmer Estate and made a definite point of forgetting the past.[174]

Black writing frequently reported like this on how differences in material circumstances and meanings attached to them reflected and reinforced sometimes subtle gradations in Black urban identity. Such gradations could be a matter of, precisely, where you lived, what dress you wore, form of Christianity you practised, soccer team you played for, what language you spoke or how exactly you spoke it. English might be accented, creolised or 'code switched' in tandem with another language. The adult Rive spoke English with 'received pronunciation'.

Complexities of urban identity and belief in common humanity

White academic studies of the 1960s investigated identity among urban Africans in particular in great detail. Some found a bifurcation between 'Tribesman and Townsmen' or 'Red Blanket', for those who maintained rural traditions and 'School' for those who did not.[175] Others discovered more subtle distinctions expressed by African residents themselves in Langa, Cape Town. Here UCT anthropologists found the population divided into three roughly equal components: migrants (*amagoduka* or 'those who go home'), the semi-urbanised and proper townsmen. Townsmen were further sub-divided into *ooscuse-me* or 'decent people' and the less respectable or *tsotsi* type, whose older members or *ooMacs* were less rough than the younger ones. Language, religious beliefs, kinship, rural origins, political and civic associations further influenced identity, as did residence in Langa compared to shanties or the new

Market Street, to be eligible for accommodation in Meadowlands, rather than being removed from the city entirely, residents had to demonstrate they had lived in Sophiatown for fifteen years.

[174] Rive, *Emergency*, 75; see also 39–40, 43, 53, 55, 92–3. Modisane, *Blame Me on History*; Themba, *Requiem for Sophiatown*.

[175] B.A. Pauw, *The Second Generation: A Study of the Family among Urbanized Bantu in East London* (Cape Town: Oxford University Press, 1963); Philip Mayer, *Townsmen or Tribesman: Conservatism and the Process of Urbanization in a South African City* (Cape Town: Oxford University Press, 1971).

township of Nyanga.[176] A few of these divides harked back to those expressed in '*Ematawini* or Excuse Me Please', a popular Zulu song about Durban in the inter-war years:

> We went to Durban and we got attracted to young women and men
>   marching up and down the streets.
> They are proud of their clothes.
> . . .
> They say; 'Excuse me please, can I please pass?
> We would like a cup of tea.'
> . . .
> It is like that in town,
> There are all kinds of people.
> Ugly and beautiful people, proud and simple people,
> Some of them are embarrassing.
> And you also find dangerous people.[177]

What the Langa study also demonstrated was that the most common criteria by which residents identified other people in the Cape Town population as a whole were colour or race and gender.

Attitudes towards race, and particularly towards Whites, was a topic frequently dealt with by Black writers. Those more involved with African nationalist political organisations like Modisane (PAC) and Mphahlele (ANC) acknowledged greater difficulty in resisting bitterness towards Whites than those who were less so, like Abrahams, Nakasa, Nkosi and Themba. Themba's White lover Jean Hart acknowledged that outwardly Modisane was 'funny' and 'warm', but thought that inwardly he was 'resentful, bitter' and speculated that there 'might have been retribution in his conquest of white women'. Yet Mphahlele thought this unlikely, and Nadine Gordimer experienced little sense of bitterness when Bloke was with her.[178]

Modisane certainly wrote about feeling patronised at tea parties by privileged and wealthy White liberals 'where Africans were educated into an acceptance of their inferior position'. He claimed that Africans did not regard Whites as people, but as 'baas' and 'missis', symbols 'to be hated and feared', and that, monstrously conditioned himself in this fashion, he was prepared to kill them. But the aptly named *Blame Me on History* was written in exile, and after the Sharpeville massacre of 1960. By his own account, Modisane had his racial consciousness of being 'African'

[176] Monica Wilson and Archie Mafeje, *Langa: A Study of Social Groups in an African Township* (Cape Town: Oxford University Press, 1963).
[177] Cited in Erlmann, 'But Hope Does Not Kill', 77.
[178] See, for instance, Can Themba, 'The Boy with the Tennis Racket', in *The World of Can Themba*, 219; Nicol, *A Good-Looking-Corpse*, 290–4; Modisane, *Blame Me on History*, 247.

raised by PAC ideas. The PAC had broken from the ANC in 1959 on a programme of Africa for the Africans and held the view that no Whites should be part of their anti-apartheid struggle.[179]

Despite Modisane's militant PAC sentiments, many passages even in *Blame me on History* depicted Whites in sympathetic fashion. He acknowledged that he had English-speaking White friends in Johannesburg, several of whom were invited to his wedding. Even an uninvited Afrikaner policeman, who might have ruined the event because alcohol was illegally being served there, ended up joining the party and charming those present:

> It took the sergeant a few glasses of brandy and some coaxing from Jeanne [*sic.* Jean Hart] to release him from his Afrikaner chains, and we were to see a human being wriggle out of the uniform and the gun. Around ten o'clock there was an ease and a charm about him, the gun belt had been loosened and the gun placed on the table, and the sergeant was talking, laughing, drinking, singing and dancing as animatedly as Fiki and I.[180]

Under the editorship of Rolfes and Herbert Dhlomo, *Ilanga* expressed strong African anti-Indian sentiments in the 1940s Durban.[181] These stemmed from African resentment at the economic power some Indians had over Africans as shopkeepers, bus company owners and landlords. In the Cato Manor area, home to Indian market gardeners at the time of the First World War, Indians leased land to thousands of African shack dwellers. When an Indian store keeper in central Durban punished an African boy for shoplifting in January 1949, Africans first attacked Indian businesses then residents of Cato Manor, and Indians retaliated. More than 130 Africans and Indians were killed, and over a thousand more injured. Yet, *Ilanga* refused to condemn African participants.

However, most Black writing celebrated common humanity, informed by missionary education, cross-racial friendships, reading, cinema and the pragmatic political desire to argue in favour of a non-racial future. The hero of a short story in *Drum* by Liberal Party member Jordan Ngubane was a Zulu who sacrifices his life in the riots saving an Indian child from a burning house.[182] Richard Rive's 'Black and Brown Song' condemned

---

[179] Modisane, *Blame Me on History*, 158, 243, 247. The PAC organised the anti-pass demonstrations at Sharpeville and Langa that led to more than seventy Africans being shot by police. Along with the ANC, the PAC adopted armed resistance in the early 1960s.

[180] Modisane, *Blame Me on History*, 259.

[181] See, for example, *Ilanga*, 12 January 1946 'Indians Cheating', 12 February 1946 on overcharging, 6 April 1946 on supporting African traders over Indians in African areas, or 7 May 1949 on the emergence after the riots of an organisation calling itself Zulu Hlangwini that pitted itself against the local Indian-operated bus service and in favour of one run by Africans.

[182] *Drum*, August 1956.

Coloured racism towards Africans, optimistically concluding that one day racial division in the country would end.[183]

Racism or awkwardness with someone of a different race was exposed in Black writing as a common human failing, as in another Rive story about Coloured climbers' uncomfortable encounter with a Jewish woman on Table Mountain.[184] The old White man who is murdered in Alex La Guma's *A Walk in the Night* is sympathetically portrayed. Mphahlele recalled enjoying a 'great' party at the house of *Drum*'s editor Sylvester Stein and invited Stein and his wife to party in Orlando. He resented a (South African) *Guardian* review of his work that suggested he should write less about common human experiences and more about racial discrimination.[185] Nat Nakasa warned against blaming all that was wrong in life on the (apartheid) 'system': trains could be just as crowded in London as in Johannesburg. An African could have good and bad experiences in shops, garages or on trains depending on the particular White person they were faced with.[186]

Peter Abrahams wrote that though he might be a 'nigger' in body, he was a 'person in mind'. He admitted that after reading Langston Hughes he briefly became a 'colour nationalist'; but that following a temporary flirtation with Marxism he had rejected racial prejudice. His characters reflected this belief. He had a White policeman with 'tired eyes', who speaks fluent Zulu, showing compassion to Dick in *Song of the City*; a White woman in 'Jewish Sister', one of his *Dark Testament* stories, treating the Black protagonist as an equal. A White detective in *Mine Boy* has no hesitation in mingling with Blacks. In his autobiography, Abrahams revealed that he was in fights with racist White boys as a child, but later met decent Whites, and he fondly recalled a 'Mad Boer poet' genuinely interested in educating Coloured children.[187]

Shared cross-racial perceptions of urban place in the 1950s

All South African perspectives on city life were informed by the transnational circulation of ideas about cities. White perspectives influenced Black ones and, noticeably so from the 1940s onwards, the opposite was also true. In challenging earlier visions of the city, Black writers did not discard them in their entirety. After all, both White and Black

---

[183] *Drum*, May 1955.   [184] Rive, 'Riva', in *Advance, Retreat*, 59–72.
[185] Mphahlele, *Down Second Avenue*, 165–6, 198–9.
[186] Patel, *Nat Nakasa*, 20, 33, 100.
[187] Abrahams, *Tell Freedom*, 36–6, 152, 196–7, 250–1; Abrahams, *Song of the City*, 75–6; *Dark Testament*, 27–33; *Mine Boy*, 136.

representations were often describing the same real, physical features of a city's topography, built structures, flora and fauna or climate. Common ground could be found in determining that the mine dumps, skyscrapers or afternoon thunder storms of Johannesburg, when 'heat mists rose from the macadamised streets', were distinctive characteristics of that place; or, for Peter Abrahams at least, that Table Mountain and flower-sellers were iconic of Cape Town.[188] Indeed, Black writing on occasion was clearly also influenced by the narrative devices of White representations of urban place. This was evident, for instance, in the Jim Comes to Joburg narrative structure of Herbert Dhlomo's *An African Tragedy* or much of Peter Abrahams' *Song of the City* and *Mine Boy*. It was also apparent in the biblical tone, reminiscent of Paton, in Richard Rive's short story 'African Song':

God Bless the children in the Great Cities, for they have no beards but are as men. And there is sadness in Africa for the children who no longer play in the streams but follow the ways of the Great Cities. And the laughter of the veld is lost in the sorrow of the towns, and the little ones swagger and laugh insolently. And there is a knife in the hand and hatred in the eye, and mistrust, for the ways of the Great Cities are not good.[189]

In turn, some White authors and film makers came themselves to be influenced by Black city writing. This helps explain the mixture of condemnation and celebration of 'slum' life that emerged in White literature and films between the 1940s and early 1960s. In 1948, the year that *Cry the Beloved Country* was published, the young Nadine Gordimer wrote a short story for *The South African Saturday Book*, an anthology of comments on the country 'old and new' modelled on its British equivalent. 'The Defeated' drew on Gordimer's childhood experience of growing up on the Rand and had her narrator envying the liveliness around stores that catered for Africans: 'noise and movement and – yes, bad smells . . . The signs of life that I craved . . . rich and careless of its vitality, it overflowed from the crowded pavement of the stores.'[190]

Post-Second World War British immigrant Donald Swanson saw cinematic and commercial possibilities in this liveliness. He made a pioneering film with a predominantly African Johannesburg cast called *African Jim* or *Jim Comes to Joburg*, released in 1949. As its alternative title

---

[188] Abrahams, *Song of the City*, 138, 159.

[189] R. Rive, 'African Song', in Chapman (ed.), *Drum Decade*, 119.

[190] Nadine Gordimer, 'The Defeated', in Eric Rosenthal and Richard Robinow (eds), *The South African Saturday Book: A Treasury of Writing and Pictures of South Africa, Old and New, Homey and Extraordinary* (Cape Town: Hutchinson, 1948), 169–82. The quotation is from page 169. The British *Saturday Book* was an annual compendium of essays on British life that ran between 1941 and 1975.

implies, the first part of the film was in keeping with the eponymous genre that depicted rural Africans struggling to adapt successfully to city life. The narrative departure came with the protagonist (played by Daniel Adnewmah), in Rooney-Garland Hollywood musical style, obtaining a job in a nightclub, falling in love with the beautiful and talented resident singer (Dolly Rathebe) and winning a music contract.[191] The commercial success of *African Jim* inspired three more films within the next couple of years with African casts. Swanson's follow-up film, originally called *The Pennywhistle Blues* but renamed *The Magic Gardens*, was a township fairy tale about the discovery of a hidden horde of money and the chain of events this unleashes. As the original title suggests, the score featured contemporary township music. Two African Film Productions musicals, *Zonk* and *Song of Africa*, attempted to emulate Swanson's success, with both consisting mainly of staged musical performances.[192]

What all these films had in common was that none attempted to capture the combination of creativity and hardship in African urban life in realist fashion. There was no depiction of White racism, explanation of segregation or *Cry, the Beloved Country*-style investigation of Black poverty. It was the combined realities of misery and liveliness that photographers and Black writers captured in contributions to *Drum* magazine and other publications. The same combination can be found in *Come Back Africa* (1959). The film was a collaboration between American film maker Lionel Rogosin (of *On the Bowery* fame) and *Drum* writers Modisane and Nkosi, who appear with Themba in the film. *Come Back Africa* depicts intellectually lively shebeen life, penny-whistle playing, brass bands, church parades, gumboot dancing and African Elvis impersonators. The 'White' Johannesburg city centre is shown as literally devoid of life until Africans from the townships enter and enliven it. The film also depicts White racists (played by White communists), the pass laws, Black poverty and violence. But the overall argument is that Africans belong in the city and have a right to belong.[193]

Black and White writing had been instrumental in relaying this message beyond South Africa. Anthony Sampson did so in an account of his time as editor of *Drum* published in 1956.[194] Sampson gave an interview to

[191] D. Swanson (dir.), *African Jim* (Johannesburg: Erika Rutherford Production, 1949).
[192] E. Nofal (dir.), *Zonk* (Johannesburg: African Film Productions, 1950); H. Kirsten (dir.), *The Magic Garden* (Johannesburg: Swanson, Swan Films, 1951); and E. Norval (dir.), *Song of Africa* (Johannesburg: African Film Productions, 1951). All three films have been analysed by others in detail elsewhere. See for instance Davis, *In Darkest Hollywood* and Maingard, *South African National Cinema*.
[193] Rogosin (dir.), *Come Back Africa*; see also L. Rogosin, *Come Back Africa: Lionel Rogosin – A Man Possessed* (Johannesburg: SET Publishers, 2004).
[194] Sampson, *Drum*.

BBC radio in 1957 in which he described township liveliness while reporting that Sophiatown, which he likened to a steep Italian village, was being 'knocked down'. The interview was accompanied by the playing of township music, with Sampson remarking that the title of hits like 'The Flying Squad Boogie', 'Pick-up Van Blues' and 'Police Station' reflected the grim side of township life. He admitted that Black Johannesburg could be 'depressing' but that it had

a bubbling energy and enthusiasm, bursting out of the squalor and poverty, which makes a stimulating and bizarre contrast to one's ordinary rather pedestrian European life there ... [Sophiatown] was gay, squalid, dangerous and intensely human, and full of the most wonderful people, of the kind that seem to have dropped out of English life since Dickens ... so full of life that you didn't at first notice the awfulness of the cardboard and corrugated iron shacks that people were living in ... streets were always packed, at any time of the night and day, with people talking, shouting, singing, even jiving ... weddings, funerals ... brass bands, political marches, gangsters.

Sampson mentioned Themba, 'quoting Milton and gangster slang equally fluently'; also a resident known as Oubas who quoted Dante and Bra Lucky, a gangster, 'who drawled Chicago slang picked up from Peter Cheyney'.[195] Sylvester Stein, a successor of Sampson as *Drum* editor, was on BBC radio a year later also talking about Sophiatown, whose streets were 'just about the liveliest part of Africa, and the noisiest too'. He revealed that he had once 'passed himself off' as a Black resident to experience an overnight stay there.[196] Gordimer's novel *World of Strangers* compared Sophiatown with South African tourist brochures depicting Africa in all its 'savage glory', whether in the form of the Kruger Park, mine dances or a Black girl with bare breast advertising Zululand. The novel's protagonist Toby, a British immigrant, parties in Sophiatown with Steven Sitole, 'a journalist on a paper for Africans'. Toby feels stiff in comparison to those he finds there and wants to feel 'that the age-old crystals of the North were melting away in my blood ... their joy was something wonderful and formidable, a weapon I didn't have'. Like parts of Sophiatown, Alexandra also had the 'aged look of all slums'; yet it was lively: 'people bounced over the rutted road on bicycles, women, endless women, yelled, threw buckets of slop into the road, laughed and thumped at tubs of washing'. White Johannesburg is dull and unreal in comparison.[197]

[195] BBC Written Archives Centre (WAC), Reading: HS 17.4.55, Home Service, 17 April 1957.
[196] BBC WAC: HS.222.58, Home Service, 22 February 1958. See also Sylvester Stein, *Who Killed Mr Drum?* (Bellville: Mayibuye Books, 1999).
[197] Nadine Gordimer, *A World of Strangers* (London: Jonathan Cape, [1958] 2002), 91, 129–30.

A BBC television investigation into the current state of South Africa, broadcast two months after Sampson's interview, described the possible future African children faced there in stark terms. Either they would grow up as 'second class citizens' or 'in a few years' time [there would be] a great African revolt and those children could be taking part in it'. The programme reported on the Treason Trial of Congress leaders, church apartheid (previously investigated by *Drum*), that 100,000 people lived in shanty towns, showing a row of corrugated iron toilets used by 'a thousand people'. Visiting Alexandra, the presenter nonetheless commented 'even in dingy surroundings like these . . . I felt the pulsating vitality of the Africans'. Equally, while Sophiatown 'does not look much', there was 'great anguish' when Africans were forced to leave their homes, and this was seen by residents as part of making them 'non-citizens' even if the new housing was better.[198]

Huddleston's indictment of apartheid, *Naught for Your Comfort*, described new township housing as monotonous compared to Sophiatown, which had more vitality than White suburbs, and whose residents possessed a sense of belonging.[199] Publishing similar thoughts on South Africa to Huddleston, Michael Scott wrote about his experiences working in the shanty town Tobruk, given the name in his account because of the wartime headlines 'Tobruk Shall Never Fall': 'In these breeding grounds of every kind of slum viciousness, there is even yet a certain African quality, an exuberance of life and music amidst death and pain.'[200] Jan Morris agreed: 'in the modern housing schemes, excellent though they sometimes are, [there is] almost no variety, colour, or individuality'; shanty towns were 'less subtly depressing' if 'more obviously gruesome'.[201]

Two broadcasts from Johannesburg by the BBC, to mark decadal anniversaries of the city, suggest ways that perceptions of the city, at least for some, had changed during the intervening years. The first happened in 1946:

Hello BBC, Hello Radio Newsreel, This is Dennis Whalley calling from Johannesburg. Today Johannesburg starts its diamond jubilee celebrations, and in front of me now I've got two photographs. One is the city sixty years ago, and the other of Johannesburg now. The first . . . shows a bare piece of dusty ground on which is littered – and littered is the word – a huddle of tents, tin shacks and mud huts, all very drab and squalid. In today's photograph – well it shows a modern,

[198] www.bbc.co.uk/archive: *Panorama: Union of South Africa*, 24 June 1957.
[199] Trevor Huddleston, *Naught for Your Comfort* (London: Collins, 1956).
[200] Michael Scott, *A Time to Speak* (London: Faber & Faber, 1958), 168.
[201] Morris, *South African Winter*, 34–6.

clean city of baby sky-scrapers fitting into the blue South African sky. An amazing change – sixty years.[202]

The second in 1956 featured Nadine Gordimer:

When, at sunset, the city empties, the Africans go home to the vast, smoking townships ... where they live, and which ring the rich city. The best birthday present Johannesburg has received on her seventieth birthday is the news that the mining houses are to finance a three million pound loan which will see these slums cleared ... No-one will be sorry to see them go; but some good things, some contributions to the savour of life in Johannesburg has come out of them too. Music for example. Only this year, the passion of jazz that has given expression to all the African's irrepressible drive towards the joy of living, even while his surroundings are the dreariest and darkest, has burst the bounds of the townships and become part of the city itself ... concerts of township jazz ... have astonished white audiences ... so it has come about that the tin whistle, which is made to give eight notes, but out of which young African boys get thirteen, has taken its place with impudent appropriateness in this city of impossible achievement – Johannesburg.[203]

---

[202] BBC WAC: Eye Witness Dispatch programme, 28 September 1946: 'Johannesburg Jubilee, 1946 by Dennis Whalley'.

[203] BBC WAC: This Day and Age programme, 17 September 1956: 'Johannesburg's 70th Anniversary by Nadine Gordimer'.

6   Remembrance of things past: an epilogue

The more optimistic portrayals of Black urban life just described were overtaken by events. Withdrawal of government aid to Mission institutions and their replacement with 'Bantu' education undermined the system that had fostered the Black literary elite of the 'fabulous decade'. The destruction of long-standing Black residential areas during the apartheid era destroyed community support networks and was seen by residents as endangering their right to belong in the city. Insensitivity in the official place (re-)naming of old areas or new townships added insult to injury. Sophiatown was replaced by the White working-class suburb Triomf. Some ex-residents of District Six found themselves in places on the Cape Flats called Hanover Park and Lavender Hill, named after District Six streets.

Cato Manor, Durban, known as *Mkhumbane* by African residents, was another place declared a White group area despite having a long history of Black occupation and ownership. Its Indian inhabitants were moved to Chatsworth, a new development on the south-west edge of the city for Indians removed from areas closer to its centre. African shack-dweller tenants were relocated in stages from 1958 to what became KwaMashu, a large township on the city's northern periphery. This removal to a monitored township threatened the livelihood of African women involved in illegal liquor brewing, who attacked the local municipal beer hall in June 1959 shouting 'We are the Zulu warriors' and '*Yinj'umlungu! Yinj'umlungu!*' (Whites are dogs). At least three Africans were killed in the ensuing riots.[1] The following January, with tension in Cato Manor running high, nine White policemen were killed by a crowd during a liquor raid.[2]

---

[1] Iain Edwards, 'Cato Manor, June 1959: Men, Women, Crowds, Violence, Politics and History', in Maylam and Edwards (eds), *The People's City*, 102–42. The cries mentioned are cited on page 129. The exact number of rioters killed ranged from an official figure of three to the belief of some residents that it may have been more than twenty.
[2] Davenport, *Modern History*, 357.

Illustration 6.1: Cato Manor, Durban, c.1950s (Mary Evans Picture Gallery)

This may help to explain why on 21 March 1960 police in the southern Transvaal township of Sharpeville fired indiscriminately on African pass protestors, killing sixty-nine and seriously wounding more than one hundred. Many were shot in the back. Film footage and photographs taken in the aftermath of the massacre were seen around the world. The killing of two more Africans in Langa and the arrest of political leaders led to residents embarking on a work stayaway in which they were joined by inhabitants of Nyanga, a nearby township established in the 1940s. The government declared a State of Emergency on 30 March, attempting to end the stayaway with a brutal raid on Langa that morning. In response, 30,000 Africans marched to Caledon Square police station in the centre of Cape Town. A violent confrontation was narrowly avoided when the PAC's Philip Kgosana was promised a meeting with the minister of justice. The crowd dispersed. But when Kgosana returned to meet the minister, he was arrested. Following a military blockade of the townships the stayaway was broken.[3]

---

[3] Philip Kgosana, *Lest We Forget* (Johannesburg: Skotaville Press, 1988); Lodge, *Black Politics*, 201–30; Tom Lodge, *Sharpeville: An Apartheid Massacre and Its Consequences* (Oxford: Oxford University Press, 2011).

The National Party banned the ANC and PAC, who responded by establishing military wings and a political presence outside the country. The government imprisoned leaders from both organisations and other opposition parties on Robben Island, introduced detention without trial and greatly extended the state security apparatus. 'Suicides' of political detainees in police custody soon followed. There was certainly now more torture than in Nkosi's fabulous decade. The consequence of such events was increased international criticism of apartheid over the next three decades, encouraged by South Africans exiled to other parts of Africa, Europe and North America. South African policies were condemned at the United Nations, and the country was gradually subjected to cultural, sporting and diplomatic isolation as well as economic sanctions.

Yet the combination of political repression and, after initial capital flight, rapid economic growth for the rest of the 1960s meant that the National Party control of the country grew stronger in the medium term. Under Verwoerd then Vorster, a further onslaught was launched against 'illegal' Africans in the cities, now deemed to be citizens not of South Africa but of their own 'homelands' such as the Transkei. With the Western Cape declared a Coloured Labour Preference area, Africans in shanty settlements on the Cape Flats such as Modderdam and Crossroads became particular targets.[4] But for all its efforts the National Party could not stop Africans seeking employment from coming to the city, sometimes walking hundreds of miles to do so. Africans voting with their feet against urban 'influx control' played a major part in making apartheid unworkable. So too did the actions of Black youths, particularly after the Soweto uprising of 1976, ensure that townships were intermittently 'ungovernable'.

By the mid-1960s already, the majority of Black Baudelaire writers had gone into self-imposed exile, and many of them died early, Can Themba and Nat Nakasa of drink-induced ill-health and suicide respectively. With them went their complex, bitter-sweet humanist city writing. This was replaced by the early 1970s with uncompromisingly bleak 'Freedom Poem' denunciations of oppressive urban conditions. James Matthews, still living in Cape Town, supplied some of the bleakest in a collection called *Cry Rage!* One was a meditation on life in Manenberg, a Coloured township on the Cape Flats, which went in part:

> Shifting sand suffocating my soul
> manenberg, oh manenberg

---

[4] Andrew Silk, *A Shanty Town in South Africa: The Story of Modderdam* (Johannesburg: Ravan Press, 1981); Josette Cole, *Crossroads: The Politics of Reform and Repression 1976–1986* (Johannesburg: Ravan Press, 1987).

Seated at the window of my
Concrete slum in the wasteland
Staring at a sand-track street
Unlit and deserted of people
Listening to the wind moaning
The woes and pain of those
Exiled from where they stayed
. . .
To watch children grow into
Beings without hope of a tomorrow
. . .
Despair driving them beyond reason
Reason replaced by fearsome rage.[5]

Wally Serote's poem 'City Johannesburg' contained the lines:

Jo'burg City, Johannesburg,
Listen when I tell you,
There is no fun. Nothing in it,
When you leave the women and men with such frozen expressions
Expressions that have tears like furrows of soil erosion,
Jo'burg City, you are dry like death,
Jo'burg City, Johannesburg, Jo'burg City.[6]

This unremitting bleakness was echoed in much international coverage of
South Africa, especially after 1976 as the Soweto uprising was followed by
intermittent low-level civil war up to the early 1990s. A detailed survey of
resulting depictions of the main cities is beyond the parameters of this
book: a brief overview must suffice. Images of urban conflict appeared
repeatedly in television news, documentaries, feature films and even
music videos broadcast across the world. Many images were of young
Black South Africans, often in school uniforms, being brutally attacked by
policemen armed with teargas, long whips and guns. As one analysis put
it, this was 'a reality . . . often so brutal and alive' that it was possible to
'package and market it directly on to film'.[7] Other post-1960 urban
realities captured on film included shanties and houses being
bulldozed and their inhabitants forcibly removed, or defiant singing of
freedom songs at township funerals. Capturing this reality was made
easier because it happened in the major cities where international

---

[5] James Matthews and Gladys Thomas, *Cry Rage!* (Johannesburg: Spro-cas Publications, 1972), 24.
[6] Wally Serote, 'City Johannesburg', in B. Feinberg (ed.), *Poets to the People: South African Freedom Poems* (London: George Allen and Unwin, 1974), 68–9.
[7] Harriet Gavshon, '"Bearing Witness": Ten Years Towards an Opposition Film Movement in South Africa', *Radical History Review* 47, 7 (1990), 331–45.

correspondents were based, and through the introduction of video technology in the late 1970s.[8]

South African cities were shown as bifurcated between crowded, dusty and desperately poor African townships and leafy and luxuriant White suburbs. Any nuances within urban social geography, such as more modest White housing or the high-rise apartments of Hillbrow (Johannesburg), Sea Point (Cape Town) and Durban's Berea, were usually absent. So were the relatively wealthier homes in Soweto, or Indian and Coloured residential areas each with their own considerable gradations in material conditions.

The iconography of newsreel footage was reinforced by international feature films made in the 1980s, even when they were filmed in Zimbabwe, with Harare standing in for South African cities. The commercially most successful *Cry Freedom* and *Dry White Season* portrayed aspects of mid-1970s apartheid South Africa. They reconstructed urban conflict of the period for which there was little or no actuality footage, including police raids on squatter camps and the massacre of Soweto schoolchildren on 16 June 1976. *Cry Freedom* re-enacts Sam Njima's picture of the dying thirteen-year-old schoolboy Hector Pieterson being carried away by Mbuyiso Makhubo; *Dry White Season* has its Afrikaner protagonist learning something of the reality of apartheid by seeing the photograph and reading the accompanying report of what was happening in Soweto in the *World* newspaper. It was an image that became as iconic of apartheid brutality in South African cities as Nick Ut's photograph of nine-year-old Phan Tim Phuc – naked and burnt by Napalm bombing – was for the horrors of the Vietnam War.[9]

The coming of democracy in 1994 saw dystopian depictions of cities scarred by apartheid give way to numerous cinematic portrayals of 'marginal lives and painful presents' in democratic South Africa.[10] They reflected continued rapid urbanisation of the country's urban poor as well as movement to South Africa's cities by political and economic migrants from north of the Limpopo. The expansion of informal settlements resulted in an insufficient supply of well-paid employment and the inability of municipalities to deliver sufficient housing and other services. This led to thousands of service delivery protests by city residents. There

[8] Vivian Bickford-Smith, 'Picturing Apartheid', in Vivian Bickford-Smith and Richard Mendelsohn (eds), *Black and White in Colour: African History on Screen* (Cape Town, Oxford and Athens, OH: James Currey, Double Storey and Ohio University Press, 2007), 256–78, for analysis of some of these films.

[9] Richard Attenborough (dir.), *Cry Freedom* (UK: Marble Arch Productions and Universal Pictures, 1986); Euzhan Palcy (dir.), *Dry White Season* (USA: Sundance Productions, 1989); Chris Menges (dir.), *A World Apart* (UK: Atlantic Entertainment, 1988).

[10] Botha (ed.), *Marginal Lives and Painful Presents*.

were also high rates of violent crime, with many who could afford it building high walls, installing security systems and employing armed response companies. Feature films such as *Hijack Stories* (2001), *Shooting Bokkie* (2003), *A Boy Called Twist* (2004), *U-Carmen eKhayelitsha* (2005), *Tsotsi* (2006), *District 9* (2009) and *Safe House* (2012) showed Cape Town and Johannesburg in combination as places of gangsters, street children, violence, poverty and xenophobia. Many documentaries did the same.

But there was also a resurgence of utopian representations of South African cities, if especially of topographically picturesque Cape Town. These accompanied democratic South Africa's international respectability and the rapid acceleration of mass tourism that went with it. There was also a return to positive economic growth, and the revered presence of Nelson Mandela as the country's first Black president. Vigorous promotion of tourism through travelogues, online material, attractive postcards and beautiful coffee-table photographic collections was aided by positive global coverage of events. Most notable in this respect were the peaceful elections of 1994, and the rugby and football world cups staged in South Africa in 1995 and 2010 respectively.[11]

The coming of democracy also saw South African cities become part of academic and political debate about the urban future of Africa and the global south in general. Optimists emphasised the economic, cultural and social creativity of residents of the continent's burgeoning cities, even within ever growing 'shadow town' shanty settlements. Employment possibilities in the city, however meagre, were at least better than in the countryside. Pessimists saw in contrast vast cities of slums, places of growing inequality, misery and deprivation in a neo-liberal, post-industrial world that prevented the possibility of progress.[12]

[11] Bickford-Smith, 'Creating a City of the Tourist Imagination'.
[12] For an optimistic perspective on informal settlements and cities of the South see Robert Neuwirth, *Shadow Cities: A Billion Squatters, A New Urban World* (New York and Oxford: Routledge, 2005); for a pessimist's view, see Mike Davis, *Planet of Slums* (New York and London: Verso, 2006). For work specifically on the debate surrounding African cities see Freund, *African Cities*; AbdouMaliq Simone and Abdelghani Abouhani, *Urban Africa: Changing Contours of Survival in the City* (London and New York: Zed Books, 2005) and Garth Myers, *African Cities: Alternative Visions of Urban Theory and Practice* (New York and London: Zed Books, 2011). For an optimistic if largely culturalist approach to twenty-first-century Johannesburg, see Sarah Nuttall and Achille Mbembe (eds), *Johannesburg: The Elusive Metropolis* (Durham and London: Duke University Press, 2008); For a Davis-style pessimist alternative see Martin J. Murray, *Taming the Disorderly City: The Spatial Landscape after Apartheid* (New York: Cornell University Press, 2008); for two collections that lie somewhere in between in tone and approach see Richard Tomlinson, Robert A. Beauregard, Lindsay Bremner and Xolele Mangcu (eds), *Emerging Johannesburg: Perspectives on the Postapartheid City* (New York and London: Routledge, 2003) and Jo Beall, Owen Crankshaw and Susan Parnell, *Uniting*

The past was seldom referred to in any detail in this debate. This was despite the fact that History Workshops at Wits and UCT mined it extensively in the wake of the Soweto uprising to explain problems of the present such as segregation and urban conflict.[13] Yet both before and after 1994, the urban past was much referred to at a popular level for personal and communal validation, the education and entertainment of others, commercial reasons or as an imaginative escape from difficult circumstances of the urban present.[14] Black as well as White South Africans often recalled aspects of everyday city life within the apartheid era in nostalgic fashion. Their memories reveal an intimate relationship between social identity, territorial belonging and loss.

Numerous popular city histories written by Lawrence Green and many others constituted a South African publishing phenomenon in the post-Second World War period. Green's books sold over 500,000 copies up to 1971, 50,000 for *Tavern of the Seas* alone, one of his four books on Cape Town.[15] These histories helped promote a sense of urban place for White anglophone South Africans during decades of heightened threat from both Afrikaner and African nationalism. A growing sense of international isolation began in the 1950s: the SABC ceased to relay BBC news; South African passports replaced British ones; Empire day ceased to be a national holiday, as did the British monarch's birthday after 1960. Popular city histories like those by Green provided comfortable tales of antiquarian detail, local colour, progress and conflicts confined to the past, and taught English-speaking White South Africans that they belonged in 'their' cities. Expensive and weighty official city histories by the likes of John Shorten, as well as council-commissioned films – such as *A New Horizon* for Cape Town or *A Million Cities of Gold* for Johannesburg – related municipal achievements in eradicating slums.[16] They defended South African urban life as conforming to what they took to be normal British metropolitan standards. In doing so, and distinguishing municipal from central government, they formed an important

---

a *Divided City: Governance and Social Exclusion in Johannesburg* (New York and London: Routledge, 2002).

[13] Bickford-Smith, 'Urban History in the New South Africa' explains how the urban past was explored in this way in the apartheid-era 'old' South Africa, with accompanying references.

[14] This point was first explored in 'Those were Wonderful Days', chapter three of Bickford-Smith et al., *Cape Town in the Twentieth Century*, especially 135–41.

[15] The dust jacket and title pages of Green, *Taste of South-Easter* provide this information.

[16] Shorten, *Cape Town*; Shorten, *Johannesburg*; Anon (dir.), *A New Horizon* (South Africa: Stafford Smith Films, 1960); Sven Perrson (dir.), *A Million Cities of Gold* (South Africa: City of Johannesburg, 1966).

component of local authority defence against external criticisms in the 1960s.[17]

But in particular, and in great profusion, oral and written accounts of places destroyed under apartheid conveyed a sense almost of paradises lost. A brief exploration of this remembrance might serve as a suitable epilogue for this book. Accounts that mourned the loss of places destroyed in the apartheid era were expressed in print, song, plays and interviews almost as soon as the 'slum' was being cleared, its destruction determined. 'Requiem to Sophiatown' was Can Themba reminiscing on the past as he wandered around what remained of the place in 1959. 'Long ago I decided to concede, to surrender to the argument that Sophiatown was a slum ... But the sheer physical fact of Sophiatown's removal has intimidated me ... so much has gone – veritable institutions.' He recalled those institutions and people associated with them: Fatty, the coquettish proprietor of the Thirty-Nine Steps shebeen; Mabeni's, another shebeen where 'Dolly Rathebe once sang the blues to me ... It was delicious'; listening to jazz records at Ah Sing's; or walking a 'Coloured girl of an evening down to the Odin cinema and no questions asked'. This was the 'magic' of a Sophiatown that was 'different and itself. You don't just find your place here, you make it and you find yourself.'[18]

Bloke Modisane's autobiography published in 1963 opened with the words: 'Something in me died, a piece of me died, with the dying of Sophiatown.' He went on to explain that Sophiatown's destruction was 'because it was a political corn inside the apartheid boot'. Modisane conceded that there was poverty and overcrowding in Sophiatown, but blamed 'sociologists and the race relationists [who] saw only textbook solutions – new townships' rather than the possibility of improving the place: 'Sophiatown belonged to me.'[19]

Similar sentiments were expressed about District Six. In 1972, as its buildings and inhabitants were disappearing, even the usually acerbic James Matthews wrote in *Cry Rage!* that this was a place of 'fire' that radiated 'love and lust' where 'shebeens operate a twenty-four hour service ... [and] mosques and churches serve the spiritual needs', but that 'now the embers are slowly dying'.[20] Interviewed in the 1980s, ex-resident Mr C.B. was unequivocal:

---

[17] For a more extended discussion of the nature and politics of these White local histories see Vivian Bickford-Smith, 'The Purposes and Politics of Local History Writing: A South African Perspective', *International Journal of Regional and Local History* 8, 1 (2013), 11–16.

[18] Can Themba, 'Requiem to Sophiatown', in Thema, *Requiem to Sophiatown*, 49–55. The piece was first published in *Africa South* 3, 3 (April–June 1959), and soon after republished in Langston Hughes (ed.), *An African Treasury*, 10–15.

[19] Modisane, *Blame Me on History*, 5, 14–15.   [20] Matthews and Thomas, *Cry Rage!*, 18.

There will never come another place like District Six. There were very good people and there were fair people ... It was a happy family that lived in District Six. Everybody knew from everybody. And then if there is any trouble, they come together quickly, not like here.[21]

There were similar comments on other predominantly Coloured Cape Town places that fell victim to the Group Areas Act. Of one of these, Tramway Road in Sea Point, Mrs G.E. asserted,

Everybody was happy. That time we never even thought about 'we too cramped out. We must move out.' We were so happy with each other that we just stayed close ... the entire road was a close-knitted family.[22]

Recalling Die Vlak, a neighbourhood of Claremont, Mrs V.D. said,

This was my street, where I belonged. People constantly dropping in to Pop's shebeen, our next-door neighbour, always keeping a friendly eye on me, the corners where everyone stopped to chat ... The place was a hive of activity from morning to night. People riding up and down, green carts [vegetables], fish-mongers, the wood cart, it was like a moving flea market.[23]

Comments of those who had lived in Cape Town's bulldozed shanty towns also expressed feelings of loss. Mrs S.C. said of Windermere:

It was very nice there. It was dung floor houses, not like houses today. We used to fetch our dung, and we had to smear our houses. We plastered paper in the zinc houses. You could make a fire when it was cold ... that place was like Sun City [a luxury resort to the north-west of Johannesburg].[24]

Writer Sindiwe Magona's *To My Children's Children* fondly remembered growing up in another informal settlement in the Retreat area of Cape Town:

The vastness of it, its vibrancy, throbbing aliveness ... filth, squalor, poverty, shabbiness, sharpened one's senses. You knew who you were in Blaauvlei ... sprawled proudly in a splendid ocean of tin shacks, or *pondoks* as we called them. I was very happy there. Each *pondok*, each humble structure of wood, zinc, card-board and paper artistically held together by nail, starch, rope, wine, and deter-mination, bespoke poverty. But it also proclaimed the will to be. I was a child, happy in the knowledge of the love of my parents and brother.[25]

The recollection of lost urban places often contained this nostalgia for a vanished childhood that Magona evokes. Fond remembrance was also

---

[21] UCT, Centre for Popular Memory (CPM), District Six transcripts, Mr C.B.

[22] UCT, CPM, Tramway Road transcripts, Mrs G.E.

[23] CPM, Claremont files, Mrs V.D.

[24] Cited in Sean Field, 'Remembering Experience, Interpreting Memory: Life Stories from Windermere', *African Studies* 60, 1 (2001), 123 (whole article 120–33).

[25] Sindiwe Magona, *To My Children's Children* (Cape Town: David Philip, 1990), 37–8.

influenced for many by a political desire to counter official 'slum clearance' justifications for their destruction, particularly when recollection was expressed before the end of apartheid. This was already evident in Black and White description and reminiscence of Sophiatown in the late 1950s. The same can be said of *Mkhumbane*, a musical about a day in the life of the place also known as Cato Manor, written by Todd Matshikiza and Alan Paton. Paton described Cato Manor as 'a squalid suburb of Durban' but one that, though poor, was 'full of life'. His contribution to the musical followed a request by the local branch of the Institute of Race Relations (IRR) to write something about the place given impending removals. *Mkhumbane* opened seven days after the Sharpeville massacre in the Durban City Hall, and was performed in front of multi-racial audiences for the rest of the week.[26]

In the same year (1960), the Cape Town branch of the Black Sash commissioned a documentary, *Notice to Quit*, which argued that because of apartheid respectable and viable communities were under imminent threat of removal in the name of 'slum' demolition.[27] A detailed study of English-language newspapers in Cape Town demonstrates that depictions of District Six as a dangerous slum began to change after National Party victory and the passing of the Group Areas Act. As early as 1950, *Cape Times* articles portrayed the District as poor but harmlessly 'boisterous', the rightful 'home' of largely decent and hard-working Coloured people.[28] Part of the reason for the volte-face on places such as District Six was doubtless pragmatic, the result of antipathy to the National Party and desire to portray apartheid as more heinous than pre-1948 segregation. Yet changing attitudes towards inhabitants of such areas and opposition to apartheid forced removals also reflected more enlightened principles. Some Whites, such as many veterans of the fight against Nazism and liberal or left-leaning students and staff at English-medium universities, kept in step with developing international distaste for racism and racial discrimination in the post-Second World War world.

By the early 1970s, District Six was the subject of literary tribute, beyond Matthews' *Cry Rage!*, in an illustrated anthology of poems by fellow Coloured Capetonian Adam Small.[29] It also appeared in benign form in a novel by liberal Afrikaner André Brink. The playwright protagonist of *Looking on Darkness* – about individual human tragedy caused by

---

[26] Alexander, *Paton*, 315–16.
[27] African Studies Library, University of Cape Town: E. Frost (dir.), *Notice to Quit* (Cape Town: Black Sash, 1960).
[28] A.Q. Marquard, 'The Political Significance of the Liberal Media Coverage of District Six from 1949 to 1970' (Unpublished MA thesis, Rhodes University, 1996).
[29] Adam Small, *Oos Wes Tuis Bes Distrik Ses* (Cape Town: Human & Rousseau, 1973).

apartheid's prohibition against cross-racial sexual relationships – sees the District as akin to a stage set for *Carmen* or *Streetcar Named Desire*: 'the entire cycle of life unfolded itself in front of my rickety window'. In a small courtyard where 'all the girls from the neighbourhood used to play hopscotch or skip with flying plaits and bobbing dresses', he rehearses plays watched by an uninvited audience who 'never left before the end'.[30]

The nature of further commemoration in the 1980s, against the backdrop of ongoing civil war in the country, went far in ensuring that the destruction of District Six would become synonymous with the inhumanity of apartheid. Photographic exhibitions, collections and paintings now lent an aesthetic of beauty to the District absent from La Guma's writing.[31] Residents of wealthy suburbs bought attractive pictures of the place to hang on their walls, akin to Gerard Sekota's highly acclaimed and beautiful paintings of Sophiatown. A documentary about one of the final families forced to leave District Six was given the evocative title *Last Supper in Horstley Street* and broadcast in Britain, Germany and the Netherlands.[32] *District Six: The Musical*, written by ex-resident Taliep Petersen and Afrikaner folk singer David Kramer, premiered in 1986. It became one of the most successful productions ever staged in South Africa and also toured internationally. Several more musicals by the pair followed with a District Six theme. Richard Rive's *Buckingham Palace, District Six*, a semi-autobiographical account of his childhood, published the same year, was another popular homage to the District and prompted its own musical version.[33] Many other reminiscences included several hundred oral histories collected for the Western Cape Oral History Project at UCT from the mid-1980s.[34] Remembering became part of political defiance, summarised in the popular slogan: 'You can take the people out of District Six, *ou pellie*, but you'll never take District Six out of the heart of the people.'

---

[30] André Brink, *Looking on Darkness* (London: Flamingo, [1974] 1988), 116–17. It was published in both English and Afrikaans versions. Brink was also author of the eponymous novel on which the film *Dry White Season* was based.

[31] See for example Adam Small and Jansje Wissema, *District Six* (Cape Town: Fontein, 1986), a limited-edition combination of literary and photographic evocations published to coincide with the exhibition of Wissema's beautiful photographic record of the built structures and people of the District.

[32] Lindy Wilson (dir.), *Last Supper at Horstley Street* (South Africa: Lindy Wilson Productions, 1983).

[33] Rive, '*Buckingham Palace*', *District Six*.

[34] The oral histories collected by the project were absorbed within the archives of the Centre for Popular Memory at UCT. Published reminiscences by ex-residents include Linda Fortune, *The House in Tyne Street: Childhood Memories of District Six* (Cape Town: Kwela Books, 1996); Noor Ebrahim, *Noor's Story: My Life in District Six* (Cape Town: The District Six Museum, 1999); Yousuf S. Rassool, *District Six – Lest We Forget* (Cape Town: Faculty of Education, University of the Western Cape, 2000).

Illustration 6.2: Promoting myth or reflecting reality? Photograph of graffiti on a wall in District Six published in *Drum* magazine in the 1960s (Mary Evans Picture Gallery)

One of *District Six: The Musical*'s songs, '7 Steps', named after a District landmark, suggested that the next generation would wreak revenge:

> For they too have been broken
> And scattered like the bricks
> The stones, cement and concrete
> That once was District Six.[35]

Sophiatown! The Play was about the place's 'life, history and destruction', part of Johannesburg's version of 1980s District Six remembrance. It

---

[35] Cited in Richard Rive, 'District Six: Fact and Fiction', in Jeppie and Soudien (eds), *The Struggle for District Six*, 114.

premiered in the same year as the Petersen-Kramer musical, and was created by the Junction Avenue Theatre Company, whose previous work had included a play called *Marabi!* (1982). Like the publication of a novel called *The Marabi Dance*, based on its author's reminiscences of growing up in Doornfontein yards and Sophiatown, this demonstrated renewed cross-racial interest in township history and culture similarly manifest in the History Workshops held at UCT and Wits.[36] *Sophiatown!* was created from interviews, also published in book form, with ex-residents and people who knew the area, such as Mphahlele, Gordimer, Huddleston, Sampson and Don Mattera.[37] In 1987, Mattera published extended recollections in an autobiography whose suggestive title was *Memory is the Weapon. A Good Looking Corpse*, an even more substantial compendium of interviews, illustrations and extracts from *Drum*, followed.[38]

Cato Manor was also warmly remembered in the 1980s. Indian ex-resident Ronnie Govender wrote and staged numerous historical plays about the place, such as *At the Edge* and *1949*. Collections of these plays, as well as short stories about Cato Manor that Govender began writing soon after his eviction, were published in the 1990s.[39] Contemporary academic interest in explaining earlier forms of resistance explains why oral histories were also collected from African ex-residents in the 1980s. As with Govender's work recalling the Indian community, they describe an African Mkhumbane society that was complex, creative and tolerant towards its own insiders. As with Sophiatown and District Six, fashion was influenced by American cinema and musical styles. John Wayne and Roy Rogers were seen as masculine role models while women imitated Marilyn Munroe and Zsa Zsa Gabor. As in District Six, male homosexuality or *Izitabane* was openly expressed. Mrs Phewa recalled Saturday wedding ceremonies, which any resident could attend, where one partner would dress up in 'long dress, stockings, high heels'. Mrs Phew would 'teach the "women" to do make-up, sewing and cooking'.[40]

Positive remembrance of place and times lost were enhanced for some by initial lack of amenities and community in places they were moved to. Mr K.T. remembered being 'brought into this Cape Flats. It was a barren land. There was nothing.' Ex-residents of District Six in particular often experienced removal as expulsion from the city proper, referred to as

[36] Modikwe Dikobe, *The Marabi Dance* (London: Heinemann, 1973).

[37] Pippa Stein and Ruth Jacobson, *Sophiatown Speaks* (Johannesburg: Junction Avenue Press, 1986).

[38] Nicol, *A Good Looking Corpse*.

[39] Harold Joseph, *An Edition of the Collected Plays of Ronnie Govender: With a Biographical and Critical Introduction* (Pietermaritzburg: University of Natal Press, 1991); Ronnie Govender, *At the Edge and Other Cato Manor Stories* (Pretoria: Manx, 1996).

[40] Edwards, 'Cato Manor', 119.

either Cape Town or 'the Cape', even though they remained within the municipal boundaries. Mrs A. remembered that 'if we stood on our verandas, then we could see the whole of the docks. And it was really nice to live there. We did not want to move out . . . it was really nice to stay in the Cape.' Mrs G.J. put it like this:

What they took away they can never give it back to us again [weeps]. Oh! I want to cry so much, all over again . . . I cannot explain how it was when I moved out of Cape Town and I came to Manenberg . . . What did we do, that they chuck us out like this? We wasn't murderers, we wasn't robbers . . . It was wrong what the White people did . . . They broke us up. They broke up the community. They took our happiness from us. The day they threw us out of Cape Town, that was my whole life tumbling down . . . I couldn't see my life in this raw township far away from the family. All the neighbours were strangers. That was the hardest part of my life, believe me.[41]

Academic analyses suggest that the sense of community relayed in recollections was not purely imagined.[42] It had both a social and territorial component. A sense of common ties with others in the community was underpinned by social networks built up over time, sometimes over generations. These networks included kinship ties and neighbourly reciprocity whose loss may have been particularly keenly felt by women.[43] Family income could be supplemented by making and selling goods within the neighbourhood. Local shopkeepers often extended credit or sold in small amounts to people they knew there.

Shared occupations, membership of civic associations and recreational activities contributed to perceptions of common ties. One activity much commented on in interviews was going to the cinema, an often boisterous communal activity. Another mentioned in many Cape Town interviews was the New Year Carnival.

Oh, oh, those were wonderful days. That days I never forget, because that was when we had a lot of pleasure, man. We were so happy. It was in Hanover Street from the start at Castle Bridge right up to the Catholic Church. Now tonight, its

---

[41] CPM, District Six files, interviews with Mrs G.J., Mr K.T. and Mrs A.

[42] See for instance Western, *Outcast Cape Town*; Claire Keeton, 'Aspects of Material Life and Culture in District Six, c.1930–1950' (Unpublished BA Hons thesis, UCT, 1987); Bill Nasson, 'Oral History and the Reconstruction of District Six', in Jeppie and Soudien (eds), *The Struggle for District Six*, 44–66; Uma Dhupelia-Mesthrie, 'Dispossession and Memory: The Black River Community of Cape Town', *Oral History*, 28, 2 (2000), 35–43. Sean Field (ed.), *Lost Communities, Living Memories: Remembering Forced Removals in Cape Town* (Cape Town: David Philip, 2001); Vivian Bickford-Smith, Sean Field and Clive Glaser (eds), 'Special Issue: Oral History in the Western Cape', *African Studies* 60, 1 (July 2001).

[43] This is suggested in Western, *Outcast Cape Town*, from the evidence contained in interviews he conducted with ex-residents of The Valley, Mowbray.

Old Year's Eve, then my Auntie would make all ready, food and everything, then she would say we must go down and keep our places.[44]

A sense of shared territory could be expressed by the parading of 'home' troupes in places such as Die Vlak, Claremont or District Six. Territorial identity with one's own place compared to someone else's was enhanced by familiarity with local institutions and landmarks. This was facilitated by the different names given to each shanty settlement, neighbourhood, township or suburb, whether these names were officially recognised or not. Roads, railways, rivers and open spaces frequently helped mark the boundaries of communities. So too could perceptions of racial difference between inhabitants of your area and another, especially if that other area was seen as unwelcoming or actively hostile.

By the beginning of the twenty-first century, District Six, Sophiatown and Cato Manor were commemorated by either a museum or heritage centre. Yet nostalgia for the urban past has not been confined to residents of places destroyed under apartheid or to Whites who may lament apartheid's demise. An account of growing up during the 1980s in Katlehong, a poorly serviced township situated some thirty-five kilometres east of Johannesburg, goes under the self-consciously ironic title *Native Nostalgia*. Its author, Jacob Dhlamini, is aware that for a Black South African to remember urban life under apartheid in other than entirely negative terms challenges prevailing wisdom. He acknowledges that Katlehong was dirty and dangerous. But he also chooses to recall the enjoyment of listening to dramas on Radio Zulu, American rock music on Radio 5, and watching football on one of the township's first televisions. More provocatively, Dhlamini admits having enjoyed Afrikaans literature and the language itself and adopting Gerhardus (Gerrie) Coetzee as his hero. This was because White Afrikaans-speaking Coetzee, who won a world heavyweight boxing title, was born in nearby Boksburg.[45]

Native Nostalgia asserts Dhlamini's right to recollect both the good and bad of 'slum' life. It suggests, as do the other reminiscences mentioned in this chapter, that a sense of place plays an important role in individual and collective identity. Such reminiscences frequently also demonstrate that this identity is influenced by the national and international circulation of ideas and popular culture. Unlike Evans thinking about Durban in 1910, Dhlamini is able to think beyond racial categorisation. These are all topics explored throughout this book. For their part, memories of those forcibly removed during apartheid suggest that the past in general is often remembered as a 'Lost Eden' myth, the 'reverse image' of the difficult present.

[44] CPM, District Six files, Mrs G.J.
[45] Jacob Dhlamini, *Native Nostalgia* (Johannesburg: Jacana, 2009).

Within such mythology in memories of ex-residents across the globe, the 'slum' is commonly transformed into a 'warm and homely place, a little commonwealth where there was always a helping hand'. The experience of urban life for the majority living in 'slums' surely lies somewhere between the grimmest judgements of external observers and this nostalgic insider remembrance.[46] More certainly, the number of those living in such places in South African cities has never been higher.

[46] Samuel and Thompson (eds), *The Myths We Live By*, 8–9.

Bibliography

Primary sources

Archive and library collections

African Studies Library, University of Cape Town
BBC Archives (online), www.bbc.co.uk
British Broadcasting Company (BBC) Written Archives Centre, Reading
British Film Institute (BFI) National Archives, London
British Library, London
Cambridge University Library
Centre for Popular Memory Archives, University of Cape Town
Cape Town Archives Repository, Cape Town
Don Africana Central Reference Library, Durban
Killie Campbell Library, University of KwaZulu-Natal, Durban
Modern Records Collection, Warwick University
National Archives Repository, Pretoria
South African National Film Video and Sound Archive, Pretoria
South African Public Library, Cape Town
University of Cape Town Library, Special Collections

City histories and autobiographies of city residents

Cartwright, A. P., *The Corner House: The Early History of Johannesburg*, Johannesburg and Cape Town: Purnell and Sons, 1965
Chilvers, Hedley A., *Out of the Crucible: Being the Romantic Story of the Witwatersrand Goldfields and the Great City which Arose in Their Midst*, London: Cassell, 1929
Chilvers, Hedley A., *Out of the Crucible: Being the Romantic Story of the Witwatersrand Goldfields and the Great City which Arose in Their Midst*, Cape Town: Juta and Company, 1948
Dhlamini, Jacob, *Native Nostalgia*, Johannesburg: Jacana, 2009
Ebrahim, Noor, *Noor's Story: My Life in District Six*, Cape Town: The District Six Museum, 1999
Faure, D. P., *My Life and Times*, Cape Town: Juta, 1907
Fortune, Linda, *The House in Tyne Street: Childhood Memories of District Six*, Cape Town: Kwela Books, 1996

Green, Lawrence, *Growing Lovely, Growing Old*, Cape Town: Howard Timmins, 1975

Green, Lawrence, *A Taste of South-Easter*, Cape Town: Howard Timmins, 1971

Green, Lawrence, *Tavern of the Seas*, Cape Town: Howard Timmins, 1947

Henderson, W. P. M., *Fifty Years' Municipal History*, Durban: Robinson and Co., 1904

Hirson, Baruch, *Revolutions in My Life*, Johannesburg: Witwatersrand University Press, 1995

Honikman, Alfred H., *Cape Town: City of Good Hope*, Cape Town: Howard Timmins, 1966

Ingram, Joseph Forsyth and Frank A. Sams, *The Story of an African Seaport: Being the History of the Port and Borough of Durban, the Seaport of Natal*, Durban: G. Coester, 1899

Laidler, P. W., *A Tavern of the Ocean*, Cape Town: Maskew Miller, 1926

Leendertz, Martin, 'The Vanished City', unpublished memoir, 1953

Macmillan, Allister (ed.), *Durban Past and Present*, Durban: William Brown and Davis Ltd, 1936

Magona, Sindiwe, *To My Children's Children*, Cape Town: David Philip, 1990

Malherbe, Janie, *Port Natal*, Cape Town: Howard Timmins, 1965

Manuel, George, *I Remember Cape Town*, Cape Town: Don Nelson, 1977

Maud, John, *City Government: The Johannesburg Experiment*, Oxford: Clarendon Press, 1938

Modisane, Bloke, *Blame Me on History*, London: Thames & Hudson, 1963

Mphahlele, Ezekiel, *Down Second Avenue*, London: Faber & Faber, 1959

Neame, L. E., *City Built on Gold*, Johannesburg: Central News Agency, 1960

Nkosi, Lewis, *Home and Exile*, London: Longman, Green and Co. Ltd, 1965

Picard, H. W. J., *Grand Parade: The Birth of Greater Cape Town: 1850–1913*, Cape Town: Struik, 1969

Rassool, Yousuf S., *District Six – Lest We Forget*, Cape Town: Faculty of Education, University of the Western Cape, 2000

Reunert, Theodore, *Forty Years of Progress*, Johannesburg and London: Reunert and Lenz Ltd and Albion Publishers, 1928

Rosenthal, Eric, *Fishorns and Hansom Cabs*, Johannesburg: A. D. Donker, 1977

Rosenthal, Eric, *Schooners and Skyscrapers*, Cape Town: Howard Timmins, 1963

Roux, Eddie and M. Winifred, *Rebel Pity: The Life of Eddie Roux*, London: Rex Collings, 1970

Shorten, John, *Cape Town*, Cape Town: John R. Shorten Ltd, 1963

Shorten, John, *The Johannesburg Saga*, Johannesburg: John R. Shorten, 1970

Stark, Felix, *Durban*, Johannesburg: Felstar Publishing Ltd, 1960

Stark, Felix, *Johannesburg: Seventy Golden Years, 1886–1956*, Johannesburg: Felstar Publishing, 1956

Wagener, F. J., *Rondebosch Down the Years, 1657–1957*, Parow: Cape Times, 1957

Wentzel, John Brunette, *A View from the Ridge: Johannesburg Retrospect*, Cape Town: David Philip, 1975

Films

Albrecht, Joseph (dir.), *Die Bou van 'n Nasie*, South Africa: African Film Productions, 1938

Albrecht, Joseph (dir.), *The Man Who Was Afraid*, South Africa: African Film Productions, 1920

Albrecht, Joseph, (dir.), *On Tour in South Africa: Land of Sunshine and Romance*, South Africa: African Film Productions, 1936

Anon (dir.), *The Cape of Good Hope*, South Africa: African Film Productions Company (for the Publicity Department, SAR&H), 1932

Anon (dir.), *Coloured Folks Carnival*, Britain: Topical Film Company, 1928

Anon (dir.), *Durban and Its Environs*, France: Production Company Unknown, 1914

Anon (dir.), *The Great Kimberley Diamond Robbery*, South Africa: Springbok Film Company, 1911

Anon (dir.), *Harbours of History*, Johannesburg: African Film Productions Company, 1946

Anon (dir.), *Johannesburg's Golden Jubilee*, South Africa: African Film Productions, 1936

Anon (dir.), *Land of the Springboks*, South Africa: African Film Productions Company, 1945

Anon (dir.), *A New Horizon*, South Africa: Stafford Smith Films, 1960

Anon (dir.), *News in a Nutshell: Johannesburg Celebrates Its Jubilee*, Britain: Pathe Gazette, 1936

Anon (dir.), *The Opening of the Empire Exhibition at Johannesburg*: African Film Productions, 1936

Anon (dir.), *Scenes in and around Cape Town*, Great Britain: Butcher and Sons, 1911

Anon (dir.), *Sixty Years After*, South Africa: African Film Productions, 1947

Anon (dir.), *Slum Clearance in Johannesburg*, Britain: British Pathe Gazette, 1937

Anon (dir.), *Sold to the Malays*, South Africa: African Film Productions, c.1915

Anon (dir.), *Train Ride from Cape Town to Simonstown*, Great Britain: Co-Operative Cinematograph, 1911

Attenborough, Richard (dir.), *Cry Freedom*, UK: Marble Arch Productions and Universal Pictures, 1986

Best, J. (dir.), *My Song Goes Forth*, UK: Gilbert Church Production Company, 1937

Cruickshanks, Dick (dir.), *The Symbol of Sacrifice*, South Africa: African Film Productions, 1918

Frost, E. (dir), *Notice to Quit*, Cape Town: Black Sash, 1960

Kirstein, Hyman (dir.), *Zonk*, South Africa: African Film Productions, 1950

Korda, Zoltan (dir.), *Cry the Beloved Country*, UK: London Film Productions, 1951

Korda, Zoltan (dir.), *Sanders of the River*, UK: London Film Productions, 1935

Lauste, Emile (dir.), *Sunday Morning Scenes, Kaffir Compound, Johannesburg*, UK: W. Butcher and Sons Production Company, 1911

Menges, Chris (dir.), *A World Apart*, UK: Atlantic Entertainment, 1988

Mitchell, R. A. (dir.), *Adderley Street, Cape Town*, UK: Mitchell 1898

Nofal, Emil, (dir.), *Song of Africa*, South Africa: African Film Productions, 1951
Orenstein, Dr. A. J. (dir.), *The Dust that Kills*, South Africa: African Film Productions, 1921
Palcy, Euzhan (dir.), *Dry White Season*, USA: Sundance Productions, 1989
Peacock, Michael (dir.), *Panorama: Union of South Africa*, BBC, 24 June 1957
Persson, Sven (dir.), *A Million Cities of Gold*, South Africa: City of Johannesburg, 1966
Porter, Edwin S. (dir.), *The Great Train Robbery*, USA: Edison Manufacturing Company, 1903
Rogosin, Lionel (dir.), *Come Back Africa*, USA: Lionel Rogosin Films, 1959
Scott, Michael and Clive Donner (dir.), *Civilisation on Trial in South Africa*, UK: Scott and Donner Production, 1950
Smith, Howard (dir.), *Ed Murrow's See It Now: African Conflict*, New York: CBS, 1954
Swanson, Donald (dir.), *African Jim*, Johannesburg: Erika Rutherford Production, 1949
Swanson, Donald (dir.), *The Magic Garden*, Johannesburg: Swan Films, 1951
Viertel, Berthold (dir.), *Rhodes of Africa*, UK: Gaumont British Picture Corporation, 1936
Weaver, H. C. (dir.), *South Africa: A Preview*, Johannesburg: South African Tourist Corporation, 1954
Wetherell, M. A. (dir.), *Livingstone*, UK: Butcher's Film Service, 1925
Wilson, Lindy (dir.), *Last Supper at Horstley Street*, South Africa: Lindy Wilson Productions, 1983

Guidebooks and travel literature

Anon, *Cape Town and the Picturesque Peninsula*, Cape Town: Cape Times, 1912
Anon, *The Guide to Cape Town: With Information Covering Kimberley and Johannesburg*, Cape Town and Johannesburg: J. C. Juta & Co., 1890
Anon, *A Nutshell Guide to Cape Town*, Cape Town: Queen's Hotel, 1897
Anon, *Six Thousand Miles of Sunshine Travel over the South African Railways*, Pretoria: SAR&H, 1937
Anon, *Souvenir of Cape Town*, Cape Town: J. C. Juta & Co., 1889
Blount, Edward, *Notes on the Cape of Good Hope: Made during an Excursion in that Colony in the Year 1820*, London: John Murray, 1821
Cape Peninsula Publicity Association (CPPA), *Cape Town for Health and Pleasure*, Cape Town: CPPA, 1913
CPPA, Bulletin No. 62, *The Call of the Camp's Bay Coast*, Cape Town: CPPA, undated, c.1920
CPPA, Bulletin No. 63, *The Climate of South Africa*, Cape Town: CPPA, undated c.1914
CPPA, Bulletin No. 66, *Table Mountain: Some Easy Ways to the Summit*, Cape Town: CPPA, 1914
CPPA, *The Cape Peninsula*, Cape Town: CPPA, c.1920
CPPA, *The Land of the Golden South*, Cape Town: CPPA, 1927
CPPA, *The Riviera of the South*, Cape Town: CPPA, 1929
CPPA, *The Summit*, Cape Town: CPPA, 1913

Duff Gordon, Lady, *Letters from the Cape*, Cape Town: Maskew Miller, 1925

Durban Publicity Association (DPA) and South African Railways and Harbours (SAR&H), *Delightful Durban: Sunny South Africa's Seaside Resort*, Durban: DPA, 1926

Edgar, Robert R. (ed.), *An African American in South Africa: The Travel Notes of Ralphe J. Bunche*, Johannesburg: Witwatersrand University Press, 1992

Edwards, Dennis, *The Transvaal and How to Reach It*, Cape Town: Dennis Edwards and Co., 1890

Fairbridge, Dorothea, *Along Cape Roads: The Wanderings of a Stranger at the Cape of Good Hope*, Cape Town: Maskew Miller Ltd, 1928

Fairbridge, Dorothea, *Gardens of South Africa*, London: A&C Black Ltd, 1924

Fairbridge, Dorothea, *Historic Houses of South Africa*, Cape Town: Maskew Miller, 1922

Finch, J. R., *Cape of Good Hope: Being the Official Handbook of the City of Cape Town*, Cape Town: CPPA [1909], revised edition 1926

General Manager, South African Railways and Durban Corporation, *Durban by the Sea: Official Illustrated Handbook*, Durban: Durban Municipality and Natal Railways, 1908

General Manager, South African Railways and Durban Corporation, *Durban. The White City. Official Illustrated Handbook*, Durban: South African Railways and Durban Corporation, n.d. (c.1914)

Gibbs, Henry, *Twilight in South Africa*, London: Jarrolds Publishers, 1949

Glanville, Richard, *Glanville's Guide to South Africa: Being a Cheap Hand-Book to the South African Colonies*, London: Richards, Glanville and Co., 1878

Hope, Henry, *With Your Car at the Cape*, Cape Town: CPPA, 1936

Johannesburg Municipality and SAR&H, *Johannesburg, South Africa*, Johannesburg: Johannesburg Municipality and SAR&H, 1924

Kennedy, David, *Kennedy at the Cape: A Professional Tour through the Cape Colony, Orange Free State, Diamond Fields and Natal*, Edinburgh: Edinburgh Publishing Company, 1879

Lewis, Cecil and Gertrude Edwards, *Cape Town: Treasures of the Mother City*, Cape Town: Speciality Press of South Africa, 1927

Mayson, J. S., *The Malays of Cape Town*, Manchester: Cave and Sever, 1855

McQuade, James J., *Durban: The Brighton of South Africa, a Souvenir from the Marine Hotel*, Durban: Marine Hotel, c.1910

Morris, James, *South African Winter*, London: Faber & Faber, 1958

Morton, H. V., *In Search of South Africa*, London: Methuen and Co. Ltd, 1948

Noble, John, *Descriptive Handbook of the Cape Colony: Its Condition and Resources*, Cape Town and London: J. C. Juta and E. Stanford, 1875

Pratt, Ambrose, *The Real South Africa*, Milton Keynes: General Books [1912], 2010

Reed, Douglas, *Somewhere South of Suez*, London: Jonathan Cape, 1950

Scully, William Charles, *The Ridge of White Waters*, London: Stanley Paul & Co., 1912

Simms, Katherine L., *Springbok in Sunshine*, London: Hutchinson and Company, 1946

St John, Robert, *Through Malan's Africa*, London: Victor Gollancz Ltd, 1954

Tingsten, Herbert, *The Problem of South Africa*, London: Victor Gollancz Ltd, 1955

Trollope, Anthony, *South Africa*, Gloucester: Alan Sutton Publishing [1877], 1987

Twain, Mark, *Following the Equator: A Journey Around the World*, Hartford, CT: American Publishing Company, 1897

Tyrell, Eleanor, *South African Snapshots for English Girls*, London: Gay and Hancock, 1910

Waugh, Evelyn, *A Tourist in Africa*, London: Chapman & Hall, 1960

Wells, A. W., *South Africa*, London: J. M. Dent & Sons [1939], 1947

Literature (magazine articles, novels, plays, poetry, short stories)

Abrahams, Peter, *Dark Testament*, London: Allen and Unwin, 1942

Abrahams, Peter, *Mine Boy*, London: Faber & Faber, 1946

Abrahams, Peter, *Return to Goli*, London: Faber & Faber, 1952

Abrahams, Peter, *Song of the City*, London: Dorothy Crisp, 1943

Abrahams, Peter, *Tell Freedom*, London: Faber & Faber, 1954

Baudelaire, Charles, *The Flowers of Evil*, Oxford: Oxford University Press [1857], 2008

Baudelaire, Charles, *Paris Spleen*, New York: New Directions [1869], 1970

Brink, André, *Looking on Darkness*, London: Flamingo [1974], 1988

Blackburn, Douglas, *Leaven: A Black and White Story*, Pietermaritzburg: University of Natal Press [1908], 1991

Blackburn, Douglas, *Richard Hartley, Prospector*, Edinburgh: William Blackwood and Sons, 1905

Boonzaier, F. W., *Die Stad Sodom*, Cape Town: H.A.U.N., 1931

Campbell, Roy, *The Wayzgoose: A South African Satire*, London: Jonathan Cape, 1928

Campell, Roy, William Plomer and Laurens van der Post (eds), *Voorslag: A Magazine of South African Life and Art: Facsimile Reprint of Numbers 1, 2 and 3 (1926)*, Durban and Pietermaritzburg: Killie Campbell Africana Library, University of Natal Press, 1985

Chapman, M. (ed.), *The Drum Decade*, Pietermaritzburg: University of Natal Press, 2001

Christie, Agatha, *The Man in the Brown Suit*, London: John Lane and the Bodley Head Ltd, 1924

Comptesse de Bremont, Anna, *The Gentleman Digger: Being Studies and Pictures of Life in Johannesburg*, London: Greening and Co. [1890], 1899

Comptesse de Bremont, Anna, *The Ragged Edge: Tales of the African Gold Fields*, London: Downey and Co., 1895

De Beer, L., *Half Hours of Leisure in South Africa: A Holiday Book*, Cape Town and Amsterdam: Jacques Dusseau, 1896

Dhlomo, R. R. R., *An African Tragedy: A Novel in English by a Zulu Writer*, Alice: Lovedale Press, 1928

Dickens, Charles, *Hard Times*, London: Penguin [1854], 2003

Dikobe, Modikwe, *The Marabi Dance*, London: Heinemann, 1973

Ensor, J. D., *Sitongo: A South African Story*, Cape Town: A. Richards and Sons, 1884

Feinberg, B., (ed.), *Poets to the People: South African Freedom Poems*, London: George Allen and Unwin, 1974

Gordimer, Nadine, 'The Defeated', in Rosenthal and Rabinow (eds), *The South African Saturday Book*, Cape Town: Hutchinson, 1948, 169–82

Gordimer, Nadine, *A World of Strangers*, London: Jonathan Cape [1958], 2002

Govender, Ronnie, *At the Edge and Other Cato Manor Stories*, Pretoria: Manx, 1996

Gray, Stephen (ed.), *Stephen Black: Three Plays*, Johannesburg: A. D. Donker, 1984

Grenfell Williams, J. and Henry John May, *I am Black: The Story of Shabala*, Johannesburg: Juta, 1935

Hardy, G. W., *The Black Peril*, London: Holden and Hardingham, 1914

Hernekin, Baptist R. (pseudonym of Ethelreda Lewis), *Wild Deer*, London: Faber, 1933

Heyer, Albert E., *The Mysteries of the Secret Phial: An Original South African Story of Afirkander Sedition, Rebellion, and Continental Conspiracy Against the Paramountcy of Great Britain in South Africa; Including Startling Disclosures Concerning a Bubonic Plague Camp in the Cape Division*, Cape Town: C. Heyer, 1902

Hughes, Langston (ed.), *An African Treasury: Article, Essays, Stories, Poems by Black Africans*, London: Victor Gollancz, 1961

Joseph, Harold, *An Edition of the Collected Plays of Ronnie Govender: With a Biographical and Critical Introduction*, Pietermaritzburg: University of Natal Press, 1991

Junod, H. A., *Zidji, étude de moeurs Sud-Africaines*, Saint Blaise: Foyer Solidariste, 1911

La Guma, Alex, *The Stone Country*, Cape Town: David Philip [1967], 1991

La Guma, Alex, *A Walk in the Night and Other Stories*, Cape Town: David Philip [1967], 1991

Matshikiza, Todd, *Chocolates for My Wife*, London: Hodder and Stoughton, 1961

Matshikiza, Todd and John Matshikiza, *With the Lid Off*, Johannesburg: M & G Books, 2000

Matshikiza, Todd, Pat Williams and Harry Bloom, *King Kong*, Johannesburg: Bernhardt Production, 1959

Matthews, James and Gladys Thomas, *Cry Rage!* Johannesburg: Spro-cas Publications, 1972

Millin, Sarah Gertrude, *God's Step-Children*, London and New York: Constable and Co. and Boni and Liveright, 1924

Millin, Sarah Gertrude, *The South Africans*, New York: Boni and Liveright [1927], 1928

Mogale, A. [Arthur Maimane], 'Crime for Sale', in M. Chapman (ed.), *The Drum Decade*, Pietermaritzburg: University of Natal Press, 2001, 28–31

Mphahlele, Ezekiel (ed.), *African Writing Today*, London: Harmondsworth, 1967

Mutloatse, M., *Casey and Co., Selected Writings of Casey 'Kid' Motsisi*, Johannesburg: Ravan Press, 1980

Nakasa, Nat, 'The Life and Death of King Kong', in Chapman (ed.), *Drum Decade*, 166–70

Odendaal, A. and R. Field (eds), *Liberation Chabalala: The World of Alex La Guma*, Cape Town: Mayibuye Centre, 1993

Patel, Essop (ed.), *The World of Can Themba*, Johannesburg: Ravan Press, 1985

Patel, Essop (ed.), *The World of Nat Nakasa*, Johannesburg: Ravan Press, 1975

Paton, Alan, *Cry, the Beloved Country*, New York and London: Charles Scribner's Sons and Jonathan Cape, 1948

Paton, Alan, *Cry the Beloved Country*, Harmondsworth: Penguin, 1971

Plomer, William, *Turbott Wolfe*, New York: William Morrow and Company Inc., [1926], 1965

Rive, Richard, *Advance, Retreat: Selected Short Stories*, Cape Town: David Philip, 1983

Rive, Richard, *Buckingham Palace, District Six*, Cape Town: David Philip, 1986

Rive, Richard, *Emergency*, Cape Town: David Philip [1964], 1988

Rutherfoord, P. (ed.), *African Voices: An Anthology of Native African Writing*, New York: Grosset and Dunlop, 1958

Schreiner, Olive, *The Story of a South African Farm*, London: Chapman and Hall, 1883

Schumann, P. W. S., *Hantie kom huis-toe*, Pretoria: J. L. van Schalk, 1933

Scully, William Charles, *Daniel Vavanda: The Life Story of a Human Being*, Cape Town: J. C. Juta & Co., 1923

Small, Adam, *Oos Wes Tuis Bes Distrik Ses*, Cape Town: Human & Rousseau, 1973

Small, Adam and Jansje Wissema, *District Six*, Cape Town: Fontein, 1986

Themba, Can, *Requiem to Sophiatown*, London: Penguin, 2006

Van der Post, Laurens, *In a Province*, London: L. and V. Woolf, 1934

Vine Hall, Arthur, *Poems of South Africa*, London: Longmans, Green and Co., 1935

Williams, John Grenfell and Henry John May, *I am Black: The Story of Shabala*, London: Cassell and Co., 1936

Wilson-Moore, C. and A. P. Wilson-Moore, *Diggers; Doggerel Poems of the Veld and Mine*, Cape Town: Argus Co., 1890

Newpapers and magazines

Bantu World
The Bioscope
Cape Argus
Cape Times
Cowley Evangelist
Daily Express
Daily Mirror
Daily Telegraph
Drum
Evening Express
Excalibur
Film Renter

Huisgenoot
Ilanga
Illustrated London News
Natal Mercury
New Era
Pall Mall Gazette
Rand Daily Mail
South Africa Pictorial Stage and Cinema
South African News
Standard and Diggers News
The Star
Trek
Voorslag

Newsreels

African Mirror
British Gaumont
British Pathé News
Gaumont Graphic

Official publications

Transvaal colony

South African Native Affairs Commission, 1903–1905, 3 vols
TG 11–1908, *Transvaal Indigency Commission, 1906–1908*

Union Government of South Africa (UG)

UG 32–1912, *Census for 1911*, Pretoria: Government Printers, 1912
UG 39–1913, *Report of the Commission Appointed to Enquire into Assaults on Women*, Cape Town: Cape Times Ltd, Government Printers, 1913
UG SC 35–1914, *Report of the Select Committee on Tuberculosis*, Cape Town: Cape Times Ltd, Government Printers, 1914
UG SC 3–1919, *Report of the Select Committee on the Public Health Bill*, Cape Town: Cape Times Ltd, Government Printers, 1919
UG SC 17–1934, *Report of the Select Committee on the Subject of the Slums Bill*, Cape Town: Cape Times Ltd, Government Printers, 1934
UG 28–1948, *Report of the Native Laws Commission [Fagan Report], 1946–8*, Pretoria: Government Printer, 1948

Other primary sources

Albertyn, J. A., P. Du Toit and H. S. Theron (eds), *Kerk en Stad: Verslag van Kommissie van Ondersoek oor Stadstoestande*, Stellenbosch: Pro Ecclesia, 1947
Angas, G. F., *Kafirs Illustrated*, London: J. Hogarth, 1849
Anon, *Cape of Good Hope Teachers' Annual 1900*, Cape Town: J. C. Juta & Co., 1900

Anon, *Official Report of the Social Survey Conference*, Cape Town: Paul Koston, 1942

Anon, *Today's News Today*, Cape Town: Argus, 1956

Anon, *Urban Residence in the Union of South Africa*, Pretoria: SAR&H, 1929

Baden Powell, Lieut.-General R. S. S., *Scouting for Boys: A Handbook for Instruction in Good Discipline*, London: Horace Cox, 1907

Barnes, Leonard, *Caliban in Africa: An Impression of Colour-Madness*, London: Victor Gollancz Ltd, 1930

Barnett-Clarke, Henry Purefoy, *The Life and Times of Thomas Fothergill Lightfoot, BD, Archdeacon of Cape Town*, Cape Town: Darter, 1908

Bigelow, Poultney, *White Man's Africa*, London: Harper, 1898

Bolsmann, E. H., *The Mount Nelson*, Pretoria and Cape Town: Haum, 1978

Broekmann, Elizabeth and Gail Weldon, *There are Stories to be Told: St Cyprian's School 1871–1996*, Cape Town: Gavin and Sales, 1996

Brookes, Edgar H., *The Colour Problems of South Africa: Being the Phelps-Stokes Lectures, 1933, Delivered at the University of Cape Town*, London and Alice: Kegan Paul, Trench, Trubner, & Co., Ltd, and Lovedale Press, 1933

Carnegie Commission, *The Poor White Problem in South Africa: Report of the Carnegie Commission*, Stellenbosch: Ecclesia, 1932

Chalmers, J. A., *Tiyo Soga: A Page of South African Mission Work*, Edinburgh, London, Glasgow and Grahamstown, Cape Colony: Andrew Eliot, Hodder and Stoughton, David Bryce and Sons, and James Hay, 1878

Clarke, James (ed.), *Like it Was: The Star 100 Years in Johannesburg*, Johannesburg: Argus Printing Company, 1987

Cornelius, H., 'Ons Werkers in Agterbuurtes en Waroom?', *Die Klerewerker*, October 1938

De Kiewiet, C. W., *A History of South Africa, Social and Economic*, London and New York: Oxford University Press [1941], 1946

De Villiers, R. and S. Brooke-Norris, *The Story of the Rand Club*, Johannesburg: The Rand Club, 1976

Fairbridge, Dorothea, *Lady Anne Barnard at the Cape of Good Hope 1797–1802*, Oxford: Clarendon Press, 1924

Gardener, John, *Bishops 150: A History of the Diocesan College, Rondebosch*, Cape Town: J. C. Juta & Co., 1997

Geddes, Patrick, *Cities in Evolution*, London: Williams & Norgate, 1915

Grosskopf, J. W. F., *Economic Report: Rural Impoverishment and Rural Exodus*, Carnegie Commission vol. 1, Stellenbosch: Ecclesia, 1932

Harrison, Wilfrid H., *Memoirs of a Socialist in South Africa, 1903–1947*, Cape Town: Stewart Printing Company, 1947

Hellmann, Ellen, *Rooiyard: A Sociological Survey of an Urban Native Slum Yard*, Cape Town: Oxford University Press, 1948

Hopkinson, Tom, *The Fiery Continent*, London: Victor Gollancz, 1962

Howard, Ebenezer, *Garden Cities of Tomorrow: Being the Second Edition of 'Tomorrow: a Peaceful Path to Reform'*, London: Swan Sonnenschein & Co., 1902

Huddleston, Trevor, *Naught for Your Comfort*, London: Collins, 1956

Immelman, R. F. M., *Men of Good Hope: The Romantic Story of the Cape Town Chamber of Commerce: 1804–1954*, Cape Town: Chamber of Commerce, 1955

Jennings, Hubert, *The D. H. S. Story 1866–1966*, Durban: Durban High School and Old Boys' Memorial Trust, 1966

Joelson, Annette, *South African Yesterdays*, Cape Town: Unie-Volkspers Beperk, 1940

Joshi, P. S., *The Tyranny of Colour*, Durban: EP and Commercial Printing Co., 1942

Keppel-Jones, Arthur, *When Smuts Goes: A History of South Africa from 1952 to 2010, First Published in 2015*, London: Victor Gollancz, 1947

Kgosana, Philip, *Lest We Forget*, Johannesburg: Skotaville Press, 1988

Kirwan, Daniel, *Palace and Hovel*, Hartford CT: Belknap and Bliss, 1870

Langham-Carter, Reginald R., *Under the Mountain: The Story of St Saviour's Claremont*, Cape Town: Southern Press, 1973

Lavis, S. W., *Cape Town's Underworld*, Alice: Lovedale Press, 1943

Lenta, Margaret and Basil le Cordeur (eds), *The Cape Diaries of Lady Anne Barnard 1797–98 vol. 1*, Cape Town: Van Riebeeck Society, 1998

Lenta, Margaret and Basil le Cordeur (eds), *The Cape Diaries of Lady Anne Barnard 1799–1800 vol. 2*, Cape Town: Van Riebeeck Society, 1999

Lewin Robinson, A. M. (ed.), *The Cape Journals of Lady Anne Barnard 1797–8*, Cape Town: Van Riebeeck Society, 1993

Lowndes, E. E. K., *Every-Day Life in South Africa*, London: S. W. Partridge, 1900

Luthuli, Albert, *Let My People Go: An Autobiography*, London and Glasgow: Fontana, 1965

Macmillan, William Miller, *Complex South Africa: An Economic Foot-Note to History*, London: Faber & Faber, 1930

Mandela, Nelson, *Long Walk to Freedom*, Johanneburg: Macdonald Purnell, 1995

Mayer, Philip, *Townsmen or Tribesman: Conservatism and the Process of Urbanization in a South African City*, Cape Town: Oxford University Press, 1971

McCracken, J. L., *The Cape Parliament 1854–1910*, Oxford: Clarendon Press, 1967

Meer, Fatima, *Portrait of Indian South Africans*, Durban: Avon House, 1969

Mehrtens, A., *Cape Town: 50 Photographs*, Cape Town: A. A. Balkema, 1950

Morris, Jan, *Stones of Empire: The Buildings of British India*, London: Penguin, 1983

Morris, Michael, *Paging Through History: 150 Years of the Cape Argus*, Cape Town: Jonathan Ball, 2007

Mulford Robinson, Charles, *The Improvement of Towns and Cities; or the Practical Basis of Civic Aesthetics*, New York and London: Putnam's Sons, 1901

Mulford Robinson, Charles, *Modern Civic Art*, New York: Putnam [1903], 1918

Mumford, Lewis, *The Story of Utopias*, New York: Boni and Liveright, 1922, 19

Murray, R. W., *South African Reminiscences*, Cape Town: J.C. Juta, 1894

National Vigilance Association, *The White Slave Trade: Transactions of the International Congress on the White Slave Trade*, London: Office of the National Vigilance Association, 1899

Pama, C., *Bowler's Cape Town: Life at the Cape in Early Victorian Times 1834–1868*, Cape Town: Tafelberg, 1977

Pauw, B. A., *The Second Generation: A Study of the Family among Urbanized Bantu in East London*, Cape Town: Oxford University Press, 1963

Phillips, Ray E., *The Bantu are Coming: Phases of South Africa's Race Problem*, London: Student Christian Movement Press, 1930

Phillips, Ray E., *The Bantu in the City*, Alice: Lovedale Press, 1939

Plomer, William, *The South African Autobiography*, Cape Town: David Philip, 1984

Raikes, Joan, *Honneur Aulx Dignes: Roedean School 1903–1978*, Johannesburg: Lorton, 1978

Ranby, W. E., *The City Club, Cape Town: A Supplementary History to 1955*, Cape Town: Galvin & Sales, 1955

Robinson, C. M., *The Improvement of Towns and Cities. Or the Practical Basic of Civic Aesthetics*, New York: Putnam's, 1901

Robinson, C. M., *Modern Civic Art or the City Made Beautiful*, New York: Putnam's, 1903

Rosenthal, Eric, *Milnerton*, Milnerton Cape Town: Milnerton Municipality, 1980

Rosenthal, Eric and Richard Robinow, *The South African Saturday Book: A Treasury of Writing and Pictures of South Africa, Old and New, Homey and Extraordinary*, London: Hutchinson, 1948

Sachs, Wulf, *Black Hamlet*, Baltimore and London: John Hopkins University [1937], 1996

Said, Edward W., *Orientalism*, New York: Vintage Books, 1978

Sampson, Anthony, *Drum: The Making of a Magazine*, Johannesburg: Jonathan Ball [1956], 2005

Schapera, Isaac, *Married Life in an African Tribe*, London: Penguin [1940], 1971

Scott, Michael, *A Time to Speak*, London: Faber & Faber, 1958

Smethurst Evans, Maurice, *Black and White in South East Africa: A Study in Sociology*, London: Longmans and Co., 1911

Stein, Sylvester, *Who Killed Mr Drum*, London: Corvo Books, 2003

Strutt, D. H., *The Story of the Durban Club: From Bafta to Baroque*, Cape Town: Howard Timmins, 1963

Thomson, D. H., *The Story of a School: A Short History of Wynberg Boys' High*, Cape Town: Wynberg Old Boys' Union, 1961

Toynbee, A., *Civilization on Trial*, Oxford: Oxford University Press, 1948

Valentine, C., *The Christ Visits the World's Wonder City: The Home of a Thousand Witcheries*, Johannesburg: C.L.D. [Pty] Ltd, 1936

Vos, K., *The Church on the Hill: St John's Parish Wynberg*, Cape Town: Struik, 1971

Whalley, Mary Frances and A. Eames-Perkins, *Of European Descent*, Cape Town: J. C. Juta & Co., 1909

Whiteside, Rev. J., *A New School History of South Africa: With Brief Biographies and Examination Questions*, 12th edition, revised, Johannesburg and Cape Town: J. C. Juta & Co., 1916

Wilks, Terry, *For the Love of Natal: The Life and Times of the Natal Mercury, 1852–1977*, Durban: Robinson, 1977

Wilmot, Alexander, *History of the Cape Colony for Use in Schools*, Cape Town: J. C. Juta & Co., 1871
Wilson, Monica and Archie Mafeje, *Langa: A Study of Social Groups in an African Township*, Cape Town: Oxford University Press, 1963

Secondary sources

Adhikari, Mohamed (ed.), *Dr. Abdurahman: A Biographical Memoir by J. H. Raynard*, Cape Town: Friends of the National Library of South Africa in Association with District Museum, 2002
Alegi, Peter, *Laduma! Soccer, Politics and Society in South Africa*, Scottsville: University of KwaZulu-Natal Press, 2004
Alexander, Peter, *Alan Paton: A Biography*, Oxford and Cape Town: Oxford University Press, 1995, 187–214
Alexander, Peter, 'Campbell, Plomer, Van der Post and *Voorslag*', *English in Africa* 7, 2 (September 1980), 50–9
Alter, Robert, *Imagined Cities: Urban Experience and the Language of the Novel*, New Haven and London: Yale University Press, 2005
Anderson, Benedict, *Imagined Communities: Reflections on the Origin and Spread of Nationalism*, London: Verso, 1983
Anderson, David and David Killingray (eds), *Policing the Empire*, Manchester: Manchester University Press, 1991
Anderson, David and Richard Rathbone (eds), *Africa's Urban Past*, Oxford and Portsmouth, NH: James Currey and Heinemann, 2000
Arscott, Caroline, 'Representations of the Victorian City', in Martin Daunton (ed.), *Cambridge Urban History of Britain: Volume Three (1840–1950)*, Cambridge: Cambridge University Press, 2000, 811–32
Badenhorst, Cecile and Charles Mather, 'Tribal Recreation and Recreating Tribalism: Culture, Leisure and Social Control on South Africa's Gold Mines, 1940–1950', *Journal of Southern African Studies* 23, 3 (1997), 473–89
Baines, Gary F., *A History of New Brighton, Port Elizabeth, South Africa, 1903–1953: The Detroit of the Union*, Lewiston, NY: Edwin Mellen Press, 2002
Bayly, C. A., *Empire and Information: Intelligence Gathering and Social Communication, 1780–1870*, Cambridge: Cambridge University Press, 1999
Beall, Jo, Owen Crankshaw and Susan Parnell, *Uniting a Divided City: Governance and Social Exclusion in Johannesburg*, New York and London: Routledge, 2002
Beavon, Keith, *Johannesburg: The Making and Shaping of a City*, Pretoria and Leiden: University of South Africa Press, 2004
Beinart, William, *Twentieth Century South Africa*, Oxford: Oxford University Press, 2001
Benjamin, Walter, *Reflections: Essays, Aphorisms, Autobiographical Writings*, New York: Shocken Books, 2007
Berman, Marshall, *All That is Solid Melts into Air*, London: Penguin Books, 1988
Bickford-Smith, Vivian, 'African Nationalist or British Loyalist? The Complicated Case of Tiyo Soga', *History Workshop Journal* 71 (Spring 2011), 74–97

Bickford-Smith, Vivian, 'The Betrayal of Creole Elites 1880–1920', in Morgan and Hawkins (eds), *Black Experience and the Empire*, 194–227

Bickford-Smith, Vivian (ed.), 'Cities and Nationalisms', Special Issue, *Journal of Urban History* 38, 5 (2012)

Bickford-Smith, Vivian, 'Creating a City of the Tourist Imagination: The Case of Cape Town, "The Fairest Cape of Them All"', *Urban Studies* 46, 9 (2009), 1763–85

Bickford-Smith, Vivian, *Ethnic Pride and Racial Prejudice in Victorian Cape Town: Group Identity and Social Practice, 1875–1902*, Cambridge: Cambridge University Press, 1995

Bickford-Smith, Vivian, '"Keeping Your Own Council": The Struggle between Houseowners and Merchants for Control of the Cape Town Municipal Council in the Last Two Decades of the Nineteenth Century', *Studies in the History of Cape Town* 5 (1984), 189–208

Bickford-Smith, Vivian, 'Leisure and Social Identity in Cape Town, British Cape Colony, 1838–1910', *Kronos: Journal of Cape History* 25 (1998/1999), 103–28

Bickford-Smith, Vivian, 'The Origins and Early History of District Six to 1910', in Jeppie and Soudien (eds), *The Struggle for District Six*, 35–44

Bickford-Smith, Vivian, 'Picturing Apartheid', in Bickford-Smith and Mendelsohn (eds), *Black and White in Colour*, 256–78

Bickford-Smith, Vivian, 'Protest, Organisation and Ethnicity among Cape Town Workers, 1891–1902', *Studies in the History of Cape Town* 6, 1994, 84–108

Bickford-Smith, Vivian, 'Providing Local Colour? "Cape Coloureds", Cockneys and the Identity of Cape Town from the Late Nineteenth Century to the 1970s', *Journal of Urban History* 38, 1 (January 2012), 133–51

Bickford-Smith, Vivian, 'The Purposes and Politics of Local History Writing: A South African Perspective', *International Journal of Regional and Local History* 8, 1 (2013), 11–16

Bickford-Smith, Vivian, 'Revisiting Anglicisation in the Nineteenth Century Cape Colony', *Journal of Imperial and Commonwealth History* 31, 2 (2003), 82–95

Bickford-Smith, Vivian, 'Urban History in the New South Africa: Continuity and Innovation since the End of Apartheid', *Urban History* 35, 2 (2008), 287–315

Bickford-Smith, Vivian, 'Writing about Englishness: South Africa's Forgotten Nationalism', in Graham McPhee and Prem Poddar (eds), *Empire and After: Englishness in Postcolonial Perspective*, Oxford and New York: Berghahn, 2007, 57–72

Bickford-Smith, Vivian and Richard Mendelsohn (eds), *Black and White in Colour: African History on Screen*, Cape Town, Oxford and Athens, OH: James Currey, Double Storey and Ohio University Press, 2007

Bickford-Smith, Vivian, Sean Field and Clive Glaser (eds), 'Special Issue: Oral History in the Western Cape', *African Studies* 60, 1 (July 2001)

Bickford-Smith, Vivian, Elizabeth Van Heyningen and Nigel Worden, *Cape Town in the Twentieth Century*, Cape Town: David Philip, 1999

Birmingham, David, 'Carnival at Luanda', *Journal of African History* 29, 1 (1988), 93–103

Bjorvig, A. C., 'Durban 1824–1910: The Formation of a Settler Elite and Its Role in the Development of a Colonial City', University of Natal PhD thesis, 1994

Bloomberg, David, *The Chain Gang: Mayors Who Served in Cape Town's City Hall*, Cape Town: Ampersand Press, 2011

Bonner, Philip, 'The 1920 Black Mineworkers' Strike: A Preliminary Account', in Bozzoli (ed.), *Labour, Townships and Protest*, 273–97

Bonner, Philip and Noor Nieftagodien, *Alexandra: A History*, Johannesburg: Wits University Press, 2008

Bonner, Philip and L. Segal, *Soweto: A History*, Cape Town: Longman, 1998

Botha, M. P. (ed.), *Marginal Lives and Painful Presents: Cinema after Apartheid*, Cape Town: Genugtig, 2007

Bottomley, Edward-John, *Poor White*, Cape Town: Tafelberg, 2012

Bozzoli, Belinda, *Labour, Townships and Protest: Studies in the Social History of Witwatersrand*, Johannesberg: Ravan Press, 1979

Breckenridge, Keith, 'No Will to Know: The Rise and Fall of African Civil Registration in 20th Century South Africa', in Keith Breckenridge and Simon Szreter (eds), *Registration and Recognition: Documenting the Person in World History*, Oxford: Oxford University Press, 2012, 357–83

Brewer, John D., *Black and Blue: Policing in South Africa*, Oxford: Clarendon Press, 1994

Briggs, Asa, *Victorian Cities*, London: Odhams Press, 1963

Brink, Elsabe, 'Man-Made Women: Gender, Class and the Ideology of the Volksmoeder', in Walker (ed.), *Women and Gender in Southern Africa*, 273–92

Bruno, Giuliana, *Atlas of Emotion: Journeys in Art, Architecture and Film*, New York and London: Verso, 2002

Bruno, Giuliana, 'City Views: The Voyage of Film Images', in Clarke (ed.), *The Cinematic City*, 46–58

Buckner, Phillip, 'The Royal Tour of 1901 and the Construction of an Imperial Identity in South Africa', *South African Historical Journal* 41, 1 (1999), 324–48

Bull, M. and J. Denfield, *Secure the Shadow: The Story of Cape Photography from Its Beginnings to the End of 1870*, Cape Town: Terence McNally, 1970

Burke, G. and P. Richardson, 'The Profit of Death: A Comparative Study of Miners' Phthisis in Cornwall and the Transvaal, 1876–1918', *Journal of Southern African Studies* 4, 2 (1978), 147–71

Calvocoressi, P., 'The Africa Bureau', *Journal of Modern African Studies* 2 (1964), 292–4

Campbell, J. T., 'The Americanization of South Africa', in E. T. May and R. Wagnleitner (eds), *Here, There, and Everywhere: The Foreign Politics of American Popular Culture*, Hanover, NH: University Press of New England, 2000, 34–63

Cannadine, David, 'The Context, Performance and Meaning of Ritual: The British Monarchy and the "Invention of Tradition", c. 1820–1977', in Hobsbawm and Ranger (eds), *The Invention of Tradition*, 101–64

Cannadine, David, *Ornamentalism: How the British Saw Their Empire*, London: Penguin, 2001

Chatterjee, Partha, *Nationalist Thought and the Colonial World*, Minneanapolis: University of Minneapolis Press, 1993

Chipkin, Clive M., *Johannesburg Style: Architecture and Society 1880s–1960s*, Cape Town: David Philip, 1993

Chipkin, Clive M. and Shirley Zar, *Park Town: A Social and Pictorial History: 1892–1972*, Johannesburg: Studio Thirty-Five, 1972

Clarke, D. B. (ed.), *The Cinematic City*, London and New York: Routledge, 1997

Clingman, Stephen (ed.), *Regions and Repertoires: Topics in South African Politics and Culture*, Johannesburg: Ravan Press, 1991

Cobley, Alan Gregor, *The Rules of the Game: Struggles in Black Recreation and Social Welfare Policy in South Africa*, Westport, CT: Greenwood Press, 1997

Coetzee, A. J., 'White South African Literature after World War 2 – Afrikaans', in Gerard (ed.), *European-Language Writing in Sub-Saharan Africa*, 217–29

Coetzee, Ampie, '"They All Went Down to Gomorrah": An Episode in the Demise of the Afrikaner', in C. N. Van der Merwe (ed.), *Strangely Familiar: South African Narratives on Town and Countryside*, Cape Town: contentlot.com, 2001

Coetzee, J. M., *White Writing: On the Culture of Letters in South Africa*, New Haven, CT, and London: Yale University Press, 1988

Cole, Josette, *Crossroads: The Politics of Reform and Repression 1976–1986*, Johannesburg: Ravan Press, 1987

Colley, Linda, *Britons: Forging the Nation, 1707–1832*, New Haven, CT: Yale University Press, 1992

Colls, R. and P. Dodd (eds), *Englishness: Politics and Culture 1880–1920*, Beckenham: Croom Helm, 1986

Comaroff, Jean and John Comaroff, *Of Revelation and Revolution*, vol. 1, Chicago: Chicago University Press, 1991

Comaroff, Jean and John Comaroff, *Of Revelation and Revolution*, vol. 2, Chicago: Chicago University Press, 1997

Coombe, Ed., *Beard-Shavers' Bush: Place Names in the Cape*, Cape Town: Baarskeerder and Peter Slingsby , 2000

Cooper, A. A., *The Freemasons of South Africa*, Cape Town: Human & Rousseau, 1986

Coplan, David, 'The Emergence of an African Working-Class Culture', in Marks and Rathbone (eds), *Industrialisation and Social Change*, 358–75

Coplan, David B., *In Township Tonight: South Africa's Black City Music and Theatre*, Johannesburg: Ravan Press, 1985

Coquery-Vidrovitch, Catherine, *Histoires des villes d'Afrique noire dès origins à la colonisation*, Paris: Albin Michel, 1993

Cornwell, Gareth, 'George Webb Hardy's *The Black Peril* and the Social Meaning of "Black Peril" in Early Twentieth Century South Africa', *Journal of Southern African Studies* 22, 3 (1996), 441–53

Couzens, Tim, '"Moralizing Leisure Time": The Transatlantic Connection and Black Johannesburg 1918–36', in Marks and Rathbone (eds), *Industrialisation and Social Change*, 314–37

Cresswell, Tim, *Place: A Short Introduction*, Oxford: Wiley-Blackwell, 2004

Cuthbertson, G., A. Grundlingh and M.-L. Suttie (eds), *Writing a Wider War: Rethinking Gender and Identity in the South African War, 1899–1902*, Cape Town and Athens, OH: David Philip and Ohio University Press, 2002

Davenport, T. R. H., *The Afrikaner Bond: The History of a South African Political Party 1880–1911*, Cape Town: Oxford University Press, 1966

Davenport, T. R. H., *South Africa: A Modern History*, 4th edition, London: Macmillan, 1991

Davidson, Joyce and Christine Milligan, 'Embodying Emotion Sensing Space: Introducing Emotional Geographies', *Social and Cultural Geography* 5, 4 (December 2004), 523–32

Davies, R. J., 'The Growth and Development of the Durban Metropolitan Area', *South African Geographical Journal* 45 (December 1963), 17–22

Davis, Mike, *Planet of Slums*, New York and London: Verso, 2006

Davis, Peter, *In Darkest Hollywood: Exploring the Jungles of Cinema's South Africa*, Johannesburg and Athens, OH: Ravan Press, 1996

Delaney, D., *Territory: A Short Introduction*, Oxford: John Wiley & Sons, 2008

Dennis, Richard, *Cities in Modernity: Representations and Productions of Metropolitan Space, 1840-1930*, Cambridge: Cambridge University Press, 2008

Dhupelia-Mesthrie, Uma, 'Dispossession and Memory: The Black River Community of Cape Town', *Oral History* 28, 2 (2000), 35–43

Dick, Archie L., *The Hidden History of South Africa's Book and Reading Cultures*, Toronto: University of Toronto Press, 2012, 54–61

Driver, F. and D. Gilbert (eds), *Imperial Cities*, Manchester: Manchester University Press, 1999

du Toit, Marijke, 'The Domesticity of Afrikaner Nationalism: Volksmoeders and the ACVV, 1904–1929', *Journal of Southern African Studies* 29, 1 (2003), 155–76

Dubow, Saul, *A Commonwealth of Knowledge: Science, Sensibility and White South Africa, 1820–2000*, Oxford: Oxford University Press, 2006

Dubow, Saul, *Scientific Racism in Modern South Africa*, Cambridge: Cambridge University Press, 1995

Dubow, Saul, 'South Africa and South Africans: Nationality, Belonging, Citizenship', in Ross et al. (eds), *The Cambridge History of South Africa*, 17–65

Dyos, H. J. (ed.), *The Study of Urban History*, London: Edward Arnold, 1968

Edwards, Elizabeth (ed.), *Anthropology and Photography, 1860–1920*, New Haven: Yale University Press, 1992

Edwards, Iain, 'Cato Manor, June 1959: Men, Women, Crowds, Violence, Politics and History', in Maylam and Edwards (eds), *The People's City*, 102–42

Elbourne, Elizabeth, *Colonialism, Missions, and the Contest for Christianity in the Cape Colony and Britain, 1799–1853*, Montreal: McGill-Queen's University Press, 2002

Elphick, R. and H. Giliomee (eds), *The Shaping of South African Society*, Cape Town and London: Longman, 1989

Erll, Astrid, 'Travelling Memory', *Parallex* 17, 4 (2011), 4–18

Erlmann, Veit, *African Stars: Studies in Black South African Performance*, Chicago: Chicago University Press, 1991

Erlmann, Veit, 'But Hope Does Not Kill: Black Popular Music in Durban, 1913–1939', in Maylam and Edwards (eds), *The People's City*, 67–101

Evans, Ivan, *Bureaucracy and Race: Native Administration in South Africa*, Berkeley: University of California Press, 1997

Feinstein, Charles H., *An Economic History of South Africa: Conquest, Discrimination and Development*, Cambridge: Cambridge University Press, 2005

Field, Sean (ed.), *Lost Communities, Living Memories: Remembering Forced Removals in Cape Town*, Cape Town: David Philip, 2001

Field, Sean, 'Remembering Experience, Interpreting Memory: Life Stories from Windermere', *African Studies* 60, 1 (2001), 120–3

Foster, Jeremy A., *Washed with Sun: Landscape and the Making of White South Africa*, Pittsburgh, PA: University of Pittsburgh Press, 2008

Fransen, H., *A Cape Camera*, Cape Town: A. D. Donker, 1993

Freestone, Robert, *Designing Australia: Cities, Culture, Commerce and the City Beautiful, 1900–1930*, London: Routledge, 2007

Freund, Bill, *The African City*, New York: Cambridge University Press, 2007

Freund, Bill, 'The City of Durban: Towards a Structural Analysis of the Economic Growth & Character of a South African City', in Anderson and Rathbone (eds), *Africa's Urban Past*, 144–61

Freund, Bill, *Insiders and Outsiders: The Indian Working Class of Durban 1910–1990*, Pietermaritzburg, Portsmouth, NH, and London: University of Natal Press, Heinemann and James Currey, 1995

Freund, Bill, 'South Africa: The Union Years, 1910–1948', in Ross et al. (eds), *Cambridge History of South Africa, 226*

Freund, Bill, 'Urban History in South Africa', *South African Historical Journal* 52 (2005), 19–31

Furlong, Patrick J., *Between Crown and Swastika: The Impact of the Radical Right on the Afrikaner Nationalist Movement in the Fascist Era*, Hanover, NH: Wesleyan University Press, 1991

Gaitskell, Debbie, 'Devout Domesticity? A Century of African Women's Christianity in South Africa', in Walker (ed.), *Women and Gender in Southern Africa*, 251–72

Gaul, William, 'The Atkinsons at Home', *Johannesburg Heritage Journal* 1 (June 2014), 4–5

Gavshon, Harriet, '"Bearing Witness": Ten Years Towards an Opposition Film Movement in South Africa', *Radical History Review*, 47, 7 (1990), 331–45

Gerard, Albert S. (ed.), *European-Language Writing in Sub-Saharan Africa*, Budapest: Akademiai Kiado, 1986

Giliomee, Hermann, *The Afrikaners*, Cape Town: Tafelberg, 2003

Gilroy, Paul, *The Black Atlantic*, London: Verso, 1993

Gordon, Robert, 'Not Quite Cricket: "Civilization on Trial in South Africa"': A Note on the First Protest Film Made in South Africa', *History in Africa* 32 (2005), 457–66

Graham, S. and J. Walters (eds), *Langston Hughes and the South African Drum Generation: The Correspondence*, New York: Palgrave Macmillan, 2010

Greenberg, Stanley E., *Race and State in Capitalist Development: South Africa in Comparative Perspective*, Yale: New Haven, 1980

Greenfeld, Liah, *Nationalism: Five Roads to Modernity*, Cambridge, MA: Harvard University Press, 1992

Grosby, Steven, *Nationalism: A Very Short Introduction*, Oxford: Oxford University Press, 2005

Grundlingh, Albert, *Potent Pastimes: Sport and Leisure Practises in Modern Afrikaner History*, Pretoria: Protea Book House, 2013

Gunn, Simon, *The Public Culture of the Victorian Middle Class: Ritual and Authority and the English Industrial City, 1840–1914*, Manchester: Manchester University Press, 2008

Gutsche, Thelma. *The History and Social Significance of Motion Pictures in South Africa, 1895–1940*, Cape Town: Howard Timmins, 1972

Hall, Peter, *Cities of Tomorrow: An Intellectual History of Urban Planning and Design in the Twentieth Century*, Oxford: Blackwell, 1998

Hallett, Robin, 'The Hooligan Riots: Cape Town August 1906', *Studies in the History of Cape Town* 1 (1979), 42–87

Harland-Jacobs, Jessica L., *Builders of Empire: Freemasonry and British Imperialism, 1717–1927*, Chapel Hill: The University of North Carolina Press, 2007

Harper, Marjory and Stephen Constantine, *Migration and Empire*, Oxford and New York: Oxford University Press, 2010

Harries, Anne, *Manly Pursuits*, London: Bloomsbury, 2000

Harries, Patrick, *Butterflies and Barbarians: Swiss Missionaries and Systems of Knowledge in South-East Africa*, London: James Currey, 2007

Harries, Patrick, 'Imagery, Symbolism and Tradition in a South African Bantustan: Mangosuthu Buthelezi, Inkatha and Zulu History', *History and Theory* 32 (1993), 106–25

Harries, Patrick, *Work, Culture and Identity: Migrant Labourers in Mozambique and South Africa, c.1880–1910*, Portsmouth, NH, London and Johannesburg: Heinemann, James Currey and Witwatersrand University Press, 1994

Hayden, Dolores, *The Power of Place: Urban Landscapes as Public History*, Cambridge: MIT Press, 1997

Hebdige, Dick, *Subculture: the Meaning of Style*, London and New York: Routledge, 1979

Hemson, David, 'In the Eye of the Storm: Dock-Workers in Durban', in Maylam and Edwards (eds), *The People's City*, 145–73

Heyningen, E. Van and Peter Merrett, '"The Healing Touch": The Guild of Loyal Women of South Africa, 1900–1912', *South African Historical Journal* 47 (2003), 24–50

Hobsbawn, Eric, *Nations and Nationalism since 1780: Program, Myth, Reality*, Cambridge: Cambridge University Press, 1990

Hobsbawm, E. and T. Ranger (eds), *The Invention of Tradition*, Cambridge: Cambridge University Press [1983], 1996

Hodgson, Janet, 'Zonnebloem College and Cape Town: 1858–1870', *Studies in the History of Cape Town* 1 (1879), 125–52

Hofmeyr, Isabel, 'Building a Nation from Words: Afrikaans Language, Literature and Ethnic Identity, 1902–1924', in Marks and Trapido (eds), *Race, Class and Nationalism in Twentieth Century South Africa*, 95–123

Hofmeyr, Isabel, 'The Mad Poets: An Analysis of an Early Sub-Tradition of Johannesburg Literature and Its Subsequent Developments', in Bozzoli (ed.), *Labour, Townships and Protest*, 117–42

Holt, R., *Sport and the British*, Oxford and New York: Oxford Studies in Social History, 1990

Home, Robert, *Of Planting and Planning: The Making of British Colonial Cities*, London and New York: Routledge, 1997

Hughes, Heather, *First President: A Life of John L. Dube, Founding President of the ANC*, Cape Town: Jacana, 2012

Hughes, Heather, '"A Lighthouse for African Womanhood": Inanda Seminary, 1869–1945', in Walker (ed.), *Women and Gender in Southern Africa*, 197–220

Hunt, Tristram, *Building Jerusalem: The Rise and Fall of the Victorian City*, London: Weidenfeld & Nicolson, 2004

Hyslop, Jonathan, 'The Imperial Working Class Makes Itself "White": White Labour in Britain. Australia, and South Africa before the First World War', *Journal of Historical Sociology* 12, 4 (1999), 398–421

Hyslop, Jonathan, 'Scottish Labour, Race, and Southern African Empire c.1880–1922: A Reply to Kenefick', *International Review of Social History* 55 (2010), 63–81

Iliffe, John, *The African Poor: A History*, Cambridge: Cambridge University Press, 1987

Iliffe, John, *Honour in African History*, Cambridge: Cambridge University Press, 2004

Jacobs, Jane, *The Death and Life of American Cities*, New York: Random House, 1961

Jeffrey, Keith, 'Crown, Communication and the Colonial Post: Stamps, the Monarchy and the British Empire', *The Journal of Imperial and Commonwealth History* 34, 1 (2006), 45–70

Jeppie, Shamil, 'Aspects of Popular Culture and Class Expression in Inner Cape Town, c.1939–1959', MA thesis, University of Cape Town, 1991

Jeppie, Shamil and Crain Soudien, (eds), *The Struggle for District Six Past and Present*, Cape Town: Buchu Books, 1990

Jonathan Hyslop, *'The Notorious Syndicalist': J.T. Bain, A Scottish Rebel in Colonial South Africa*, (Cape Town: Jacana Media, 2005)

Jones, Emrys, *Metropolis*, Oxford: Oxford University Press, 1990

Journal of Southern African Studies, Special Issue on 'Urban Studies and Urban Change in Southern Africa', 21, 1 (March 1995)

Kasinitz, Philip, *Metropolis: Centre and Symbol of Our Times*, London: Palgrave Macmillan, 1995

Kaul, C. (ed.), *Media and the British Empire*, London: Palgrave Macmillan, 2006

Keeton, Claire, 'Aspects of Material Life and Culture in District Six, c.1930–1950', unpublished BA Hons thesis, UCT, 1987

Killingray, David, "'A Good West Indian, a Good African, and, in Short, a Good Britisher": Black and British in a Colour-Conscious Empire, 1760–1950', *The Journal of Imperial and Commonwealth History* 36, 3 (2008), 363–81

King, Anthony D., *Urbanism, Colonialism, and the World-Economy: Cultural and Spatial Foundations of the World Urban System*, London and New York: Routledge, 1990

Kolb, B.M., *Tourism Marketing for Cities and Towns: Using Tourism Marketing Branding and Events to Attract Tourists*, Burlington MA: Butterworth-Heinemann, 2006

Kotler, P., D.H. Haider and I. Rain, *Marketing Places: Attracting Investment, Industry, and Tourism to Cities, States and Nations*, New York: The Free Press, 1993

Krause, Linda and Patrice Petro (eds), *Global Cities: Cinema, Architecture and Urbanism in a Digital Age*, New Brunswick and London: Rutgers University Press, 2003

Krikler, Jeremy, *White Rising: The 1922 Insurrection and Racial Killing in South Africa*, Manchester: Manchester University Press, 2005

La Hausse, Paul, "'The Cows of Nongoloza": Youth, Crime and Amalaita Gangs in Durban, 1900–36', *Journal of Southern African Studies* 16, 1 (1990), 79–111

La Hausse, Paul, "'Mayihlome": Towards an Understanding of Amalaita Gangs in Durban, c.1900–1930', in Clingman (ed.), *Regions and Repertoires*, 30–59

La Hausse, Paul, 'The Struggle for the City: Alcohol, the Ematsheni and Popular Culture in Durban, 1902–1936', in Maylam and Edwards (eds), *The People's City*, 33–66

Lambert, John, 'Britishness, South Africanness, and the First World War', in P. A. Buckner and R. D. Francis (eds), *Rediscovering the British World*, Calgary: Calgary University Press, 2005

Lambert, John, 'An Identity Threatened: White South Africans, Britishness and Dominion South Africanism, 1934–1939', *African Historical Review* 37, 1 (2005), 50–70

Lambert, John, "'Loyalty Its Own Reward": The South African War Experiences of Natal's "Loyal" Africans', in Cuthbertson, Grundlingh and Suttie (eds), *Writing a Wider War*, 119–31

Lambert, John, "'Munition Factories … Turning Out a Constant Supply of Living Material": White South African Elite Boys' Schools and the First World War', *South African Historical Journal* 51 (2004), 66–86

Lambert, John, 'South African British? Or Dominion South Africans? The Evolution of an Identity in the 1910s and 1920s', *South African Historical Journal* 43, 1 (November 2000), 197–222

Lambert, John, "'The Thinking is Done in London": South Africa's English Language Press and Imperialism', in Kaul (ed.), *Media and the British Empire*, 37–54

Lambert, John, "'An Unknown People": Reconstructing British South African Identity', *Journal of Imperial and Commonwealth History* 37, 4 (December 2009), 599–617

Landau, Paul S., 'With Camera and Gun in Southern Africa: Inventing the Image of the Bushmen c.1880 to 1935', in P. Skotnes (ed.), *Miscast: Negotiating the Presence of the Bushmen*, Cape Town: University of Cape Town Press, 1996

Landsberg, Alison, *Prophetic Memory: The Transformation of American Remembrance in the Age of Mass Culture*, New York: Columbia University Press, 2004

Lange, Lis, *White, Poor and Angry: White Working-Class Families in Johannesburg*, Aldershot: Ashgate, 2003

Law, Christopher M., *Urban Tourism: Attracting Visitors to Large Cities*, London and New York: Mansell, 1993

Lees, Andrew, *Cities Perceived: Urban Society in European and American Thought, 1820–1940*, Manchester: Manchester University Press, 1985

Lennon, John and Malcolm Foley, *Dark Tourism: The Attraction of Death and Disaster*, New York and London: Continuum, 2000

Lester, Alan, *Imperial Networks: Creating Identities in Nineteenth Century South Africa and Britain*, London and New York: Routledge, 2001

Lester, Alan and David Lambert (eds), *Colonial Lives Across the British Empire: Imperial Careering in the Long Nineteenth Century*, Cambridge: Cambridge University Press, 2006

Lewis, Gavin, *Between the Wire and the Wall: A History of South African 'Coloured' Politics*, Cape Town: David Philip, 1987

Lewsen, Phyllis, 'The Cape Liberal Tradition – Myth or Reality?' *Race and Class* 13 (July 1971), 65–80

Lodge, Tom, *Black Politics in South Africa since 1945*, Johannesburg: Ravan Press, 1987

Lodge, Tom, *Sharpeville: An Apartheid Massacre and Its Consequences*, Oxford: Oxford University Press, 2011

Mabin, Alan, 'Suburbs on the Veld: Modern and Postmodern', unpublished paper, University of Witwatersrand, 2005

Mabin, Alan and Dan Smit, 'Reconstructing South Africa's Cities? The Making of Urban Planning 1900–2000', *Planning Perspectives* 12 (1997), 193–223

Maingard, Jacqueline, *South African National Cinema*, London and New York: Routledge, 2007

Marks, Shula and Richard Rathbone (eds), *Industrialization and Social Change in South Africa: African Class, Culture and Consciousness, 1870–1930*, London: Longman, 1982

Marks, Shula and Stanley Trapido (eds), *The Politics of Race, Class and Nationalism in Twentieth Century South Africa*, Harlow: Longman, 1987

Marquard, A. Q., 'The Political Significance of the Liberal Media Coverage of District Six from 1949 to 1970', MA thesis, Rhodes University, 1996

Marshall, M., 'The Growth and Development of Cape Town', MA thesis, University of Cape Town, 1840

Martin, Denis-Constant, *Coon Carnival, New Year in Cape Town, Past and Present*, Cape Town: David Philip, 1999

Martin, Denis-Constant, *Sounding the Cape: Music, Identity and Politics in South Africa*, Cape Town: African Minds, 2013

Marx, Karl, *The Eighteenth Brumaire of Louis Bonaparte*, Rockville, MD: Arc Manor [1852], 2008

Maylam, Paul, *The Cult of Rhodes: Remembering an Imperialist in Africa*, Cape Town: New Africa Books, 2005

Maylam, Paul, 'Explaining the Apartheid City: 20 Years of Urban Historiography', *Journal of Southern African Studies* 21, 1 (March 1995), 19–38

Maylam, Paul and Iain Edwards (eds), *The People's City: African Life in Twentieth Century Durban*, Pietermaritzburg and Portsmouth, NH: University of Natal Press and Heinemann, 1996

Mayne, Alan, *The Imagined Slum*, Leicester: Leicester University Press, 1993

McAdam, Anthony, 'Leonard Barnes and South Africa', *Social Dynamics* 3, 2 (1977), 41–53

McArthur, Colin, 'Chinese Boxes and Russian Dolls: Tracking the Elusive Cinematic City', in Clarke (ed.), *The Cinematic City*, 19–45

McKenzie, Kirsten, 'Gender and Honour in Middle-Class Cape Town: The Making of Colonial Identities: 1828–1850', PhD thesis, University of Oxford, 1997

Meller, Helen, *Patrick Geddes: Social Evolutionist and City Planner*, London and New York: Routledge, 1990

Mendelsohn, Richard and Milton Shain, *The Jews of South Africa: An Illustrated History*, Johannesburg: Jonathan Ball, 2008

Merrett, Christopher, *Sport, Space and Segregation: Politcs and Society in Pietermaritzburg*, Scottsville: University of KwaZulu-Natal Press, 2009

Merrington, Peter, 'Maps, Monuments and Masons: The 1910 Pageant of the Union of South Africa', *Theatre Journal* 49, 1 (1997), 1–14

Merrington, Peter, 'Pageantry and Primitivism: Dorothea Fairbridge and the "Aesthetics of Union"', *Journal of Southern African Studies* 21, 4 (1995), 643–56

Metcalf, Thomas, 'Herbert Baker and New Delhi', in R. Frykenberg (ed.), *New Delhi through the Ages: Essays in Urban History, Culture and Society*, New Delhi: Oxford University Press, 1986, 392–8

Moodie, T. Dunbar, *The Rise of Afrikanerdom: Power, Apartheid, and the Afrikaner Civil Religion*, Berkely: University of California Press, 1975

Moore, James, 'Between Cosmopolitanism and Nationalism: The Strange Death of Liberal Alexandria', *Journal of Urban History* 38, 5 (2012), 879–900

Mordechai, Tamarkin, *Cecil Rhodes and the Cape Afrikaners: The Imperial Colossus and the Colonial Parish Pump*, London: Frank Cass, 1996

Morgan, Philip D. and Sean Hawkins (eds), *Black Experience and the Empire*, Oxford and New York: Oxford University Press, 2004

Morrell, Robert, *From Boys to Gentlemen: Settler Masculinity in Colonial Natal, 1880–1920*, Pretoria: Unisa Press, 2001

Murray, Bruce, *Wits, the Early Years: A History of the University of the Witwatersrand, Johannesburg, and Its Precursors 1896–1939*, Johannesburg: Wits University Press, 1982

Murray, Martin J., *Taming the Disorderly City: The Spatial Landscape after Apartheid*, New York: Cornell University Press, 2008

Myers, Garth, *African Cities: Alternative Visions of Urban Theory and Practice*, New York and London: Zed Books, 2011

Nasaw, David, *Going Out: The Rise and Fall of Public Amusements*, Boston: Harvard University Press, 1999

Nasson, Bill, *Abraham Esau's War: A Black South African War in the Cape, 1899–1902*, Cambridge: Cambridge University Press, 1991

Nasson, Bill, 'Oral History and the Reconstruction of District Six', in Jeppie and Soudien (eds), *The Struggle for District Six*, 44–66

Nasson, Bill, *Springboks on the Somme: South Africa in the Great War, 1914–1918*, Johannesburg: Penguin, 2007

Nasson, Bill, *The War for South Africa: The Anglo-Boer War 1899–1902*, Cape Town: Tafelberg, 2010

Nattrass, Nicola and Jeremy Seekings, 'The Economy and Poverty in the Twentieth Century', in Ross et al. (eds), *Cambridge History of South Africa*, 531–3

Nauright, John, *Sport, Cultures and Identities in South Africa*, Cape Town and Johannesburg: David Philip, 1997

Neuwirth, Robert, *Shadow Cities: A Billion Squatters, A New Urban World*, New York and Oxford: Routledge, 2005

Nicol, Mike, *A Good-Looking Corpse*, London: Secker & Warburg, 1991

Nightingale, Carl H., *Segregation: A Global History of Divided Cities*, Chicago and London: University of Chicago Press, 2012

Nowell-Smith, Geoffrey, *The Oxford History of World Cinema*, Oxford: Oxford University Press, 1999

Nuttall, Sarah and Achille Mbembe (eds), *Johannesburg: The Elusive Metropolis*, Durham and London: Duke University Press, 2008

Nye, David E., *Electrifying America: Social Meaning of a New Technology, 1880–1940*, Boston: Massachussets Institute of Technology Press, 1992

Parnell, Susan, 'Race, Power and Urban Control: Johannesburg's Inner City Slum-Yards, 1910–1923', *Journal of Southern African Studies* 29, 3 (September 2003), 619–37

Parnell, Susan and Alan Mabin, 'Rethinking Urban South Africa', *Journal of Southern African Studies* 21, 1 (March 1995), 39–62

Parsons, Neil, 'Towards a Broader Southern African History: Backwards, Sideways and Upside–Down', *South African Historical Journal* 66, 2 (2014), 217–226

Parsons, Timothy H., *Race, Resistance, and the Boy Scout Movement in British Colonial Africa*, Athens, OH: Ohio University Press, 2004

Phillips, Howard, *Black October: The Impact of the Spanish Influenza Epidemic of 1918 on South Africa*, Pretoria: Government Printer, 1990

Phillips, Howard, 'Locating the Location of a South African Location: The Paradoxical Pre-History of Soweto', *Urban History* 41, 2 (2014), 311–32

Phillips, Howard, *The University of Cape Town 1918–1948: The Formative Years*, Cape Town: University of Cape Town Press, 1993

Picton-Seymour, Desiree, *Victorian Buildings in South Africa*, Cape Town and Rotterdam: A. A. Balkema, 1977

Pike, Burton, *The Image of the City in Modern Literature*, Princeton: Princeton University Press, 1981

Piper, Nicole, *Racism, Nationalism and Citizenship: Ethnic Minorities in Britain and Germany*, Aldershot: Ashgate Publishers, 1998

Pirie, Gordon, 'South African Urban History', in *Urban History Yearbook* (1985), 18–29

Pogrund, Benjamin, *Sheer Cussedness: A History of the 'Rand Daily Mail'*, Cape Town: David Philip, 2003

Pogrund, Benjamin, *War of Words: Memoir of a South African Journalist*, New York: Seven Stories Press, 2000

Posel, Ros, 'Amahashi: Durban's Ricksha Pullers', in Maylam and Edwards (eds), *The People's City*, 202–21

Preston-Whyte, R. and D. Scott, 'Urban Tourism in Durban', in Rogerson and Visser (eds), *Urban Tourism in the Developing World*, 202–22, 245–64

Rive, Richard, 'District Six: Fact and Fiction', in Jeppie and Soudien (eds), *The Struggle for District Six*, 110–16

Robinson, Helen, 'Beyond the City Limits: People and Property at Wynberg 1895–1927', PhD thesis, University of Cape Town, 1995

Robinson, Helen, *Wynberg: A Special Place*, Cape Town: Formsxpress, 2001

Robinson, Jennifer, 'Johannesburg's 1936 Empire Exhibition: Interaction, Segregation and Modernity in a South African City', *Journal of Southern African Studies* 30, 3 (2003), 759–89

Robinson, Jennifer, *The Power of Apartheid: State, Power, and Space in South African Cities*, Oxford: Butterworth-Heinemann, 1996

Rogerson, C. M. and G. Visser (eds), *Urban Tourism in the Developing World: The South African Experience*, New Brunswick, NJ: Transaction Publishers, 2007

Rogosin, Lionel, *Come Back Africa: Lionel Rogosin – A Man Possessed*, Johannesburg, SET Publishers, 2004

Rosenstone, Robert A., *Visions of the Past: The Challenge of Film to Our Idea of History*, Cambridge, MA: Harvard University Press, 1995

Rosenthal, Eric, *You Have Been Listening: A History of the Early Days of Radio Transmission in South Africa*, Cape Town: Purnell & Sons, 1974

Ross, Robert, 'Cape Town (1750–1850): Synthesis in the Dialectic of Continents', in Ross and Telkamp (eds), *Colonial Cities*

Ross, Robert, *Status and Respectability in the Cape Colony 1750–1870: A Tragedy of Manners*, Cambridge: Cambridge University Press, 1999

Ross, Robert and G. J. Telkamp (eds), *Colonial Cities: Essays on Urbanism in a Colonial Context*, Leiden: Martinus Nijhoff, 1985

Ross, Robert, Anne Mager and Bill Nasson (eds), *The Cambridge History of South Africa*, 2, Cambridge: Cambridge University Press, 2011

Rubin, Margot, 'The Jewish Community of Johannesburg, 1886–1939: Landscapes of Reality and Imagination', MA thesis, University of Pretoria, 2004

Ryan, J. R., *Picturing Empire: Visualization in the British Empire*, Chicago: University of Chicago Press, 1997

Saker, H., *The South African Flag Controversy*, 1925–8, Cape Town: Oxford University Press, 1980

Samuel, Raphael and Paul Thompson (eds), *The Myths We Live By*, London and New York: Routledge, 1990

Sapire, Hilary, 'African Loyalism and its Discontents: The Royal Tour of South Africa, 1947', *The Historical Journal* 54, 1 (2011), 215–40

Sapire, Hilary, 'Ambiguities of Loyalism: The Prince of Wales in India and Africa, 1921–2 and 1925', *History Workshop Journal* 73 (July 2011), 37–65

Saunders, Christopher, 'The Creation of Ndabeni: Urban Segregation and African Resistance in Cape Town', *Studies in the History of Cape Town* 1 (1979), 165–93

Saunders, Christopher, *The Making of the South African Past: Major Historians on Race and Class*, Cape Town: David Philip, 1988

Saunders, Christopher, *Writing Urban History: South Africa's Urban Past and Other Essays*, Pretoria: Human Sciences Research Council, 1992

Shain, Milton, *The Roots of Anti-Semitism in South Africa*, Charlottesville: University Press of Virginia, 1994

Shaw, Gerald, *The Cape Times: An Informal History*, Cape Town: David Philip, 1999

Shiel, M. and T. Fitzmaurice (eds), *Cinema and the City: Film and Urban Societies in a Global Context*, Oxford: Blackwell, 2001

Silk, Andrew, *A Shanty Town in South Africa: The Story of Modderdam*, Johannesburg: Ravan Press, 1981

Simmel, Georg, *On Individuality and Social Forms*, Chicago: University of Chicago Press, 1971

Simone, AbdouMaliq and Abdelghani Abouhani, *Urban Africa: Changing Contours of Survival in the City*, London and New York: Zed Books, 2005

Simons, Harold Jack and Ray Esther, *Class and Colour in South Africa, 1850-1950*, London: International Defence and Aid Fund, 1983

Sisulu, Elinor, *Walter and Albertina Sisulu: In Our Lifetime*, Cape Town: David Philip, 2003

Sittert, L. Van, 'The Bourgeois Eye Aloft: Table Mountain in the Anglo Urban Middle Class Imagination, c.1891–1952', *Kronos: Journal of Cape History* 29 (2003), 161–90

Smith, Ken, *The Changing Past: Trends in South African History*, Johannesburg: Southern Books, 1988

Smith, Mark M., 'Consuming Sense, Making Sense: Perils and Prospects for Sensory History', *Journal of Social History* 40, 4 (Summer 2007), 841–58

Spear, Thomas, 'Neo-Traditionalism and the Limits of Invention in British Colonial Africa', *The Journal of African History* 44, 1 (2003), 3–27

Stedman Jones, Gareth, 'The "Cockney" and the Nation, 1780–1988', in David Feldman and Gareth Stedman Jones (eds), *Metropolis London: Histories and Representations since 1800*, London and New York: Routledge, 1989, 301–16

Stedman Jones, Gareth, *Outcast London*, Harmondsworth: Penguin, 1976

Stein, Pippa and Ruth Jacobson, *Sophiatown Speaks*, Johannesburg: Junction Avenue Press, 1986

Stein, Sylvester, *Who Killed Mr. Drum?* Bellville: Mayibuye Books, 1999

Steinberg, Johnny, *The Number*, Cape Town: Jonathan Ball, 2004

Stokesbury, John A., *Apartheid, Liberalism and Romance: A Critical Investigation of the Writing of Joy Packer*, Umea: Umea University Press, 1996

Stone, John, *Colonist or Uitlander? A Study of the British Immigrant in South Africa*, Oxford: Clarendon Press, 1973

Street, Sean, *A Concise History of British Radio, 1922-2002*, Tiverton: Kelly Publications, 2005

Strydom, Bronwyn, 'Belonging to Fiction? A Reconsideration of H. A. Junod in the Light of His Novel *Zidji*', *African Historical Review* 40, 1 (2008), 101–20

Sturgis, James, 'Anglicisation at the Cape of Good Hope in the Early Nineteenth Century', *Journal of Imperial and Commonwealth History* 11 (1982), 5–32

Swaisland, Cecille, *Servants and Gentlewomen to the Golden Land: The Emigration of Single Women from Britain to Southern Africa, 1820–1939*, Oxford and Providence, RI: Berg Publishers, 1993

Swanson, Maynard W., '"The Asiatic Menace": Creating Segregation in Durban, 1870–1900', *The International Journal of African Historical Studies* 16, 3 (1983), 401–21

Swanson, Maynard W., '"The Durban System": Roots of Urban Apartheid in Colonial Natal', *African Studies* 35, 3–4 (1976), 159–76

Swanson, Maynard W., 'The Joy of Proximity: The Rise of Clermont', in Maylam and Edwards (eds), *The People's City*, 274–98

Swanson, Maynard W., 'The Sanitation Syndrome: Bubonic Plague and Urban Native Policy in the Cape Colony, 1900–1909', *Journal of African History* 18, 3 (1977), 387–410

Sweet, Rosemary, *Antiquaries: the Discovery of the Past in Eighteenth-Century Britain*, London: Hambledon, 2004

Sweet, Rosemary, *The Writing of Urban Histories in Eighteenth-Century England*, Oxford: The Clarendon Press, 1997

Thompson, Andrew, 'The Languages of Loyalism in Southern Africa, c.1870–1939', *English Historical Review* 118, 477 (2003), 617–50

Thompson, Leonard, 'Great Britain and the Afrikaner Republics', in Wilson and Thompson (eds), *The Oxford History of South Africa*, 289–324

Tindall, Gillian, 'Existential Cities', in R. Fermour-Hesketh (ed.), *Architecture of the British Empire*, New York: The Vendrom Press, 1986, 78–82

Tomaselli, K., *The Cinema of Apartheid*, New York: Lake View Press, 1988

Tomlinson, Richard, Robert A. Beauregard, Lindsay Bremner and Xolele Mangcu (eds), *Emerging Johannesburg: Perspectives on the Postapartheid City*, New York and London: Routledge, 2003

Torr, Louise, 'Lamontville: A History, 1930–1960', in Maylam and Edwards (eds), *The People's City*, 245–73

Trapido, Stanley, 'White Conflict and Non-White Participation in the Politics of the Cape of Good Hope, 1853–1910', PhD thesis, London, 1970

Turrell, Robert Vicat, *Capital and Labour on the Kimberley Diamond Fields, 1871–1890*, Cambridge: Cambridge University Press, 1987

Urry, John, *The Tourist Gaze*, London: Thousand Oaks and New Delhi: Sage Publications, 2002

Valiani, Arafat, 'Recuperating Indian Masculinity: Mohandas Gandhi, War and the Indian Diaspora in South Africa (1899–1914)', *South Asian History and Culture Online* 5, 4 (2014), 1–16

Van der Walt, Lucien, 'Revolutionary Syndicalism, Communism and the National Question in South African Socialism', in Steven Hirsch and Lucien van der Walt (eds), *Anarchism and Syndicalism in the Colonial and Postcolonial World, 1870–1940*, Leiden: Brill, 2010

Van Heyningen, Elizabeth, 'The Mysteries of the Secret Phial: Spies and Plague in Cape Town in 1907', *Quarterly Bulletin of the South African Library* 34, 2 (December 1979), 53–8

Van Heyningen, Elizabeth, 'Public Health and Society in Cape Town, 1880–1910', PhD thesis, University of Cape Town, 1989

Van Heyningen, Elizabeth and Pat Merrett. '"The Healing Touch": The Guild of Loyal Women of South Africa 1900–1912', *South African Historical Journal* 47, 1 (2002), 24–50

Van Onselen, Charles, *The Fox and the Flies: The World of Joseph Silver, Racketeer and Psychopath*, London: Jonathan Cape, 2007

Van Onselen, Charles, *Studies in the Social and Economic History of the Witwatersrand, 1886–1914, Vol. 1 New Babylon*, Harlow: Longman, 1982

Van Onselen, Charles, *Studies in the Social and Economic History of the Witwatersrand, 1886–1914, Vol. 2 New Nineveh*, Harlow: Longman, 1982

Van Wyk, Johan, *Constructions of Identity and Difference in South African Literature*, Durban: C.S.A.L.L., 1995

Van-Helten, Jean-Jacques and Keith Williams, '"The Crying Need of South Africa": The Emigration of Single British Women to the Transvaal, 1901–10', *Journal of Southern African Studies* 10, 1 (1983), 17–38

Vergunst, Nicholas, *Hoerikwaggo: Images of Table Mountain*, Cape Town: South African National Gallery, 2002

Vincent, Louise, 'Bread and Honour: White Working Class Women and Afrikaner Nationalism in the 1930s', *Journal of Southern African Studies* 26, 1 (2000), 61–78

Visser, Nick and Tim Couzens (eds), *H. I. E. Dhlomo Collected Works*, Johannesburg: Ravan Press, 1985

Vosloo, Robert, 'From a Farm Road to a Public Highway: The Dutch Reformed Church and Its Changing Views Regarding the City and Urbanisation in the First Half of the 20th Century (1916–47)', *Studia Historiae Ecclesiasticae* 39, 2 (December 2013), 19–32

Walker, Cherryl, *Women and Gender in Southern Africa to 1945*, Cape Town and London: David Philip and James Currey, 1990

Wallace, Ciaran, 'Fighting for Unionist Home Rule: Competing Identities in Dublin 1880–1929', *Journal of Urban History* 38, 5 (2012), 932–49

Wallis, J. P. R., *Thomas Baines: His Life and Explorations in South Africa, Rhodesia and Australia, 1820–1875*, Cape Town: A. A. Balkema, 1976

Ward, Stephen V., *Selling Places: The Marketing and Promotion of Towns and Cities 1850–2000*, London and New York: Spon Press, 1998

Warren, Digby, 'Merchants, Commissioners and Ward Masters: Politics in Cape Town, 1840–1854', MA thesis, University of Cape Town, 1986

Watson, Graham, *Passing for White: A Study of Racial Assimilation in a South African School*, London and New York: Tavistock, 1970

Welsh, David, 'The Growth of Towns', in Wilson and Thompson (eds), *The Oxford History of South Africa*, 172–244

Western, John, *Outcast Cape Town*, Cape Town: Human and Rousseau, 1981

Whittingdale, John, 'The Development and Location of Industries in Greater Cape Town', MA thesis, University of Cape Town, 1973

Willan, Brian, 'An African in Kimberley: Sol T. Plaatje, 1894–8', in Marks and Rathbone (eds), *Industrialisation and Social Change*, 238–58

Willan, Brian, *Sol Plaatje: A Biography*, Johannesburg: Ravan Press, 2001

Willemse, Hein, *More than Brothers: Peter Clarke and James Matthews at Seventy*, Cape Town: Kwela Books, 2000

Williams, Raymond, *The Country and the City*, Oxford: Oxford University Press, 1975

Willis, Justin, 'Unpretentious Bars: Municipal Monopoly and Independent Drinking in Colonial Dar es Salaam', in James R. Brennan, Andrew Burton and Yousuf Lawi (eds), *Dar es Salaam: Histories from an Emerging African Metropolis*, Dar es Salaam and Nairobi: Mkuki na Nyota Publishers and The British Institute in Eastern Africa, 2007, 157–74

Wilson, Monica, 'Co-operation and Conflict: The Eastern Cape Frontier', in Wilson and Thompson (eds), *Oxford History of South Africa: 1870–1966*, 2, Oxford: Oxford University Press, 1971, 233–71

Wilson, Monica and Leonard Thompson (eds), *The Oxford History of South Africa: 1870–1966*, 2, Oxford: Oxford University Press, 1971

Winberg, Chris, 'The "*Ghoemalidjies*"' of the Cape Muslims: Remnants of a Slave Culture', unpublished paper, English Department Seminar, UCT, 1991

Winberg, Chris, 'Satire, Slavery and the Ghoemaliedjies of the Cape Muslims', *New Contrast* 19, 4 (1991), 78–96

Witz, Lesley, *Apartheid's Festival: Contesting South Africa's National Pasts*, Bloomington, IN: Indiana University Press, 2003

Worden, Nigel, *The Making of Modern South Africa*, Oxford: Wiley-Blackwell, 2000

Worden, Nigel, Elizabeth Van Heyningen and Vivian Bickford-Smith, *Cape Town: The Making of a City*, Cape Town: David Philip, 1998

Worger, William H., *South Africa's City of Diamonds: Mine Workers and Monopoly Capitalism in Kimberley, 1867–1895*, Johannesburg: A. D. Donker, 1987

Yates, A. and L. Chester, *The Troublemaker: A Biography of Michaels Scott*, London: Aurum Press, 2006

Index

Abdurahman, Abdullah (Dr.), 120, 150
Abrahams, Peter, 9
  cross-racial initiatives and, 249–250
  political activism of, 248
  on racism, 250
  segregation in writing of, 246
  writing by, 222, 224–5, 235, 236, 237,
    243, 245–6, 248, 250, 251
academic research, on segregation and
  urbanisation, 213, 247, 269
Adams, Thompson and Fry
  (company), 156
Adams College, 53, 60, 223
Adnewmah, Daniel, 252
African Americans
  Black South African writers and, 232
  perceptions of South Africa by, 190, 192
  visit of musicians to South Africa, 60–1
An African Tragedy (Dhlomo), 92, 95, 122,
  188, 238, 251
An African Treasury (Hughes), 224
African Conflict (CBS program), 15, 220
African Drum magazine, 224
African Film Production Company, 81,
  108, 118, 182, 252
African Jim or Jim Comes to Joburg (Film), 251
African Mineworkers Union, 202
African Mirror newsreels, 81n.8, 82, 133
African National Congress (ANC)
  apartheid and, 230–1
  banning of, 13, 258
  Black South African writers and, 248
  British identity and, 147
  Defiance Campaign of, 231
  Freedom Charter, 231
  militancy of, 142
  Women's League, 150, 242
  Youth League of, 52–3, 145–6, 201, 231
African Pathfinders, 151
African Political Organisation (APO),
  58, 150
'African Song', (Rive), 251

African Voices (Rutherfoord), 224
African Writing Today, 224
Afrikaanse Christelike Vroue Vereeneging
  (ACVV, Afrikaans Christian
  Women's Society), 107
Afrikaans language
  Afrikaner nationalism and, 107–8
  employment requirements for, 135
  Pact government recognition of, 135
Afrikaner *Broederbond* (Brother's
  League), 108
Afrikaner Party, 217
Afrikaner population. *See also* Boer
  colonialism
  apartheid and, 14, 202–4, 206
  conflicts with British and, 78, 141
  Dutch Reformed Church and, 56
  English-speaking press campaign against,
    63–4
  ethnic mobilisation of, 205
  institutions and organisations for, 151–52
  labour strikes by, 105–6
  in literature, 88–9
  nationalism of, 106–10, 112–13, 177–9,
    204–6
  politics and, 135–6
  pro-German organisations and, 205–6
  state security apparatus under, 13
Albertyn, J. R., 204
Alexander, Morris, 24
Alexander, Richard, 99, 126, 127
Along Cape Roads (Fairbridge), 177
Amalaita gangs, 97–9
American Board Missions (ABM)
  British women's emigration to South
    Africa and, 149
  influence on African Christian music of,
    60–61
  schools created by, 53
American Club (Johannesburg), 85
Americanisation, South African creolisation
  and, 19

Urban Residence in the Union of South Africa
(SAR&H), 179, 181
'The Urchin' (Themba), 225

Valentine, C., 187
Van der Post, Laurens, 210, 215–16, 227
Van der Stel, Simon, 22
Verlaine, Paul, 238
Verwoerd, Hendrik (Dr.), 205
Victoria League, 83
Vigilance Societies, 73
  as anglophone tradition, 56
Virginia Jubilee Singers, 60, 101
visual materials. *See also* cinema; media
    images of South Africa
  promotion of South Africa through,
    163, 184
Volapuk language, attempted construction
    of, 168n.149
Voorslag (Whiplash) journal, 215
Voortrekkers (Afrikaner boy scout
    organization), 151
Vorster, John, 206
voting rights
  anti-apartheid campaigns for, 231
  apartheid abolition of, 217
  early restrictions on, 25n.26
  expanded restrictions on, 146
Vrededorp, establishment of, 31–2
Vry, Andries, 88

wages, racial differences in, 134–5
A Walk in the Night (La Guma), 226,
    235, 250
Wallace, Edgar, 43
Wanderers' Athletic and Sporting Club,
    32, 58
wartime activities, anglicisation of South
    Africa through, 73
Washington, Booker, Booker T., 60
Watling, Cyril, 194
Watts, G. F., 39
Wayfarers (African girl guides), 151
The Wayzgoose (Campbell), 215–16
welfare organisations, cross-racial initiatives
    for, 152
Wellington, Arthur, 52, 54
Wells, A. W., 188
Western Cape Oral History Project, 266
Western Europe, influence on urban design
    of, 1
When Smuts Goes (Keppel-Jones),
    197–8, 206
White Christy Minstrels, 100
White Diggers, in music and literature, 92

Whiteside, Joseph (Rev.), 49–50
white slave trade
  emergence in South Africa of, 84–5
  in film and literature, 118–19
White workers
  labour conditions for, 104–5
  militancy of, 105, 109
  political radicalism of, 109, 112
  wage and employment patterns for,
    134–5
'Why our Living is so Tough'
    (Themba), 225
Wilberforce, William, 22
Wild Deer (Lewis), 210
Williams, J. Grenfell, 210
Williams, Raymond, 4, 79
Williams, Ruth, 228
Wilmot, Alexander, 49–50, 176
With Your Car at the Cape (Hope), 158
Witwatersrand gold mines, urbanization in
    South Africa and, 16Wollheim,
    Oscar, 220
women in South Africa. *See also* gender
    divide
  Afrikaner women in Boer War,
    107–8
  anglicised school traditions and, 47
  anglophone institutions and societies
    and, 47, 54
  anti-apartheid protests by, 231
  Black African writers and, 240–2
  British emigrants for domestic service,
    35, 149
  cross-racial institutions and, 149
  domestic brewing by, 99, 138–40, 142
  Garment Workers' Union formed
    by, 109
  historical accounts of, 177
  sexual threat of Black Africans for,
    113–20
  stokvel parties held by, 232
  temperance movement and, 83
  urban life and role of, 269
  wartime opportunities for elite women
    and, 73–4
  women migrant workers and, 95
Women's Christian Temperance Union
    (WCTU), 83
The Workers Herald newspaper, 143
working class in South Africa
  Black working-class, 14
  leisure activities of, 149, 151–4
  in literature, 103
  New Year Carnival and, 99–101
  racism and segregation in, 112